Forms of Conflict

Forms of Conflict is a full-length study of the representation of contemporary warfare on the British stage. It investigates the strategies deployed by theatre practitioners in Britain as they meet the representational challenges posed by the 'new wars' of the global era.

Sara Soncini questions how dramatists have responded aesthetically to the changing nature of conflict, focusing on plays written and performed after the September 11 terrorist attacks. Soncini examines how the works of playwrights such as Caryl Churchill, David Hare, Martin Crimp and Simon Stephens have provided an interpretative means to enlarge our understanding of the new patterns of conflict, ensuring theatre's continued cultural and political relevance.

Forms of Conflict explores the relationship between new forms of warfare and new forms of drama, illustrating what dramatic form can reveal about the post-9/11 landscape and complementing a rapidly growing field of contemporary war studies. An appendix contains a complete list of war-related plays staged in Britain between 1991 and 2011, with a brief description of their topic and approach.

Sara Soncini is a researcher in the Department of Philology, Literature and Linguistics at the University of Pisa. Her research interests include twentieth- and twenty-first-century British drama and theatre, with specific emphasis on the representation of war and conflict, and the aesthetics and politics of intertextual and metatheatrical strategies.

Exeter Performance Studies

Series editors: Peter Thomson, Professor of Drama at the University of Exeter; Graham Ley, Professor of Drama and Theory at the University of Exeter; Steve Nicholson, Professor of Twentieth-Century and Contemporary Theatre at the University of Sheffield.

British Theatre and the Red Peril: The Portrayal of Communism 1917–1945
Steve Nicholson (1999)

Grand-Guignol: The French Theatre of Horror
Richard J. Hand and Michael Wilson (2002)

Freedom's Pioneer: John McGrath's Work in Theatre, Film and Television
edited by David Bradby and Susanna Capon (2005)

John McGrath: Plays for England
selected and introduced by Nadine Holdsworth (2005)

Theatre Workshop: Joan Littlewood and the Making of Modern British Theatre
Robert Leach (2006)

Making Theatre in Northern Ireland: Through and Beyond the Troubles
Tom Maguire (2006)

"In Comes I": Performance, Memory and Landscape
Mike Pearson (2006)

London's Grand Guignol and the Theatre of Horror
Richard J Hand and Michael Wilson (2007)

Theatres of the Troubles: Theatre, Resistance and Liberation in Ireland, 1980–2000
Bill McDonnell (2008)

British South Asian Theatres: A Documented History
edited by Graham Ley and Sarah Dadswell (2011)

Critical Essays on British South Asian Theatre
edited by Graham Ley and Sarah Dadswell (2012)

Victory over the Sun: The World's First Futurist Opera
edited by Rosamund Bartlett and Sarah Dadswell (2012)

Marking Time: Performance, Archaeology and the City
Mike Pearson (2013)

Singing Simpkin and Other Bawdy Jigs: Musical Comedy on the Shakespearean Stage
Roger Clegg and Lucie Skeaping (2014)

Ancient Greek and Contemporary Performance: Collected Essays
Graham Ley (2014)

The Censorship of British Drama 1900–1968
Steve Nicholson
Volume One 1900–1932 (2003)
Volume Two 1933–1952 (2005)
Volume Three, The Fifties (2011)
Volume Four, The Sixties (2015)

Eighteenth-Century Brechtians: Theatrical Satire in the Age of Walpole
Joel Schechter (2016)

Performing Grand-Guignol: Playing the Theatre of Horror
Richard J Hand and Michael Wilson (2016)

Forms of Conflict

Contemporary Wars on the British Stage

Sara Soncini

UNIVERSITY
of
EXETER
PRESS

First published in 2015 by
University of Exeter Press
Reed Hall, Streatham Drive
Exeter EX4 4QR
UK
www.exeterpress.co.uk

British Library Cataloguing in Publication Data
A catalogue record for this book is available from the British Library.

Hardback ISBN 978 0 85989 993 2
Paperback ISBN 978 0 85989 994 9

Typeset in Plantin by Carnegie Book Production, Lancaster
Printed in Great Britain by TJ International Ltd, Padstow

Contents

Illustrations

To the memory of my grandfather Cesare Cavagnini,
a kind-hearted, peace-loving man who was drafted to fight
under Fascist rule and spent the best part of his youth
enmeshed in the horrors of war

Acknowledgments

I owe a debt of gratitude to a number of people who have contributed, both directly and indirectly, to my work on this book.

Firstly I would like to thank the friends and colleagues who generously gave their time to read some of the material: Caroline Patey, for her very helpful and encouraging comments on the initial proposal, and Carla Dente and Sylvia Greenup for their invaluable feedback on chapter drafts. The fourth member in this valiant task force, Cristina Cavecchi, was not only an engaged and sympathetic reader throughout my long and protracted grapple with this project, but also an inseparable companion in a long line of brief but invigorating theatre binges in London. Thank you for the good times, my dear Rosencrantz – or is it Guildenstern?

I am very grateful to the series editors at UEP, Peter Thomson, Graham Ley and Steve Nicholson for welcoming this book in the Exeter Performance Studies series and for their expert advice and constructive criticism. In Steve's case, this acknowledgment must be supplemented with a very heartfelt thanks for his enduring friendship and readiness to help. I am deeply obliged, too, to the anonymous reader who gave such supportive and stimulating feedback on both the proposal and the final typescript, and whose detailed and thoughtful response was a huge boost during the more daunting moments of the writing process. Finally, a big thanks goes out to Simon Baker for his commitment to this project and for his patience in responding to my many queries, and to Helen Gannon for her attention and admirable poise in seeing my bulky typescript through production.

My deepest thanks are due to my family, of course. I am grateful to my parents and in-laws for their day-to-day help and support, both moral and material, and their willingness to provide extra childcare in order to allow me to carve out those all-important visits to theatres and archives in the UK. A very special mention of thanks goes to Alessandro for his liberal supply of love, good sense and lightness, and also for occasionally letting me win at tennis when in desperate need of some cheer (what if I had hit the doldrums more often, though?). Viola and Nina have gracefully waved aside their suspicions about a mother who spends so much time in front of a computer screen yet insists she's not a game-addict; their trust, forbearance and bounteous cuddling deserves my grateful acknowledgment. Above all, however, I am profoundly thankful to my beautiful girls for making my life so much more complicated, and yet so incredibly simple.

Many thanks, too, to the writers and artists who have contributed with their time and work to the making of this book: to Mimi Poskitt, for providing me with the unpublished script of her documentary piece *Yesterday Was a Weird Day* and for our lively and enlightening conversation in London back in 2011; to Simon Stephens, for kindly replying via email to my queries about his play, *Pornography*; to Peter Mumford, Arno Declair, Manuel Harlan and John Haynes for giving me their photographs to include in the book; and last, but by no means least, to Anselm Kiefer for allowing me to use his astonishingly visionary painting, *Lilith* as a cover image.

The following people have been of huge assistance in locating material and assisting with reproduction issues: Nadine Koller at the Fondation Beyeler; Eva König at the Atelier Anselm Kiefer; Daria Wallace at the Lebrecht Picture Gallery; and Emma Schad at the National Theatre of Scotland Press Office. I am also very grateful to the staff at the V&A National Video Archive of Performance and at the National Theatre archive in London for arranging repeated viewings of the recordings in their collections and for their prompt supply of material and information. Finally, many thanks, too, to the librarians at Centro Interbibliotecario LM2, University of Pisa: to Anna Bonechi, in particular, for her highly benevolent management of library funds and uninterrupted supply of books, and to Laura Matteoli for running a highly efficient interlibrary loan service.

Earlier versions of material used in some of the chapters have appeared in the following articles and book chapters:

"War in words: The Tricycle Theatre's re-voicing of the Bloody Sunday Inquiry", *Pólemos: Journal of Law, Literature and Culture* 9:2 (Aug. 2015), pp. 393–409.

'"This is Not a War": le neoguerre nel teatro di Caryl Churchill', in M. Cavecchi and M. Rose (eds), *Caryl Churchill. Un teatro necessario* (Florence: Ed.it, 2012), pp. 77–100.

'The "Translation Turn" in Contemporary War Plays: Tony Kushner's *Homebody/Kabul*', in F. Ciompi (ed.), *One of Us. Studi inglesi e conradiani offerti a Mario Curreli* (Pisa: ETS, 2009), pp. 367–84.

Preface

Forms of Conflict: Contemporary Wars on the British Stage investigates a range of formal strategies deployed by theatre practitioners in Britain in response to the representational challenges created by the 'new wars' of the global age. By positing a connection between modes of conflict and modes of representation, this study seeks to assess the impact on dramatic form and theatrical presentation of what has been generally described as a full-fledged paradigm shift in the way of waging and perceiving war. In so doing, it ultimately sets out to fathom the theatre's capacity for providing some interpretive means to enlarge our understanding of the new patterns and mechanisms of conflict—a much-needed skill for the uneasy denizens of a world enmeshed in permanent war.

There is broad consensus among specialists and commentators from a variety of fields that the final years of the twentieth century mark a watershed between 'old' and 'new' wars, that is to say between traditional, Clausewitzean modes of conflict—emerging out of the evolution of the modern nation-state in Europe between the fifteenth and the eighteenth centuries—and the new forms of organized violence that have come to characterize the global era.[1] This volume focuses mainly on plays written and performed around or after the terrorist attacks of 11 September 2001, a time when the inadequacy of traditional strategic and cultural models to account for the changed nature of contemporary warfare became all too palpable, but it also directs attention to plays that have prefigured these developments and, in parallel, have provided innovative artistic answers to a number of aesthetic problems which were only then beginning to come into focus. The body of work considered in *Forms of Conflict* reveals that theatre practitioners have often proved more receptive than policy-makers in grasping the changed nature of war, a fact that arguably casts an auspicious light on the epistemological wager of new war drama. It also shows that this heightened sensitivity has produced a readiness to direct the dramatists' inquisitive, perceptive gaze inwards, as much as outwards. In trying to figure out and give scenic shape to the new forms of warfare, the writers and theatre-makers discussed in this book have been willing to embrace a self-reflexive scrutiny of the limits and possibilities of the medium they work with, prompted by the need to secure its continued cultural and political relevance at this highly critical historical juncture.

Forms of Conflict is not conceived as an exhaustive account of contemporary war drama. The amount of new war plays written and/or staged in Britain over the past two decades is impressive and ever on the increase, and it has therefore been necessary to select a more limited and manageable corpus for closer inspection. This approach does not simply answer to practical considerations but tallies with the overall purpose of this volume, which is to provide a phenomenological account of formal strategies elicited by the subject of the new wars, rather than a chronological, contextual one. Instead of dealing with individual conflict situations and their symptomatic portrayal on the British stage, this study identifies some distinguishing features and patterns of global conflict and connects them with a range of formal responses to the issues of representation they raise. The choice of plays examined below was therefore primarily dictated by their paradigmatic value with respect to the overall conceptual framework of the book, i.e. their ability to exemplify new tendencies and provide insight into formal developments as stimulated by the onset of a new paradigm of warfare.

In more than one respect, this guiding principle has resulted in significant levels of heterogeneity. For a start, my discussion combines the close reading of individual plays with their exemplary use to illustrate specific arguments, with the balance between the two notably shifting depending on the nature of the issues addressed in each chapter. The select group of dramatists included in the book are also very much a mixed bag, ranging from prominent figures of the British theatrical mainstream to emerging companies and young writers at their debut; canonical works are covered alongside unpublished plays, and small-scale performances in fringe venues often receive the same amount of in-depth analysis as widely-reviewed, major productions. The decision to limit my investigation to the British stage does provide a unifying frame for my discussion, but that was not the main reason behind the narrowing of focus. In fact, this choice was primarily motivated by the book's emphasis on formal innovation and the related need to emphasize the dramatists' more or less conscious negotiation with a particular tradition and what they might perceive as its distinctive theatrical vocabulary. For this reason, while the vast majority of the plays considered in *Forms of Conflict* have been written by British or British-based dramatists, there are some notable exceptions, such as plays by British writers that received their world premiere elsewhere, or works by American writers staged in Britain and also, in some cases, British productions of foreign-language plays in translation.

The selection of primary material was to some extent influenced by a more extrinsic factor that also accounts for the partial London-centrism of this investigation. While the material examined is principally textual, I have generally felt more comfortable discussing plays that I was able to see performed: by attending productions whenever possible, but often also through the invaluable aid of video recordings. As a non-UK-based researcher, resources such as the V&A National Video Archive of Performance, the National Theatre archive and the Drama and Literature Recordings collection at the British Library have been of tremendous help in getting a firmer grasp of the plays and their possibilities in performance; yet the fact that these collections are almost exclusively focused on productions staged in the London area has inevitably had some impact on the orientation of my study.

The two-decade span (1991–2011) covered by the contemporary war plays listed in the Appendix is somewhat deceptive in its promise of an even chronological distribution. In fact, the temporal frame of my investigation tends to be rather more approximate and basically mobile in its extent. The distinguishing feature of the new wars is precisely their tendency to elude boundaries, both spatial and temporal. As shall be discussed in the introductory chapter, the demarcation line between 'old' and 'new' wars is an essentially porous one. True, the events of 9/11 have tended to be construed as an ontological event ushering into a new geopolitical era, but the rupture they have come to epitomize is more symbolical than real, given the patent continuities between the logic of twenty-first-century global warfare and some noticeable mutations in the patterns of violent conflict during the previous decade or so. The authoritative 'new war' theory that was already widely current at the time of the terrorist attacks on the Twin Towers had been formulated as a response to the new forms of organized violence that emerged during the Balkan Wars of the 1990s; and the reconceptualization of war as a 'virtual', 'global' and 'permanent' phenomenon likewise predated the supposed historical watershed of 11 September 2001, having already begun with specialist analyses of the First Gulf War at the opening of the previous decade and the NATO intervention in Kosovo at its close. At the same time, it would be wrong to underestimate the capital role played by the al-Qaeda attacks on America in making the rupture manifest. Though not in itself a moment of origin, 9/11 must be acknowledged as a consolidating and an intensifying one, a vantage point that enabled a retrospective grasp of the fundamental (and frightening) interconnectedness between phenomena previously detected in a variety of seemingly discrete conflict situations. Because of their media-enhanced symbolical magnitude, moreover, the events of 11 September had an undeniable propulsive function in bringing war to the fore as the major political and cultural issue of the present day, as is also demonstrated by the considerable and steady growth in the output of war-related drama in Britain throughout the 2000s. *Forms of Conflict* has been conceived to reflect this historical pattern: while its primary focus is on the 'coming of age' of new war drama during the first decade of the twenty-first century, it also frequently gazes backwards in order to emphasize a common lineage between post-9/11 dramatic responses and a number of seminal plays that were produced before the paradigm shift had become fully visible.

The start date chosen for these analepses—1991—is supported by the widely consensual perception of the First Persian Gulf War as ushering into a new age of warfare. By contrast, the practical need to set an end date for this study felt strongly at odds with the open-ended, professedly 'infinite' nature of the forms of conflict which the plays attempt to capture. There has been a tendency, in the critical literature on new war drama, to restrict the temporal frame to the period between the 9/11 attacks and Barack Obama's election to the American presidency in 2008, taking the latter date as officially marking the conclusion of the global war on terror launched by his predecessor at the White House. This is the case, for example, of Jenny Spencer's edited volume *Political and Protest Theatre after 9/11* (2012). The same kind of periodization is adopted in Jenny Hughes's monograph *Performance in a Time of Terror,* published in 2011, although the author concomitantly stresses the 'temporal and spatial formlessness' that defines the new paradigm.[2] Crucially, however, if President Obama and his Defense Department may be seen to have inaugurated a new rhetoric when they dropped the term 'War on Terror' in favour of a less blatantly aggressive 'Overseas Contingent Operations', the strategic priorities of the United States and its allies have remained fundamentally unchanged to this very day. Just like terrorism in its various shapes has not ended with the assassination of Osama bin Laden in 2011, so the global pre-emptive mandate of the war on terror has continued to live on in the massive drones campaign launched by the Obama administration or, closer to Europe, in the 'regime change' policy informing the NATO-led bombing of Libya in 2011. By the same token, while never entirely disappeared from media language,[3] the widely-criticized phrase 'war on terror' has been forcefully resurrected in official political discourse following the recent terrorist attacks in Paris: in January 2015, the French Prime Minister Manuel Valls could be heard declaring France's 'war against terrorism, against jihadism, against radical Islam, against everything that is aimed at breaking fraternity, freedom, solidarity',[4] in a language that distinctly echoed the lexicon used by President Bush in the aftermath of the 9/11 strikes. In light of the proven durational quality of the new wars, I have felt that an historically-motivated end date would be no less arbitrary than the decade periodization proposed for this study, which has at least the advantage of openly advertising its conventional nature. As the tenth anniversary of the al-Qaeda attacks on America, moreover, 2011 was a year of commemorations but also an occasion for reviewing and reassessing a whole decade of fear, insecurity and violence. The rich crop of new war plays written and performed during that year testifies to a climate of renewed, rekindled interest and was another element that tilted the balance in favour of this particular chronological marker.

The research presented in *Forms of Conflict* originates from a deep-felt need to find out whether the theatre can provide some means to understand and maybe even counter the seemingly irreversible process whereby violence—national or transnational, virtual or real, emanating from state actors or from small groups of individuals—is becoming 'the central regulative principle of everyday life' for an increasing number of people across the globe.[5] I am aware that my desire to provide a critical analysis of phenomena that are still very much ongoing may have resulted in some degree of methodological looseness. It is possible, and highly to be wished, that in a not too distant future the world will steer away from this totally insane course. When that happens, it will presumably be easier to pause and take stock of our times of crisis and the theatrical responses they have generated; this book, however, felt too urgent to wait any longer.

Pisa, October 2015

CHAPTER ONE

Introduction: mapping the terrain

New wars? New *wars*?

Writing in the wake of the al-Qaeda attacks on New York and Washington, the French philosopher and controversial political commentator Alain de Benoist famously announced that the twentieth century had ended on 11 September 2001, and that the launch of the war on terror marked the outbreak of 'the first war of globalization'. This new war, he argued,

> no longer has any limits, either territorial or in the choice of means. The main feature of globalization is that it cannot be subordinated to, controlled or regulated by any superior power. For the first time in history, it establishes a world without borders. In the era of globalization, there are no longer 'sanctuaries', or safe countries. Since there are no more borders, the battlefield expands over the whole world ... The traditional distinction between friend and enemy does not make sense anymore, because now there is no way to know who is a friend and who is an enemy, who is 'inside' and who is 'outside' ... Ultimately, in a globalized world there are no longer any foreign wars, but only civil wars.[1]

While de Benoist insisted on the radical novelty of this 'first post-modern and "furtive" war', his description of its key features is in fact of a piece with the paradigm shift registered by Mary Kaldor in the bloody ethnic conflicts that ravaged the Balkans during the 1990s. Akin to de Benoist's analysis, Kaldor's new war theory emphasizes the 'blurring of the distinctions between war … organized crime … and large-scale violation of human rights'[2] as the epitomic feature of political violence in the post-Clausewitzean era. In bringing to the fore the utterly globalized nature of apparently localized conflicts, Kaldor shows that the new wars defy traditional notions of foreign and domestic, internal and external, public and private, laying bare the political and strategic blunders that can result from the failure to grasp the obsolescence of these conceptual boundaries. Kaldor's criticism is mainly substantiated via her case study of the war in Bosnia-Herzegovina, where humanitarian intervention was not only delayed, but also irredeemably vitiated by a lengthy and specious debate within the international community about whether the conflict in the former Yugoslavia was of an intra- or an inter-state nature.

Throughout the 2000s and beyond, Kaldor has continued to defend the applicability of her theorization to the age of global warfare, classifying both the events on 9/11 and the political and military responses they have triggered as manifestations of the new wars on a spectacularly grand scale.[3] Other commentators who have stressed the same historical and conceptual continuities have similarly underscored the unprecedented extremity of the confrontation,[4] and Kaldor herself sees a genuine element of novelty in the accelerating, radicalizing and consolidating impulse given by the new information and communication technologies to the instalment of the new paradigm and its elevation into a state of global permanent war.[5] During the fateful decade that spawned the 9/11 attacks and the global war on terror, the tearing down of the last barrier standing, that between war and peace, was definitively and conspicuously consummated, exposing the glaring inadequacy of our inherited conceptual dichotomies when it comes to accounting for the 'furtive' character of the new modes of warfare. In this new breed of violent conflict, combat operations are no longer tied to a declaration of war and tend to rage on after their official cessation. In strategic terms, too, peace simply becomes another way to pursue hostilities—as already shown, for example, by the appalling number of civilian deaths caused by UN sanctions in Iraq during the theoretically 'peaceful' interval between the first and the second Gulf War[6] or, closer in time, by the soaring violence in Afghanistan and Iraq after the official ending of military operations. To return to de Benoist's formulation, the consolidation of the paradigm has fully revealed the contours of a world order where the Clausewitzean maxim is reversed and 'politics and peace extend war by other means'.[7]

In an even more extreme way, the traditional perception of peace and war as oppositional frames has been made untenable, in the post-9/11 landscape, by the utter normalization of what was once experienced as a devastating breakdown in the ordinary course of social life. The first decade of the twenty-first century has witnessed the transformation of war from a state of exception into the new *modus vivendi*. As Arjun Appadurai has remarked, the ultimate rationale of global terrorism in all its manifestations is precisely that of collapsing the distinction between military and civilian space in order to 'replace peace with violence as the guaranteed anchor of everyday life'. From this point of view, the new model of warfare far surpasses in fierceness and scale the total wars of the twentieth century on account of its 'quotidian' character, its quintessentially terrorist endeavour to install 'war as an everyday possibility, waged precisely to destabilize the idea that there is an "everyday" for anyone outside the space and time of war'.[8] While Appadurai is mainly referring to the civilian targets of potential or actual terrorist violence, his observations equally apply to those who actively engage in combat. The phenomenon of 'domestic' terrorism is an obvious case in point here, but striking levels of quotidianization are also detectable in acts of violence executed by members of the military as part of official, 'regular' combat operations. American and RAF drones flying over Afghanistan are operated from Creech US Air Force Base in Nevada, several thousand miles away from the actual battlefield, by air force members who sit before a computer screen and use a games console-style joystick to hit targets and kill suspect terrorists. During a flight, drone pilots can make phone calls, go to the lavatory or get a coffee; like ordinary office employees, they work five days a week and drive home to their families at the end of their shift.[9] Under these arrangements, the notion of war and peace as mutually exclusive frames of experience appears indeed very hard to sustain.

This blurring of ontological and conceptual boundaries finds a correspondence in the variable and often disputable nomenclature of the new forms of conflict. Especially after 9/11 the term 'war' has been employed to designate the use of political violence for purposes that are not, strictly speaking, political. This is the case, most notably, of the 'global war on terror' declared against an enemy that the United States is unable to identify, and waged with no attainable geopolitical goal in sight. As Derrida pointed out in the aftermath of 9/11, when Afghanistan was bombed and invaded in retaliation for the terrorist attacks on America, neither its civilian population nor its army were held to be enemies of the United States or the coalition countries. Though al-Qaeda claimed responsibility for the strikes, Osama bin Laden, like the hijackers, was not Afghan; in fact, he had been officially disavowed by his own country and by practically every other country in the world given that, then as now, the states who help and harbour terrorist networks do not do so as states. What is more, the 9/11 attacks proved beyond doubt that 'the United States and Europe, London and Berlin, are also sanctuaries, places of training or formation and information for all the "terrorists" of the world'.[10] Conversely, the massive aerial bombardment of Yugoslavia in 1999 was accompanied by the careful avoidance of the term 'war', although this was an operation conducted by a military alliance and expressly targeting the military infrastructures and armed forces of the Serb state. The designation of war would not have been out of place here; yet, at the same time as they were unleashing an impressive tonnage on Kosovo and Serbia, NATO leaders spoke of strikes, coercive diplomacy and humanitarian intervention in order to bypass legal restrictions on the exercise of state violence. The volatile lexicon of the new wars has alternatively been used to turn the virtual into the real, as with the 'war on terror', or the real into the virtual, as happened during the NATO campaign in Kosovo, ultimately making void the distinction between the two domains.

Indeed, a further development that has been seen as symptomatic of the full-blown identity crisis undergone by war at the turn of the millennium is the extreme degree of virtualization that has accompanied its startling rise to the omnipresent, all-encompassing foundational 'reality' of the new global order. Ever since Jean Baudrillard's provocative statement, in 1991, that the Gulf War had not taken place, the notion that we live in an age of virtual war has been generally understood in reference to the heavily mediatized nature of contemporary warfare. This is probably the most prominent feature of the new paradigm, and as such it will be discussed at length in the following paragraph and elsewhere in the book; however, the idea of the new wars as a quintessentially virtual affair has been likewise invoked in connection with some deep modifications in their mechanisms of conflict or, more precisely, to denounce the outright supersession of the conflict principle that these wars have allegedly brought about. The new types of warfare, it has been observed, are totally asymmetrical contests that no longer involve any real measure of antagonism; therefore, our continued recourse to the term 'war' may be inappropriate or even misleading when it comes to accounting for its latest incarnation in an array of 'hybrid', 'degenerate', or 'residual' forms.[11] The insightful corollary to this perspective is that it invites us to approach with the same caution the manifestly 'unlawful' and 'irregular' violence of terrorism, which we are accustomed to seeing as something different from war, and the 'legitimate' military operations undertaken by sovereign nation-states, often under the aegis of international organizations like the UN or NATO.

In this respect, an influential template for virtual war was established as early as the Gulf War of 1991. The first major military operation of the post-bipolar era offered a brutal demonstration of the markedly non-antagonistic, non-dialectical quality of the then emerging paradigm of warfare. The overwhelming technological and military superiority of Western coalition forces turned Operation Desert Storm, as the US-led campaign was sensationally branded, into an out-and-out punitive expedition. In downgrading the war against the Iraqi regime to the rank of 'a well-organized butchery', Italian literary critic and political thinker Alberto Asor Rosa pointed out that an event that was presented by the media and generally apprehended by the viewing public in the coalition countries as a muscular confrontation between opposed armies was in fact no more than a fiercely unilateral affirmation of 'the social and civil hierarchies regulating the new world order', and of global inequality as its primary organizing principle.[12]

The First Gulf War also set an important example for casualty-free warfare, another crucial and related aspect of the drift towards the virtual typified by the new forms of belligerence. Superior technology enabled coalition forces to impose their supremacy upon the enemy while barely paying the human cost of war; meanwhile, over one hundred thousand Iraqi military casualties were 'quietly incorporated in disembodied language', their corpses effectively removed from the battlefield in a sanitized war of '"targets", in which "installations", "assets" and "units" were "attrited", "neutralized" and "pounded" by remote-controlled missiles'[13] carrying video cameras that reframed a morally illegitimate turkey shoot as a rousing *Top Gun*-style movie. In parallel, the same verbal and visual rhetoric of technological cleanliness and 'collateral damage' was deployed to conceal the real impact of 'smart' weaponry and 'surgical' strikes upon the civilian population of Iraq.

Only a couple of years later, the oxymoronic 'humanitarian wars' of the mid-1990s brought to the fore the troublesome moral implications of this new virtual brand of war, while at the same time giving an intimation of the alarming geopolitical scenario that lay ahead. The ever more robust peacekeeping operations in Somalia, Rwanda and the former Yugoslavia laid bare the profoundly iniquitous assumptions about the value of human life upon which the doctrine of risk-free warfare is founded. These interventions were undertaken in the name of universal human rights, but the apparently well-meaning and strategically-sound efforts to minimize military casualties turned out to imply a very selective apprehension of the right to safety. In the former Yugoslavia, for example, the prioritization of the security of armed UN soldiers over the defenceless civilians they were mandated to protect infamously resulted in the failure to avert the massacre of over eight thousand Bosnian Muslims in Srebrenica. Like many other instances of culpable nonfeasance on the part of UN peacekeepers, the shame of Srebrenica provided damning evidence of the privilege accorded to international military lives over those of the civilian victims of ethnic cleansing.

The military and moral asymmetries of risk-free warfare came spectacularly together in the humanitarian intervention in Kosovo at the close of the century. This was a virtual(ized) war waged with unprecedented, and thus far unsurpassed, levels of impunity: NATO's high-altitude bombing campaign achieved its strategic objectives without a single combat fatality to our side. This meant that while the violence of the 'humanitarian' bombs had a very real impact on the soldiers and the civilians of all ethnicities on which they were dropped, the citizens of the NATO countries, including the members of the armed forces engaged in combat operations, were exclusively mobilized as spectators. In his widely-known analysis of Kosovo as the epitome of a virtual conflict, Michael Ignatieff explains that when technological mastery removes death from our experience of war, war 'ceases to be fully real to us'; this, in turn, carries heavy political repercussions in that democratic electorates in whose name virtual wars are waged may be more willing to consent to their governments' resort to 'precision lethality',[14] particularly when state violence is moralized as humanitarian. In light of America's uncontested global military supremacy, Ignatieff warned in the immediate aftermath of Kosovo, the prospect of risk-free military interventions posed a serious security threat because it paved the way for a planetary escalation of armed conflicts.

The alarm sounded by Ignatieff and others about the possible geopolitical consequences of virtual war proved well-founded in view of subsequent developments. During the first two decades of the twenty-first century, with the world's superpower and its allies policing the globe and controlling rogue states in the name of democracy and humanitarian principles, risk-free warfare has increasingly shown a regrettable proneness to fuel violence on a planetary scale. Far from making the world a safer place (or even a safer place only for some), the dispensation of violence from a position of impunity—reaching a new frontier with the recent emergence of drone warfare—has been paralleled by a fearsome escalation of savage acts of terrorism that target precisely our sense of safety and, with it, the misplaced belief that virtual war can guarantee immunity from violence. The political narrative of jihad against the West that is commonly advocated to account for contemporary terrorism loses much of its hold the moment one considers that the bombing of Manhattan on 11 September 2001, for all its indisputable moral contemptibility, followed a decade of terror from the air as America's tactic of choice, and that this tactic was premised on the 'assumption that the perpetrators could go on indefinitely making war from a distance, with no need to "fear vengeance in their homeland from the peoples whose homelands were their theatres of war"'.[15]

The 'old' model of conflict implied in the 'clash of civilizations' rhetoric is in effect one of the main conceptual targets of the theory championed by Kaldor and widely espoused by the current critical literature. As has been convincingly argued, the Clausewitzean notion of war as a mighty adversarial struggle fuelled by opposed interests and irreconcilable positions founders historically as well as conceptually when applied to the current geopolitical landscape. Advocates of the 'jihad against the West' scenario too readily forget that the birth of Islamic fundamentalism as a modern political project dates from America's support to Afghani mujahedeen against the Soviet Union at the height of the Cold War. When the same project was resurrected by Osama bin Laden at the turn of the millennium, it became remoulded as the global, viral phenomenon that often goes by the name of Islamic terrorism; undeniably, though, the history of the al-Qaeda network, and later of ISIS, is one of intense interchange between Islam and the West. Many al-Qaeda members were educated in Western countries or spent considerable time there, like the terrorists who carried out the 9/11 strikes. The organization itself was conceived as 'a contemporary, global, and networked enterprise, with a flattened hierarchy and cellular structure characteristic of drug cartels and some multinational business companies';[16] its affiliates showed a remarkable command of computer technology and a full grasp of the power of media for global refraction. Finally, the West's attempts at wiping out the 'disease' of Islamic extremism—as British Prime Minister David Cameron recently dubbed it[17]—has considerably aided and accelerated its global spread. The most striking demonstration of this mechanism is provided by Iraq, where al-Qaeda formed in response to the US-led intervention there and then morphed into ISIS, spreading to Syria and quickly extending its operations to Northern Africa and other areas of the Middle East and South Asia. Taken together, these elements unequivocally point to contemporary jihadism as a 'modern, hybrid creation of Islam's encounter with the West',[18] rather than an atavistic manifestation of radical cultural alterity. This critique of traditional conflict theory as embodied in the 'clash of civilizations' model is best summarized in Jean Baudrillard's definition of twenty-first-century global warfare as the ultimate expression of '*triumphant globalization battling itself*'.[19]

Even though they advocate an understanding of the nature of the new wars 'through hybrid categories of mutual constitution',[20] new war theorists continue however to insist on the political character of the new forms of organized violence: Kaldor's decision to persist with using the term 'war' to describe them is expressly motivated by her perception of identity politics as a key ingredient of the new model of conflict. The lesson that can be drawn from the identity-driven ethnic conflicts of the 1990s, Kaldor argues, is that polarized identities are a product of the new wars, rather than their root cause: identitarian narratives are politically constituted and/or accentuated for the specific purpose of mobilizing people and expanding networks of extremism by emphasizing 'cleavages of tribe, nation and religion'.[21] If we fail to understand that 'political mobilisation around identity is the aim of war rather than an instrument of war',[22] we become blind to a fundamental aspect of the current forms of belligerence, namely, that the political polarization between the West and the rest is highly beneficial to the functioning and the empowerment of the terrorist networks—that both global terror and the global war on terror share a self-perpetuating interest in the reproduction of identitarian antagonisms. In Kaldor's lucid formulation,

> if we understand the 'War on Terror' as a mutual enterprise—whatever the individual antagonists believe—in which the American Administration shores up its image as the protector of the American people and the defender of democracy, those with a vested interest in a high military budget are rewarded and extremist Islamists are able to substantiate the idea of a Global Jihad and to mobilise young Muslims behind the cause, then action and counterreaction merely contribute to 'long war', which benefits both sides.[23]

Kaldor concludes her defence of the 'new wars' model by explaining that the hermeneutic value of the adjective 'new' has to do less with the particular features of the present forms of belligerence than with the need to develop a fresh approach to the phenomena it seeks to address. The term 'new', she explains, is 'a way to exclude "old" assumptions about the nature of war and to provide the basis for a novel research methodology'.[24] As this book seeks to demonstrate, the British stage has shown a remarkable readiness to take up this call and re-examine existing categories whereby we frame and understand violence and war. Being undertaken from inside a representational art form, this inquiry is intrinsically animated by a sharp awareness of the constitutive power wielded by representations in the contemporary theatre of operations and, in parallel, by a sustained self-reflexive engagement with the problem itself of representability.

Frames of violence

> "There is no war ... without representation".
>
> (Paul Virilio)[25]

In his landmark study *The Great War and Modern Memory* (1975), Paul Fussell provides compelling evidence about the way existing literary models shaped first-hand accounts of the First World War and actually predetermined writers' perception of its traumatic modernity. Today we have become accustomed to thinking that representational regimes of all kinds concur in the construction of a discourse on war which then becomes the omnipresent filter through which the material reality of war is apprehended and understood. The idea that existing discursive formations define our experience of war was a critical truism endlessly repeated at the time of the attacks on the Twin Towers, when commenting on the widespread impression that the events on 9/11 had been eerily anticipated by Hollywood blockbusters. And yet, whereas the mutual implications of war and representation are plain for all to see, the operations of power that are embedded in these interpretive frameworks tend by their very purpose to remain hidden. The cultural framing of violence is a politically saturated act: war relies on discursive accompaniment to give it meaning and legitimacy, and to regulate our affective and ethical disposition towards it. In this sense, the way in which we perceive the violence of war, or are induced to perceive it, carries substantial political consequences. This is typically the case of the war on terror, where only a 'differential and selective framing of violence'[26] can account for our divergent responses to the horrors of suicide bombing, on the one hand, and of state-sponsored brutality, on the other. One would otherwise be at a loss to explain the failure of Western public opinion to react to the US Senate report of December 2014 detailing the atrocities perpetrated on detainees in CIA black sites around the world (Europe included) with even a fraction of the moral outrage rightly aroused by the *Charlie Hebdo* shootings in Paris only a few weeks later.

Of course, the mobilization of cultural constructs to legitimize killing (and being killed) in war is rooted in the history itself of armed conflict: in its material dimension, war is a matter of rival narratives and adversarial stances becoming—literally—embodied as physical damage.[27] The element of novelty about contemporary conflict that is more frequently stressed in critical analyses is the unprecedented hold that representations have acquired over the reality of war, and the concomitant establishment of perception management as the ultimate mode of military conduct in today's theatre of war. This can be seen in part as a consequence of the overwhelmingly rhetorical quality of contemporary warfare—of the hypertelia that has been diagnosed as a co-morbid condition of the hypertrophic proportions assumed by global permanent war.[28] Already a prominent feature of the nuclear age, of the eminently speculative and 'fabulously textual' mode of warfare that characterized the virtual belligerence during the Cold War, the displacement of conflict onto the discursive plane soared to stunning new heights in the post-bipolar era, with the disappearance of the 'structuring' enemy and its replacement with 'a mobile multiplicity of potential interchanging metonymic entities'.

From this point of view, the war on terror provides a prime example of a radical alterity 'without measure or end'[29] being conjured up discursively in order to justify the unleashing of proleptic violence on an equally measureless, endless scale.

A further, massive factor behind the rise of representations to a constitutive component of the new paradigm of belligerence is, needless to say, the ever more prominent role played by the media in the global battlefield and their by now complete integration in contemporary warfare as the principal means *and* space of military action. According to theorists, the transition from a mode of military conduct tied to the mobilization of images to one based on their out-and-out weaponization began with the First Gulf War in 1991 and was already fully accomplished by the time of the second intervention in Iraq in 2003. The kind of 'image warfare' exemplified by the al-Qaeda strikes on 11 September has been seen to mark a watershed between a centralized mode of controlling images and knowledge, still attached to twentieth-century notions of propaganda and mass media, and a deterritorialized war of images that both reflects and exploits the rhizomatic condition installed by the new communication and information technologies.[30] Through global interconnectedness, enhanced interactivity and widespread media literacy, in the twenty-first century the deep entanglement of war and representation announced by Virilio has become reconfigured as a fundamental identity between the media used to wage war and the media used to view it, reaching an extreme where the material reality of war can no longer be separated by the discursive regimes through which it operates.

In specialist literature, the current paradigm of 'image warfare' has been generally described as at once a consequence of and a reaction to the new regimes of visibility and invisibility attendant upon the advent of 'spectacular secrecy' as the signature politico-military strategy of the information age.[31] The lesson learned from Vietnam—a war lost in the living rooms of America, according to Marshall McLuhan's famous remark—loomed large behind the strategic importance attached to the management of the collective imaginary during the First Gulf War of 1991. Operation Desert Storm was sold to the global public through a highly professionalized management of the flow of information that relied simultaneously on the exclusion of independent, first-hand witnesses from the theatre of operations (particularly photojournalists), and the parallel reshaping of news coverage according to the narrative and visual codes of entertainment television. The first intervention in Iraq was conceived as a media spectacle which fomented the illusion of total visibility and accessibility created through real-time global broadcasting while exerting a very strict control over the public's apprehension of the war. In this respect, this first major virtual war of the post-bipolar age offered a powerful demonstration of the decline of the knowability of things in proportion to their accessibility which William Leiss has diagnosed as the defining syndrome of our information society.[32]

After 9/11, this heightening of the visible and its systematic management have continued to prove strategic assets in manufacturing consent around armed interventions in Afghanistan and Iraq. The same public relations consultant who stage-managed the globally televised scene of the liberation of Kuwait City in 1991, the self-styled 'information warrior and perception manager' John W. Rendon, was again hired by the US Department of Defense in 2001, allegedly 'to help it explain US military strikes in Afghanistan to global audiences';[33] shortly afterwards, the Rendon Group was assigned to the short-lived Office of Strategic Influence created by the US administration as part of a hearts and minds campaign to promote support for the war on terror.[34] Consequently, when Saddam Hussein's statue on Firdous Square was toppled by US soldiers on 9 April 2003, strong—though as yet unconfirmed—suspicions arose about the contribution given by perception managers of the likes of Rendon to the orchestration of a spectacle that seemed to have been designed to symbolically counter the bombing of the Twin Towers, and to do so moreover through an iconic image of America's successful liberation of Iraq. As has been amply established, a closely cropped framing of the large Baghdad square and a selective use of close-ups transformed a few dozen bystanders, mainly foreign journalists and soldiers, into a massive crowd of Iraqi citizens spontaneously celebrating their newly-found freedom; this heavily manipulated scene then lent backing to the politically expedient comparison, made by US Secretary of Defense Donald Rumsfeld, between regime change in Iraq and the fall of the Berlin Wall.

Even more importantly, in the post-9/11 context the discursive regimes instated and enforced through the control of the visible have been crucial to the transformation of war from the state of exception into the 'New Normal'.[35] The First Gulf War, as already mentioned, was marked by a verbal and visual rhetoric that replaced the human element with the inanimate: weapons counts—how many Iraqi tanks, airplanes, Scud missiles had been destroyed—instead of body counts; high-tech strikes in place of armed combat; video footage of bridges and buildings being blown up, aerial photographs of jagged metal and shattered machinery in lieu of the physical destruction of human lives.[36] The war on terror has continued to rely on spectacular obscurantism in order to pre-empt moral assessment of the inhumanity of war by 'coalition' audiences. In a gesture that emblematically captures the importance attached to the control of images, on 5 February 2003, the day when US Secretary of State Colin Powell presented the case for war against Iraq at the United Nations, a blue curtain was placed over the tapestry reproduction of Picasso's *Guernica* that hung in the anteroom to the UN Security Council Chamber, reportedly under pressures from US administration officials who saw the inappropriateness of this most iconic denunciation of the barbarity of war as a backdrop for official statements to the world media. Even before 'Shock and Awe' was meted out to the Iraqi population, then, the victims of the bombing campaign had already become shrouded in invisibility.

When compared with the saturation coverage received by the terrorist strikes in New York and Washington on 9/11, in Madrid on 11/3, or in London on 7/7, the obscurity that envelops the operations of state-sanctioned terrorist warfare becomes all the more striking. During the war on terror, the blanket of invisibility that has fallen on violence executed by state actors has done more than virtualizing war and its consequences; perception management has been strategically employed to naturalize an 'antidemography of the discounted' that has accompanied and sustained the rise of exceptionalism as the dominant form of government in the current world order.[37] In her insightful analysis of contemporary biopolitics, Judith Butler maintains that for a life to be accorded a value, it must be perceived as a life in the first place. Pointing to the different levels of 'grievability' accorded to Western and non-Western casualties in contemporary conflict, Butler underlines the different entitlement to personhood that is attendant upon these regimes of visibility and invisibility. The management of perception, she concludes, is an issue of the utmost political significance: if representation and representability contribute to define who qualifies as a human subject in the political arena, their differential regulation can be used to undermine the universalistic premise of fundamental human rights which lies at the basis of ethical, legal and constitutional restrictions to the exercise of political violence by democratic governments.[38] This is clearly the case of the war on terror, a war whose pre-emptive remit necessitates the bypassing of constitutional and international prohibitions against wars of aggression, and the creation of categories of people who can be kept outside the law and subjected to indefinite detention, extraordinary rendition and torture. In this context, the monopoly on invisibility has been a key asset in normalizing the state of exception whereby global permanent war justifies its practices and sustains itself.

According to theorists, it is precisely in connection with this tactical alliance of visibility and power that the 'highly optical character'[39] of contemporary terrorism should be understood. The West's reliance on the production and the control of images as a preferred method of statecraft, it has been suggested, has in turn generated a vulnerability to acts of image warfare such as those epitomized by the horrendous spectacle of September 11. The attacks on the World Trade Center were designed above all to be visible: as Richard Schechner points out, the hijackings were timed 'as a one-two punch for maximum spectacular effect, synchronized to the morning news cycle in New York and midday in Europe' in order to reach as large a spectatorship as possible.[40] The 9/11 terrorists have exposed the element of vulnerability involved in the logic of image-control and adroitly exploited the media's collusion in its operations, ushering into a new era of 'mediatized terrorism' in which, as Freedman and Thussu explain, 'media are not simply external actors bringing the news of terrorist incidents to global audiences but are increasingly seen as active agents in the conceptualization of terrorist events' and therefore wield 'not simply ... definitional but constitutive power'.[41] Seen in this light, what the jihadists effectively hijacked on September 11 was the formidable firepower of representations to inflict perceptual damage, and the immense potential of global communications as a force multiplier. Following this epitomic moment of 'image-defeat',[42] the spectacle of terrorism has continued to take full advantage of the opportunities provided by electronic and digital media for message amplification and rapid dissemination on the one hand, and community building, engagement and proselytism on the other.

With both state and non-state actors equally versed in image warfare, in the contemporary theatre of war acts of belligerence are increasingly carried out according to escalating patterns of visual tit-for-tat. To go over but the more salient steps in the spiralling perceptual violence during the initial phase of the war on terror, the destruction of the Twin Towers was answered by the spectacle of 'Shock and Awe' in the Baghdad sky, a pyrotechnical military campaign named like a Hollywood blockbuster and seeking to counter the symbolical damage perpetrated by al-Qaeda's screening of its own macabre disaster movie in New York; the spectacular bombing of Baghdad was followed, a couple of weeks later, by the globally televised 'beheading'[43] of Saddam Hussein's imposing statue on Firdous Square, a major media event to which the Iraqi insurgency responded with a spate of crude DIY videos of the executions of prisoners; shortly afterwards, the peer-to-peer dissemination of the chilling digital images of the brutalization of detainees in Abu Ghraib jail by American soldiers showed that the rise of the 'terrorist as impresario' had been matched by the advent of the 'torturer as video artist'.[44] Over the years, the deployment of atrocity footage has not only moved well beyond Iraq, but has become increasingly professionalized; today, jihadist image warriors can rely on ISIS's own media arm, Furqan Media Corporation, to produce and disseminate their horrific visual assaults through video clips featuring carefully scripted beheadings, or slick propaganda films like the very recent 'Flames of War'. This fifty-two-second video was released in

September 2014, in the wake of President Obama's turn towards greater intervention in his Iraq strategy. Purporting to be the trailer of yet another disaster movie 'coming soon'—as according to its closing caption—if American combat troops were to be again deployed to Iraq, the ISIS clip featured images of wounded American soldiers, exploding tanks and kneeling men waiting to be savagely executed; its pre-emptive strike was executed in patent blockbuster style, complete with slow motion replays, fast-paced editing, spectacular visual effects and sensational titles in block letters. By overtly targeting the very conventions of atrocitainment through which the war on terror has been fed to 'coalition' audiences, and the perceptual frames that these conventions have contributed to generate, this recent episode in a long row of visual attacks and counter-attacks went one step further in that 'Flames of War' overtly flaunted the insurgents' cognizance of the 'representation turn' in contemporary conflict, transforming the warriors' command of perceptual weaponry into integral part of the threat of terror.

In a rather uncanny way, this is not entirely dissimilar to the theatre's own self-conscious way of trafficking in representations. The contemporary stage, too, directly targets discursive formations about war and the cognitive and affective frames they generate and/or enforce. It does so, however, with the intent of reclaiming representations from the warmongering party and in order to see if and how they can still be used to produce knowledge, rather than violence. As will be shown, the terms of engagement in this perceptual battle revolve around the question of whether the theatre possesses the means for an effective intervention in the public sphere—a question leading to a comprehensive stocktaking of the representational arsenal at hand, and a strategic analysis of how best to mobilize it.

'Our theatre of cruelty'

Probably more than any other art form, the theatre can draw on a long-standing, intense conceptual commerce with war to bolster up its epistemological claims. The very nature of the vocabulary that is commonly used to describe armed conflict would seem to point to the theatre's strengths as a heuristic device: our reliance on expressions like 'theatre of war' or 'theatre of operations' to designate the space in which military activity takes place speaks of a deep-seated habit of understanding war as an activity that is largely isomorphic to stage practice. This conceptual framework is a legacy of nineteenth-century military strategists and, more directly, of Antoine-Henry de Jomini's attempt at providing the first comprehensive theory of modern warfare in his *Précis de l'art de la guerre* (1830). In de Jomini's treatise, strategic thinking is predicated upon the stage-like quality of the battlefield, an enclosed, circumscribed zone susceptible to visual survey and therefore enabling an exact choreography of military manoeuvres based on abstract, almost geometrical calculations.[45] Like Carl von Clausewitz's *Vom Kriege*, de Jomini's theory was influenced by his experience of the Napoleonic wars, an example of military strife founded on the direct clash of massed troops 'within restricted spatiotemporal parameters that almost seemed designed to respect the Aristotelian unities'.[46] And yet, at the very same time as they provided the culminating point of the so-called 'chessboard model' of warfare, the grand open-field battles of the early nineteenth century also marked the beginning of the tactical obsolescence of the model itself. The supposed observability of the classical battlefield, it has been suggested, was greatly reduced by the very literal 'fog of war' created by discharge from artillery and muskets: the kind of visual prowess ascribed to field commanders in these foundational theories of warfare, and their attendant claim to insight through observation, should probably be understood more as a theoretical abstraction or even a 'popular fantasy'[47] than a real possibility.

Commenting on the cognitive deficit that affects the panoptic spectatorship afforded by media today, Petra Rau similarly traces the historical point of origin of this aporia to the Napoleonic wars, classifying the omniscient panoramic view typically assumed by war painting and military historiography from the early nineteenth century onwards not only as a 'myth', but as a telling symptom of the mystifying drive that inheres the commonplace equation of visibility with knowability.[48] If the dissolution of the classical battlefield was already underway at the beginning of the nineteenth century, and was greatly accelerated by the growing industrialization of warfare during the rest of the century and the following one, with the new wars of the global age the observability of the theatre of operations has become completely detached from whatever residual spatiotemporal materiality the latter might still retain. Even when armed conflict seems to be tied to a specific territorial location, as in the case of Iraq and Afghanistan, the ubiquity and simultaneity produced by real-time media coverage flatten time and space into a 'homogeneised surreal non-space',[49] a thoroughly virtualized scopic field in which war takes places simultaneously all over the world before the 'universal eyewitness' of the global public.[50] As a result, one of the major aesthetic and political questions faced by contemporary dramatists is how to continue to harness the cognitive-critical power of the theatrical gaze under these circumstances. Although they are keen to retain the epistemological potential of the stage as *theatron*, a 'place for seeing' according to the Greek etymon, and therefore a space where fixed modes of seeing can be defamiliarized and unsettled, their work is marked by a strong circumspection about the potential pitfalls in the current alliance between virtual war and the cognitive ruse of visibility.

This wariness about the tools of the trade and their possible collusion with the new modes of belligerence extends beyond the field of performance as scenic space to include also the field of performance as environmental, phenomenal space. The massive utilization of processes, practices and frameworks associated with performance within the new paradigm of belligerence has been aptly registered by recent scholarship in this area. The most authoritative critique to date dealing with the 'performance turn' in contemporary warfare, Jenny Hughes's *Performance in a Time of Terror* (2011), provides an extensive discussion, supported by a broad range of examples, of the 'institutionalization of performance as a strategy and tactic of violence' by global terror and the global war on terror alike. As evidence of the truly bipartisan appropriation of the language of performance by the warring factions, Hughes points to the theatricalization of violence by insurgents and state actors alike, observing moreover that the most radical acts of performance are 'those taking place as part of the shock and awe tactics, covert military operations and torture scenarios'.[51] Hughes's position is shared by Jeanne Colleran, who further adds to the list of weaponized performances the illocutionary acts carried out by political and military leaders through the media. Taking as a case in point the 'Mission Accomplished' speech delivered in May 2003 by George W. Bush, in *Top Gun*-style combat gear, from the deck of the USS *Abraham Lincoln*, and Osama bin Laden's reply to that speech through a globally televised message in which he predicted never-ending war for the invaders of Iraq, Colleran suggests that the US president's attempt at 'replacing the spectacle of 9/11 loss with the spectacle of American triumph' and bin Laden's eventual rebuttal by means of a low-tech pre-recorded video should both be regarded as performative utterances, speech acts functioning to all effects as acts of war: 'Bin Laden's tape was not ancillary to the War on Terror; it was itself an act of terrorism. Bush's declaration was not just an announcement; it was a battlefield manoeuvre played out on a landscape more important than the Iraq desert or Afghan mountains: the television screen.'[52]

A similar conclusion about the weaponization of performance in the age of global terror is reached by the doyen of performance studies, Richard Schechner, in his well-known analysis of the spectacle of 9/11. Schechner starts from the incendiary statement made by the German composer Karlheinz Stockhausen when he described the terrorist action of 11 September as 'the greatest work of art imaginable for the whole cosmos',[53] and then proceeds to review this controversial case from inside his discipline; much to his discomfort, Schechner is finally brought to adjudicate that 'from the perspective of performance studies, the attack on the World Trade Center was a performance: planned, rehearsed, staged, and intended both to wound the US materially and infect the imagination', and should therefore be understood as standing 'in direct succession to futurist, anarchist, and other *avant-garde* manifestos and actions'.[54] More specifically, throughout his analysis Schechner sees a distinctly Artaudian component in the spectacular violence staged by the al-Qaeda militants in New York. Physical destruction, he remarks, was not the primary objective of their strikes; far more than the actual victims of the bombings, the terrorists were targeting media audiences worldwide and working on their states of mind and feeling—the province of art, he then goes on to remind us. In what Schechner sees as a textbook example of Artaudian cruelty, the suicide bombers seized on the ability of performance to collapse the barriers between the virtual and the real and used it as a formidable force multiplier, magnifying the impact of their violence over space and time in a potentially infinite extension of its destructive capability.

But is not only as a form of communication between senders and receivers that the language of performance has been seen to support and enact war in the contemporary battlefield; an equally troubling aspect concerns the mobilization of the cognitive and affective force of theatre as an immersive, embodied experience for those who take part in it. The collaboration between play-making and war-making goes a long way back in history: simulations, role-playing, re-enactments have been traditionally employed, alongside theatrical vocabulary and metaphors, to conceptualize conflict and to envisage and rehearse military strategies. In parallel—and with growing intensity from the mid-twentieth century onwards, following the establishment of conflict analysis as a specialist field—the epistemic potential of practices and frameworks associated with theatre and performance has been leveraged by diplomats, strategic analysts and peace-brokers in the attempt to avert or address situations of violent conflict.[55] The latter category, in particular, see the power of the theatrical experience to untangle and transform conflicts as premised on the cognitive and affective possibilities opened up by role-taking and role-playing, on the revelatory quality of the embodied experience of inhabiting a different self. In a thought-provoking article calling for an urgent re-evaluation of the role of theatricality in contemporary warfare, Diana Taylor denounces the perverse self-referential logic in which performance practices have seemingly become mired in our age of simulation.[56] Taylor substantiates her argument by discussing the strange surprising case of Fort Irwin, a US army base in California's Mojave Desert hosting the National Training Center, America's premier military training facility. Over the past decade or so, a huge number of American soldiers from all services have prepared for war at the NTC through theatre immersion. Prior to their deployment in Iraq, for example, troops were required to spend two weeks in the so-called 'Sandbox', a one-thousand square mile reproduction of an Iraqi province. The full-size simulations designed for their training followed episodic, interchangeable plots and involved exposure to guerrilla warfare, convoy ambushes, car bombings and videoed beheadings but also interaction with Iraqi civilians engaged in their everyday activities. For this purpose, the Sandbox featured several mock villages filled with Arabic-speaking Iraqi expatriates who were hired to play townspeople and insurgents (the latter, a more demanding role requiring coaching from a Hollywood professional). After a new Commanding General took charge of the NTC in 2007, the ranks of the Iraqi other were engrossed through the recruitment of some three hundred homeless people from the nearby town of Barstow to perform non-speaking parts.

As Scott Magelssen observes, theatre immersion at the NTC is strikingly different from traditional wargaming techniques for the importance it assigns to the human element and to face-to-face interaction with the Iraqi 'enemy', whether potential or actual. Through this strange, simulacral form of theatre, troops prepare for war in 'a ludic, ritualized space of play where identities are performatively forged and stabilized through re-enactment, or *pre-enactment*, on the limen of actual Iraq'. The behaviour of each Iraqi character in the scenario is produced in detail by professional scriptwriters and actors are instructed to 'keep the simulation watertight' no matter what happens.[57] Because one can only prepare for things one already imagines, Taylor concludes, scenario thinking of the kind epitomized by the Fort Irwin training tends to envision conflict (and resolution) in our own image and to project a fixed image of the Other modelled on our fears and imaginings; as they literally step into their cultural representations and play them out, participants in theatre immersions are trapped in a 'tautological circle' where performance forecloses transformation, rather than enabling it.[58]

In the eyes of the theatre-makers who seek to bring contemporary warfare on stage, the unprecedented overlap between the constituents of theatre and the constituents of war in the current historical juncture is perceived both as an empowering factor and as a daunting aesthetic and political problem. On the one hand, the sense of urgency and commitment with which playwrights have taken up the challenge of giving scenic shape to the new forms of war is itself testament to their enduring faith in the cognitive value of the medium they work with. On the other, however, the belief that the field of performance can prove 'invaluable for understanding not only what the 9/11 terrorists did, but also for understanding much of what has happened before and after

9/11, and what will happen in the years to come', in the words of theatre historian John Bell,[59] is never detached from an equally pressing need to re-evaluate the role of theatre from inside its context of practice. The dilemmas of representation generated by the new wars, the experiments in form through which contemporary dramatists have attempted to navigate these tensions, and the outpouring of creative and theatrical possibilities that have emerged out of these times of crisis are the main lines of investigation pursued throughout the rest of this volume.

Following this introductory reconnaissance of the field of research, the second chapter ('This is not a war') sets out to fathom the reverberations of the increasingly virtual nature of contemporary wars on the visual and verbal texture of their dramatic reconfigurations. In the first part of the discussion, the accent falls principally on theatre aesthetics and on responses triggered by what Baudrillard has described as the 'implosion of meaning' in the age of simulacra.[60] Reacting to a radical crisis of representation in general, and of the visual authority of images in particular, the new dramaturgy of war is marked in different degrees by a disappearance of the representational imaginary. In this new landscape of conflict, war is conspicuously absent from the stage, having been entirely re-encoded in metaphorical analogues or mediated through narrative reconstructions. More often than not, this tendency to shun mimetic reproduction is closely connected with the expression of a critical stance towards the rhetoric of presence, immediacy and referentiality flaunted by the media. Built on the disjunction of word and image, this distinctive brand of new war plays denounces a radical coming apart of sign and object, art and referent, questioning at one and the same time our notion of 'the real' and, by extension, the very epistemology of theatre as a mimetic art form. For its paradigmatic value, the work of Caryl Churchill forms a constant point of reference throughout the discussion; but the same mechanisms are charted in the dramaturgy of Martin Crimp, Mark Ravenhill and Simon Stephens, while the first section, 'Mimesis in the age of simulacra', draws attention to the anticipatory quality of First Gulf War drama in terms of its deliberate problematization of visibility.

In parallel, Chapter Two investigates a further layer of the problem of mimesis by considering the impact of these new dilemmas of representation on the configuration of the drama text and the dialogical structure. With their profoundly asymmetrical and hence fundamentally unilateral nature, the new wars of the post-bipolar era have put a heavy strain on the traditional model of dramatic conflict as expressed through verbal interaction. In the work of the dramatists discussed in this chapter, the issues surrounding the representation of war as scenic action are typically associated with the doubts raised by dialogue as the standard formal embodiment of dramatic conflict. The last three paragraphs explore some representative answers to the crisis of the relational/intersubjective model implied in verbal interaction. Here, I start from the erosion or outright supersession of the conflict principle in dialogue, and then move on to consider the monologization of dramatic discourse and the alternative formal arrangements produced through the postdramatic reorganization of the drama text and its components.

In the next two chapters, 'Why fabulate?' (Three) and 'The performance of witnessing' (Four), I turn momentarily away from fictional recreations of contemporary conflict by switching the focus onto the recent resurgence of documentary forms of drama on the British stage. A considerable share of plays written after 9/11 and the onset of the war on terror are marked by an urgent return to questions of reference and reality. Reacting to the heavily mediated and mediatized apprehension of contemporary wars, theatre-making in Britain has characteristically turned to modes that purportedly relinquish 'fiction' for the sake of 'truthfulness'. The introductory section assesses the crucial role played by the subject of war in triggering the new upsurge in documentary theatre and, most importantly, in stimulating the redefinition and renewal of this genre. This leads to an examination of two modes of documentary practice which differ significantly in terms of the source material used and its formal organization. I begin by considering tribunal plays based on the official transcripts of public inquiries, the format that comes closest to a realist epistemology, and then turn to hybrid forms of documentary which mix factual reportage and imaginative reconstruction. While registering substantial differences in their respective rules of engagement, my analysis also foregrounds some defining features and concerns that are common to the new wave of verbatim drama and have specifically emerged in connection with the new paradigm of belligerence. By focusing their attention on language, verbatim plays turn words into exhibits, bring them to the bar and subject the evidence to cross-examination; in so doing, they direct their gaze self-reflexively onto the nature of documents, the problem of documentation, and more in general the tension, inherent to the form, between factual accuracy and dramatic efficacy, aesthetical considerations and ethical obligations.

Proceeding in the critique of the documentarian approach to contemporary conflict, Chapter Four places centre stage the figure of the witness and the act of bearing witness, two basic constituents of verbatim theatre across its main currents: interview-based plays, testimonial solo performances and tribunal dramas. The rendering of testimony is here explored as a discursive position that can lend authenticity and authority to a particular account of the real, but does so by paradoxically foregrounding the subjective nature of testimony and putting the witness in the dock. By looking at 'The performance of witnessing', then, this chapter aims to delve into another conflict zone inhering today's culture of documentary, namely, the tension between impersonality and impersonation, between the factual, objective quality of testimony as knowledge and the inescapable subjectivity of testimony as performance. The introductory section traces the rise to prominence of the figure of the witness in contemporary accounts of war, foregrounding some areas of ambivalence that surround the testimonial act and its representation. This is followed by 'The talking cure', a discussion of issues tied to the mediation of testimony in plays based on interviews and other oral source material. This topic is developed with specific reference to the documentary practice of Robin Soans and of London-based theatre company, Look Left, Look Right, looking at the strategies of presentation whereby their plays textualize the moment of intersubjective encounter between the primary witnesses and those who record their testimony and transmit it to a theatre audience. The second section, 'The artist is present', turns to consider the problem of actorly intermediation by looking at David Hare's travelogue about the Israeli-Palestinian conflict, *Via Dolorosa*, and its symptomatic response to the problem of the 'witness capacity' of the performer's body when it comes to mediating the testimony of real people. Finally, in 'Technologies of recollection' the problem of testimonial presence and its authenticating function is brought to bear on the competition between live and recorded performances of witnessing in documentary versions of contemporary conflict.

In the fifth and final chapter, 'Figures of mediation', the twin issues of the intermediary and the act of (re-)mediation are approached from yet another angle. Here, I turn attention to a growing body of plays that point to language mediation as a key feature of the new wars and, at the same time, an embodiment of their mechanics. The British stage has been quick to recognize the special relevance taken on by the management of language difference in contemporary conflict, and the extent to which interlingual mediators have become implicated in the informational economy of the new wars. Translators and interpreters feature regularly as the characters, and sometimes the protagonists, of new war drama, with the operations of translation, and particularly its failures, inadequacies and inevitable compromises, becoming yet another voice in the play. More often than not, in these plays, the representation of translation *in* the war zone entails the representation of translation *as* a war zone, a conflict-ridden practice that can shed light on the situations of violent conflict in which it is enacted. With its focus on the amount of role-taking and role-playing involved in the act of translating, this new breed of multilingual and meta-lingual theatre work represents a high-water mark of the critical self-reflexivity that runs through the other formal configurations considered in previous chapters, thus providing an ideal conclusion for the trajectory drawn throughout the book.

Following an initial discussion of the mutual implications of war and translation within the current paradigm of belligerence, I then chart the rise to prominence of interlingual mediation in contemporary British theatre, looking also at the more or less overt presence of the (mis-)translation theme and trope in some plurivocal, polycentric and plurilingual works considered earlier on in the book. In the three sections that follow, I concentrate on three distinct incarnations of the wartime translator, privileging one particular thread of analysis for each typology. 'The translator's invisibility' offers a parallel discussion of Gregory Burke's *Black Watch* and George Packer's *Betrayed*, two plays that deal with the fate of locally-hired linguists during the Iraq war from a documentary (or semi-documentary) angle, but choose diametrically opposed ways of constructing the translators' onstage presence. These modulations, I argue, have important repercussions on the framing of the act of textual mediation performed by the verbatim editor. In 'The combat linguist' I examine David Greig's *The American Pilot*, a provocative parable play that denounces the full and definitive integration of language mediation in the institution of war, while at the same time employing the dramaturgy of (non-)translation as an eloquent formal analogue of today's asymmetrical warfare. Finally, in 'Uncanny bodies' I deal with Tony Kushner's *Homebody/Kabul*, a precursor of the 'translation turn' in the military and the dramatic field alike, and its most archetypical incarnation so far. With his emphasis on translation as an embodied activity, I suggest, Kushner gives a markedly performative slant to the play's parallel investigation of the violence of war and the violence of translation, infusing his dramaturgy of war with a radical interrogation of the theatrical medium and its specific means for engaging with our Babelian, conflict-ridden world.

CHAPTER TWO

This is not a war

Mimesis in the age of simulacra

Royal Court Theatre at the Duke of York's, London, June 1997. Music. A heading scrolling on to a screen above the set announces: 'The War in Bosnia'. The scene: a London street, a man waiting with flowers; his date arrives, apologizes for double booking and their evening together is called off. 'Byebye' and on to the next scene. With its coming apart of word and image, object and sign, the opening of Caryl Churchill's *This is a Chair* can be seen as the emblematic forerunner of a new breed of plays wherein war is announced, discussed, thematized but programmatically banished from the stage.

Of course, since the very beginnings of Western dramatic tradition the representation of war has systematically raised the issue of representability, testing both the limits and the potential of the theatrical medium, and calling into question its founding principles of mimesis and verisimilitude. As the Prologue to Shakespeare's *Henry V* famously reminded its audience, war is too vast a subject to squeeze it onto an 'unworthy scaffold'; and from the Greeks onwards dramatists have had to resort to a number of devices to negotiate the representational shortcomings of the stage—the most common of which, *teichoscopia*, is attested already in the first complete Western tragedy to have reached us, Aeschylus's *Persians*, which features a Messenger's graphic report of the battle of Salamis. Throughout the twentieth century, the increasingly technological nature of warfare on the one hand, and the competition of cinema and the media on the other, have put ever increasing pressure on those dramatists who have tried to come to grips with the traumatic modernity of the Great War, the indiscriminate mass violence of total warfare during the Second World War, the threat of Armageddon, the paranoid stalemate of the Cold War, the absurd hell of Vietnam. More often than not, this has resulted in bold experiments with dramatic form and stage language(s) and in a thoroughgoing questioning of current theatre aesthetics.[1]

My specific contention here, however, is that there is something both quantitatively and qualitatively different to the aesthetic challenge faced by the writers and theatre-makers who have sought to give scenic shape to contemporary conflict. Today, it is not only a matter of seeking to translate into material, embodied terms an endless war fought on a global battlefield against an invisible, faceless enemy—arguably, a more demanding task than having to accommodate 'the vasty fields of France' into a theatrical 'cock-pit' and 'cram/Within this wooden O the very casques/That did affright the air at Agincourt'.[2] Unlike Shakespeare's paradigmatic representational disclaimer, and unlike the pervasive trope of adynaton in war writing past and present, denouncing the difficulty yet the need to find words to convey war,[3] the aesthetic issue at stake here is not limited to finding an adequate representational analogue for the event of war, but involves instead a more radical reconsideration of the very representative basis of theatre.

War as we have come to experience it in the global media age is an aestheticized commodity specifically designed for spectatorial consumption, a clear instance of the 'implosion of meaning' in the age of simulacra.[4] This is a process that many cultural commentators, and most notably Baudrillard, see as originating from the First Gulf War—the 'Ur-production' of total television, according to Tom Englehardt[5]—and culminating with 9/11. Broadcast and experienced simultaneously all over the world, in real time, via digital technologies and television screens alike, and uncannily resembling the spectacular scene of a Hollywood disaster movie, the attacks on the Twin Towers have been taken to mark the definitive onset of what Baudrillard calls the age of simulation: the event of war, irredeemably hijacked by its mediatized images and repackaged for consumers, is ultimately replaced by a 'pseudo-event' in which the interpretative model precedes and eclipses the event.[6] At the same time, while disposing of referentials altogether, today's images of war predicate their appeal upon the capacity of technology to offer immediate and unmediated access to the 'reality' of war. By bringing contemporary warfare onto a theatre stage, therefore, today's dramatists do more than engage in a fierce competition with the mighty spectacle of media-produced images; if the power of the virtual rests precisely in the illusion of presence built through its aesthetics of real space and real time, this inevitably throws a problematic light on the representational imaginary *per se*, raising the troubling question of whether it is still possible to provide a visual recreation of war that will be immune from the logic of simulacra.

As David Edgar appositely observed, British theatre at the turn of the millennium was perfectly equipped with 'a vocabulary to deal directly with an international crisis that started with a terrorist outrage and moved on to shock and awe'.[7] The defining play of the 1990s, Sarah Kane's *Blasted*, had proven beyond doubt the power to provoke and unsettle unleashed through the onstage display of the violent realities of war. The vindication of the materiality of the war body against its obfuscation and sanitization by the media was one the main strategies enacted by Kane's play in order to reclaim the Bosnian conflict from the non-European otherness to which political and public discourse were conveniently consigning it. At the same time, Kane's in-yer-face aesthetics managed to steer clear of whatever disingenuous form of mimicry. In *Blasted*, the shocking stage images of war's atrocities that turned Kane overnight into a standard-bearer for 'New Brutalist drama' come across as deeply problematic signifiers: their referentiality is simultaneously affirmed and undercut, materialized and theatricalized so that, at the very same time as they gesture towards the offstage reality from which they have originated, they point to the inevitable mediation of representations. Conversely, the kind of aesthetic terror that *Blasted* enacts on its audience, through its powerful combination of extreme violence and the blowing apart of the familiar dramaturgical landmarks that might help contain and explain this violence, strikes us as eloquently isomorphic to the operations and the premises of twenty-first century political terror.[8]

In light of the currency and the attested efficacy of this formal template, the resolute ban on visual representation on the part of the dramatists examined in this chapter reads as a very deliberate change of track and a forceful declaration of intents. Their mobilization of mimesis as a world-creating model to destabilize, defamiliarize and unsettle habitual frames of perception is predicated upon an uncompromising rejection of the metonymy of presence that can derive from mimesis as a world-reflecting model.[9] While more directly prompted by a widespread suspicion of images, moreover, the dramatists' interrogation of mimesis in the age of simulacra has encompassed not only the domain of drama as the imitation of *action*, as according to Aristotle's traditional definition, but also that of drama as the imitation of *interaction*,[10] leading to a radical reconfiguration of the dialogic structure and its cardinal components and functions.

The theatre's aptitude to represent war, at least as far as Western culture is concerned, has been historically predicated on the common antagonistic principle underlying their respective grammars. The structural analogies between Clausewitz's theory of war and the classical notion of dramatic conflict as embodied in verbal interaction are only too easy to detect. The notion of war as an antagonistic confrontation between adversaries in pursuit of opposed, irreconcilable ends—'*an act of force to compel our enemy to do our will*', according to the definition given at the opening of *Vom Kriege* (1832)[11]—is wholly consonant with Hegel's coeval theorization of drama as a dialectical process originating from '*collisions* of circumstances, passions, and characters' that trigger off 'actions and then … the reactions which in turn necessitate a resolution of the conflict and discord'.[12] Like Hegel's *Aesthetics*, Clausewitz's classic analysis of the constitutive elements of war places distinctive emphasis on the relational, reciprocal character of conflict, as well as on its dynamic and transformative quality.[13] Similarly, a dialectical principle of internal contradiction has traditionally been seen as the basis of drama, a form which relies on the performative/actional dimension of speech for the construction of plot, situation and character.

With its spectacular demise of the conflict principle, the First Gulf War provided a clear example of the transformation of armed combat from an antagonistic and potentially destructive confrontation between adversaries to a clean, high-tech process of electrocution of the enemy, an impossible communication travelling one-way from a sender to a receiver who was always conveniently confined to the other side of the screen.[14] One decade later Jürgen Habermas, writing in the wake of the al-Qaeda strikes on 11 September, found it necessary to reassess his theory of communicative action and the centrality therein ascribed to linguistic exchange among the relations which concur in the intersubjective construction of the self. According to the German philosopher, the unilateral act of violence involved in the attack on the Twin Towers ought to be classified as a form of 'communicative pathology', in that it foreclosed the possibility for mutual perspective-taking upon which human communication depends.[15] Seeing terrorism as the most extreme manifestation of a collapse of reciprocal interaction in the age of globalization, Habermas wondered whether dialogue could be still thought of as 'a universal tool of communication', or if it should not rather begin to be envisaged as a culturally-specific practice which might not always or no longer be 'a feasible option'.[16]

In the dramatic works discussed in this chapter, Habermas's doubt is reframed in aesthetic terms, resulting in a full-scale reconsideration of the dialectical basis of drama. The systematic disruption of the dialogic texture that characterizes these new war plays seems deliberately meant to raise the issue of whether speech exchange can still provide an accurate formal embodiment for forms of organized violence that no longer appear to hinge on relational patterns of conflict. This refiguring or outright removal of interaction also extends to the other elements of drama which enable the intersubjective construction of the self, in particular the spatial and temporal continuity which is necessary to bind the conflicting selves within the shared enclosing frame of the scenic situation. As we shall see, the transition to the post-dialogic in these texts is also, under many respects, a transition to the postdramatic, especially when the latter is understood as an aesthetic stance involving 'a rupture and a beyond that continue to entertain relationships with drama and are in many ways its analysis and anamnesis'.[17]

Far Away, so close

Trevor Griffiths's *The Gulf Between Us* and Naomi Wallace's *In the Heart of America* are the two most notable exceptions to the almost complete reticence of the British stage about the First Gulf War.[18] If this omission seems to point to the theatrical intractability of the first truly mediatized postmodern war, it is also highly significant that Griffiths's and Wallace's plays, while not entirely eschewing the scenic re-enactment of the desert conflict, should be marked by a common tendency to challenge the integrity of the referential image through its juxtaposition with competing and conflicting frames of re-presentation, thus prefiguring the more systematic and thoroughgoing redefinition of the mimetic in subsequent dramatic responses to fully-blown global warfare.

Premiering at Leeds's West Yorkshire Playhouse in January 1992, *The Gulf Between Us* is the first intervention into the 1991 Iraq War by a British playwright, expressly written to mark the anniversary of the start of operations. While still featuring scenic recreations of Operation Desert Storm, Griffiths's play is a seminal attempt at placing visual representation in inverted commas and questioning media images through the theatrical medium. In its arresting opening scene, after a narrative prologue by the enigmatic storyteller-cum-craftsman O'Toole, a Westerner in Arabian attire, the audience are presented with '*mute cockpit-videos of famous strikes on* [*Baghdad's*] *bridges, buildings, installations*'.[19] The sadly popular 'videogame' footage of the bombing of the Iraqi capital, however, is muted and preceded by a kind of ghost soundtrack, a cacophony of human voices, languages and discourses, ranging from '*commercial jingles*' to '*a moral litany from First World leaders justifying the punitive use of force against Third World intransigents*' (2). This Babelian confusion is heard amidst complete stage darkness until a very dim light gradually thickens to herald dawn, and the flurry of voices gives way to a muezzin's call to prayer which then morphs into a siren's wail warning Iraqis of the coming air raid. In her thoughtful analysis of Griffiths's play, Jeanne Colleran points out that the splitting of sound and image, and the initial replacement of the visual with the aural, effectively work to 'fold ... technology into the frame of theatrical presentation' and thereby estrange and critique 'the act of medial transformation'.[20] In turn, this self-reflexive juxtaposition of different and competing modes of representation sets the tone for Griffiths's extended exploration, throughout his 'dreamplay' (as advertised in the introduction), of the divide, or indeed the gulf, between war as apprehended from the safe distance afforded by technology, and the raw reality of human grief, mangled bodies, death and devastation into which the 'spectacle' translates for those who experience it from the ground.

A similar and equally polemical foregrounding of the violence of the virtual forms the backbone of Naomi Wallace's *In the Heart of America* (London, Bush Theatre, 1994). Although the play bears the subtitle 'A Gulf War Drama' and is actually set in a war zone, armed conflict remains significantly peripheral to the main action, which alternates between naturalistic scenes that take place in the Saudi desert at the time of Operation Desert Storm, and the surreal reverberations of the Iraq war in an unspecified present ridden with ghosts, troubling memories and eerie nightmares. Even in the actual theatre of operations, moreover, war turns out to be a spectral presence: anticipating an enemy attack that never seems to come, the dialogues between Craver and Remzi, two young US soldiers, reconfigure scenes of armed combat as verbal fictions, playful simulations, and surreal erotic fantasies fuelled by the thrill of high-tech weaponry. The only first-hand contact the soldiers ever have with their unseen enemy is with the charred bodies of the retreating Iraqi troops bombed on the infamous 'Highway of Death', whom they have now been ordered to bury or rather, as the American-Palestinian Remzi provocatively puts it, 'cover ... up';[21] ironically, the only fire that really kills, for them, is friendly fire: the brutal, and this time close-up, violence directed against Remzi's sexual and racial difference by his own fellow soldiers. This displacement of the epicentre of conflict from faraway Kuwait into 'the heart of America' is mirrored, on the other hand, by the deliberate defamiliarization of the spectacular signposts of Operation Desert Storm: at the beginning of Act Two, the endlessly televised sounds of '*deafening ... jets, bomb, guns*' (117) are conjured up by Lue Ming, a ghost from the Vietnam War; to a similar estranging effect, the deathly fireworks setting ablaze the Baghdad night sky are watched from a distance by Craver and Remzi, the appalled, yet flippantly wisecracking spectators of this '*beautiful awe-inspiring*' (119) show.

With its ironic play on war's simultaneous proximity and distance, and its partial replacement of stage images with verbal reconstructions, Wallace's *In The Heart of America* prefigures two key structural principles of the dramaturgy of war authored by Caryl Churchill from the mid-1990s onwards, a body of work that must be credited with a unique propulsive force with respect to the emergence of the new war play as a distinctive genre, and with an equally crucial role in defining and redefining its concerns and contours. In Churchill's new war drama—and in her by now canonical masterpiece, *Far Away*—the dramatic strategies adumbrated in Wallace's and Griffiths's Gulf War plays are more systematically and self-consciously deployed to question generally-held assumptions about visual representation, leading to a sweeping critique of the very epistemology of theatre as a scopic field.

Over the past two decades or so, Caryl Churchill's engagement with the topic of war has been impressive and ever on the rise. From her manifesto-like piece *This is a Chair*, presented in 1997, through to her last short play to date, *ding dong the wicked* (staged at the Royal Court in October 2012), Caryl Churchill's theatrical oeuvre comes across as an extended, engrossed meditation on the aesthetic, ethical and epistemological problems involved in the theatrical representation of the new forms of warfare. This steadfast commitment to rethinking and redefining the dramaturgical frames whereby the new wars can be mediated on stage has been paralleled by Churchill's very active and visible role as a political campaigner in the public arena and by her growing involvement, as an artist and a citizen, in a number of anti-war initiatives nationally and internationally.[22] When one considers the remarkable space taken up by the issue of war in Churchill's public utterances, then, the concomitant disappearance of war in her staged plays becomes all the more conspicuous and meaningful.

In Churchill's more recent work, the sparing, minimalist strategy of displacement inaugurated with *This is a Chair* has increasingly acquired a sharp political edge, as eloquently shown by her bitter protest piece against the massacre of Gaza, *Seven Jewish Children*, written for the Royal Court and staged there in February 2009. In the course of seven short scenes, an unspecified number of adults, '*the parents and if you like other relations of the children*',[23] debate over what and how much should be told to a Jewish child about the violence perpetrated against Jews in the past, and the brutality of the Israeli-Palestinian conflict in the present. Chronologically, the seven chunks of text that compose *Seven Jewish Children* draw a trajectory leading from the Nazi persecutions up to the attack on Gaza after the victory of Hamas, and touching upon the foundation of Israel, the Six-Day War, the occupation of the Territories, the Intifada, the bulldozing of Palestinian homes, the plight of West

Bank residents at checkpoints. Churchill's condensed, poetically distilled account of victims turning perpetrators makes it all the more difficult to explain, justify or even cover up the horrors of war. At the same time, the seven Jewish children mentioned in the title, and constantly evoked through the repetition of the imperative 'Tell her'/'Don't tell her', are denied any kind of stage presence, either visual or aural: Churchill turns them into the hollow centre of a discourse on war which polemically confines them to invisibility, just like the hundreds of Gaza children killed by Israeli bombs during the siege.

A similar mechanism of displacement and denial is at work in *Far Away*, by almost general consensus the defining war play of the post-9/11 era. Staged at the Royal Court Theatre in 2000, but retrospectively acclaimed as a visionary prefiguration of the age of global warfare,[24] *Far Away* depicts a snug domestic universe that is gradually, stealthily infiltrated by escalating violence and finally plunged into a Hobbesian permanent war of all against all. Typically, however, this all-pervasive war is never shown on stage, where it is replaced by scenes of domestic or professional strife that function as metaphorical analogues and invite the audience to reflect on the meaning of the play's wilful dislocation of its 'primal scene'.

In the original Royal Court production, the play pointed to the slippages of mimesis since its very inception. The first stage image was that of a painted front cloth showing a picture-postcard scenery of the English countryside. As audience members were still taking their seats, the accompanying pastoral soundtrack of birdsong and streaming water was joined by a female voice singing of a 'Happy Land, Far Far Away'. After a few minutes, the cloth rose, curtain-like, to reveal the domestic interior where Churchill's opening scene takes place. Harper, her song now over, is trying to comfort her niece Joan who has woken up in the middle of the night. A feeling of unease gradually creeps in the apparent normality of the situation as the ten-year-old girl rebuts her aunt's hackneyed reassurances and, instead of returning to bed, begins to pose questions about things she has seen outside the house. Proving a relentless prosecutor, Joan skilfully delays the disclosure of evidence in order to lead Harper into self-contradiction and force her to admit that there are men, women and children in the shed who have been brutally tortured by her husband and will be carried away in a lorry at dawn.

The gradual uncovering of the truth is cleverly used by Caryl Churchill to place the equation of seeing and understanding under a very problematic light. The mystery in which Harper's family is involved invites the audience to become vicariously engaged in Joan's brave questioning. As they do so, however, spectators are resolutely denied the privilege of eyewitnessing upon which the success of Joan's truth-seeking endeavour is predicated. What is more, the relentless Harper deals a magisterial blow to the power inherent in Joan's gaze, mobilizing the 'just war' rhetoric in order to steer her young niece away from empathy with the victims. Towards the end of the scene, Joan's spectatorial status comes very close to the one prefigured by Harper while pressing her into the war effort: 'I'm not surprised you can't sleep, what an upsetting thing to see. But now you understand, it's not so bad. You're part of a movement now to make things better.'[25]

The second part of *Far Away* takes place '*Several years later*' (16) and is set in a hat factory where Joan, fresh from her milliner's degree, manages in the course of a week to overcome the diffidence of her more senior colleague, Todd, and win the much-coveted first prize at the Friday parade for which, we learn, the hats are meant. In James Macdonald's production, the silent scene featuring '*A procession of ragged, beaten, chained prisoners, each wearing a hat, on their way to execution*' (24) was choreographed to resemble a catwalk show, the convicts almost crushed under the bulk of the hats which they paraded downstage and which the audience had watched grow more '*enormous and preposterous*' (22) with each day of their manufacturing.

After the ceremony, a new week starts; Joan continues to urge Todd to fight corruption within the hat industry, while at the same time lamenting with shocking callousness the fleetingness of their elaborate creations, since all but the musealized winner are burnt together with the prisoners' bodies. With like-minded flippancy, Todd praises art's transience—'You make beauty and it disappears. I love that' (25)—at the same time as he more cogently reminds the newcomer that the destruction of the hats is essential to the consumerist logic upon which the whole economy that rewards their creativity is founded.[26] In the central section of Churchill's play, then, the violence of war is subjected to a double and complementary dislocation: on the one hand, it is replaced by Joan and Todd's scenes of professional micro-conflict (a symptom, also, of their by now ingrained habit of repression and displacement); on the other, it is absurdly sublimated into the ghastly art show involving the prisoners—a form of aestheticized, spectacularized violence identical to the one which informs the televised trials against the enemies of the regime that Todd likes to watch late at night 'drinking Pernod' (18). The brutality of state terrorism has become a central but inconspicuous feature not only of the characters' everyday life, but of cultural production as well: as Elin Diamond aptly notes, this marks the first occurrence, in Churchill's production, of an explicitly self-reflexive scene featuring 'committed artists who work for an apparatus'.[27]

In the third and final part of *Far Away*, the crucial role played by representations in creating, sustaining and perpetuating situations of belligerence becomes fully exposed. Following a further time lapse of a few years, Churchill takes us back to Harper's house. The symmetry with the first act is reinforced by the fact that this part, too, is composed of a single long scene that opens in *medias res*—here, with Harper's eerie line: 'You were right to poison the wasps' (28). The first words spoken by Harper in her exchange with Todd, who is now married to Joan, reintroduce the issue of the ideological justification of violence; her rhetorical manoeuvres, however, are now explicitly situated in the context of a 'war' (29) of global proportions. In the realistic, everyday tones of family chatter, Harper and Todd's words conjure up an apocalyptic scenario where every single living creature is enmeshed in a bloody conflict. Meanwhile, Joan is asleep, exhausted by the long march: to Harper's huge dismay, she has left the battlefront to join her husband who is on furlough. Joan's probable desertion drives a worried Harper to sound out Todd's loyalty by dragging him in a tricky review of allies and enemies, an almost impossible task given the constantly changing configurations of the opposing fronts. As the ideologue of the trio, it is Harper who is mostly responsible for the rhetorical construction of the conflicting parties according to ever more fragmented and exclusive parameters of identity:

> HARPER: The cats have come in on the side of the French.
>
> . . .
>
> TODD: But we're not exactly on the other side from the French. It's not as if they're the Moroccans and the ants.
>
> HARPER: It's not as if they're the Canadians, the Venezuelans and the mosquitoes.
>
> TODD: It's not as if they're the engineers, the chefs, the children under five, the musicians.
>
> HARPER: The car salesmen.
>
> TODD: Portuguese car salesmen.
>
> HARPER: Russian swimmers.
>
> TODD: Thai butchers.
>
> HARPER: Latvian dentists.
>
> TODD: No, the Latvian dentists have been doing good work in Cuba. They've a house outside Havana.
>
> HARPER: But Latvia has been sending pigs to Sweden. The dentists are linked to international dentistry and that's where their loyalty lies, with dentists in Dar-es-Salaam. (29–31)

The closing monologue in which Joan, on waking up, describes her journey across a terrifying landscape of violence seems to validate the scenario evoked by Harper and Todd's stichomythic catalogue of comically mismatched particularisms at war: with a further, surreal escalation of the conflict, Joan describes a world plunged into total warfare, a nightmare where 'everything has been recruited', including the weather, light, gravity and noise, and it remains to be seen 'who's going to mobilise darkness and silence' (38). While never straining from its unsettlingly plain tone, Joan's narrative reaches a potential climax when her progress is halted by a river. Unable to tell whether she is facing an enemy, an ally, or simply a river, Joan recounts how she testily set foot into the stream: 'It was very cold but so far it was all. When you've just stepped in you can't tell what's going to happen. The water laps round your ankles in any case' (38).

Joan's last words, and the last words of the play, leave the audience in complete uncertainty as to the real nature of the river. The fact that Joan is still alive to tell her story might lead us to infer that the water was harmless, but Churchill does not reveal whether or how Joan has actually gone through with the crossing—whether her 'small moment of sentient resistance'[28] has actually translated into action. Joan's account might not even end here, a possibility reinforced, in the Royal Court production, by Katharine Tozer's suspended delivery of the final line of her monologue.[29] Spectators are left groping in the dark, and resolutely denied an ocular proof which could confirm or disprove Joan's testimony. As with Harper and Todd before, Churchill's war is entirely mediated by unverifiable verbal representations that are very slippery in their truth-claims: Joan's eyewitness account, after all, is delivered after waking up from a long sleep, and retains the oneiric quality of a nightmare, or a reverie.

In the ultimate analysis, moreover, the same cognitive muddle is shown to envelop the characters in the play. In the closing section it becomes clear that their apprehension of the war they wage, watch and report is in fact no less shrouded in representations than it is for the audience. For Joan, Todd and Harper the enemy remains throughout a convenient blank which can strategically take on the identity that best serves their needs at any given time. Tellingly, none of them ever mentions a single instance of violence suffered at the hands of the enemy forces:[30] indeed, their battlefield reports are fundamentally self-incriminating in that they only attest to atrocities perpetrated *by* them on apparently harmless enemy combatants:

> TODD: I've shot cattle and children in
> Ethiopia. I've gassed mixed troop

> of Spanish, computer programmers and
> dogs. I've torn starlings apart with my
> bare hands. (34–35)

This arbitrary, unilateral violence is just as far away from the referent 'war' as the media-produced evidence that Harper appeals to, during her conversation with Todd, in order to corroborate her rhetorical construction of a bloodthirsty enemy. When she asks Todd whether he has 'seen the programme about crocodiles' (31), she is clearly tapping into televisual authority in order to back up her charges against the enemy species. Whereas young Joan's inquisitive gaze in the first act still seemed able to penetrate the mist of ideology, here verbal and visual representations appear to have definitively joined sides in neutralizing the cognitive power of eyesight. In this respect, Joan's hesitation before the river betrays her state of induced blindness. Faced with a life-or-death situation, she is unable to ascertain the truth from the visual evidence that is available to her: a group of Chilean soldiers upstream, cows watering downstream, and the slight cloudiness of the water at the river's centre, where the stream runs faster. By the end of the play, Joan's gaze is exposed as no less defective than the audience's restricted visual scope: both sighted and sightless are equally blind in Churchill's dreamscape.

In addition to denouncing the increasingly virtual and mediated nature of contemporary conflict, Churchill's avoidance of referentiality also proves strategic in other respects. By steering her representation of war towards Aesopic fable and literary dystopia, Churchill would seem to be inducing spectators to consider the situation of universal and permanent belligerence at the end of the play as a purely speculative fiction, safely and reassuringly confined to a different ontological dimension from reality. This mode of reception, however, is difficult to sustain once one realizes that those very same aspects of Churchill's war that appear to be at the farthest remove from reality ultimately bear a disturbing resemblance to the current state of military affairs. Todd's identification of 'the children under five' as a potential enemy, for example, powerfully resonates with the notorious statement made in 1996 by the then American Secretary of State, Madeleine Albright when she classified half a million Iraqi children who had died in consequence of the embargo as legitimate war targets.[31] Along the same lines, the regime's techniques for the rhetorical construction and demonization of the enemy in *Far Away* resemble recent historical cases of information warfare. Drawing on a classic topic in the historical demonization of the Other—be it the Jews in Nazi propaganda, or Communists during the Cold War—Harper often points to the alleged killing and even eating of babies as the ultimate proof of the enemy's evil nature. In the months preceding the First Gulf War, the trump card dealt by Hill & Knowlton, the world's largest public relations company, in the US-backed propaganda campaign against Saddam Hussein was the horrifying report of war crimes committed by Iraqi soldiers against premature babies who were wrenched from their incubators and left to die on the floor of Kuwaiti hospitals. This ghastly story, aptly supported by unverified evidence given by supposed eyewitnesses, circulated for months and was even repeated by the US President, George (H.W.) Bush, before it was finally exposed as a hoax; in the meantime, though, the ensuing media hype had been decisive in securing public opinion support for armed intervention in the Gulf.[32] As a further example of Churchill's analogical reconfiguration of patterns of conflict, the grotesque proliferation of particularisms on a global scale in the third part of the play is underpinned by the same logic of 'glocalization'[33] informing the post-bipolar world, although in *Far Away* religion is significantly and polemically excluded from the set of identitarian grounds for conflict. Even the mobilization of the animal realm in *Far Away* finds an unexpected mimetic equivalent: with characteristic prescience, Churchill anticipated the news media's insistence on the military potential of the animal realm in the age of global war. News stories about animal fighters were heard regularly during the run-up to the Iraqi campaign in early 2003: to quote but a few cases from Italian media sources, readers and viewers were informed of an averted plot by an Egyptian Jihad cell involving pigeons that had been programmed to carry remote-controlled explosive charges on to the rooftops of buildings; of sea lions trained in a San Diego base to perform underwater actions against terrorists; and of an irritating desertion when Tacoma, a mine clearer dolphin drafted into US Marines, went unpatriotically AWOL in the Gulf.[34]

While at the time of its debut, in November 2000, it was still possible to classify *Far Away* as an 'absurdist' play and the war represented in it as 'pure theatre',[35] after 9/11 Churchill's oneiric yet disturbingly accurate play has been widely hailed for its topicality. This turnabout in the reception of *Far Away* is appositely condensed in the comment, made by Churchill's colleague and admirer Simon Stephens, that while the play felt 'absurdist' when he first read it in 2000, after the onset of the war on terror 'it seemed like social realism'.[36] When observed from a post-9/11 perspective, then, Churchill's fairy tale world appears far less remote, both chronologically and spatially, than its deliberately misleading title initially appeared to claim. In the first production this Magrittean trick was underscored through the use of the small studio space of the Royal Court Theatre Upstairs, where Churchill's dystopian fantasy was all but far away from the reality of the spectators.

Dramaturgically, this mechanism of displacement reads as a slightly modified version of the one at work in *This is a Chair*. In Churchill's earlier inquiry into the slipperiness of mimesis we gradually become aware, underneath the apparently random juxtaposition of word and image, of a synecdochic connection whereby the dynamics of human behaviour presented in each scene function as a miniature version of the larger issue announced by its running headline. In *Far Away*, the correspondence is based less on a quantitative relationship than on the effect of estrangement produced through the interplay of distance and proximity, disjunction and conjunction which is the ruling principle of metaphor and the source of its cognitive potential.

This is all the more relevant since, through another directorial addition, in the Royal Court production the play's ending unmistakably connected the invisibility of war to the problem of the (theatrical) gaze. Joan's last words were followed by a moment of silence; the stage went dark and then, suddenly, the idyllic curtain which had been lifted at the beginning dropped back down with a loud bang. This *coup de théâtre* lent itself to two opposed yet complementary readings: on the one hand, it felt like a rude awakening from a nightmare, an abrupt return to normality after the distressing stay in one of the possible worlds of fiction; the painted cloth, however, also resembled a huge eyelid which suddenly blocked the audience's view after a brief glimpse of the disconcerting truth about their world. At the time of the first performance, in 2000, the ending was arguably meant to shock audiences awake and force them to acknowledge that the era of global conflict had already begun, although they might have failed or refused to realize it. In its ambivalence, the final stage image forced spectators to reconsider the categories of the 'real' and the 'fictional' in their application to contemporary conflict, and to become aware of the risk, denounced by Baudrillard at the time of the First Gulf War, that a real war might well go unnoticed for habitual consumers of its 'artificial dramatisation'.[37] The unmistakable Englishness of the idealized countryside painted on the curtain clearly reinforced the impression that this was a state-of-the-nation play; the iconography also evoked British recruitment posters of the First and Second World War, which typically depicted rural arcadias in order to symbolize the homeland and the set of values that patriots were being called upon to fight for.[38] Through these suggestions, the depicted idyll with which *Far Away* parted from its spectators pointed to war as an essential precondition of what passes off as peacetime civilization, and to the human cost involved in keeping up the pretence.

This ending powerfully encapsulated the war of images that in *Far Away* replaces the image of war and challenges the authority of the visual and the visible in the contemporary battlefield. In the closing sequence, as in the rest of the play, war is ostensibly absent from the field of vision but is at the same time a pervasive presence; having been fully established as the 'New Normal', it is both nowhere and everywhere. In Churchill's play, however, the barriers between the virtual and the real are not only undermined, but further exposed as the product of a politically-inflected gaze. That this final blow at the ontology of the visible should be dealt on and through a stage curtain is a powerful indicator of the self-reflexive dimension embedded in Churchill's critique of visual representation. With its closing eyelid, the ending of *Far Away* confirms Churchill's resolute refusal to address war directly, while at the same time pointing to a wholehearted embrace of theatricality as strategic vantage point for engaging with its simulacra.

Fragments from a warrior's discourse

Churchill's next take on the new wars premiered at the Royal Court on 10 November 2006. In her first post-9/11 play proper, the disjunction between word and image acquires an even sharper ironic edge and is directly related to the war on terror and a whole genealogy of historical antecedents. Whereas in *Far Away* the contrast between the invisibility of war and its totalizing scenic presence builds gradually until it reaches a climax in the apocalyptic third act, in *Drunk Enough to Say I Love You?* the reality of global, never-ending war is presented as a given from the start. The play covers half a century of (dirty) wars fought or supported by the United States by charting the ups and downs of a homosexual affair. Along eight short dialogues, Sam and Jack fall in love, become a couple, fall out, break up, reconcile, and again part.

In the opening scene, Jack calls on Sam, who has forgotten or feigns to have forgotten about their night together, and accepts to leave his family and job in order to start a relationship with him; in return, he is sparingly warned that this will require a readiness to go 'anywhere'[39] and do anything. For all of Churchill's disclaimers that the love story between (Uncle) Sam and (Union) Jack was not intended as an allegory of the Special Relationship and, specifically, of the political alliance between Bush and Blair during the Iraqi campaign,[40] in the post-Iraq climate the power dynamics inside the couple, and the intimate pact stipulated as a prologue to their joint war efforts, had inevitable resonance with the debates around Britain's involvement in the invasion of Iraq and the British prime minister's infamous tête-à-tête with George W. Bush in the American president's Texas ranch. Similarly, the increasing strain within Sam and Jack's romance and the progressive deterioration of their entente could be seen to reflect the increasing discomfort, in British public opinion, over the American-led war on terror and particularly the military campaign in Iraq. By 2006, the initial trauma of the terrorist attacks on 9/11 had cooled off, and with it the initial upsurge of unconditional support for whatever retaliatory actions had been undertaken in the wake of those attacks. In Iraq, the supposed threat posed by Saddam Hussein's weapons of mass destruction had been exposed as a colossal hoax, and the demanding toll involved in the exportation of democracy was becoming ever more evident, especially after repeated clashes between British troops and enraged Iraqi mobs in the Basra area. After his recent re-election, George W. Bush had come to bear an even stronger resemblance to Churchill's despotic Sam, dragging his subservient British ally into a gangrenous conflict with no evident payoff other than honouring a highly burdensome alliance.

Having established the terms of engagement in the opening scene, the 'lover's discourse' that makes up the rest of *Drunk Enough to Say I Love You?* is entirely made up of references to conflict situations involving the American superpower, along a timeline which begins with Korea and Vietnam, moves on to Lumumba's assassination in Congo and US-backed military coups in Greece and Chile, and reaches up to Afghanistan, Gaza and Guantanamo. Sam and Jack's lines are filled exclusively and obsessively with weapons, military strategies, destabilization tactics, more or less overt acts of aggression and control; yet they are spoken by two lovers sitting comfortably at home on their cosy leather couch. In James Macdonald's production at the Royal Court, the jarring contrast between the nano-scale domesticity of the context of enunciation and the macro-scale politics of its content was further offset by Eugene Lee's brilliant set design. The sofa, the only prop on stage, was enveloped in darkness and literally floated in a spaceless void. As Sam and Jack recited the seemingly endless catalogue of bloody conflicts troubling our world, the couch rose by a few inches at each conversational reprise, reaching about the height of the gallery in the closing scene; meanwhile, invisible stage hands hastened to dispose of the coffee cup or cigarette butt discarded with sublime insouciance by these two lords of the universe. The sense of remoteness was further increased by the proscenium which framed this absurd domestic double act with dressing-room light bulbs that dimmed between scenes.[41]

While hinting at the public and artificial dimension of Sam and Jack's relationship, the deliberate theatricality of the stage arrangement also gestured self-reflexively towards the play's own aesthetic framing of the violence and brutality of war, thereby implicitly questioning the role and position of the audience. Like Sam and Jack, our reflection in the mirror, we too are 'couch warriors', spectators in a theatre of war which recruits us as global consumers of a rich repertoire of dirty wars that become duly sanitized and aestheticized in the process of dishing them

1. Floating in cosmic darkness: Sam (Ty Burrell) and Jack (Stephen Dillane) in the Royal Court production of Caryl Churchill's *Drunk Enough to Say I Love You?* (2006). Photography by Peter Mumford. © Peter Mumford.

up as atrocitainment. This parallel becomes even more apparent in Scene Six, when Sam and Jack are explicitly characterized as TV viewers as they mention the Twin Towers being hit before their eyes. At the same time, however, the image of the two world superpowers enjoying from their living room seat the spectacle of an all-encompassing conflict of their own making is also an ironical reference to an earlier foundational moment in the concomitant mediatization of war and weaponization of media in contemporary warfare: as Jeanne Colleran pointedly reminds us, the live broadcast of the first strikes of Operation Desert Storm, in 1991, was intercut with shots of the American and the British presidents (George Bush Senior and John Major) as they watched on television the military campaign they had just launched.[42]

More in general, in her determination to keep off the stage the landscapes of war that are mentioned in the play, Churchill polemically declares her distrust of images, her awareness of their inescapable simulacral component. In their place, Churchill offers us a scenic metaphor which, by its very concealment of the referent 'war', at once denounces the invisibility of the countless conflicts that are ignored by the media industry and subtly captures the voyeuristic premises of the relationship we entertain with images. Whether by lack or by excess of visibility, the global war of *Drunk Enough to Say I Love You?* remains shrouded in the cosmic darkness which surrounds the snug safety of Sam and Jack's surreal drawing room.

At a closer look, moreover, the eclipse of war from Churchill's stage turns out to be not only a visual but also a linguistic phenomenon. Tellingly, the word 'war' never figures in Sam and Jack's conflict-crammed verbal exchanges: the only two occurrences of the term are highly ironical in their displacement of war into the past ('second world war', 16) or into the sci-fi domain of 'star wars' (24). This refusal not only to show war but also to name it is symptomatic of Churchill's endeavour to account for the surreptitious quality of today's diffused and degenerate warfare, with its simultaneously polymorphous and amorphous nature.[43] As Elin Diamond fittingly remarks in her discussion of Churchill's 'terror dramaturgy', *Drunk Enough to Say I Love You?* is an emblematic instance of the way 'the spatial logic of terror's dissemination, from here to there, from there to here, has worked its way into the form of Churchill's plays'.[44]

In this post-9/11 play, indeed, Churchill's critical mimesis goes one step further by spilling onto the drama text, enacting a rupture of its dialogical basis. The key dramaturgical feature of *Drunk Enough to Say I Love You?* is the erosion of dialogue in parallel to and in connection with the destabilization of the temporal and spatial coordinates of the scenic situation. Churchill's plot is built upon a major chronological disjunction in that the love affair between Sam and Jack unfolds sequentially, whereas the story of America's endless wars is organized thematically and develops according to principles of circularity and contiguity. In this way, the play stresses substantive historical continuities between the United States' steady recourse to war in order to achieve and consolidate the global supremacy of American 'democracy', and the more recent elevation of this pattern into a state of permanent war. Each individual scene is devoted to a specific form or technique of belligerence and its diverse manifestations across time and space: examples include the use of (mis-)information and black propaganda to overthrow politically-opposed governments and favour regime change (Scene Two), carpet bombing and other 'shock and awe' tactics targeting the civilian population (Scene Three), protectionism and trade wars (Scene Four), environmental warfare (Scene Eight). Each section pinpoints some key episodes that testify to America's intense commerce with an impressive array of conventional and especially unconventional weapons from the Second World War to the present day: for example Scene Seven, dealing with the systematic use of torture, covers an historical frame ranging from the military Junta in Greece, on to the Vietnam War, Central and South-American dictatorships, Afghanistan and then Guantanamo Bay. In terms of political references, the story rewinds and restarts from the beginning with each new conflict scenario, albeit with different actors and a changed setting, and comes to a new climax as it again reaches the present. In the original Royal Court production, these narrative interruptions and re-starts were marked through a short musical intermission.

The overall effect created by Churchill's arrangement of the political narrative is of a genealogy of forms of contemporary conflict that proceeds in endless loops and ultimately subsumes the linear narrative of the love story within its repetitive circular motion: at the end of Scene Six, Jack leaves Sam to return to his family; in the following scene, he comes back, declares he cannot live without him, and the couple resume their ménage, and their warmongering, simply picking up at the point where they had left off. The final scene, where Jack again threatens to leave, seems to prefigure in Beckettian fashion the endless repetition of a by now consolidated pattern. As if to symbolize the impossibility of drawing the romantic plot to an end, the play closes with a dangling line, as Sam demands of his wavering partner that he should 'love me love me, you have to love me, you' (42). Similarly, Sam and Jack's interlaced litany of bombings in Scene Three does not properly end but is simply broken off at the end of the scene, conveying the impression of a proliferation of conflicts that exceeds the formal limits of the text:

> SAM: bombing Vietnam now, bombing
> Grenada, bombing Korea, bombing Laos,
> bombing Guatemala, bombing Cuba,
> bombing El Salvador, bombing Iraq,
> bombing Somalia, bombing Lebanon
> JACK: but it's Israel bombing
> SAM: so? bombing Bosnia, bombing Cambodia,
> bombing Libya, bombing
> JACK: used to be a village and now
> SAM: because we want it gone
> JACK: need a coffee
> SAM: get a coffee
> JACK: exhausting
> SAM: thrilling
> JACK: exhausting being so thrilled
> SAM: coffee but keep
> JACK: bombing China, bombing Panama
> SAM: good at this
> JACK: well
> SAM: did a whole lot before like second world
> war and going right back

JACK: all the back killings like the indians
SAM: never sure how many we started
JACK: maybe twenty million, fifty
SAM: got them down to a quarter million so
JACK: not looking at that
SAM: no just get on with the job which is bombing
JACK: bombing Peru, bombing (15–16)

Both the time and the space of war stretch well beyond the boundaries of scenic fiction, in a potentially endless expansion. Yet, at the same time, all the conflict situations alluded to by Sam and Jack are comprised within the claustrophobic space of their intimate relationship. By making war the sole topic of the lovers' verbal interaction, Churchill compresses half a century of belligerence into the here and now of their unfolding affair; docked onto their private love story, history acquires a paradoxical dual temporality, a simultaneously diachronic and synchronic quality. In Scene Six, for example, the acts of terrorism punctuating the last fifty years of American foreign policies are all listed as happening within the present tense of Sam and Jack's dialogue:

SAM: got to plant bombs in the hotels in Havana
JACK: yes ok ok the Cuban exiles in Miami are just
SAM: and get the money to Iraq
JACK: done it, the Iraqi National Accord have the
SAM: and have they destabilised Saddam yet? No
JACK: car bombs
SAM: giving them millions
JACK: hundreds civilians dead
SAM: not enough to
JACK: ok
SAM: fucking results
JACK: off my back, will you?
SAM: desperate for
JACK: mujahedeen
SAM: yes yes train the
JACK: so ok that's something really good
SAM: stop at nothing, flaying, explosions, whole villages
JACK: and here we're getting on with the assassinations (29–30)

Only a few lines later, roles are swapped for a moment as Sam and Jack, having just learnt about the 1998 American embassy bombings in Africa, watch in astonishment the Twin Towers collapse in a brilliantly laconic rendition of the defining twenty-first century trauma, and of the political lexicon in which it became instantly encapsulated:

> JACK: look out we're being
> SAM: no no no the towers
> JACK: wow
> SAM: evil (32)

In the ultimate analysis, the historical conflicts crammed inside *Drunk Enough to Say I Love You?*—perpetual yet instantaneous, localized yet boundless—turn out to be the manifold facets of an infinite, protean war that swallows up time and space, erodes the boundaries between past, present and future, and collapses the distance between the safe haven of Sam and Jack's drawing room and the murky vastness that surrounds it. Strategically, moreover, the chronotope of war that emerges from the lovers' discourse articulated in Churchill's play stands in sharp contrast to the disappearance of war from the play's visual frame, making this absence even more conspicuous.

Another effect of Churchill's relocation of global conflict within a dysfunctional relationship is to specifically link the paradoxical (omni) presence/absence of war on stage to issues of relationality. The state of permanent belligerence thematized in *Drunk Enough to Say I Love You?* is entirely played out inside the couple. More than fifty years of historical wars with their million dead are absorbed in a private relationship which, while not utterly conventional, is nevertheless rather predictable and commonplace. A whole history of massacres, atrocities, genocides is turned into the subject matter of Sam and Jack's cliché-ridden dialogues and banal sentimental masturbations. Sam, the dominant partner, puts pressure on Jack, urges him to be more active and enthusiastic, is irritated by his hesitations which he dismisses as mere surliness, and doubts his love at the first feeble hint of unpatriotic dissent. On the other hand, the potentially moral or political objections raised by Jack are primarily a way of expressing his personal unhappiness and resisting the power imbalance in their ménage. Scene Four, for example, opens with Jack vindicating his right to keep in touch with friends and family; Sam's impatience, however, soon puts paid to his complaints, and Jack rather more wisely decides to try and chase the blues away by resuming 'work' (17) on trade agreements designed to open up Third World markets for US exports.

Amelia Howe Kritzer sees a problem with the play's political effectiveness because 'although the love affair framework highlights the link between the personal and the political, use of narrative to deliver the critique of U.S. imperialism suggests that the invasion of Iraq, as well as other acts of aggression—and the support to this aggression by ordinary people—are the result of personal obsessions, fears, and desire.'[45] I would argue, rather, that the relational dynamics underpinning Churchill's ironic romancing of war provide a very eloquent correlative of the 'totalitarian dramaturgy'[46] of asymmetrical warfare: the violence emanating from the couple onto the rest of the world is a truly one-way affair, a punishment inflicted from high above by the world superpower and its servile and serviceable ally that excludes any real 'collision', to use Hegel's term, or retort. This situation of radical unilateralism, which divests dialogue of its dialectical prerogatives, also informs the confrontation between Sam and Jack. Their verbal combat is far more apparent than real, and their 'war', too, is a matter of consensual, rather than conflictive, violence: an imposition of conformity through overwhelming force and dissuasion. Jack has entered into a contract which binds him to unconditional love; every time he ventures a potentially critical comment on Sam's foreign policy, putting a strain on their consensual sadomasochism, Sam does not deem it necessary to engage in dialectical argument with his partner in order to bolster up his position: he just curtly reminds him that dissent is simply not an option. Jack is not entitled to agree or disagree but only to love or not to love; to be with Sam on his terms or leave him and sink in the terrifying void surrounding the floating sofa. In Sam's formulation, their romantic attachment is regulated by the same Manichean paranoia underpinning the war on terror, with anything short of full commitment to the cause becoming equated to complicity with an 'axis of evil'. As is quite clear from his chilling monologue on torture techniques at the opening of Scene Seven, moreover, Sam is quite prepared to dispense with Jack's cooperation and go on solo with his warrior's discourse. In the end, then, even the conversation that provides the only form of dramatic action in *Drunk Enough to Say I Love You?* is revealed as a mere simulacrum of verbal interaction, a dialogue that has been entirely drained of its dialectical essence.[47]

Linguistically, this erosion of the conflictive basis of drama finds its counterpart in the pervasiveness of ellipsis. Following a process already adumbrated in *This is a Chair*, the characters' utterances in *Drunk Enough to Say I Love You?* are not naturalistic dialogue lines but rather a sampling of shreds from longer conversations which spectators are tasked to reconstruct. In *This is a Chair*, this mechanism was displayed in the scene called 'Hong Kong', featuring a homosexual couple who are having a row until the arrival of a common friend sparks off an insider/outsider opposition that leads to their renewed alliance. The dialogue between the two partners, Tom and Leo, is made up of fragments from a longer conversation taking place over a twenty-four hour period[48] and mainly consists of incomplete sentences almost entirely devoid of punctuation; Leo's final line, 'love it when you' (27), reads indeed as a prefiguration of Sam's dangling injunction at the close of *Drunk Enough to Say I Love You?*. In the later play, Churchill's editing serves to further foreground the power imbalance inside the couple: for Sam, the possessor of truth, details are redundant; Jack, for his part, responds to his partner's imperious laconism by compliantly confirming or completing his utterances. This element of cooperation, however, also sheds light on the complementarity between partners, their steady adherence to the scripted roles (active/passive, dominating/dominated) that regulate their relationship. Instead of engaging in the cut and thrust of dialogue, Sam and Jack speak almost as one, their non-conflictive, additive language yielding rather the impression of a choral structure. While their peculiar scenes from a marriage unfold, Sam and Jack's lines shrink progressively: the two lovers need to use ever fewer words to understand each other and we witness the gradual development of what ultimately turns into a 'private or "special" form of communication, impenetrable to others'.[49]

This process reaches a climax in the final moments of the play, when Sam and Jack come to an extreme form of stichomythia in which language is entirely divested of its relational components:

> JACK: carbon
> SAM: can't see it in the air, so
> JACK: Kyoto?
> SAM: price of electricity in California
> JACK: but
> SAM: nuclear
> JACK: danger
> SAM: efficient
> JACK: waste
> SAM: solution
> JACK: Iran? (40)

With this reduction of the dialogical structure to a sequence of single isolated words, Churchill gives textual form to the ultimately non-dialectical quality of Sam and Jack's speech exchange and the totalitarian premises upon which it rests. But the ellipses in *Drunk Enough to Say I Love You?* are also loaded with implications for the audience. A few syncopated fragments may be enough to ensure effective intrascenic communication between Sam and Jack, but on the *theatron* axis spectators are instead called upon to complete, unpack, contextualize these remnants of dramatic dialogue. This interpretive task requires an effort of intralingual translation which strategically constructs audience members as partners, or indeed accomplices, in the verbal transactions occurring on stage. By casting spectators as active co-participants in Sam and Jack's defective conversation, Churchill astutely intimates that one can subscribe to a 'way of life' (23) that needs global permanent belligerence to sustain itself even without an explicit assent like the one given by Jack at the beginning of the play: just because we are there, Sam's invisible yet omnipresent war surreptitiously recruits us all, whether we like it or not, whether we are aware of it or not.

Media narratives

The dialogue with media images, which is conducted *in absentia* and by inferences in Churchill's theatre of war, forms the explicit theme of a number of plays written in and about the post-9/11 landscape. In these works, the issue of mimesis becomes directly related to the modes of production and reception that have become dominant in the age of global media, and to their impact on the way we apprehend, construe and respond to the event of 'war'.

A seminal quality here must undoubtedly be ascribed to Martin Crimp's *Attempts on her Life* (1997), a play in which the critique of media representations becomes fully integrated into a probing interrogation of the theatre as a representational art form. Devised against the backdrop of the new forms of 'degenerate warfare' of the 1990s, and filled with references to ethnic cleansing, Crimp's 'Seventeen scenarios for the theatre'—as they are defined on the contents page of the play text—combine the ellipsis, or indeed the eclipse, of the subject of the performance, the enigmatic Anne, with her reflections in a kaleidoscope of disembodied images that are verbally recreated by the anonymous speakers on stage. Each scenario tackles the invisible female protagonist of the narrative from a different angle. As parents, lovers, friends, police interrogators, art critics, film-makers and many other unidentified voices take turns at defining her, Anne morphs into Anya, Annie, Anny, Annushka; in the process, she becomes everything from a 'megastar' to the survivor of ethnic slaughter, from a scientist to a terrorist, from a mythical heroine to the 'girl next door', as according to the title of the fourteenth scenario, structured as a farcical sequence of rhyming conjectures:

> She's an artificial tan
> She's the fat in the pan
> She's the film in the can
> She's the shit in the fan.[50]

In Crimp's play, each 'attempt' stakes a claim for Anne's presence while at the same time spotlighting her absence; by the same token, war is thematically present in a number of scenarios whose titles point elsewhere and, conversely, it is conspicuously absent from the ones which allegedly address 'The threat of international terrorism™' or focus on 'The occupier'—a striking analogue of the Magrittean trope we find in Caryl Churchill's *This is a Chair.* This game of hide and seek with the referent 'war' is also masterfully embedded in the play's punning title, with the word 'attempts' evoking the elusiveness of the central character and the aggressiveness of the mediations through which she is apprehended, as well as the more literal violence of war, terror, ethnic cleansing which is one of the principal motifs punctuating, and holding together, Anne's impossible biography. In the revised edition of the script, published in 2005, the 'murderous capacity of images' displayed in Crimp's scenarios is explicitly placed within the context of Baudrillard's media critique through a direct quotation from his 1990 essay, *The Transparency of Evil*: 'No one will have directly experienced the actual cause of such happenings, but everyone will have received an image of them.'[51] The pervasiveness of images, and the way they engulf the real while offering it up for consumption, is identified by the play's epigraph as the underlying theme of the play, again establishing the primacy of representational conflicts over representations of conflict.

Crimp's intermedial discourse was given overt scenic form in Katie Mitchell's superb revival at the National Theatre in 2007. The performance was conceived as a live TV show in which Crimp's scenarios were played out according to different media formats which oriented, and indeed constrained, the actors' apparently improvised storytelling. As the company engaged collectively in the activity of media production, Crimp's narrative fragments were turned into one long, continuous scene which took place on a multi-tasking, multi-focal stage split into several *loci deputati*, and cluttered with recording and broadcasting technology. The actors' performances were filmed and relayed in real time as live feed on screens placed in different areas of the stage; live and recorded media were shown competing for space and for the audience's attention, in a constant attempt to frame and overrule each other. This friction was eloquently conveyed by the performance's finale. The shrill cacophony of multiple voices, sounds and noises drowning the stage was comfortingly neutralized by a return to the bare set and the 'unplugged' choral delivery with which the play had opened. Released from the pressures of media production, the company went on cheerfully to weave their joint narrative; until, with a final ironic twist, the orchestra pit began to slowly descend and the actors were literally swallowed by the stage, their initial excitement turning into worried agitation as they sensed the imminent fade-out.

When connected with Crimp's homage to Baudrillard's media theory, the final *coup de théâtre* devised by Katie Mitchell comes across as a striking visual rendition of the 'implosion of meaning' theorized by Baudrillard as the core mechanism of simulation. Crimp's text does not specify the number of speakers involved in the delivery of each scenario and leaves the attribution of lines blank; the only indications provided are about turn-taking, with dashes at the beginning of a line indicating a change of speaker. On the page, some scenarios feel like duologues while others appear to have a more choral structure. While the original Royal Court production, directed by Tim Albery, sought to invent a different realistic setting for each scenario—the cabin of a plane that is about to crash, a restaurant where actors are having a post-performance dinner, or a military roadblock in a Third World country[52]—in her revival at the National Theatre Mitchell opted instead for the dislocated ensemble delivery which she had already tried out when directing the play in an Italian production at Milan's Piccolo Teatro in 1999. In this seminal version, a cast of eight performers, four men and four women, played 'a group of young writers who had to improvise all the play's scenarios under pressure from an unseen force'.[53] Although the highly mediatized stage of the National was a far cry from the stripped-back theatre at the Piccolo, Mitchell's new production retained the rehearsal feeling of the earlier Milan run. But in the 2007 revival the actors' constrained, pre-formed improvisations gestured more clearly towards the simulacral quality of media production and reproduction: more than enacting scenarios they were enacted by them, betraying their fundamental entrapment in a closed circle of performative speculation in which the model precedes and generates the referent.

Nothing outside the (media) text

Crimp's deft combination of the embargo on visual representation with the display and critique of popular media formats set the tone for a number of post-9/11 war plays. This influence is probably nowhere as manifest as in Mark Ravenhill's *Product*, which premiered at the Edinburgh Fringe in 2005 before embarking on an international tour. In many respects, Ravenhill's hilarious one-acter reads as a spin-off from the brainstorming session which opens *Attempts on Her Life*.[54] The essential ingredients of the hackneyed sentimental plot that Crimp's speakers are intent on devising in the scenario called 'Love and Ideology' are picked up and expanded in the film script which Ravenhill's protagonist, a film producer, recounts to Olivia, the actress he hopes to cast as the female lead, in order to convince her of the global saleability of his 'product'. With even greater deliberateness, moreover, Ravenhill builds upon the work-in progress dimension of Crimp's playlet in order to estrange the signifying practices of the popular media: adding yet another mystifying title to the list, what we witness here is the process, rather than the product, of translating war into the language of Hollywood blockbusters.

The surreal mix of 'love and ideology' which James pitches to Olivia in *Product* is a riot of trite clichés and stereotypes, as the script respectfully follows the well-established formulas that have secured substantial box office revenue to countless commercial movies. When Amy and the 'tall, dusky fellow'[55] sitting next to her on the flight back to London end up in her ultra-cool Docklands loft, it quickly becomes clear that the sexual encounter between civilizations is sadly doomed to revert to a more customary clash. As was to be expected, the jihadist's commitment to the cause proves highly incompatible with Amy's duty towards the defence of Western values and her righteous vengeance for the attack on the Twin Towers. Through his narrator, Ravenhill presents us with a wickedly funny assemblage of prevailing stereotypes about Islamic fundamentalism, shabby Freudian symbolism, mawkish tabloid romance, soft-porno fantasies, Hollywood-style populism, cheap melodrama and predictable special effects. The definitive and complete absorption of contemporary conflict into its media images is comically mirrored, inside the film script, by the ridiculously self-centred attitude of the heroine: before takeoff, as she places her Gucci luggage in the overhead locker, Amy spots the jihadist's prayer mat (an item no genuine Muslim ever parts with!) and asks the mysterious man with dark good looks to whom it belongs whether he does yoga—a Bridget Jones moment without the redeeming self-consciousness. Later on, the discovery that Mohammed is a follower of al-Qaeda, and that his suicidal terrorist attack on Disneyworld Europe has been ordered by Osama bin Laden in person, is treated by Amy as a side issue with respect to her overwhelming need to love and be loved in order to heal from her inner wound (caused, needless to say, by the death of her boyfriend Troy on 9/11, as we discover through a melodramatic replay of his last voice message on Amy's mobile phone).

While the more direct target of Ravenhill's biting satire is mass film and TV production, the accumulation effect which originates from this 'trans-global and trans-cultural'[56] agglomerate of media formats and discourses effectively conveys the all-encompassing sweep of the act of mediatization: in the world of *Product* there is, literally, nothing outside the (media) text. In this respect, the double level of mediation to which war is subjected in Ravenhill's play—filtered through media discourses which then become the subject of James's narrative feat—is a very effective way of estranging the markers of fictionality which tend to be subsumed in the 'pure performing present' of minute-by-minute coverage of live events.[57] Although we may fail to recognize it, from the First Gulf War onwards we have become accustomed to watching war as a mini-series told by reliable, authoritative anchors who act as the 'omniscient narrators of a daily novel'.[58] By doubly emphasizing its 'artificial dramatization' of war, to return to Baudrillard's expression, *Product* directs the audience's attention towards the narrative devices which James's plot of 'love in the time of Jihad' shares with news media versions of Islamist terrorism, thereby unmasking the illusion of immediacy and transparency which these familiar formal devices are expressly designed to bolster up.

In this way, the thorough narrativization of war and its media images in *Product* becomes in itself a form of mimetic criticism of, at one and the same time, the solipsistic dimension of the West's engagement with Islamic otherness, and the concomitant hypertrophy and hypertelia of contemporary conflict. Just as happens in Crimp's *Attempts on Her Life*, the event of war has been here completely swallowed up by its simulacra, placing a heavy burden on its stage reproduction; at the same time, the invisibility and unknowability of the enemy in the so-called war on terror is shown to have engendered a representational overload that Ravenhill himself explicitly relates to a cognitive deficit:

> An al-Qaeda bomb, or planes going into a tower, doesn't have a story, unlike an IRA bomb. That had a story, in that the IRA would say, 'This is going to happen', then there would be a bomb, and afterwards there would be a claim saying, 'Yeah we did it, and we want troops out of Ireland'. That's your beginning, middle and end. But with al-Qaeda, there's nothing like that, they just do it. I think that's one of the things that unsettles us, because we want a story. So my character tries to give suicide bombing a story.[59]

In performance, the play's estrangement of representations was further sustained through repeated breaches of stage illusion. The first and most evident one stemmed from Ravenhill's idea to play James himself, allegedly in order to find 'a route into the impossibly big issue of two whole cultures meeting',[60] but with obvious repercussions on the reality/fiction divide. James, the authorial figure in the text, coincides with the real-life author of a play in which a film producer explains that a theatre writer has been hired to work on a weak bit in the script. In the enlarged 'World Remix' version of the play (2007), this tongue-in-cheek self-reflexivity was reinforced through Ravenhill's frequent acknowledgment of the audience, either by delivering his lines out front or by way of tactical pauses and emphases and knowing glances.[61]

Towards the end of the performance, James's mention of a muezzin's call to prayer provoked a sound effect and a brief light change which were external to the narration: for a moment, and with yet another added frame, James and her silent partner were transported inside the movie. By systematically juggling with levels of fictionality, Ravenhill's staging deftly contributed to defamiliarize mimetic reproduction, which thereby became held up as just another special effect in the discursive configuration of 'the real' in today's representational battlefield.

The rest is silence

Caryl Churchill's *Drunk Enough to Say I Love You?* received its long-awaited Italian premiere on 28 February 2012 in a production by Carlo Cecchi, a veteran *avant-garde* figure of the Italian theatre scene. During the initial Milan run and the national tour that followed, Churchill's play (*Abbastanza sbronzo da dirti ti amo?*, in Giorgio Amitrano's remarkable translation) was double-billed with a revival of Mark Ravenhill's *Product*, which Cecchi had already staged in 2010, and now presented as the second part of the evening. When seen together and in this order, the complementarity of Churchill's and Ravenhill's plays becomes striking. One shows the process and the other, precisely, the product, of the demise of dialectic within the current paradigm of conflict. Whereas Churchill's *Drunk Enough* still stages dwindling vestigial stubs of dialogue, in Ravenhill the removal of interaction is complete, and its residues can only be inferred *ex negativo* from the dramatic situation.

As James recounts his film scenario, his potential interlocutor, Olivia, never breaks her silence. Although James constantly acknowledges her presence, by way of direct address and the occasional question, the possibility of conversation is always absurdly pre-empted by his unilateral management of the floor. This reaches a hilarious climax when, for the first time after over forty minutes of uninterrupted monologue, James suddenly feels the need to fathom Olivia's reaction to his daring narrative turn towards 'fucking edgy stuff' ('What do you think? What are you thinking? I'd love a word here. Just a word to let me know how I'm ...'). Even this ridiculously belated cue for turn, however, is quickly overruled: typically, James does not wait for Olivia's reply (and probably does not even expect one), hurrying instead to comment on her supposed turn lapse by calling her a 'bitch' who enjoys her power over him; and when the much-coveted film star appears to be opting out for good, he calls on her to stay and 'hear the end of the story', which he resumes with customary relish (173). With this injunction, James ratifies the fixity of their respective roles of speaker and hearer, a fixity which excludes the mutual perspective-taking which ought to be the precondition of speech situations.

In formal terms, then, *Product* presents us with the monologized version of a typical situation of realistic drama—two people in a room—which is habitually construed as conducive to dialogue. Like *Attempts on her Life*, it deploys storytelling as a weapon to deconstruct the dramatic form, albeit through an opposite approach: whereas Crimp's play framed realistic dialogues within a dramatic situation depleted of character, setting and plot, Ravenhill reintroduces all the familiar signposts of drama and raises expectations for a mimesis of interaction that is then ironically denied to the audience. In *Attempts on Her Life*, moreover, the replacement of mimesis with diegesis does not exclude dialectic, but simply relocates it or, better still, displaces it: as Crimp himself has explained, 'this is simply a play in which the story is being told and the drama in the play is about conflicts within the teller about telling the story'.[62] Ravenhill's model of non-dialogue, by contrast, shows a closer kinship to the monologization of Sam and Jack's verbal interaction in *Drunk Enough to Say I Love You?*, where the expression of dialogue is prevented by excessive consensus of the speakers, rather than an insurmountable gulf of conflict. In Churchill's play, however, the communicative pathology affecting the dialogic structure has a discernible cause, in that it is offered up as the analogue of the asymmetry and unilateralism characterizing the new paradigm of warfare or the 'hegemonologue' of the post-9/11 era.[63] While similarly rooting the lack of interaction between James and Olivia in a discourse of war, *Product* is far more ambivalent in its aetiology: the reasons for Olivia's silence and its meaning are equally difficult to pinpoint. On one level, her failure to participate in the speech situation is readable as a sign of overwhelming power imbalance. James is consciously using his story to keep Olivia in his grip, turning his narration into a virtuoso one-man show in which he acts out the film's scenario, impersonating characters, miming actions, turning into props the objects in his office. The play's emphasis on James's command of narrative, however, also betrays his determination to project the image of a master storyteller. This element of self-consciousness, underscored in performance through Ravenhill's ironical overacting, points to the producer's anxiety about Olivia's possible refusal, which might result in the frustration of his narrative urge: as James himself must admit, donning the mask of the show-business savvy,

> There are powers greater than me. There is a Higher Power. I cannot greenlight. And I have been to the Power and I have said: 'This is the one, this is the … I want to produce this script, I have wept like a woman at this script and now I must tell this story,' and the Power has said to me: 'Get someone big attached.' (161)

Whereas in *Drunk Enough to Say I Love You?* Jack's unconditional subscription to Sam's totalitarian dramaturgy placed him in a no-win predicament, Ravenhill's Olivia still seems to have some bargaining power left which she however refrains from wielding. Olivia's puzzling lack of response is open to a range of contradictory interpretations. Is her silence a sign of passive acquiescence, a behaviour acquired through professional training and gender conditioning? While completely unrevealing as to her actual state of mind, throughout the telling of the story Olivia's body responds compliantly to James's directorial prompts, performing the (silent) tasks he assigns her: although there are no stage directions in the published script, some actions can be inferred from James's words, and in performance Olivia was often pressed into assisting with the staging. Her demeanour, however, provides no conclusive answer to the questions that keep ringing in the audience's mind: is she aware of the preposterousness of the female part James is offering, and of the utter insanity of the script with its reductionist stereotyping, Manichaean morals, irresponsible egotism and shameful spectacularization of war and violence? Is she so disgusted by James's story that an icy 'no comment' is all the attention she is prepared to give it? Does she actually like the script? Or, more discomforting still: does she give a damn? In the 2007 revival at the Bush Theatre, Jo Lobban was a sphinx in her ordinariness, her body language and facial expressions an unfathomable blank: her initial nods of acknowledgment were equally interpretable as genuine interest, bored 'default' appreciation, or ironic mockery; even as James's story gained momentum and became ludicrously far-fetched, it was impossible to tell whether a raised eyebrow was meant to suggest enthrallment or astonishment. Spectators were tantalizingly left without the least clue for disambiguating Olivia's silence and determining whether it was of a consensual or a conflictive nature. Any judgment would have been just as arbitrary as James's final assessment of her dumb show when he triumphantly announces over the phone, after she has left: 'Hey! Loved it. Loved it. She loved it' (178).

By selecting a female addressee as the empty centre of the play, both in moral and in formal terms, Ravenhill follows a similar path to Crimp's *Attempts on Her Life* and Churchill's *Seven Jewish Children*, with the obvious and telltale difference that here Olivia does appear on stage, paradoxically signalling absence by way of her presence. In *Product*, that is to say, the blind spot in the text is actually brought on stage and connected to the problem of visibility and viewing. As the passive addressee of the play's one-way communication, Olivia is also a figure of spectatorship, the unresponsive recipient of James's mass-media version of war and terror. Her bewildering mode of reception becomes far more explicable once one imagines a screen which separates her from the sender of the message. While the eclipse of Crimp's Anne and Churchill's children from the scene alluded, albeit in different ways, to the 'murderous capacity' of media images with respect to the object of representation, Olivia's silent relinquishing of agency and response-ability is a mirror held up to the global media spectator. In Ravenhill's play, then, narrative is both a strategic asset in the dismantling of the dialogical principle of drama and a target of critique. The outright monologization of verbal interaction in *Product* effectively captures the non-dialectical, non-conflictive nature of the current paradigm of war, while at the same time indicating spectatorial passivity as a by-product, or even an intended effect, of mainstream narrative emplotments of the post-9/11 scenario.

The 7/7 bombings and the pornography of the media gaze

If the entire body of work considered in this chapter can be seen to be making a precise aesthetic and political statement through its avoidance of the representational imaginary, the programmatic nature of this questioning of theatrical mimesis achieves even greater prominence in dramatic responses to the London bombings of 7 July 2005, an act of belligerence that happened in the here and now of present-day Britain and whose substantial character could hardly be a matter of contention. The fact that the British stage held on firmly to metaphorical, analogical or narrative reconstructions when reporting the London bombings can perhaps be read as a measure of the rootedness of this attitude—a sign, arguably, that by the mid-2000s the banishment of war from scenic space had already become a signature formal feature of contemporary war drama.

The output of dramatic takes on 7/7 is remarkably scarce when compared with, for example, plays about the Iraq war, pointing to the fact that homegrown terrorist violence has been perceived as a particularly sensitive subject by British theatre-makers. The earliest 7/7 play to make its way onto a British stage was *Yesterday Was a Weird Day*, a verbatim piece by documentary theatre company Look Left, Look Right which premiered at the 2005 Edinburgh Fringe, presenting a mosaic of testimonies culled from the aftermath of the terrorist attacks in London (see Chapter Four for an extended analysis). After this blitz response, British audiences had to wait two more years before Mark Ravenhill ventured another comment on the subject with *Shoot/Get Treasure/Repeat*, an epic cycle of plays initially staged as a series of readings at the 2007 Fringe Festival with the title *Ravenhill for Breakfast*, and subsequently given full production at several London venues throughout April 2008. Though they do not form the main subject of Ravenhill's cycle, the London bombings feature among the various acts of terror scattered across the plays, and references to them are particularly evident in the opening choral playlet, *Women of Troy*. As will be discussed in more detail below, the belated British premiere of Simon Stephens's *Pornography*, a play that entirely centres on the events of 7/7, is another telling sign of the unease surrounding their representation on stage; crucially, Ravenhill's and Stephens's plays remain to date the only exception to the overall silence of British mainstream drama about the terrorist attacks in London.

It is also symptomatic that this reluctance to address the sensitive topic of the 7/7 bombings should become considerably attenuated when topicality could be seen or made to emerge in more indirect ways. This happened, for example, with Frank McGuinness's historical drama *Speaking Like Magpies*, written to mark the quatercentenary of the Gunpowder Plot. When the play opened at the RSC in Stratford in September 2005, reviewers promptly connected the averted Catholic conspiracy to blow up the English Parliament to the recent terrorist events in London, emphasizing the fact that in both cases the attackers were English born and bred. A similar kind of contemporary currency was ascribed to Edward Kemp's *5/11* (Chichester Festival, August 2005); here, the connection between Guy Fawkes and the attacks of 7 July is more explicitly suggested through the play's title and further expounded in the Foreword to the published script, showing the writer's readiness to tap into the trauma of 7/7 for added relevance, when this could be done from the safe distance of the past.

Plays about contemporary terrorism that opened in the wake of the 7/7 attacks were also inevitably framed by the context of the attacks in London; in this case, however, the new topicality they gained was not always beneficial in terms of their critical appreciation. The mixed reception of Robin Soans's documentary piece, *Talking to Terrorists* is case in point here (see Chapter Three for an in-depth discussion); but Dennis Kelly, too, has spoken of his misgivings when he realized that his imagined scenario of a simulated terrorist attack in *After the End* had been overtaken, and possibly made irrelevant, by the dire reality of the events in London.[64] Kelly's play, a co-production between new writing theatre company Paines Plough and the Bush Theatre, was in rehearsal at the Traverse Theatre in Edinburgh, where it eventually opened on 5 August, when the bombings took place; on the day of the second, failed attack on London's public transport system on 21 July, the company were working on the opening scene of the play, which is set in '*a 1980s nuclear fallout shelter with a wheel hatch in the ceiling, but in the present day*'.[65] Here, Mark recounts to her workmate Louise how he managed to rescue her from the fallout after their city was razed to the ground by a terrorist nuclear attack and she lay unconscious from the blast. As the play progresses, we discover that the suitcase bomb is a fiction and that the nerdish Mark has enacted this paranoid fiction for the purpose of bringing the all-popular, cool Louise to like him. The process of re-education he has envisaged for her is a comprehensive one, and is meant to ensure Louise's adherence to his lifestyle and his values, including the 'clash of civilizations' worldview that she and her liberal cronies are so irresponsibly fond of mocking. At all levels, Kelly's plot explicitly invites a reading of Mark's simulation as a miniature version of the war on terror. One the home front, Mark mobilizes the spectre of weapons of mass destruction to exert control over Louise and get her to play along with his scenario of fear and threat; at the same time, as he turns to ever more brutal methods to tame his recalcitrant partner in the wargame he has devised, Mark continues to insist that he is acting in Louise's best interest, in an obvious parallel with the oxymoron of democracy installed through illegal wars of aggression.

While it is easy to understand Kelly's concern that the grim reality of the London attacks might weaken the play's argument about the simulacral quality of the war on terror, on the other hand those same events could be seen to have offered a powerful demonstration of the violence of the virtual that is explored in *After the End*. The overall positive reviews of the Edinburgh performances and of the subsequent transfer at London's Bush Theatre in September show that British audiences were willing to recognize in Kelly's story a metaphor of our age of anxiety and a warning against war's tendency to remake people and societies in its own image. Critics, however, were oddly silent about the play's potential relevance, or even irrelevance, to the very recent events in London: one is left to wonder therefore whether the favourable reception met by *After the End* is not at least in part a consequence of a more or less conscious mechanism of denial.

In the case of Simon Stephens's *Pornography*, the London bombings were subjected to a more literal form of displacement. The play was jointly commissioned by the Schauspiel Hannover and Theaterformen Festival in Hanover and the Deutsches Schauspielhaus in Hamburg, and made its debut in Hanover in June 2007, in a German version directed by Sebastian Nübling. Stephens had by then established a reputation as one of the most exciting talents of British new writing: he had won an Olivier Award for Best New Play with *On the Shore of the Wide World* in 2005, followed in 2006 by a box office hit at the Royal Court with his Iraq war drama, *Motortown*. In spite of this, it took more than one year before *Pornography* received its British premiere at Edinburgh's Traverse Theatre in July 2008—a delay which the author himself admitted to finding 'rather bewildering'.[66] This difficulty in getting the play produced may be attributed to Stephens's provocative view of the terrorists as 'absolutely a product of the same Britain I'd grown up in',[67] as well as to the formal experimentalism of a play written for a German theatre director of proven postdramatic inclinations; it is also symptomatic, however, of a wish to keep at a reassuringly safe distance the artistic reproduction of an event which still felt so close in time and space.

This is all the more remarkable since *Pornography*, despite its declarative title, is very careful to avoid any voyeuristic exploitation of the tragic events in London by keeping them resolutely out of both the visual and the verbal texture of the performance. The play text is divided into seven sections, or 'chapters' according to Stephens's own definition,[68] corresponding to six separate stories which take place in and around London during the first seven days of July 2005, followed by a list of obituaries of the fifty-two victims of the attacks. Four of the sections are monologues, while the remaining two consist of bits of conversations taking place over a period of time comprised within the seven-day frame and involving, respectively, a middle-aged professor and his former pupil (Three), and two siblings who commit incest (Five). The protagonists of the other stories are a working mother vexed by her boss (Seven), a racist teenager with a crush on his teacher (Six), a suicide bomber making his journey to central London (Four), a misanthropic old lady (Two). With the exception of Jason, the teenage stalker, characters do not have names and they do not necessarily identify with the narrator(s): a prefatory note to the script specifies that scenes 'can be performed by any number of actors' and 'in any order' (214).

While never intersecting, all the stories refer to the same timeline of historical events, which include the Live 8 concerts in Hyde Park on 2 July 2005, the opening of the G8 summit in Gleneagles, Scotland on 6 July, and the announcement of London's successful bid for the 2012 Olympics on the same day, but they all refrain from describing or even mentioning the final and capital event on 7 July that they appear to be heading towards. The six plots convey a sense of linear progression towards a specific target, also enhanced by the numbering of scenes from seven to one as in a countdown, yet each segment ends on the narrative threshold of the London bombings which happen on the seventh and final day: either because the story stops exactly at the point where the speakers would start talking about the attacks or their reactions to them; or because the narrator fails to register the impact of what has happened. Indeed, even when the protagonists of the stories are affected by the bombings, their lives are touched in very marginal and/or individualistic ways. In the fifth section, we sense that the brother's decision to end the incestuous relationship is somehow related to the tragedy he has witnessed, but the dramatist wittingly refrains from introducing a causal link between the individual story and the terrorist attacks. As she heads towards the university department she has long retired from for an appointment with a former colleague whom she keeps pestering with unsolicited articles, the embittered 83-year-old lady of Chapter Two realizes that something extraordinary must have happened since all tube lines are closed; but she never for a moment stops to inquire and obdurately walks all the way from Hammersmith to central London only to find out that nobody has come into the department that morning, nor has bothered to let her know. Even as she drags herself home amidst a mass of stranded Londoners, her mind remains invariably focused on her private world, her memories, her blistered feet, and it is already late evening when the smell of barbecued chicken coming from a house she passes by prompts her to knock on the strangers' door and ask for some. While this sudden, irresistible need to reach out to others is clearly met with suspicion and condescension by the person who gets the door, the story closes on a note of hope for this lonesome widow who as a rule does not 'see anybody … speak with anybody' (269). The old lady's parting words, though, confirm her inability to work out the impact of that eventful day: 'I walk home. The chicken tastes good. I can't feel my feet anymore. I can't understand why there are tears pouring down the side of my face. This makes absolutely no sense to me at all' (274–75).

In Stephens's play, the failure of Londoners to connect with others, and their lack of response-ability towards the 7/7 bombings as both individuals and members of a community, is directly related to a 'pornographic' mode of perception enabled and induced by the media. While pornography as we commonly intend it does occasionally surface in some of Stephens's stories, the consumption of internet porn or hard-core videos is seen as just another symptom of a more widespread erosion of the act of communication in the age of global media: the interaction of distant partners nurtured by technology greatly reduces the awareness of being answerable and bound to others; the act of perception is dissociated from the event perceived; empathy recedes in favour of reification. Moreover, as if confirming Susan Sontag's remark that 'being a spectator of calamities happening in another country is a quintessentially modern experience',[69] most of Stephens's characters are consumers of war-related atrocitainment which they approach with the same casual attitude that they display towards pornography. Having a little earlier informed us, in her characteristic matter-of-fact tone, that the coverage of the war in Iraq gives her 'the same kind of thrills as do exciting video games' (269), the old lady of Chapter Two proceeds to illustrate, with almost scientific detachment, the genre conventions of the paedo-pornographic trailers she habitually watches on the internet. In the first episode, Lenny's mother returns home from another difficult day in the office to find her husband watching the news; bored with the umpteenth car bomb in a Baghdad market, she takes up a magazine wishing they could switch on to the glitzy soft porn of *Sex and the City.*

This inability to connect with distant, and distanced, wars has seemingly become so ingrained that empathic response is equally blocked when suicide bombers target the very heart of London. With the exception of the brother in Scene Five, and akin to the vast majority of Londoners on 7 July 2005, the characters' experience of the destruction wreaked by the bombs on their city is entirely mediated by technology—the sister in the incest story confirms that she has watched the news, but she still cannot see why and how the hell raging in the outside world should affect their private relationship; Jason, the racist schoolboy, has spent the whole morning watching the 'tantalising' (230) flux of CCTV camera images of the bombed sites, and wishing his teacher had been on the tube that morning; the working mother, who has decided to stay at home with her baby after divulging her boss's all-important top-secret report, hears about the Russell Square explosion from a radio phone-in show. In all cases, the characters' reactions are either left blank or remain unfathomable: 'Are you laughing or are you crying?' (230), Jason's sister asks him twice.

Even the story that comes closest to the narrative epicentre, the suicide bomber's monologue in the fourth and central 'chapter', is similarly marked by a detached, affectless attitude. Throughout his momentous journey into London, the terrorist's thoughts are steadfastly tuned onto the mundane and the everyday; he never mentions the bomb, the projected outcome of the journey of death he and his comrades have undertaken, and the reasons which move them. There is no attempt at pondering about the meaning, import and impact of the act he is about to perform; no mention of moral, religion, politics, American imperialism or al-Qaeda. His mind is set on entirely different matters: his family, the people around him, his physical sensations, the habits and routines of commuters, the food they (all) eat, the dreary impersonality of the suburbs, the decadent, defiant majesty of the war-worn city which rises before him as the train approaches St Pancras Station:

> London rises. It takes you by surprise. Cut out of the edges of bomb blasts. And a thousand years of fire. This is a city that is forever under attack. (254)

After the terrorist boards the Tube, taking his fateful load into the busiest carriage, the monologue ends with the matter-of-fact notation that 'The train pulls out of Liverpool Street and moves towards Aldgate' (255). There is no blast, no pain, no spectacle in this deliberately subdued climax. In the 2008 production at Edinburgh's Traverse Theatre, the actor simply walked off the stage and disappeared into the auditorium, turning himself into a void which pointed to another conspicuous absence from drama and performance text alike.

This final vanishing act should be seen in conjunction with Stephens's deliberately elliptical characterization of his militant. The text is reticent about the cause-and-effect relationships which would be necessary to establish motive. In the end, we are left wondering whether there is indeed a connection between the things the terrorist sees and the act of violence he commits; between, for instance, this hyperbolic explosion of hatred against suburban life in the Midlands and the bomb he is about to detonate:

> Disused Jet garage forecourts sit side by side with double driveways. Here there are food-makers and the food they make is chemical. It fattens the teenage and soaks up the pre-teen. Nine-year-old children all dazzled up in boob tubes and mini-skirts and spangly eyeliner as fat as little pigs stare out of the windows of family estate cars. In the sunshine of mid-morning in the suburbs of the South Midlands heroin has never tasted so good. Internet sex contact pages have never seemed more alluring. Nine hundred television channels have never seemed more urgent. And everybody needs an iPod. And nobody can ever get a *Metro* anymore.
>
> If I had the power I would take a bomb to all of this. To every grazing horse and every corrugated-metal shed and every wind-blasted tree and every telephone mast and every graveyard. Wipe it all off the skin of the world. Scratch it away. (252–53)

We are also left wondering, more mundanely, whether improved coffee and an adequate supply of almond croissant at Upper Crust could have made any difference in the speaker's outlook on life on that particular morning. The whole play pivots around an empty moral and ideological centre, a blank which audience members are left to fill in with their own reactions (or lack thereof) to the countless other irritants, big or small, which Stephens's terrorist mentions throughout his narrative journey into this metropolitan heart of darkness. The play normalizes the suicide bomber, placing him within a larger pattern of increasing isolation and atomization, and thereby invites its spectators to see the supposed otherness of terrorism as part and product of a prevailing culture of pornography which allows people to erase the humanity of others and turn them into abstracts—a process which, according to the dramatist, is likewise operative in the 'production and consumption of pornography' and in 'the objectification needed to commit an act of terrorism, and kill fifty-two strangers'.[70]

These two aspects of the 'pornography' of contemporary war are brought together in the final section of the play. As already hinted, Scene One consists of a list of fifty-two obituaries of the actual victims of 7/7. The text of the biographies is an edited verbatim reproduction of the obituaries published on the *Guardian* website shortly after the attacks.[71] The dramatist has indicated the Vietnam Veterans Memorial Wall in Washington as a direct source of inspiration,[72] but unlike the display on the Wall, the names of the victims are here omitted and replaced by numbers. This is in keeping with the overall anonymity of Stephens's characters, but the reduction of individuals to abstract figures also powerfully foregrounds the dehumanization which is implicit in the indiscriminate mass violence of terrorism, with the numbers further gesturing towards genocidal wars past and present.

On one level, then, Stephens's list painfully exposes the dire consequences of pornographic objectification on human beings. At the same time, however, the obituaries are themselves provocatively pornographic in their spectacularization of pain and in their voyeuristic reification of the victims. The fragments are offered up to the audience as unadulterated exhibits of 'the real', yet they are the result of an editorial process carried out on a text which is itself a translation of the lives of fifty-two people into a formulaic narrative compatible with media exposure. The obituaries' original media provenance was underscored in the British production through the fact that the words were not spoken but just projected as text after the curtain call, like the end credits of a film or TV show. The representational aporia inhering this irruption of the real in the fictional situation is probably best captured by obituary number forty-three, which is left disturbingly blank.

A further, related performative blank concerns the 'images of hell' evoked by the only stage direction in the play, which were given a different visual translation in the original German production and in the British premiere. Significantly, though, neither of the two opted for a straightforward rendition in terms of the havoc wreaked by the 7/7 attacks. In Sean Holmes's production at the Traverse, the play was set in an empty interior whose potential realism was undermined by the indeterminacy of spatial and temporal markers. Light bulbs flashing on and off in the darkness, exposed wires and dangling cables suggested a space that was still being fitted or had been blown apart. The presence of television sets and sound boxes seemed to imply a room or a flat, but a recurrent humming noise pointed instead to a train carriage or a tube tunnel—a hint of referentiality which was then immediately disowned by the presence of an onstage sound engineer who managed these effects live.

Sebastian Nübling, instead, set the playlets against the backdrop of an imposing digital reproduction of Brueghel's *Tower of Babel* made of

2. 'Images of hell': Muriel Gerstner's set for Sebastian Nübling's production of *Pornography* (Hanover, June 2007). Photography by Arno Declair. © Arno Declair.

crumbling mosaic tiles. As the play progressed, actors added tiles to the mosaic, thus linking their joint narrative effort to the building, and imminent destruction, of the Biblical tower. In the closing scene the cast continued working on the mosaic while a speaker read out the obituaries. The terrorist opened up the bag he had been carrying around, scattering thousands of new tiles onto the stage; the company picked them up and resumed their task. Nübling's set, designed by Muriel Gerstner, offered a powerful visual counterpart to the picture of the chaos, loneliness and alienation of city life that emerges from the play's fragmentary tales. The vengeful wrath that has fallen or is about to fall on this modern-day Babel/Babylon only adds another tile to the mosaic of a millennial history of sin and punishment, a mythical dimension which is also poetically evoked in the text by the suicide bomber's awestruck description of the hellish London sighted from the train. Projected into an almost timeless dimension, the London bombings were then metaphorically recreated through an 'explosion' of tiles from the terrorist's ominous bag: a metatheatrical allusion to the play's own substitution of mimetic reproduction with narrative fragments, but also a final acknowledgment of the fundamental fellowship of the suicide bomber with the disjointed community of storytellers imagined by the writer.

There is method in this randomness

While reflecting the dramatist's critical engagement with the 'murderous capacity' of images, the diegetic drift of *Pornography* is also the expression of a thoroughly postdramatic take on the representation of contemporary war, involving a full-scale reconfiguration not only of the constituent parts of drama, but of the very formal framework that binds them. As noted above, *Pornography* is conceived as a sequence of playlets that present a narrative structure and, occasionally, even scenes featuring dialogue and action, yet are arranged within a dramatic construction that defies teleology by replacing the linear-successive model of conventional plot development with the non-hierarchical and seemingly random connectivity of parataxis. Significantly, the writer himself has characterized his postdramatic preference for 'juxtaposition' as a deliberate attempt at 'creat[ing] plays that demand a position of interpretation from their audience rather than reception' (xii). In a play tackling the 7/7 London bombings through a kaleidoscope of reactions to those events, this statement of aesthetics can be more straightforwardly read as a challenge to the overwhelming dominance of conventional narrative frames in popular media versions of war, and to the modes of perception and response they are designed to elicit.

A similar call for the receivers' participation in the meaning-making process also extends to the first and privileged reader/interpreter of the text, that is to say the director. The postdramatic openness of *Pornography*, itself instigated by the fact that the play was expressly written for the German experimental scene, cuts out a far more important role for its stage interpreters, placing upon them the responsibility of creative co-authorship in the signification process; in the playwright's own words, the text

> not only invites directorial interpretation, it is unstageable without it. There are only a few stage directions and they are frankly impenetrable. There are no character names. It is a play that can be staged in any order using any number of actors. (xix)

This interpretative openness belongs to the very logic of the postdramatic paradigm as theorized by Hans-Thies Lehmann, that is to say to the transition from theatre as representation, 'the "making present"' (*Vergegenwärtigung*) of speeches and deeds on stage through mimetic dramatic play', to theatre as presentation of discourses that the individual performers convey to the audience.[73] Although in both the German and the British productions *Pornography* was staged using eight actors (the current 'default number' according to Simon Stephens[74]), the lack of specified characters even in the more naturalistic duologues, as well as the total freedom granted by the author in terms of casting and lines allocation, allow in principle for choral productions in which the disjunction between character and performer, and the characterization of the latter as a speaker or text-bearer,[75] would be more emphasized. This also applies to the two fragments which still retain a more evident dramatic quality, that is to say the speech situations involving the middle-aged professor and his former student (Three) and the incestuous siblings (Five), where the dialogue is productive of stage action that develops sequentially, albeit in an elliptical manner. Still, in a script which envisages, or indeed invites, a mode of staging in which the performers/speakers would not be attached to the situation being portrayed, even the mimetic potential of these two fragments inevitably becomes relativized.

In its way of simultaneously suggesting and undercutting a dialogic structure, *Pornography* deploys a combination of the strategies discussed in connection with Caryl Churchill's *Drunk Enough to Say I Love You?* and Mark Ravenhill's *Product*. Stephens's play is an assemblage of duologues which share some of the formal qualities of Sam and Jack's verbal interaction, and of first-person narratives that—like the film script recounted by James—encompass and often also enact sections of dialogue. The two duologues in *Pornography* are marked by frequent conversational ellipses, with dashes signalling turn lapses at moments of particular strain, as when the brother and sister commit incest, or the professor's advances become more aggressive and probably also violent:

> What knickers are you wearing? Tell me.
> Be quiet.
> Are you wearing any?
> Christ.
> Come on. I'm noticing you. This is me noticing you.
> –
> Ow.
> –
> Ow. You fucking. You. That fucking hurt.
> –
> I should beat the crap out of you for doing that.
> –
> Don't tell me that you didn't want exactly what –
> Is there a lock on that door?
> What?
> Is there a lock on the bedroom door?
> –
> Can it be locked from the inside?

> Yes. Of course it can.
> I need to sleep somewhere.
> –
> –
> –
> You're quite little, aren't you?
> Little?
> I've never noticed before. (266–67)

These gaps in the conversation are often associated with a shrinking of the speakers' utterances which recalls the stichomythic exchanges in *Drunk Enough to Say I Love You?*, as in the dialogue following the siblings' reunion:

> Where were you?
> What?
> You never told me. All this time.
> I was all over the place.
> Tell me where.
> No.
> Why? Why won't you?
> –
> Were you all right?
> –
> Were you?
> Not really.
> Why not?
> –
> What happened?
> You don't need to know.
> I'm sorry.
> What for? (236–37)

With its unallocated lines and complete lack of stage directions, Stephens's putative dialogues end up resembling the lines of a poem on the page, and lend themselves to a choral or monological rendition in performance.[76] Like the conversation between Sam and Jack in Churchill's *Drunk Enough*, moreover, the duologues in *Pornography* are not continuous but take place over a period of time during which the dramatic situation evolves, but the scenic situation remains the same. The asterisks marking these narrative ellipses in the text are a clear indication that the scene's configuration proceeds from an editing process which is external to the drama and the fictional world it projects.

Conversely, the monologues consist of first-person storytelling which however encases lines spoken by other characters, and even segments of actual verbal interaction. In the schoolboy's playlet (Six), this alternation of diegesis and mimesis is established already from the opening lines:

> I wasn't born here. They tell me I was born here, it's not true.
> 'What the fuck are you talking about, Jason, eh? What the fuck are you like?'
> I'm Italian, I'm half Italian. How can I be Italian if I was born around here? (222)

The snatches of dialogue that are recurrently interpolated within Jason's narrative sometimes stretch into longer conversations, as when we hear him discussing Live 8 and the Olympics with his teacher (227), or in the tense exchange when she finds him stationed on her doorstep:

> How did you find out where I live? Jason, this is serious.
> It's in the phone book, Miss. It's not difficult. Do you want a cigarette?
> What are you doing here?
> I'm just sitting here.
> Can you move, please?
> You were wrong about the Olympics, Miss.
> I was what?
> I can't fucking believe it myself. I think they must all be insane. Did you see them? Don't you think they're insane? Don't you think Lord Sebastian Coe is insane, Miss? And David Beckham.
> Jason, can you move away from my house, please?
> Where were you at the weekend, Miss?
> Where, what?
> Where were you at the weekend? You weren't in all weekend. Did you go away for the weekend?
> Jason, get off my wall this instant. (228–29)

In performance, these lines could be spoken by an actor playing a character who tells Jason's story and impersonates his fictionalized interlocutor; or they could figure as a moment of actual verbal interaction between two characters staged inside a narrative frame, a kind of mimetic enclave within a diegetic text. However, given the text's openness to a variety of possible stagings, it is entirely up to the director to decide who will actually deliver the text, and whether or not to attribute the speaker or speakers' utterances to individualized human beings.

The suicide bomber's story, too, features unmarked transitions to free direct speech; revealingly, however, in these snatches of conversations we only hear the protagonist's voice, never that of his actual or potential interlocutors:

> I turn out and away from Piccadilly Gardens.
> I climb up the hill towards the railway station.
> I could do with a coffee.
> I really need a cup of coffee.
> Can I have a cup of coffee, please? Thank you. Great. Thanks. Thank you. (250)

Unlike Olivia's puzzling silence in *Product*, the monologization of the terrorist's lines of dialogue is directly presented as a formal correlative of human alienation. The suicide bomber's attempts at interaction during his fateful journey to London are frustrated by the apparent unresponsiveness of his selected interlocutors: the bus driver who fails to return or even acknowledge his greeting on getting off the bus; the tube station assistant who does not smile back. Ironically, however, the protagonist of the story is also debarred from face-to-face communication with his comrades-in-arms travelling on the same train—for obvious strategic reasons, contact within this fellowship of death must be limited to text messaging. In either case, and within the apparently opposed categories of terrorists and potential victims, strangers and companions, live interaction no longer appears to be a feasible option.

The same picture of an atomized, fractured world 'scorched by a need and inability to connect' (xxi) is suggested through the dramatic structure that holds together the individual stories. Like Churchill's *Far Away*, *Pornography* reproduces some elements of the traditional formal architecture of drama at the same time as it enacts its disruption, with the notable difference that here the tearing apart or the overturning of conventional plot construction is not a consequence of the irruption of total warfare into the fictional realm of the play, but is rather presented as a given, a more accurate reflection of a world which, like the city 'cut out of the edges of bomb blasts' (254) evoked in the suicide bomber's story, already bears the scars of ageless, endless conflict. In Stephens's London the chaos of war is a permanent, endemic condition, and the final catastrophe that the six stories appear to be heading towards is only the last in a long line of calamities that have fallen upon the city, turning its collective narrative into a Babel of uncomprehending voices, an apparently random assemblage of disjointed fragments.

On one level, then, the play's claim to truthfulness rests on its refusal to impose order and meaning upon the London bombings by rearranging the messy reality of war as a linear sequence of events developing according to a cause-and-effect scheme. At the same time, however, and in truly postdramatic fashion, the play engages critically with dramatic modes of emplotment and their unwavering grip over contemporary audiences. This markedly self-reflexive quality is specifically tied to the simultaneous reproduction and disavowal of the conventions of classical tragedy. In a recent study, Elizabeth Kuti has convincingly detected an underlying classical dramaturgy in some representative plays of the 1990s and 2000s, implicitly inviting a reassessment of the degree of formal innovation with which they have been credited.[77] Unlike the cases discussed by Kuti, though, in *Pornography* the presence of tragic tropes is overtly acknowledged and held up for scrutiny, with their distinctly residual character pointing to formal innovation as a quintessentially dialectical process.

Stephens's six fictional fragments are almost formulaic in their adherence to the tragic form: their characters are all moral trespassers who defiantly break social rules and taboos (including incest); and the real protagonist of the play, the city of London, falls from a great height like a true tragic hero, moving in a brief time span from the euphoria of Live 8 and the Olympics announcement to the catastrophe of the 7/7 bombings. In formal terms, the individual stories are based on a linear-successive narrative that is arranged as a gradual build-up of events leading towards a climactic and defining act of transgression: the working mother faxes the confidential report, the schoolboy harasses his teacher, the siblings commit incest, the professor's sexual interest in his former pupil turns aggressive, the misanthropic old lady knocks at the strangers' door. In the play's narrative epicentre, the suicide bomber's monologue, the momentous journey of the protagonist towards his target provides an eloquent spatial correlative for the chronological thrust and (con-)sequential progression of events informing all episodes. The numbering of chapters in descending order, as in a countdown, further adds to the sense of urgency and finality. The ultimate irony, of course, is that the heart of the play's narrative—in thematic, formal and symbolical terms—should stop short of actually hitting its appointed target. The centripetal force giving impetus to the terrorist's progress towards a tragic epilogue is thwarted by the inconclusive suspended ending of his story.

The other fragments, too, seem to gesture towards a classical plot only to make its demise more conspicuous. As already mentioned, the expected tragic denouement is either withheld or shown to be of little or no consequence, therefore failing to produce the new awareness that comes with anagnorisis. This turning of the tables is perhaps nowhere so clear as in the old lady's story, which presents a reprise of the parallel between the linear-progressive drive of the unfolding narrative and the protagonist's journey, here spurred on by the perspective of a long-awaited meeting that fails to take place. As if to mirror the play's downward movement into ever more dismal circles of hell, the frustrating anti-climax of this last fictional chapter is compounded by the additional punishment, for the elderly woman, of the long and exhausting march home, back to where both her story and her journey had started off, in a kind of rewinding or undoing of the earlier forward movement towards the centre of London.

Similarly, at the macro-textual level, the linear trajectories traced by the stories are superseded structurally by the circular pattern established through the principle of juxtaposition. As in Churchill's *Drunk Enough to Say I Love You?*, the story of those first seven days of July comes to a halt and then begins all over again in the following episode; the linear continuum is twisted into loops, conveying a similar impression of narrative blockage and of repetitive cycles of violence which elide time and space into an eternal present and an indeterminate everywhere.[78] While providing, as in Churchill's case, a formal correlative for the sprawling formlessness of contemporary war, in *Pornography* this systematic rupture of dramatic conventions is more specifically aimed at the hermeneutic model underpinning them. The tragic scheme that the play appears to embrace would enable a neat causal reading of the indiscriminate violence of terrorism: London as a modern-day Babylon; the carnage of 7/7 as a capital punishment visited upon its inhabitants for their collective sins, a nemesis commensurate with the hubris and overreaching exposed through the play's random yet representative sampling. However bleak, this narrative would afford the comfort of teleology—a comfort which the writer is clearly determined to withhold by invalidating both the master narrative and the dramatic structure which might sustain it. The cause-and-effect scheme of the classical plot is evoked only to reveal its inability to capture the random logic of terrorism, implicitly suggesting that new forms of warfare require new dramatic models to be conceptualized.

It is this cognitive investment in formal innovation which arguably provides the rationale for the set of correspondences between the postdramatic architecture of the play and the paradigm of warfare underlying the London bombings. Adriana Cavarero has pointed to the semantic exactness of the term 'casualties' when applied to the indiscriminate logic of terrorism;[79] and as the obituaries in Chapter One pointedly remind us, the victims of the 7/7 attacks were not chosen according to political, moral or identitarian distinctions but on purely accidental grounds: the bombers' violence eschewed causal attribution and was instead directed against random targets who attained exemplary status precisely on account of this randomness. Yet, even as it wages war on dramatic form with the aim of offering a more accurate conceptual framework for the apprehension of contemporary conflicts, Stephens's writing does not entirely surrender to formlessness. The play's offensive against conventional emplotment should be seen in parallel with, or perhaps as conducive to, an emphasis on alternative forms of connectivity that manifest themselves in bizarre, unexpected and often paradoxical ways. Stephens's dramaturgical structure is clearly designed to dig out patterns in chaos—or 'method' in randomness. Unlike the totalizing narrative of the linear-teleological plot, however, Stephens's formal organization of events is immanently dialogical and imbued with self-deconstructing potential.

The first and more noticeable way in which Stephens establishes an overarching pattern of resonance among the playlets is through the presence of shared narrative elements. While each individual story remains confined within its self-enclosed chapter, a cluster of leitmotifs travels across the different narratives creating an uncanny sense of interrelatedness. As the play progresses, we gradually become aware that the protagonists of the individual stories speak a common language as a result of their shared experience of London life. These verbal echoes are only partly linked to the contingencies of the time frame (like the recurrent mention of Live 8, the Pink Floyd, the Olympics and G8), but actually extend to a whole collection of realia (from food brands and chains to place names, from newspapers to lines and stations of the London Underground) and a sizeable amount of shared urban jargon. In Chapter Four, for instance, the obsession with 'polish' and 'R&D' that the working mother ascribes to her boss in Chapter One is picked up, rather ironically, by the terrorist when he arrives at the train station and describes his fellow London commuters:

> All of a sudden, as if by magic, there are people everywhere. Turning away from train platforms. Suited and smart and elegant and crisp. Weary eyed and bloated. Breakfasting on McDonalds or Breakfast Bars or Honey and Granola. Lugging their lap tops. Clicking their heels. Pulling their shirt cuffs. Pressing their phones. They've been working all night on a polish. They've been driven by the R&D. Their attention to detail and their R&D is breathtaking. (250)

In these moments, it feels as if the alienated characters of *Pornography* know each other, or at least are part of a discursive community that might enable intersubjective communication. The ultimate irony, of course, is that although we sense the permanence of a common language underneath the Babelian confusion of uncomprehending voices, the speakers remain totally unaware of this and the dramaturgical structure keeps them stubbornly locked inside their own segregated context of utterance.

This contradiction was powerfully visualized in the Traverse production. As already hinted above, Sean Holmes's set was cluttered with a mess of electronic equipment—television screens, loudspeakers, exposed lights—which suggested the disconcerting solipsism of metropolitan life but at the same time created an image of untidy organic interconnectedness: a tangle of wires and extension cables stretching out from the auditorium like a network of veins and arteries around the pulsing heart of London. A similar kind of duplicity was also highlighted dramaturgically, through the director's decision to further cut up the six fictional playlets and present them as interlaced fragments. On one level, the rearrangement of the discrete stories into an amalgam of 'interwoven non-sequiturs'[80] added to the impression of disorderly cacophony; on another, though, the simultaneous presence of all the actors on stage, spinning what began to resemble a collective yarn, suggested the possibility of turning the jumbled fragments into a communal/choral narrative. Holmes's staging vividly conveyed the characters' need for and incapability of reaching out to others, making it very clear that for Stephens's Londoners the fact of inhabiting the same space was something that at once enabled and foreclosed interaction: when delivering their portions of text, the speakers sometimes addressed the audience directly, but steered clear of communicating with their fellow storytellers, even though they were watched and sometimes even touched by the other members of the cast.

This ambivalence is a key feature of Stephens's dramatic architecture as a whole. On the one hand, through its web of internal correspondences, the play seems to have been designed to reveal an immanent logic or even an intrinsic order in chaos; in this respect, then, *Pornography* would still be ascribable within a classical paradigm of drama in which meaning emanates autonomously from a totalizing fictional universe where form and content are organically joined in a hermeneutic circle. On the other hand, though, this intensional model is systematically counterpointed by a number of other formal palimpsests that are clearly extrinsic to the dramatic materials and therefore draw attention to the act of textual construction through which meaning is artificially asserted. It is through this formal gesture that Stephens's 'method' for giving artistic shape to terror and its random logic sheds all pretence to immanence and ontology, declaring instead its contingent and arbitrary nature.

This is already apparent in the replacement of a dramatic plot, in which the course of action would be organically shaped by an internal dialectical principle, with more abstract geometrical patterns: the division of the play into seven chapters allows the suicide bomber's monologue to maintain its central position (three-one-three) even if the order of presentation is reversed; the terrorist's centripetal journey towards London, the city centre, and finally the 'heart of the carriage' finds its structural counterpart in the numbering of the scenes in descending order, with the countdown offering a neat spatial representation of the plunge into chaos. This use of symmetry as a formal principle to balance or hold together contradictions places in a clearly self-conscious light the writer's formal endeavour: plot construction is wholly entrusted to an external agency, replacing logical necessity with a deliberate act of formal construction; dramatic conflict and its management are relocated from the content of the actual drama scenes onto their extra-dramatic container.

This ironic desemiotization of *Pornography*'s particular method for revealing patterns of chaos becomes even more emphasized when the formal palimpsests are apparently loaded with symbolical value in connection with the dramatized events. Stephens plays with and builds upon the numerological density of 7/7, a date which was to all likelihood chosen by the terrorists for its symbolic potential and impact (not least in media terms). The triple seven in the date of the London bombings, which took place on the seventh day of the seventh month of the year 2005 (whose figures also add up to seven) is replicated in the three symbolic narratives which are alluded to in *Pornography*. As the dramatist himself has explained (xviii), the original arrangement of the seven chapters was modelled on the chronological sequence of the different parts played by human actors on the world stage as outlined by Jacques in *As You Like It*: Shakespeare's infant, schoolboy, lover, soldier, justice, pantaloon and the 'second childishness/and mere oblivion' of old age all find a correspondent in the fictional playlets, with the telling omission of the 'justice .../With eyes severe and beard of formal cut,/Full of wise saws and modern instances'.[81] The analogy also works in structural terms given that the narrative of the seven ages of man is only apparently progressive, closing as it does on a return to the point of departure, and is therefore a particularly apt literary/philosophical antecedent for the narrative loops that block the linear development of the stories in *Pornography*, as well as for the play's ironic countering of the idea of successive stages of being with the regressive numbering of the chapters. Since each of these paradigmatic stages is characterized, in *Pornography*, by a defining act of transgression, and given also the play's depiction of London as a modern-day Babel/Babylon, the seven ages of man become blended here with the seven deadly sins of medieval theology and, more ironically, with the Christian myth of creation: as also emphasized through the countdown, God's labour terminates here in destruction; at the same time, the connection with Jacques's histrionics throws into relief an irreverent parallel between God's six days of toil followed by rest on the seventh, and the genesis of *Pornography*, in which the writer/demiurge pens the six fictional stories and then suspends his creative effort in the final obituaries scene, where he simply appropriates other people's words. This tongue-in-cheek self-reflexivity also extends its debunking effect onto the hermeneutic claims which *Pornography* might seem to be making through its formal associations with the mystical number seven and the related idea of illumination produced through the progressive unveiling of an esoteric truth. Stephens builds his alternative model of connectivity upon numerological correspondences which raise expectations for the revelation of some kind of symbolic order or meaning about the random violence of terrorism, but whose purported hermeneutic potential is highly attenuated by their ostensible characterization as deliberate acts of literariness.

The contrapuntal method of *Pornography* is perhaps best exemplified by the final testimonial section. The paratactic organization of the list of obituaries emphasizes the purely coincidental nature of the connections created by the London bombings: the lives of fifty-two strangers, disparate in age, profession, nationality and ethnicity, briefly collide only because they happen to intersect with the bombers' trajectory. As in the fictional biographies, though, even in this random assemblage of raw materials lifted from the 'real' world there are elements which unexpectedly, almost magically, cohere. For example, one is surprised to read how very few of the victims were actually born in London: some had been attracted by the opportunities or the excitement of metropolitan life, but a strikingly considerable share had 'made [their] home in London' (278) because they or their families were fleeing from war zones—Vietnam (no. 30 and 32), Israel (no. 38), Afghanistan (no. 42) and Iran (no. 35); following a similar pattern, two of the victims (nos 21 and 25) had been 'safely' (277) evacuated from the Tube before they fatefully boarded the Tavistock Square bus that was blown up by the fourth suicide bomber. Unlike the artificial correspondences created by the dramatist in the fictional playlets, the patterns that emerge from the micro-stories narrated in the biographical fragments would really seem to possess an immanent logic or meaning and this, in turn, might lend factual backing to the epistemological credentials of Stephens's postdramatic mode of representation.

In this respect, the verbatim section is the one that comes closest to naturalizing what is still, after all, a form of emplotment of the purportedly 'real' materials: the writer's selective editing of the actual biographies plays a crucial role in making the internal correspondences conspicuous and therefore capable of affording to the audience those thrilling, unexpected moments of significance. Unlike what happens in the rest of the play, here the logic of verbatim reproduction of factual material seems to leave no space for internal contradiction and the self-reflexive questioning of the truth-claims that are implicit in every artistic form.

The text's complete openness in terms of staging, however, affords the possibility to recover in performance the principle of counterpoint even when it is no longer operative on the dramaturgical level. Whereas in the German premiere the biographies of the victims were read out loud by a speaker, in Sean Holmes's production at the Traverse they were simply projected as text after the curtain call. According to Stephens's own estimate, in the hectic context of the Edinburgh festival only a scant ten per cent of the audience took notice of the obituaries, whereas in a subsequent performance at the Birmingham Repertory Theatre 'all audience members noticed [them] and sat throughout the ten minutes of text reading'.[82] The naturalizing stance of the testimonial scene was redeemed, so to speak, by the fact that its actual reception was subjected to a principle of casualness: whether or not the audience became aware of the eerie correspondences in the real biographies of the 7/7 victims and of their import in terms of the play's hermeneutics became entirely a matter of contingency and coincidence, depending on each specific situation in which *Pornography* was performed and on the play's variable collision angle with each individual spectator. The transparency of the author's arbitrary intervention in the verbatim section was strategically matched and offset by this surrender to arbitrariness in performance, thereby offering a further, convincing demonstration of Stephens's 'method in randomness'. Read metatheatrically, the playwright's overt engagement with the realist epistemology of verbatim and his strategic deployment of a postdramatic aesthetics to undermine any clear-cut opposition between fictional and factual testimony invite a reappraisal of the often overlooked convergences between the imaginative, metaphorical renderings of contemporary war examined thus far, and the forms of documentary and testimonial drama that form the subject of the next two chapters.

CHAPTER THREE

'Why fabulate?'

Documenting war

In February 2002, an article by David Hare published in the *Guardian* newspaper raised a timely issue which was eloquently captured by the title: 'Why fabulate?' Through a detailed exposition, the celebrated playwright authoritatively argued that fiction, which is based on the paradox whereby some form of 'poetic' or 'higher' truth is reached through the stratagem of lying, may not (or no longer) be the appropriate representational mode for the subject of war. According to Hare, the rendering of war demands an 'honesty' which can best be attained by 'dropping the familiar apparatus of play-making'.[1] This perception was elucidated through reference to Richard Norton-Taylor's 1999 documentary play, *The Colour of Justice*, a verbatim recreation of the Stephen Lawrence inquiry, and to Hare's own *Via Dolorosa* (1998), a long monologue in which the author had appeared as himself on the Royal Court stage to offer a first-person account of his visit to the Middle East, sharing with the audience his eyewitness testimony concerning the Israeli-Palestinian conflict. Hare, a veteran of political theatre with an outstanding record of fact-based investigations into a wide range of domestic and international issues, never made it clear why the Israeli-Palestinian question was unique in requiring to be rendered in non-dramatic form;[2] his subsequent return to the fictional mode in *Stuff Happens* (2004) and *The Vertical Hour* (2008), both dealing with the Iraq war, seems to corroborate the playwright's claim, in the article that gives the title to this chapter, that *Via Dolorosa* was a rejection of old models but not an attempt to impose a new one. Rather than a

Damascene conversion to a documentary orthodoxy of sorts, then, Hare's turn to the documentary form comes across as a contingent solution to the problem of art's relationship with the real; significantly for my analysis, this is a problem that for the dramatist was thrown into relief by the subject of contemporary conflict, and that instilled in his subsequent production a creative tension between alternative formal templates for the representation of war.

Over the last decade or so, British drama has witnessed the rise of an ever increasing corpus of war plays that are marked, like *Via Dolorosa*, by an urgent (and perhaps unexpected) return to questions of reference and reality. The revival of documentary drama has been a growing trend on the contemporary stage, and plays concerned with the war on terror and other related international developments after 9/11 have featured prominently among new dramatic work devised as a factual report of events, and based on edited verbatim quotations from a variety of documentary sources: from more official ones like public statements or the transcripts of judicial inquiries, to other forms of personal testimony such as letters, interviews and diaries. This form of 'neo-naturalism'—as the eminent exponent of the 1960s iconoclastic avant-garde, Charles Marowitz disparagingly dubbed it[3]—undoubtedly partakes of a more general trend towards testimonial and documentary forms in Western cultural production at the turn of the millennium, a trend that Baudrillard's seminal analysis in 1981 already polemically ascribed to a nostalgic longing for the real in the age of simulation:

> When the real is no longer what it was, nostalgia assumes its full meaning. There is a plethora of myths of origin and of signs of reality—a plethora of truth, of secondary objectivity, and authenticity. Escalation of the true, of lived experience, resurrection of the figurative where the object and substance have disappeared. Panic-stricken production of the real and of the referential, parallel to and greater than the panic of material production: this is how simulation appears in the phase that concerns us—a strategy of the real, of the neoreal and the hyperreal that everywhere is the double of a strategy of deterrence.[4]

Seen in this light, the renewed interest in a dramaturgy of the real would seem to be classifiable as a response to 'war in the age of simulacra' that is diametrically opposed to the metaphorical/analogical approach discussed in the preceding chapter, and which could be described (and has sometimes been described) as backward-looking, even naïve, after the long anti-essentialist offensive waged by postmodern art. Still, the documentarian approach to war not only quickly dislodged the 'in-yer-face' plays of the 1990s as the mainstream trend in British new writing at the beginning of the new century; it has also been credited with a very welcome rejuvenation of political theatre at a particularly critical juncture, and has been hailed as a boldly innovative formal development appearing to outclass dramatic 'mimicry' in terms of epistemological integrity, ethical credentials, and capacity for consciousness-raising.

In a recent essay Derek Paget has warned against the risk that the 'broken tradition' of documentary theatre, whose history 'is marked by a discontinuity that sharply contrasts with the continuity of stage naturalism',[5] may induce critics and academics to overestimate the novelty of 'verbatim', the term currently used to describe its latter-day incarnation in the UK. As Paget and other commentators have aptly pointed out, the contemporary culture of documentary can draw on a long line of distinguished antecedents in twentieth-century drama, with a lineage going as far back as Erwin Piscator's 1925 *Trotz Alledem!*, a theatrical reportage on the history of the German Communist Party relying entirely on verbal and visual documents. It was with specific reference to Piscator's piece that Bertolt Brecht first used the term 'documentary' in 1926, and the current designation of its more recent spate on the British stage was itself originally coined by Paget in 1987, when he used the locution 'verbatim' to describe what he then saw as the 'latest manifestation of documentary theatre', namely, the work of theatre practitioners during the 1970s and '80s who drew on taped interviews as their primary source material, following a method first developed in the mid-'60s by Peter Cheeseman in his community plays for the Victoria Theatre in Stoke-on-Trent.[6]

For its part, 'verbatim' is under many respects a slippery category. The loose application of a term originally intended to designate a specific working method to a broad variety of documentary or semi-documentary forms in the context of the present-day 'boom' has met with critical perplexity for more than one reason. To begin with, practitioners and researchers have advocated a more clear-cut demarcation between 'documentary' and 'verbatim', in order to account for substantial differences in the type of traces of the real upon which they respectively draw. Others have pointed to the unhelpful co-opting of a technique to denote a form or genre, a misnomer that ends up turning 'verbatim' into an umbrella term of impoverished critical value and one which, moreover, 'needlessly ups the ante on the promise of documentary' by placing it within a narrow orthodoxy of word-for-word authenticity that 'inevitably falls short of technical truth'.[7] Along the same lines, Christopher Innes's perception of the recent embrace of documentary by two historic figures of British political theatre like David Hare and Max Stafford-Clark as 'in many ways revolutionary' is at odds with the insistence, by playwright and director alike, on a fundamental continuity between their more recent collaboration on *The Permanent Way* (2004), a verbatim investigation into the privatization of the British railways, and their extensive use of verbatim as a research tool during the development of the Joint Stock repertoire throughout the 1970s and '80s.[8]

Definitional problems apart, however, there is general consensus among commentators that the purposeful de-fictionalization of theatre involved in the documentary turn should be understood as a reaction to the hypertheatricalization of public life in our time.[9] In this context, theatrical responses to global conflict have been at the forefront in driving the change, corroborating Derek Paget's view that the intermittent resurgence of documentary forms coincides with moments of crisis and 'situations of opposition'.[10] To a large extent, the new currency achieved by dramaturgies of the real at the turn of the twenty-first century is a result of the search for an adequate form to convey the subject of war. As already discussed in the introductory chapter to this volume, the terrorist attacks of 11 September 2001 and the ensuing war on terror partake of a shared culture of belligerence which co-opts performance as an institutionalized 'strategy and tactic of violence'.[11] In today's theatre of operations the appropriation of the language of performance as a weapon is a truly global phenomenon that cuts across warring factions, placing a heavy burden on the aesthetics and ethics of the theatrical medium. It is not surprising then that 9/11, a historical event which consolidated and above all made apparent the growing theatricalization of warfare, should also have acted as a watershed in the history of documentary drama. Whereas pre-9/11 documentary work usually centred on local narratives, as in Cheeseman's community plays, the post-9/11 revival has tended instead to focus on situations of crisis and/or conflict with an international dimension,[12] thus confirming the intimate connection that exists between the recent burgeoning of documentary forms and the dramatic changes in global politics. Following a similar path to the fictional plays discussed in Chapter Two, the initial impulse behind this new generation of docudramas originates from an oppositional stance towards the heavily mediatized apprehension of contemporary wars; their exploration of alternative modes is underpinned by a similar distrust of the referential imaginary; yet, instead of replacing mimetic reproductions with metaphorical analogues, they go to the other extreme and relinquish fiction altogether, turning to the presentation of testimony as an alternative to the ethical and epistemological pitfalls that may inhere representational art.

When one keeps this in mind, the phrase 'verbatim' acquires a new appropriateness since it precisely captures the twofold predicate that underpins the new wave of documentary drama, giving equal importance to the origin of the text spoken on stage—the words of real people—and to speaking as opposed to showing, to the replacement of visual recreation with verbal recollection. The embargo on the scenic representation of war is constant throughout the whole spectrum of documentary work considered in this chapter and over the next one: from the more realistic tribunal plays with their exact reconstructions of court proceedings, to testimonial drama where the act of bearing witness is no longer located within a fictive cosmos but takes on instead a markedly presentational quality. The reliance on witnessing as a substitute for representation can be seen as the documentarians' particular response to a common challenge faced by theatre-makers today, as they endeavour to offer a truthful account of contemporary conflict without replicating, and thereby spectacularizing, the barbarity of war. As they address an audience exposed on a daily basis to a barrage of graphic images of violence, death and mayhem, contemporary documentary-makers engage in a kind of guerrilla warfare against the spectacle of infotainment media, confiding in the incendiary, ob-scene power of the spoken word to burst through representation and wreck its foundations. In war documentaries, the non-mimetic option afforded by the presentation of verbal testimony is clearly as important in bolstering up the genre's claim to veracity as the factual origin of the materials it incorporates; it also offers considerable advantages on the ethical level since verbal reconstructions avoid the quagmire of mimicry and the further violence inflicted by mimetic repetition on the victims of trauma.

In the rest of this chapter I examine two modes of documentary theatre practice which differ significantly in the kind of source material used and the formal organization to which this material is subjected. I begin with tribunal plays based on the transcripts of official inquiries, the format that comes closest to documentary orthodoxy, and then move on to consider hybrid forms mixing factual reportage and imaginative reconstruction. Each mode is characterized by a variable degree of freedom in terms of the editing, organization and presentation of the 'signs of the real' that are brought on stage. Starting from these premises, my approach to the documentarian rendition of contemporary war develops two interconnected lines of argument. First, I try to advance beyond the surface opposition between fact-based theatre and the fictional/metaphorical approach by highlighting some crucial points of contact, in terms of shared concerns and strategies, that have been generally overlooked in the critical literature. Secondly, I argue that the current revival of documentary, while undoubtedly involving a recuperation of well-oiled methods, is also very clearly marked by an attempt at redefining and renewing the form. The impulse to explore and extend the aesthetic and epistemological limits of documentary is at its most palpable in hybrid plays mixing fact and fiction, but a self-reflexive vein infiltrates even the more orthodox examples of verbatim. Moreover, the contiguity or overlap of documentary with the non-fictional domains of journalism and historiography, on the one hand, and its aesthetics of anti-theatricality and facticity, on the other, ultimately raise the question of whether the stage presentation of unadulterated chunks of actuality can still count as theatre, thus prompting a reconsideration the very fundamentals which define the field of drama. Almost invariably, the documentarians' struggle with the contradictions originating from their determination to capture the reality of war through what remains, after all, an artistic construction resolves in a surrender to, and a self-conscious embrace of, theatricality.

The tribunal play: extending the code

The so-called tribunal plays produced at the Tricycle Theatre in Kilburn, North London have come to represent under many respects the hallmark of the present wave of documentary. Their epitomic quality rests in an uncompromising emphasis on the word: as they place the wars of our time in inverted commas and stage them through the filter of witnesses' recollections in an 'inquisitorial tribunal of inquiry',[13] these docudramas base their claim to veracity on the exact reproduction of the actually spoken; to say it with Nicolas Kent, the Tricycle's artistic director until very recently, 'the strength of verbatim theatre is that it's absolutely truthful, it's exactly what someone said'.[14] While David Hare insisted in *Via Dolorosa* that he was 'just a pen',[15] thereby stressing the verbal, as opposed to visual, nature of his performance, the verbatim plays devised by Richard Norton-Taylor for the Tricycle go one step further by designating the dramatist as the mere editor of the words spoken on stage—a specification that very deliberately shifts authorship and creative agency onto the real people to whom those words originally belonged and, in this way, acquits the artist from the suspicion of fictionalization.[16]

As David Hare himself has admitted with reference to his verbatim piece *The Permanent Way*, this form of authorial invisibility is simply an illusion, an effect:[17] any arranged presentation of facts inevitably offers a particular, invested point of view; even the more balanced editing is informed by an editorial stance. Nicolas Kent has conceded this by describing *Guantanamo: 'Honor Bound to Defend Freedom'*—the spoken evidence play he commissioned from *Guardian* journalist Victoria Brittain and novelist Gillian Slovo in order to denounce the violation of human rights and international law in the infamous detention camp for suspect terrorists—as 'blatantly a campaigning piece of work' that proved instrumental in obtaining the subsequent release of some of the British detainees.[18] That the writer's attitude functions as a crucial shaping force in the selection, organization and presentation of 'found' dialogue is also perceptively acknowledged by David Hare's laudatory appraisal of Kent and Norton-Taylor's seminal verbatim project, *The Colour of Justice*: while commenting on the impressive quality of a play generated through an 'act of editing', Hare also points to the unmistakably subjective slant involved in this act, comparing the dramatist's skill to a Picasso-like ability to paint not an object, but an attitude towards it. Accordingly, Hare maintains that in his verbatim recreation of the Stephen Lawrence inquiry 'Norton-Taylor did not paint a tribunal of a racist crime. He painted the anger you feel when you look at a tribunal.'[19]

In the Tricycle shows, where the presentation of testimony is placed within a distinctly legal frame, this tension between objective reporting and subjective investment, 'hard' facts and interpretation, often becomes the locus of dramatic conflict and the focus of self-reflexive scrutiny. As will be elucidated, underneath their emphasis on a neo-naturalistic eclipse of the artist and the factual accuracy of the material presented, the tribunal war plays invite a phenomenological understanding of the nature of documentary—one which points less to an essence emanating from the incorporated documents, and rather more to the effect produced on the audience through a particular artistic mediation of these 'found' materials.[20]

In the tribunal play, the field of factual reference on which the dramatist and the audience agree to meet is defined by strict norms that have tended to set an exacting benchmark for the recent wave of documentary. In equating truthfulness with an uncompromising adherence to the actually spoken, Kent and Norton-Taylor have collaboratively developed a rigorous editing protocol which would place a considerable share of contemporary documentary work outside the province of verbatim, in spite of an otherwise exclusive reliance on verbal testimony and commitment to 'raw' facts:

> Richard and I have always had certain rules when we work together. For example, if someone asks a question, you must never skip to another answer, you always have to give the answer to that question; you can edit the question a little bit, you can edit the answer a bit, but you've got to keep the chronology going. If you suddenly chuck in something you make up because it's easier, I think you distort the truth—what you come to may be very illuminating but it isn't, in my view, the absolute truth of what happened and what people said. And my attempt, in using verbatim, is always to get as near to the truth as you can.[21]

According to the provisions laid out by the Tricycle's artistic director, professedly non-fictional plays that nonetheless combine words from more than one source in a single speech, feature composite characters drawn from a number of real-life witnesses, or mix verbatim quotations with representative dialogue based on a conflation of spoken evidence would fall short of the technical requirements of 'pure' verbatim drama; but the tribunal plays themselves, as shall be shown, are occasionally at odds with the narrow limits established through this self-imposed orthodoxy.

This tightening of rules and procedural forms is closely correlated with the high civic aspirations driving the Tricycle's verbatim projects. The tribunal plays are expressly envisaged as theatrical interventions into the public sphere, providing a much-needed forum for participatory democracy in light of the growing sense of disenfranchisement produced by the post-democratic drift that has affected Western societies. This helps explain the thematic predominance, within the format, of the war on terror and of the burning political, legal and humanitarian questions it has raised. It is also symptomatic that two of the Tricycle plays—*Justifying War* and *Called to Account*—as well as David Hare's mixed documentary piece *Stuff Happens*, produced at the National Theatre, should have been devoted to the build-up to the war in Iraq, a historical juncture in which the ever-widening rift between the citizens of Western democracies and their elected governments was arguably at its most palpable. The patent disregard of constitutional principles and international law by world leaders, the fabrication of evidence to manipulate parliaments and public opinion, a massive anti-war protest that went practically unheeded were taken by many as damning evidence that political agency had been seized from the public arena and definitively sequestered behind closed doors or inside executive suites. With their unwavering commitment to investigate complex events of crucial public import, bring them to a wider audience, and subject them to collective scrutiny, the tribunal plays are motivated by a 'sense of obligation'[22] to redress this perceived democratic deficit. They make accessible to a community of public-minded play-goers vital information that may have been obscured, neglected or distorted and, in so doing, they very explicitly set out to compensate for the failure of journalism and the other news media to live up to their public role.

That documentary theatre work can provide a valid substitute for journalism, or at least a valuable extension of it, is a very common claim amongst practitioners and commentators alike, and one that undeniably gains weight when it comes from an editorialist of remarkable standing like Richard Norton-Taylor, who brought to the Tricycle's tribunals of inquiry his own professional signature as Security Affairs Editor for the *Guardian* newspaper. Perhaps more than any other contemporary scandal, the war on Iraq has unmistakably exposed the collusion of the mainstream news media with political spin and censorship, and the consequent failure of journalism to abide by its ethical obligation to truth-telling—a failure so glaring that the *New York Times* felt it necessary, in May 2004, to apologize with its readers for insufficient fact-checking and excessive reliance on biased sources of information in its coverage of the Iraqi campaign. While exempt from these charges, the alternative forms of journalism produced on the British stage have also invoked their independence from the logic of infotainment as a guarantee of 'fair, positive and intellectually honest' reporting.[23] In its mission to inform, the theatre is not burdened by the relentless battle for space or air time that afflicts the news media. The compression of complex information into sound-bite formats or marketable narratives can be effectively countered by the greater room for manoeuvre afforded by the theatre and its attendant opportunities for in-depth analysis and balanced reporting.

With respect to the latter, documentary theatre in particular can be credited with a proven track record for broadening the audience's base of knowledge through the inclusion of a wide variety of perspectives in its reportage: especially in its British manifestations, and most notably in Peter Cheeseman's community plays of the 1960s and '70s, documentary theatre practice has tended to place emphasis on retrieving the voices that are normally unheard in public discourse. On discussing his 2004 play *The Arab-Israeli Cookbook*—another verbatim take on conflict in the Middle East, based on recipes and stories gathered during a sort of gastronomic tour through Israel, Gaza and the West Bank—Robin Soans characterizes verbatim's research method as a profitable corrective to a typical shortcoming of today's news media, that is to say the tendency to rely on the pre-packaged 'truths' dished up by official sources or news agencies, whereas the people whose lives are most affected by the conflict are usually the least consulted. According to Soans, the promise of verbatim to deliver a truthful and revelatory experience is rooted precisely in its 'amplification of an otherwise lost voice'[24] and the nuanced insight this can provide into the intricacies of conflict.

While crucial in establishing verbatim as an extremely powerful form of political theatre, this assumption of prerogatives originally belonging to a different sphere of knowledge is not without drawbacks. To begin with, the tendency to see verbatim plays as a journalistic response to current events, rather than as works of art with an intrinsic aesthetic value, tends to place them under the aegis of contingency. This particularly applies to the tribunal play, a format that Nicolas Kent has no qualms in characterizing as inherently ephemeral: 'I'm not expecting these plays to last. They're a response to the moment. I'm not looking at them as art, I'm looking at them as a journalistic response to what is happening.'[25] On the one hand, through his comment Kent is acknowledging a paradox at the root of contemporary documentary practice, which champions the specificity of theatre on account of its epistemological and ethical advantages over the mainstream media, but at the same discounts that specificity by measuring its own success on the ability to act as a valid surrogate for journalism. By implication, the primacy of theatre in communicating the real may well cease once (or if) the news media resume their public mission. While rehearsing *Bloody Sunday: Scenes from the Saville Inquiry* (2005), Kent pointed out that the tribunal plays were created in order to provide an adequate platform for major public inquiries that were not receiving enough media attention, adding that he would highly welcome a change in this policy even if it were to render his stage reconstructions redundant.[26] More specifically, the tribunal plays are regarded as by their own creators and by some critics has having a short shelf-life because their impact is largely dependent on the moment in which they are staged. The Tricycle's forensic simulations are typically timed to appear when the real official inquiry has just closed and a verdict, though imminent, is yet to be pronounced. This lends to the performances an intense topical thrill that enhances their ritual quality as acts of collective witnessing; but once this synchronicity with the real inquiry and the surrounding events wanes, so too does—the argument goes—a considerable share of their political resonance.

These ambivalences are reflected in some contradictory drives inhering the form itself of the tribunal play. By insisting on being approached an accurate source of information, the Tricycle documentaries enter into a contract of trust with the audience that automatically binds them to an alternative jurisdiction from that of drama. The commitment to the truthful reporting of facts places a ban on aesthetic mediation, let alone invention. In the analysis that follows I focus on the pressures that this orthodoxy of documentary puts on theatre-makers, and on the ways in which the strictures of the code have been negotiated, questioned, and eventually loosened as a result. This is particularly evident in the tribunal plays dealing with the war on terror: a war increasingly fought outside legal jurisdiction, in states and spaces of exception, and which has therefore thrown into sharp relief the epistemological limits of a form of drama that is entirely dependent on the existence of legal records. A further, and related, problem concerns the presence or resilience of a dramatic structure underlying the presentation of documentary evidence, which again seems to contradict or downscale the tribunal playwrights' initial rejection of art as a means to represent and conceptualize war. This tension also expresses itself in an increasing self-questioning, over successive realizations of this formal model, of the supposed neutrality and objectivity of editing as a creative method. Partly as a consequence of the inquiry format itself, and partly because of the actual role played by the arrangement of so-called 'evidence' in creating consensus around armed intervention in Iraq, the Tricycle war plays systematically undermine the realist epistemology on which they are predicated by calling attention to their own constructedness and, particularly, to the act of editing as a meaning-making process in its own right and the inevitably manipulative dimension it entails.

For all their insistence on figuring as no more than the editors of spoken evidence, the tribunal playwrights are well aware of how ludicrously reductive this qualification sounds when applied to the mighty enterprise of condensing the transcripts of major public investigations. The Bloody Sunday inquiry dramatized by Kent and Norton-Taylor in 2005, for instance, ran for more than a decade and involved the hearing of evidence from almost one thousand witnesses. With this new official inquiry, announced in 1998 but actually started in 2000, the Blair government responded to years of campaigning by relatives of the victims and survivors of Bloody Sunday, as well as to pressures from the Irish government in the climate of political negotiations surrounding the Good Friday Agreement, by launching a fresh investigation into the events of that fateful day. The inquiry, chaired by Lord Justice Saville, aimed at establishing the truth about the killing and wounding of unarmed civilians by British paratroopers during a civil rights march in Derry. It had been long called for as a much-needed corrective to the hasty conclusions reached by the Tribunal of Inquiry established by Prime Minister Heath back in 1972—the so-called 'Widgery whitewash', as this first official report was commonly dubbed after the name of the Lord Justice then in charge. The Tricycle's *Bloody Sunday: Scenes from the Saville Inquiry* was staged in the time lapse between the conclusion of the hearings, in November 2004, and the inquiry's final report, which the time of the play's debut, in April 2005, was expected to be made public later that year or some time in 2006.[27] Kent, who had reportedly been waiting to dramatize the Saville Inquiry since its very inception, felt that in 2005 the timing was perfect because he could then bank on the enhanced resonance gained by the play's central issue—how the military is controlled in a democratic society—following the incoming evidence of murder and abuse of civilians by British troops that had been deployed in southern Iraq.

Norton-Taylor's play distils well over twenty million spoken words into the customary two hours of a theatre performance.[28] In the published script, the opening speech by the counsel to the inquiry, Christopher Clarke, takes up less than one page and is dated 27 March 2000; in the actual inquiry, it went on for forty-two days, breaking a record in British legal history.[29] Claire Spooner's set for the Tricycle's sampling of 'Scenes' from the inquiry, a meticulous reproduction of the Guildhall office in Derry where the majority of Lord Saville's hearings took place, was cluttered with desks, bookshelves, file cabinets, monitors and other technical equipment; the sense it conveyed, of too many things crammed in too small a space, provided a vivid metaphor for the huge amount of documentary evidence available to the dramatist and the need to bring it to manageable proportions.

Although the process of selection in verbatim dramaturgy is determined by quantitative considerations, editorial choices are essentially guided by the qualitative principle of relevance. Compared with the day-to-day chronicling of journalistic reportage, the tribunal play has the epistemological advantage of retrospective, which allows editors to take in the overall picture of the trial, single out its 'turning points', and extract a coherent narrative out of the sprawling verbal evidence they are working from:

> In a way it's like the précis of the trial, but it looks very carefully at the turning points. As a result you get a very rounded, unbiased overview of the evidence. If you read that evidence in great detail you might get lost, or bored, or you might not quite see its point. In this sense, our version is more coherent, and that's an enormous positive.[30]

The mere act of selection, then, already entails a *mise-en-forme* of the source material. Like a present-day Michelangelo, the playwright works by subtraction, removing excess verbal mass in order to reveal an underlying structure of meaning, a story with 'a beginning, a middle and an end'[31] that lends itself naturally to dramatic treatment. From its retrospective vantage point, the act of editing projects a dramaturgical structure that negotiates the density and opacity of the subject matter for audiences, providing them with a key conceptual aid. In this regard, the goal pursued through the editorial practice of the Tricycle tribunal playwrights, of offering 'a more compact way of disseminating a protracted story',[32] is wholly consonant with Aristotelian prescriptions about magnitude as set forth in the *Poetics*. In Aristotle's theory of drama, not only the arrangement of events but also their length and scale are a matter of the utmost importance. Spectators will only grasp the organic unity of a story, and therefore its sense, if they can easily embrace its narrative arc in a single view; the materials presented in dramatic form must be quantitatively compatible with the scope of their gaze and their memory capacity. The stringent selection carried out by the tribunal playwright is similarly aimed at bringing observability into a confusing plethora of source material in order to make it intelligible to the spectator. In Aristotle, as in the documentary practice of the tribunal playwrights, this aspiration to adjust the magnitude of the story to the gaze of the spectator is what sets the fictive cosmos of drama apart from the real world; it is also one of the crucial epistemological advantages afforded by dramatic constructions of the real over the mere recording that is the province of history.[33] Even as a 'simple' act of compression, then, the editing of judicial proceedings involves a dramaturgy that renders the tribunal playwrights liable to the charge of artistic counterfeit—a charge that they then strategically pre-empt by insisting on the presence of a 'hidden' narrative structure which emanates from the raw material itself and is simply brought to light by the editor.[34]

Another aspect of this naturalization of the editorial gaze concerns more directly the dramaturgical arrangement of the source material. While advocating the epistemological superiority of theatre over journalism (or historiography, as Aristotle would have it), Norton-Taylor points to another level of formal compatibility between the judicial inquiry and drama, one deriving from their shared dialectical quality and the effortless way in which the conflict principle can be profitably translated from one into the other:

> The theatre can be an extension of journalism in the best possible way—that is, by communicating and explaining contemporary issues, scandals and events in a unique, fair, positive and intellectually honest way. Formally, tribunal plays make use of one particular advantage. There is an inbuilt conflict to the proceedings, with both sides giving their version of events, usually determined to stick to their position, but sometimes breaking down and confessing.[35]

As a form based on an internal principle of contradiction, the Tricycle documentarians maintain, drama can let this 'inbuilt conflict' emerge and this qualifies the stage as an ideal forum for public debate around vital civic themes. (The fact that dramatic conflict is typically embodied in verbal interaction is, of course, another crucial asset given the purely verbal nature of the source material.)

At the same time, this argument is significantly qualified by Kent's admission that in their final shape, the tribunal plays co-produced with Norton-Taylor are the result of a tense, albeit useful, negotiation between the conflicting pulls towards accuracy, on the one hand, and drama, on the other.[36] The latter seems to have had the upper hand on a number of occasions: for instance, Sinn Féin's Martin McGuinness, who gave evidence before Lord Saville as the reputed leader of the Provisional IRA at the time of Bloody Sunday, was expunged by Norton-Taylor from his verbatim rendition of the inquiry on account of the fact that he 'didn't read very well as drama'.[37] Similarly, some editorial practices that are typical of the tribunal play seem expressly designed to balance the recourse to a conventional dramaturgy with the need to avoid the impression of theatricality. The dramatic architecture of *Justifying War: Scenes from the Hutton Inquiry* is a prime case in point. With this play, which opened at the Tricycle on 30 October 2003, Kent and Norton-Taylor offered a dramatic rendition of Lord Hutton's inquiry into the death of Dr David Kelly, a respected weapons expert and chief government adviser on Iraqi weapons of mass destruction who committed suicide shortly after his exposure as the source of a BBC leak that accused the Blair government of having exaggerated the threat posed by Saddam Hussein in order to press the case for pre-emptive military intervention. A Producer's Note to the published script explains that the edited transcripts presented in the play are taken from the first part only of the inquiry, which went on for almost a month and heard from seventy-five witnesses. Of the twelve witnesses that actually made it into the play, all but five were again summoned in the second part of the inquiry, where the evidence given earlier was cross-examined by counsels to the opposing parties (the Government, Dr Kelly's family, and the BBC) and further questioned by the counsel to the inquiry, James Dingemans QC. The Note also specifies that the testimonies are presented chronologically, with the exception of the one rendered by Dr Jones, who was heard after Mrs Kelly, but appears before her in the play.[38]

Reviewers who criticized the incomplete representation of the inquiry saw Norton-Taylor's decision to omit the cut and thrust of cross-examination as detracting from the play's dramatic strength. This move was generally put down, rather simplistically, to lack of time: as with the other tribunal dramas, *Justifying War* had to be produced in the short interval between the end of the hearings and the presentation of Lord Hutton's final report. The exclusion of the more dramatic and lively part of the trial, however, reads also as a very deliberate attempt to move away from the consolidated formula of courtroom drama and its typically adversarial model. In defining the format he works with, Norton-Taylor emphasizes the distinction between an adversarial trial, 'in which one party is seeking to triumph over the other by attaining the desired verdict', and an inquiry, whose aim is 'to uncover and establish the more accurate version of events.'[39] In the inquisitorial tribunal of inquiry recreated on the Tricycle stage, the classical model of dramatic conflict as embedded in verbal interaction is purposely rejected in favour of an un-dramatic, or perhaps post-dramatic, focus on the more presentational act of witnessing; the dramatic tension produced by what Hegel calls the '*collisions* of circumstances, passions, and characters'[40] is forgone and the play's grip on the audience must be secured through an alternative structuring of the material.

Norton-Taylor's selection of the inquiry transcripts appears therefore to have been influenced also by a specifically formal concern, that is to say the need of dissociating his presentation of spoken evidence from the traditional dramatic representation of a tribunal setting. This is perfectly understandable when one considers the negative press received by documentary war plays that rely too heavily or too blatantly on a recognizable dramatic build. A fitting example in this regard is the verbatim project *My Name is Rachel Corrie* (Royal Court Theatre, 2005), a one-woman show devised by Alan Rickman and Katharine Viner and based on the diary and personal correspondence of the young American activist who was crushed to death by an Israeli bulldozer in front of the Palestinian home she was trying to protect from demolition. Academic criticism has tended to overrule the almost unanimous praise bestowed by reviewers on this highly moving tribute to Corrie's passion, courage and integrity by measuring its alleged shortcomings against the standards of documentary. Strong reservations have been expressed about the one-sidedness of the account of the Israeli-Palestinian conflict that the play offers but also, more cogently, about the extent to which Rickman and Viner's documentation of Corrie's political ideals and actions is enmeshed in theatrical artifice.

As pointed out by several commendatory reviews of the Royal Court production, the unequivocal pro-Palestinian bias of Corrie's testimony is simply the logical consequence of the autobiographical register and the highly personal nature of the source material available to the dramatists: *My Name is Rachel Corrie* was built posthumously out of the private jottings of a twenty-three-year-old activist who was killed in Gaza less than two months after leaving the safety and comfort of her teenager's bedroom in Washington; documentary verisimilitude would have been indeed severely strained if the editors had attempted a composed, politically-balanced overview of the intricacies of the Israeli-Palestinian conflict like the one offered by David Hare in his carefully-honed retrospective narrative, *Via Dolorosa*. The charges brought against the editors' 'artful' arrangement of this verbal evidence, however, are rather more difficult to rebut. Commentators have mercilessly exposed the play's crescendo of emotional manipulation and the array of textual and theatrical artifice that mediates Rachel's testimony:

> the e-mail in which Rachel considers her future, which you just know, even without the gradually tightening lighting effects, is going to be the last main segment of the play; her final exit walking (literally) into the light, followed by an audio-taped extract of a

> colleague's account of her death, and topped off with a winsome video snippet of fifth-grade Rachel making a school speech about ending world hunger. By the end, I was having to remind myself that Rachel Corrie was a real, dead person, not simply an amalgam of dramatic devices. In that respect the piece does her a disservice even as it commemorates her and her beliefs.[41]

For all the undisputed genuineness of Corrie's words, their blatantly dramatic assemblage would seem to be sufficient to undermine the honesty of the subjective register and cast the play's veracity in a suspicious light.

While already severely compromised by its unorthodox mingling of verbatim and fictional scenes, the truth-claims of David Hare's *Stuff Happens*, too, are severely called into question by the detectable presence of a conventional dramatic architecture upholding this fact-based account of the political machinations leading to military intervention in Iraq. Hare's epic rendition of the run-up to war opened in September 2004 on the National Theatre's Olivier stage, in a production that under many respects marked verbatim's move into the mainstream. Availing itself of an unusually large cast, *Stuff Happens* brought before London audiences George W. Bush, Tony Blair and a number of other key figures in the American and British administration in a semi-documentary play that combined verbatim quotations with imagined (but fact-based) dialogue. Discussing the emplotment of Hare's play as tragedy, Elizabeth Kuti remarks on the dramaturgical necessity of turning Bush's Secretary of State, Colin Powell into a hero-figure whose brave but doomed resistance against the warmongering hawks in the White House becomes the main source of dramatic tension in the play, and whose individual fall triggers, in typically tragic fashion, a catastrophe of global proportions.[42] In the eyes of a notable spectator such as Robin Cook, the Labour MP who, in March 2003, resigned from his position as Leader of the House of Commons in protest at Britain's involvement in Iraq, the main drawback to Hare's decision to focus the action on the Bush administration is that the invasion of Iraq does not seem to have been a real matter of contention in Washington, and consensus hardly makes for powerful drama.[43] To many other critics and reviewers, the misrepresentation of the historical Colin Powell as a lofty spokesman for reason and political wisdom who defiantly opposes the American powerbrokers' obsession with Saddam Hussein came across as a disingenuous dramatic device sitting awkwardly with the presumed factual accuracy of Hare's 'history play', according to the author's own definition.[44] Taking the argument further, Donatella Soto-Morettini locates the play's 'vulnerability' in its selective and inaccurate historical narrative but also, more importantly, in a formal arrangement that 'imposes a kind of coherency and order onto what, for most of us, remains a strange mixture of heavily controlled media images, unlocated weapons of mass destruction, ideological tales of moral warfare and the outer reaches of weblog hysteria'.[45]

This is worth outlining as even the more rigorous tribunal plays are open to the charge of extracting a neat cause-and-effect narrative from the confusing mass of war's textual evidence. It is therefore highly significant that, for all their awareness of the incompatibility of dramatic emplotment and the documentarians' commitment to truth-telling, Kent and Norton-Taylor should have decided to re-arrange the sequence of testimonies at the end of *Justifying War* in order to build up a tragic climax. As mentioned above, the evidence given by the wife of the deceased via videoconferencing was moved forward in the play, where it figures as the last hearing. The dignified testimony rendered by Mrs Kelly adds a moving personal note that creates a powerful contrast with the dispassionate objectivity of the inquisitorial procedure. Whereas in a play like *Bloody Sunday* no adjustment was needed in order to highlight the 'contrast between the coolness of the inquisitive form and the heat of the events they seek to explicate'—the primary source of dramatic tension in tribunal plays, according to David Edgar[46]—in the case of *Justifying War* the editor's creative intervention became necessary as neither the Kelly affair nor its colourless protagonist, aptly renamed 'the Willy Loman of the weapons inspectors' by Janelle Reinelt,[47] afforded in themselves sufficient emotional intensity.

I would also suggest a further compelling reason for this reshuffling of the original sequence of the hearings in *Justifying War*. The prominence given by the play to Mrs Kelly's voice effectively spotlights one of the central concerns identified by the Hutton Inquiry and indirectly points to its implications for the tribunal format. Mrs Kelly's testimony is not only placed in a climactic position and allowed to have the final word on the story; it also stands out from the other hearings because, in an accurate reproduction of the manner in which she testified at the original inquiry, the audience did not witness a moment of direct address but only heard the actress's voice from a fluctuating phone link, while a still picture of the witness appeared on the courtroom monitors. As Jenny Hughes has pointed out, the drifting in and out of Mrs Kelly's disembodied voice provided a powerful indication of 'the failure of a forensic voice in a time of crisis'.[48] Indeed, while offering strong evidence that the Ministry of Defence outed Kelly as the source of Andrew Gilligan's BBC broadcast, the inquiry's narrow terms of reference prevented Hutton from delving into the burning issue of the government's fabrication of an evidence base for going to war. Similarly barred from the truth about the 'sexing up' of the September dossier on weapons of mass destruction, *Justifying War* nonetheless manages to shed light on another troubling reality emerging from the inquiry transcripts, that is to say the virtual impossibility of reconstructing top-level decision-making procedures leading to Britain's involvement in the Iraq war due to an alarming dearth of official records. As Hughes fittingly observes, 'it is this uncertainty in the textual and vocal record of war that constitutes the central drama of *Justifying War*'.[49] Mrs Kelly's fading voice functions as an effective reminder of this disturbing democratic deficit but also, at the same time, of the epistemological limitations of the tribunal play. Especially when dealing with the increasingly extra-legal forms of warfare of the contemporary era, the revelatory power of theatre as juridical space is considerably diminished by its self-imposed dependence on the happenstance of official documents; the tribunal playwrights' exclusive reliance on existing legal records as a guarantee of truthfulness and legitimacy ultimately works against the documentarian ambition to uncover the truth.

Unsurprisingly, the war on terror is the subject that more than any other has thrown into relief this contradiction at the heart of the tribunal play, triggering new developments within the format. An extra-judiciary detention centre like Guantanamo Bay by definition excludes the availability of official legal documents. As a consequence, Victoria Brittain and Gillian Slovo could only respond to the Tricycle's commission to investigate into the disgraceful lawlessness of Guantanamo by seeking out their own witnesses and setting up a 'moral tribunal'[50] based for the most part on unofficial evidence. Like its more orthodox predecessors, *Guantanamo: 'Honor Bound to Defend Freedom'* (2004) begins with an opening statement by Lord Justice Johan Steyn in which he harshly condemns the infringement of human rights and international law under the pretence of democracy and warns that the 'loss of liberty' involved in wartime exceptionalism is on the path to becoming a permanent feature of Western society.[51] As a projection informs the audience, though, Steyn's speech did not originate within an official court setting but was taken from the much-commented lecture on Guantanamo Bay prison given by the senior Lord Justice in November 2003.[52] That Steyn has no authority to preside over Brittain and Slovo's surrogate trial immediately becomes apparent when, after delivering his speech, house lights dim and he exits, handing over the stage to a chorus of voices singing in Arabic the pre-dawn call to prayer.

The testimonies that follow present spoken evidence collected in March/April 2004 through interviews with the relatives and lawyers of British inmates detained in Guantanamo and with two of the prisoners who had been released earlier that year. Verbatim extracts from the interviews are delivered as interwoven monologues with no intervening moderator figure to prompt or orchestrate turns, and they also include letters written by the detainees. As Ryan Claycomb points out, *Guantanamo* combines oral history sources with more traditional forms of documentation—the letters but also the official statements of public figures.[53] For the most part, though, these documents are exposed as heavily manipulated and hence inadmissible in judiciary terms. The prisoner's statements, for one, bear the clear marks of US military censorship, mimicked in the Tricycle production by the performers' mouthing of the crossed-out words. At times, they ring absurdly and sarcastically counterfeit, as in the case of the letter written by Bisher al-Rawi upon his arrival in Guantanamo:

> Dear Mother,
> I'm writing to you from the seaside resort of Guantanamo Bay in Cuba. After winning first prize in the competition, I was whisked to this nice resort with all expenses paid. I did not have to spend a penny. I and Jamil [Al Banna] are in very good health. Everybody is very nice. The neighbours are very well behaved. The food is first class, plenty of sun and pebbles, no sand I'm afraid. Give my salaam to everybody and my special salaam to Wahab. I wish him the very best with his life, religion and business. I hope to see you soon if you want. Your son, Bisher.
>
> PS: Please renew my motorbike insurance policy. (30)

With sneering irony, the detainee here corroborates Donald Rumsfeld's outrageous depiction of Camp X-Ray as a seaside resort in the infamous press conference, also quoted in the play, in which the former US Secretary of Defense vigorously rebutted allegations of inhumane treatment following the release of official photographs of the camp inmates, arguing instead that the US government was indeed very humanely treating a whole bunch of vicious terrorists to 'an eight-by-eight cell in beautiful sunny Guantanamo Bay, Cuba' (35).[54] Later in the second act, the dissonant juxtaposition of Rumsfeld's brash official statement with the narrative of fear and suffering collectively spun by the prisoners and their closest relations effectively works as a damning cross-examination of the official position of the Bush administration about America's human rights policy.

A similar jarring effect is created by Jack Straw, the only spokesman for the British government in the play. Brittain and Slovo turned to their advantage the fact that they had been unable to obtain the viewpoint of members of the government for their verbatim project:[55] the impersonal quality of their official voices as they are heard in the play is a further factor contributing to tilt the balance in favour of the detainees. The opening of Act Three quotes verbatim from the press announcement made by the British Foreign Secretary in February 2004, stating that the US government had agreed to release five out of the nine British citizens held in Guantanamo. The affectless, unapologetic officialese in which Straw announces the imminent return of the five Britons after two and half years in detention without legal representation and without charge is powerfully countered by a choral act of witnessing in which the prisoners' relatives grieve about the indelible marks left by internment on the bodies and souls of their beloved ones, while legal counsels scathingly denounce the further humiliation of gruelling identification procedures upon their return in the UK, and Moazzam Begg's increasingly frantic letters from solitary confinement painfully remind the audience of the countless other suspect terrorist still being held indefinitely in the legal black hole of Guantanamo but also, closer to home, in HMP Belmarsh Prison under the provisions of the 2001 Anti-Terrorism, Crime and Security Act.

While not abandoning the tribunal format altogether, as also testified by the summoning of Lord Justice Steyn to seal the play's ending with what sounds like a legally authoritative closing statement, the means through which *Guantanamo* pursues its truth-seeking mission are essentially extrajudicial, and only partly so by necessity. Whereas official voices were simply unavailable for questioning, Brittain and Slovo's inquiry tactfully refrained from subjecting its traumatized witnesses to the inquisitorial practices typical of the court setting, since this could amount to a form of re-traumatization in the process of vindicating their injustice. A new interrogation, even in the neutral Q&A form of an interview, would not only be objectionable on ethical grounds; it might also actively prevent the witnesses from telling the truth, since their past experience of torture and interrogation 'with a gun to your head' (52) would presumably be liable to generate unhelpful defensive reactions. As the testimonies themselves reveal, the great majority of Guantanamo detainees lied during military interrogations, pleading guilty to charges of terrorism out of fear of death or torture. So, while admittedly aware that interviewees might see the play as an opportunity for political campaigning,[56] Brittain and Slovo decided to relinquish their control over the proceedings:

> We usually met just one family member, always in their choice of territory: in pubs, hotel bars, impeccable sitting rooms, in rooms that doubled as bedrooms, in lawyers' offices, in the Tricycle's rehearsal rooms. They gave us tea, or wonderful Indian sweets, a baby to hold or a lift to the station. There were no prepared questions. We wanted the families to decide what they most wanted to say.[57]

The play, too, is explicit in grounding its truth-claims in the genuineness of testimony rendered spontaneously in an unconstrained interview setting, as opposed to the forcible extraction of dubious evidence by way of interrogation techniques. Civil rights solicitor Gareth Pierce, who appears in the play as the legal representative of the 'Tipton Three',[58] is convinced of the honesty of the account given by the released prisoners 'not because you're interrogating them, but it's tumbling out and they're reminding each other, they're telling things that they haven't told anyone' (52). Implicitly, then, Pierce's words question the appropriateness of the Tricycle's 'inquisitorial tribunal of inquiry' when it comes to dealing with the testimony of people for whom she claims equal status to that of concentration camp survivors (52). By basing their verbatim inquiry on largely uncorroborated evidence, and by refusing to cross-examine, Brittain and Slovo seem for their part prepared to relinquish the strict procedural code so far established by the other tribunal war plays and go extrajudicial, so to speak. Confronted with the utter lawlessness of the war on terror, they set up an alternative court of justice that compensates for the due process denied to the detainees; by so doing, however, they also lay bare the limitations of the tribunal play and opt for the significantly different jurisdiction of a theatre of witness.

The following Iraq play produced at the Tricycle is only superficially a return to tribunal orthodoxy. With *Called to Account*, staged in April 2007, Nicolas Kent and Richard Norton-Taylor again addressed the issue of the evidence base for Britain's involvement in the Iraq war, but the much broader terms of reference pursued by the inquiry allowed them this time to delve more directly into the issue of the government's machinations. As in the actual Iraq inquiry presided by Sir John Chilcot, in *Called to Account* we hear evidence from a variety of witnesses, including politicians, diplomats, security and intelligence officials, high-ranking military officers, lawyers; but the spotlight is on Tony Blair's manipulation of intelligence, law and Parliament in the build-up to the war: as announced in the prosecution's opening statement, the court is called upon to establish whether the evidence presented provides sufficient legal ground for the indictment of the former Prime Minister for 'the crime of aggression against Iraq'.[59] The hearings take place in a realistic courtroom setting where evidence is extracted in accordance with strict judicial procedures and duly cross-examined by four attorneys, two for the prosecution and two for the defence. Marking a sharp departure from the tribunal plays that precede it, however, *Called to Account* offers an accurate verbatim reproduction of a *fictional* legal case: the official Iraq inquiry had not even been announced when the play premiered in London. As in the case of *Guantanamo*, the Tricycle team filled in a legal gap by launching their own independent investigation into the unlawfulness of Britain's military involvement in Iraq. Norton-Taylor pointed out in an article published on the eve of the play's premiere that since the government had not allowed Parliament to carry out further investigations after the highly dubious findings of the 2004 Butler Review (entrusted to a committee whose members were personally appointed by the main defendant himself), and given that its ministers persistently declined to answer questions from MPs, 'what better than for the theatre to take on its ancient role as the people's tribunal?'[60] In light of subsequent developments, one can only subscribe to the political and civic importance attached by the tribunal playwright to his surrogate forum for public debate, considering the enervating slowness of the Chilcot Inquiry, the protracted deferment in making its conclusions known to the public, and the classified nature of part of its proceedings.[61]

With its conflation of verbatim reproduction and speculative recreation, *Called to Account* moves the tribunal play away from strict documentary orthodoxy into far more hybrid territory where the distinctions between fact and fiction become blurred. The play condenses about twenty-eight hours of spoken evidence given by real witnesses who volunteered to appear before a professional legal team in a series of interviews taking place mainly in London through January and February 2007. In order to secure maximum verisimilitude in performance, some of the actors working from the edited version of the transcripts attended the original hearings, met the real person they would be playing on stage, or were provided with footage of the original interview, as in the case of Diane Fletcher when she was cast to play former cabinet member Clare Short.[62] It is perhaps with unwitting irony that the dramatist praises the efforts made by the performers 'to be as faithful as possible to the real thing',[63] since the real thing they were attempting to replicate originated in fact within the *simulation* of a legal process.

Like the other public inquiry plays at the Tricycle, *Called to Account* predicates its epistemological authority upon the truthful and accurate reporting of a court case, but since the case only actually exists in the alternative jurisdiction of theatre, as the dramatic re-presentation of a simulated trial, its truth-claims become far more slippery. In this respect, the relationship that this documentary play establishes with the real comes closer to spoken evidence pieces in the key of *Guantanamo*, and is significantly open to similar charges of evidential incompleteness and partiality. As a note to the published script informs us, not all of the witnesses approached by the Trycicle team accepted to take part in the project. Because this was not an official public inquiry, testimony was gathered on a purely voluntary basis, and this inevitably resulted in a general predominance of hostile, pro-indictment voices. While the evidence examined is often compelling, the overall effect is ultimately closer to political campaigning than judicial debate. Moreover, while the terms of reference of the Tricycle's mock inquiry were ambitiously broad, the base of knowledge it worked from was considerably diminished by the inaccessibility of the more relevant witnesses. With the sole exception of Clare Short, Blair's Secretary of State for International Development at the time of the Iraq war, the big hitters in pre-invasion events—such as Defence Secretary Geoff Hoon, the Attorney General and, needless to say, the Prime Minister—were obviously unavailable for questioning; but also a number of other key players who might have wanted to come forward were understandably reluctant to disclose potentially incriminating evidence outside the legal protection of an official inquiry, especially with Blair still in power. This was the case, for instance, of Sir Jeremy Greenstock, the former British ambassador to the UN who held the role of Special Representative for Iraq between September 2003 and March 2004, and whose views are brought up in the play through the hearing of Juan Gabriel Valdes, Chile's ambassador to the UN at the time of the invasion. Valdes reports that Greenstock was unconvinced by the intelligence that was being used to push the case for war, and prosecutor Sands further asks the witness to confirm the ambassador's view that the conflict was illegitimate as expressed in Greenstock's notoriously censored book on Iraq.[64] It is also noteworthy that among the public figures who appear in *Called to Account*, only Clare Short was eventually summoned before the Chilcot Inquiry, where she repeated the allegations made in the play that Parliament's assent to the war had been obtained through manipulation and deceit.[65]

When measured against the expectations associated with the tribunal format, then, Kent and Norton-Taylor's dramatization of a mock Iraq inquiry inevitably shows a deficit in authoritativeness, and also authenticity, compared with its predecessors on the Tricycle stage. I suggest however that these apparent drawbacks affecting *Called to Account* as a piece of tribunal drama hold explanatory power with respect to the format itself, and should be seen in connection with the play's pervasive concern with the nature of evidence, its interpretation or manipulation, and the attendant implications for the epistemology of verbatim.

As summed up in Philippe Sands's closing statement, the prosecution's case pivots on the British Prime Minister's manipulation of documentary evidence and the law in his wilful determination to bring about regime change in Iraq, a crime of aggression under international law to which Blair had committed himself a full year before seeking parliamentary approval for the invasion. The legal justification of the Iraq war rested entirely on intelligence about Saddam Hussein's failure to comply with UN Security Council Resolution 1441; the capital security threat that Iraq's weapons of mass destruction allegedly continued to pose meant that military intervention was the only remaining option. As it turned out, however, what had been presented as—or sincerely believed to be, according to the defence's argument—incontrovertible evidence of the menace posed by Iraq to world peace proved insubstantial: an outrageous hoax considering the devastating material repercussions it had on countless human lives. Fiction, as is now well known, was the only real weapon of mass destruction deployed in Iraq; to be more precise, fiction handled as factual material. The reliability and correct use of evidence therefore becomes a key issue in the play and, as a consequence, the relationship between the real and its signs is constantly held up for self-reflexive scrutiny.

The Stuart Smith deposition is a prime case in point. As a former Security and Intelligence Services Commissioner, Sir Murray Stuart Smith had access to what he describes as 'a good deal of the raw intelligence' (31) that provided the evidence base for the legal justification of military intervention. Stuart Smith frankly admits that the sources of intelligence available about Iraq's WMD capability could not be trusted to provide conclusive evidence: human intelligence was rarely first-hand but came from 'sub-source[s]' or even 'sub-sub-source[s]', and the 'photographic imagery' that made its way into the government's September dossier was equally dubious because 'although the camera doesn't lie it's not always easy to interpret actually what … what you're seeing' (31). This observation is equally applicable to the two main sources of factual evidence on which verbatim drama founds its truth-claims, the witness and the document, and some aspects of Nicolas Kent's staging seemed deliberately designed to bring out this analogy. In addition to relying on the mediating presence of actors as sub-agents for the original witnesses, the production likewise gestured towards the surrogate nature of documents. When the counsels referred to documents, usually to ask witnesses to read from them, the actual exhibits flashed up on the large screen on the backstage wall and on the two smaller monitors downstage. For example, as prosecution counsel Philippe Sands directed Stuart Smith's attention towards a report by chief UN weapons inspector Hans Blix which was included in the Attorney General's legal advice to the Blair government just prior to the invasion, the original document on headed notepaper was projected on the screen; similarly, audiences were shown Elizabeth Wilmshurst's letter of resignation from her role as deputy legal officer of the Foreign Office, in protest against the unlawfulness of the war, complete with the crossed-out section that had initially been censored for media release. Even as they experienced the thrill of unmediated access to classified documents, however, the audience could not fail to realize that these apparent originals were obviously photocopies now made accessible through digital projection. The performance thus foregrounded the referential status of the documents only to reveal their (doubly) mediated apprehension, again undermining the solidity of 'hard' evidence as the cornerstone of documentary. Ultimately, the one truth that audiences came out with at the end of the Tricycle performance was that there is no such thing as 'hard' evidence. By the end of the play, the defence's tautological conclusion that 'Self-evidently, there is not the "hard evidence" that is necessary' (92) to prove that the Prime Minister deliberately lied to the British people about WMD gained a strange credibility in the audience's ears; meanwhile, on the large screen at the back of the scene, the former parade of documentary exhibits with their promise of facticity was dislodged by a picture of Tony Blair sporting his baffling Cheshire Cat grin.

In its parallel investigation into the manipulation of evidence and the manipulation of law, *Called to Account* also studiedly draws attention to the signature creative method of verbatim and its supposed transparency. One of the most controversial issues raised by the prosecution concerns the Attorney General's legal advice to the government on the lawfulness of the Iraq war. During the Stuart Smith hearing, the prosecution counsel points to the rather appalling U-turn taken by Lord Goldsmith, the Attorney General, between the full legal advice given on 7 March 2003 and the statement made in the House of Lords only days later, when military intervention was put to the vote. In the first official document, which was only made public after Parliament's consent had been gained, the Attorney General's position was consistent with the legal advice given to the Cabinet Office one year earlier, in March 2002, according to which 'hard evidence of non-compliance and non-co-operation' would be essential to authorize the use of force against Iraq. In the statement made on 17 March 2003, Lord Goldsmith maintained instead that Iraq was plainly in material breach of UN Resolution 1441. Since no relevant change in the intelligence basis about Iraqi weapons had intervened between 7 and 17 March, Murray Smith concedes that the advice given by the Attorney General must have been politically motivated and geared to support Blair's 'unequivocal view that Iraq is in further material breach of his obligations' (33), as phrased in a letter by the Prime Minister's private secretary to the Attorney's legal secretary. Clare Short's subsequent deposition clarifies that the sea-change in the Attorney's position on the lawfulness of the war was not only a case of bad faith but also, most importantly, one of 'bad' editing. Blair's dissenting minister provides revealing details about the emergency cabinet meeting preceding the parliamentary vote on war on 17 March. According to Short's recollection, the legal advice that the Attorney General gave on that occasion, reading out loud from a one-page document that had been handed out to cabinet members, was a distorted version of the full, and far more cautious, official legal opinion submitted on 7 March. The latter, however, was strategically not disclosed until after the Cabinet's vote had been secured. If the unabridged legal advice had been put before the Cabinet, Short argues, 'it would have been much more difficult for Tony to get the yes' (44).[66]

By insisting on the use of edited verbal evidence within the judicial context of the fictional inquiry, Norton-Taylor's dramatugy exposes some troubling affinities between the manipulation of official texts in the political arena and the work method of the verbatim playwright. This overlap was strongly foregrounded in performance, too. As already mentioned, the counsels often based their examination of witnesses on edited chunks of official or unofficial documents that were projected on the onstage screens and monitors. In Kent's production, yellow highlights were used to mark out the portions of text referred to by the attorneys, thereby drawing attention to the selective presentation of testimonial evidence as instrumental to the configuration of their opposed versions of the 'truth'. Both in the actual story of the run-up to war and in the tribunal format through which it was rendered by Kent and Norton-Taylor, then, editing comes across as one of the main weapons in the legal and political controversy surrounding the Iraqi conflict, and these forms of embedded textual manipulation are in turn loaded with implications for the primary editing practice that is responsible for the discursive frame which mediates them. The ostensibly neutral, objective re-production of the actually spoken which forms the basis of the play's claim to veracity is undercut by its concomitant emphasis on the editors' subjective agency and invested point of view. The aesthetics of documentary transparency that the play formally abides by is offered up for scrutiny as, precisely, a formal construction. Verbatim is not only infiltrated with fiction in *Called to Account*; it is also self-reflexively put in the dock, and becomes further theatricalized in the process.

Uneasy coalitions

The dialectic between factual report and imaginative reconstruction, objective presentation and subjective investment that haunts even the more orthodox forms of verbatim drama becomes a defining structural principle in *Stuff Happens*, David Hare's account of the top-level political manoeuvres leading to the invasion of Iraq. This hybrid documentary play reintroduces fiction into the formal model of verbatim and, by so doing, engages critically with it. Here, any illusion of transparency in the representation of the Iraqi conflict is undermined by a sustained dramatization of the creative process which effectively shifts the focus from documental evidence onto performative documentation: the gathering, dramaturgical arrangement and presentation of verbal testimony and the problems attached to each stage of mediation.

Under many respects, Hare's relapse into drama with *Stuff Happens* after the more 'purist' experience of *Via Dolorosa* can be interpreted as a corrective to the formal and epistemological limits of the documentary form. As already argued at the beginning of this chapter, the conventional dramatic structure which shapes his fact-based account of the run-up to the Iraq war can be understood as Hare's particular way of instilling debate and narrative into an otherwise potentially dull compilation of documentary material. In terms of topic, the play delves into the same political scenario as *Called to Account*, albeit with a more transatlantic slant, but manages to bypass the strictures of the tribunal play thanks to its straightforward trespass into fictional territory. Whereas the informational capacity of the Tricycle documentary projects is inescapably tied to the terms of reference of the inquiry they dramatize or, in the case of *Called to Account*, to the actual accessibility of witnesses, the dramatist is here able not only to present spoken evidence from the key players involved in the decision-making process leading to the invasion of Iraq, but to further complement the insight derived from the characters' public utterances through invented speech that crucially broadens the base of knowledge to which the revelatory quality of the documentary experience is tied.

Hare's method for mixing verbatim reproduction with imaginative reconstruction is briefly illustrated in the oft-quoted programme note in which the writer sets out his rules of engagement with the real:

> *Stuff Happens* is a history play, which happens to centre on very recent history. The events within it have been authenticated from multiple sources, both private and public. What happened happened. Nothing in the narrative is knowingly untrue. Scenes of direct address quote people verbatim. When the doors close on the world's leaders and their entourages, then I have used my imagination.[67]

Predictably, Hare's classifications have attracted considerable criticism for the way they credit invented dialogue with the same degree of authoritativeness and veracity as 'genuine' verbatim quotations, and have been seen as a rather underhanded attempt at 'claim[ing] truthfulness and dramatic license at the same time'.[68] To me, however, the wording of these claims and their very assertiveness seem deliberately crafted to discourage the reader/spectator from taking them at face value and foster instead a critical attitude. While concluding, a couple of lines below, that *Stuff Happens* is 'surely' not a documentary, Hare grounds his mimesis of events in the private and public sources he has consulted. Like a verbatim playwright, he relies on words borrowed from real people as an authenticating mechanism. The two statements that follow would appear to corroborate this assumption but in fact they undermine it. The sententious reassurance that 'what happened happened' sounds like a modified version of the titular 'stuff happens', itself a quotation of the outrageous official comment made by Donald Rumsfeld, the American Secretary of Defense, about the looting of Baghdad by coalition troops in April 2003. The subsequent disclaimer that 'nothing in the narrative is knowingly untrue' could have come straight from the mouth of a Blairite spin doctor; and at the time of the play's first run at the National Theatre, in autumn 2004, it had obvious resonance with the by then proven inexistence of Iraq's weapons of mass destruction, and the dawning defence argument according to which the Prime Minister had genuinely believed in what had turned out to be unreliable intelligence, and could not therefore be held accountable for dragging the nation into a war of aggression. While documentary evidence is presented as a guarantee of facticity, then, Hare's subsequent mimicry of his sources immediately raises the question of the mystificatory power of their words.

The ambivalence of the Author's Note alerts us to the complex liaison between the real and the fictional that characterizes the play—to the uneasy, unstable coalition in which they are joined. To begin with, the neat distinction between verbatim scenes and dramatic recreations is almost exclusively limited to the paratext. While the dialogue is not entirely devoid of 'taxonomic clues about how to interpret the play's truth claims'[69]—direct quotations, for instance, are generally introduced as reported speech by out-of-role actors—in performance especially, the boundaries between the actually spoken and the 'not quite spoken'[70] tend to become blurred. For one, there is fundamental continuity and consistency between the verbatim public face of characters and the dramaturgically reconstructed private one. This seamlessness is mainly established through the constant presence of actor-characters who function as a chorus, filling in crucial contextual information that is not otherwise available through the dialogue, either because it has been suppressed in official public statements, or because it lies outside the province of the dramatic narrative: in Scene Seventeen, for example, an actor refers back to the period before the First Gulf War, when Iraq was secretly supplied with biological and chemical weapons by American and French companies. The actors' mediating role between the story and the audience also extends to the presentation of characters upon their first appearance, when they are introduced by their name and qualification; this device is systematically employed in both fictional and verbatim scenes. A further element of confusion is created through the mingling of real public figures with representative generic characters who share their viewpoints with the audience—from 'A Journalist', 'A New Labour Politician' or unidentified 'Friends' of Donald Rumsfeld and Tony Blair down to the 'Iraqi Exile' who closes the play with a bitter soliloquy. It is not clear from the text whether these are real people whose identity is left undisclosed, or invented characters in their own right. In the National Theatre performance, no attempt was made at differentiating characters on the basis of their ontological status, either through style of acting (which remained in the mimetic register throughout) or mode of presentation (direct audience address was equally used by historical figures and unidentified characters).[71]

This blurring of boundaries between the authentic and the constructed effectively spotlights theatrical mimesis and the assumptions whereby truth status is granted to one representational mode over the other. *Stuff Happens* is a truly dialogical play not only because of its hybrid cohabitation of factual reproduction and dramatic invention, but also because it postulates a fundamental reversibility between the two domains. On the one hand, the indexical traces of the real are used to authenticate fiction: an aura of verbatim authority spills onto the dramatist's invented dialogue; the factual public face of characters confers veracity on their imagined private one. On the other hand, though, fictional recreation is granted a higher degree of truthfulness than factual presentation: the public evidence quoted in the play is certainly authentic but it is designed to obscure, rather than disclose, the truth about Iraq. The mimetic scope of verbatim, in *Stuff Happens*, is strictly limited to heavily massaged utterances expressly designed for a public context with the obvious purpose of persuading, manipulating and, more often than not, deceiving. By relocating factual authority entirely within official public discourse whose constructedness is self-evident, Hare completely sidesteps the '"off the record" mystique'[72] in which the reality effect of verbatim drama is commonly grounded. For their part, the unofficial sources consulted by the playwright are resolutely kept offstage; the evidence they have given, while crucial for the play's truth-claims as an accurate reflection of a complex conflict, is recast as 'counterfeit' dramatic dialogue. Whether by tapping into the self-deconstructing potential of verbal evidence or by translating it into fiction, then, the play challenges the opposition between authenticity and theatricality and in this way allows for a more complex, nuanced configuration of representational modes to emerge.

As a documentary or 'history' play, *Stuff Happens* roots its ethico-political credentials in a reassertion of the facticity of events, yet at the same time invites us to be wary of reifying material evidence as an undisputable carrier of truth. The play problematizes not only the already widely discredited notion that the 'raw' truth may be unveiled though documentary, but also the 'simple facticity' that Janelle Reinelt sees as the zero degree of its epistemology, a holding on to 'the indexical value of documents [as] the corroboration that something happened, that events took place'[73] in our age of simulation. As the title also reminds us, this is a play that clearly insists on the notion that 'stuff' has indeed happened, that the words of politicians in Washington and London have taken a massive toll in terms of human lives, yet stubbornly refuses to display the bodies of evidence: the bombing campaign marking the outbreak of hostilities is colossally dwarfed as a brief interlude of air-raid sirens wailing in the distance at the close of one scene, and already fading as the next one opens and the voices of the Western powerbrokers regain control over the play's soundscape with their collective spinning of the phoney success story about the blitz invasion. Polemically, in *Stuff Happens* the only 'facts' about the Iraqi conflict that are made accessible to the audience are the public and private verbal theatrics of the lead actors on the world stage.

At all levels in the play, a resolute heightening of theatricality seems to have been Hare's particular understanding of the documentarian 'honesty' prescribed to the war writer in 'Why Fabulate?'. This is clearly established from the very opening moments of the performance. In a kind of metadramatic prologue, a chorus of actors introduces the central characters and, just before George W. Bush joins them on stage, emphatically compares world politics to theatre: 'These are the actors, these are the men and women who will play parts in a defining drama of the new century' (9). The self-reflexive performativity of the chorus's running commentary was further sustained, in the National Theatre production, through a pervasive anti-illusory style of presentation. As already mentioned, the fourth wall was constantly breached not only by the chorus but also by the characters themselves, who used direct audience address when quoting verbatim from spoken evidence. The actors forming the chorus, moreover, also doubled as extras and their stage identity was extremely volatile as they rapidly turned from journalists at a press conference to members of the House of Commons or anti-war protesters. The same kind of fluidity characterized stage space, which was entirely non-representative and relied on lighting, music, a few movable props and especially the formalized blocking of performers to denote a change of scene or location, with seamless transitions from Washington to London, from Texas to Camp David, from public situations to behind-closed-doors conversations.

In some respects, the theatricality that permeates text and performance alike in *Stuff Happens* contributes to turn stage space into a courtroom where those responsible for the Second Gulf War stand trial on the basis of the verbal evidence gathered and presented by the playwright: the distinctly Brechtian quality of the National Theatre production has been often registered, and Ryan Claycomb is right in pointing out that the distancing effect created from the very onset of the play worked to estrange the rhetorical utterances of world leaders and their entourage and offer them up as *gestus* to the audience's critical judgment.[74] While bolstering the critical potential of the verbatim element in the play, however, the citational quality of *Stuff Happens* also operates as a self-questioning mechanism. With their active participation in the shaping of scenes, the actor-characters assume the prerogatives of a collective authorial figure through whom the performance draws attention to the very methods of verbatim dramaturgy. In addition to contextualizing the characters' statements, the actors exercise an evident control over the construction of both character and plot. In the initial expository scenes, actors provide the protagonists' back stories, mixing factual information about their professional careers with touches of colour that offer a glimpse of the private side to their political personality: Condoleezza Rice's love of 'passionate' yet 'unsentimental' Brahms (6), or Dick Cheney's readiness, as an ambitious junior assistant, to get his hands dirty by dealing with malfunctioning plumbing in the White House (5–6). In public scenes especially, the chorus's connecting role is essential to the development of narrative out of an array of illustrative quotations; actors join up the dots in story and control its pace, interrupting the action when a supply of extra-textual information is needed, or a new character requires introduction. When Paul O'Neill joins in the debate during President Bush's first Security Council Meeting in 2001, for instance, the dialogue is literally put on pause and then restarted after the Actor's explanatory comment:

> BUSH: Now let's move on. Iraq.
> O'NEILL: Iraq?
> AN ACTOR: Paul O'Neill. Secretary of the Treasury.
> O' NEILL: Iraq? (12)

As a metaphor for textual construction, the stop-and-replay technique is sometimes used in a more explicit way to underscore the documentary nature of the material presented and the uses and possible misuses of other people's words. Scene Fourteen opens with President Bush heading to the UN on 12 September 2002 to give the highly momentous speech in which he will ask for a new resolution to authorize the use of force against Iraq in case of non-compliance with disarmament obligations. The text he reads from is the result of tense negotiations between the war-thirsty hardliners in his administration and Colin Powell's valiant struggle to avoid political unilateralism and, if possible, armed intervention. As Bush reads from the agreed text, Powell begins to fear that the crucial undertaking to seek UN approval may have been removed from the final draft by his most Machiavellian opponent, Dick Cheney. The President's delay in delivering the promised words, however, is simply due to a technical failure; the line has not appeared on the teleprompter and, realizing this, Bush goes on impromptu:

> BUSH: We will work with UN Security Council for the necessary resolutions.
> AN ACTOR: The unscripted use of the plural—
> BUSH: 'Necessary resolutions.'
> AN ACTOR: —will unleash a process of diplomacy which will last six months. (66–67)

In a war that is all about the minutiae of language, even a minor slip of the tongue carries substantial consequences: in this case, it gives unexpected room for manoeuvre to the double-dealing French who first insist on two separate resolutions, ostensibly to ensure that a material breach of UN provisions by the Baghdad regime will not automatically provide the USA with a trigger for war, but later turn their back on Powell and contribute to founder the diplomatic option.

The play invites a connection between Bush's involuntary blunder and the penchant for misspeak by world leaders and their entourage. The initial part of the same scene provides ample evidence of the 'linguistic offensive' (as Powell defines it, 60) mounted by warmongers in the US and UK governments through August-September 2012 in order to pre-empt the findings of weapons inspectors and strengthen their case for an invasion prior to President Bush's speech at the UN. The dialogue quotes familiar examples of the rhetorical escalation about the Iraqi threat that was used to sell the war to public opinion: from the repeated connections between Iraq and the 9/11 attacks, to the matter-of-fact assertiveness of Dick Cheney's 'Simply stated, there is no doubt that Saddam Hussein now has weapons of mass destruction' (61), through to Condoleezza Rice's ominous warning, voiced on CNN, about the 'smoking gun' turning into a 'mushroom cloud' (62)[75] and its Whitehall version, the forty-five-minutes-from-doom claim that was one of the salient points in the sexed-up September dossier. All these quotations are spoken by the historical character from which they emanated, and are presented by the chorus as performative utterances that can conjure up realities out of verbal fictions and pro-actively determine what kind of 'stuff' happens on the world stage. In the immediate aftermath of the invasion, in a similar merry-go-round of enacted public statements, all potentates in the Bush administration (including Powell) unapologetically admit the speciousness of the justifications advanced for going to war: the epitomic White House hawk, Paul Wolfowitz is quoted candidly declaring, as early as May 2003, that the US government had harped on weapons of mass destruction for 'bureaucratic reasons' ('because it was politically convenient, because it was the one reason everyone could agree to', 116). The outrageous public statement made by Bush's Deputy Secretary of Defense is followed by Tony Blair's pathetic request of 'a little bit of patience' (116) for coalition troops engaged in a pointless search for inexistent evidence ('because Saddam's history of weapons of mass destruction is not some invention of the British security services', 116) and, a few lines later, by Dick Cheney's unashamed plea of guilty, on 14 September:

INTERVIEWER: Vice-President, this time last year you claimed Saddam Hussein was developing nuclear capability.
CHENEY: Yeah, I did misspeak. We never had any evidence that Hussein had acquired a nuclear weapon. (117)

The question of whether the content of the earlier official public statements was true or false is symptomatically treated as irrelevant by those who have made them; the only thing that counts is that they were true *performatively* and thus shaped the course of history. When asked for an official comment about going to war on fabricated evidence, White House Press Secretary Ari Fleischer replies with a sinister 'The President has moved on' (118).

These two rounds of 'true lies', before and after military intervention, have set an important precedent for subsequent uses of the same method, as is clearly the case with Simon Levy's *What I Heard About Iraq*, a spoken evidence play that presents a collage of verifiable quotes in order to expose the blatant lies of politicians during the run-up to war and the following occupation of Iraq.[76] And indeed, Hare's twin scenes offer a powerful demonstration of the critical potential of verbatim when it comes to dealing with the hypertheatricalization of the public sphere and the concomitant weaponization of (verbal) performance in the contemporary battlefield. The clever juxtaposition of mutually contradictory quotations in *Stuff Happens* is a highly effective method for making official 'misspeak' fire back upon itself; statements made in a public context make binding evidence, as the demonstrative replay of Bush's UN episode indicates. On the metadramatic level, Hare's strategy here would appear to corroborate the realist epistemology of verbatim: 'found' words need no other dramatic treatment than to be produced as forensic exhibits in order to nail down the world's political elites and make them accountable before a democratic assembly in the theatrical courtroom;

because these words were previously spoken before a world audience, they have a different ontological weight and a greater political impact than invented dialogue.

These presuppositions are simultaneously sustained and undercut through Hare's adroit mobilization of theatricality, as is apparent, once again, from the demonstrative replay of George Bush's verbal slip. Compelling as it may be, verbal evidence is also very visibly manipulated by the onstage representatives of the author in order to buttress the dramatist's political and dramatic narrative. In this respect, then, misspeak also fires back on the supposedly 'pure' facticity of verbatim. The evidential use of quotations is estranged through the chorus's (meta-) theatrics and explicitly presented as a dramatic device serving a particular discursive purpose. Hare's theatricalization of the documentary form in *Stuff Happens* thus ultimately entails a vigorous reinstatement of the author-function in the verbatim method; the self-effacing editor is placed centre stage and unmasked as a playwright in his own right—a maker of fictions that are revelatory because of their complex, conflicting ways of engaging with the reality of war.

CHAPTER FOUR

The performance of witnessing

The discourse of testimony

A rhetoric of witness has been integral to the epistemology of documentary since its very early manifestations, as a result of the more or less explicit legal rubric underpinning its truth-seeking mission, and of the value attached to individual memory as a depository of alternative narratives that can counter totalizing and/or mainstream versions of historical events.[1] The figure of the witness and the act of witnessing have also been traditionally prominent in literary and particularly dramatic versions of war. As has been mentioned in Chapter Two, the first war play of the Western tradition, Aeschylus's *Persians,* already features an epitomic reporter from the battlefield, in the person of the Messenger who brings in news of the catastrophic defeat of Xerxes's army at Salamis, and shares with the queen and an anxious chorus of elders his detailed account of a theatre of operations they cannot access. The rhetoric of Aeschylus's war witness sheds light on a key presupposition of testimonial drama. At the beginning of his address, the Messenger presents eyewitnessing in contradictory terms, as at once a curse and a blessing: a curse because of the excruciating pain involved in watching traumatic events and relating them, and a blessing because of the discursive entitlement associated with the unmediated gaze of the onlooker ('I was *there*. I can tell you, no hearsay,/the evils that sprang up hurtling against us'[2]). The burden of first-hand witnessing entails both the moral obligation to share the experience verbally with an audience and the ethical and epistemological authority to do so.

Donald McManus suggests that the truthfulness of the Messenger's account is independent from whether or not Aeschylus himself was actually a witness of the battle of Salamis in real life; in his view, the testimony is compelling not as a reflection of first-order experience, but for the way it captures 'the Greek understanding of the battle in history and their ability to empathize with the enemy rather than the facts of what occurred in the waters outside the city'.[3] The prominence achieved by the witness as a validating mechanism in recent verbatim drama, however, tends to be more specifically predicated on an actual moment of contact with the real that is stored in individual memory and then relayed through the performance of testimony. In our age of simulation, the figure of the witness seems to have provided verbatim playwrights with a kind of last resort against the utter dematerialization of 'facts' and the glaring epistemological inadequacies of documents—the last best hope of incorporating 'the indexical traces of the presence of a real past'[4] into a theatrical experience that aspires to engage with the actuality of war. Sustained by this original presence, the witness's claim to authenticity sheds its ontological authority on the performance of witnessing on stage, where the latter is in turn reinforced by the testimonial positioning of the audience in the live situation.

Derek Paget connects the rise in the authoritativeness of testimony and the parallel distrust of other possible signs of the real in the new forms of documentary to the current historico-political juncture:

> Testimony and witness have increased in importance as former certainties—and faith in facts as understood by the likes of Weiss—have drained away from 'post-documentary' cultures in mediatised societies. Documents have become vulnerable to postmodern doubt and information management (a.k.a. 'spin'). But the witness's claim to authenticity can still warrant a credible perspective.[5]

Paget further points to the performance of witnessing as a form of political resistance in the face of an ever-widening 'credibility gap' between citizens and their rulers and the widespread feeling that civic dissent is unable to challenge power in any meaningful way. From a political perspective, however, the figure of the witness does more than charge the theatrical experience with the 'legalistic and spiritual components' that are attached to the notion of testimony in Western culture, as advanced by Paget;[6] as a powerful embodiment of the author-function, the witness also foregrounds individual agency and therefore reintroduces a principle of responsibility and accountability in the production and transmission of meaning. The act of bearing witness involves standing in person before an audience in order to publicly defend a particular version of the truth; in the theatrical courtroom the witnesses' words are weighed, their demeanour scrutinized and a verdict passed. This alone accounts for a subversive moment of transparency that vigorously counters the erosion of subjectivity from the public sphere, a gesture of opposition in light of the growing difficulty, in our age of global interconnectedness and transnational networks, to locate and identify the agency behind political processes and allocate responsibility for material conditions.

While so pervasive, though, the discourse of testimony in contemporary war drama also reflects a radical crisis of (eye)witnessing in our age of the spectacle. As shown in this chapter, the presentation of witnesses upon a stage draws attention to, and implicitly questions, the reliability of the mediator upon which the ontological authority of the discourse of testimony is based; even more importantly, it foregrounds the act of mediation itself, pointing to witnessing as a performance that reproduces, or rather stands for, the original act of 'real' witnessing. With its material existence in the shared here and now of live theatrical communication, the actor's body is essential for the production of presence. Yet this very emphasis on the referentiality of the signifier paradoxically makes the absence of the signified—of the original witness—even more conspicuous; it accentuates the representational dichotomy of theatre and ultimately raises the complex issue of the 'witness capacity of the body'.[7]

The game of duplication and reduplication involved in the performance of witnessing is particularly evident in the tribunal plays: the theatrical re-enactment of a legal performance, and therefore to all effects 'a meta performance, a performance about a performance'.[8] In the live space of the courtroom, the witness performs an act of recollection of a past live situation; this original performance, already at one remove from the real experience it is meant to convey, is turned into verbal evidence which then functions as the pretext for the subsequent testimony of actors in the live space of the theatre. In the closing section to this chapter, 'Technologies of recollection', I return to Richard Norton-Taylor's *Bloody Sunday* in order to dig out the problematic implications of these successive intersemiotic translations, in both legal/political and aesthetic terms. But the problem of mediating testimony is equally central to the verbatim plays based on interviews and other oral sources, and the following section examines the strategies of presentation devised by dramatists in order to textualize the moment of intersubjective encounter between the primary witnesses and those who record their testimony in order to transmit it as a theatre experience.

The ambivalent status of eyewitnessing is also apparent in the kind of role that the current theatre of testimony cuts for its audiences. The act of bearing witness before an assembly of spectators in the live space of theatre entails a heightening of the extra-scenic axis of communication: the idea of theatre as fiction recedes compared with that of theatre as a situation of intense, direct personal contact between performers and members of the audience. In many of the plays discussed below, the audience 'becomes a key, if silent, character in the performance'[9] as the recipient of staged testimony: the act of witnessing is constructed as a collective response to the trauma of war, but its possible therapeutic effects on the psychological as well as political level are shown to be dependent on the presence of auditors and their willingness to listen. Spectators are therefore placed in a position that requires a different level of commitment from that of fictional drama, and the testimonial play actively seeks their collaboration as the receiving end of an act of communication that effectively turns them into eyewitnesses in their own right. As will be shown, this transmissibility of the witness function is also a way of calling the audience to account. The representations of secondary witnesses in the plays often invite a comparison with the audience's role as vicarious receivers of 'the pain of others', to recall the title of Susan Sontag's essential study on war images, and to recognize the possible contiguity with the voyeuristic mode that characterizes the universal eyewitness of global media public. Being 'spectators of calamities' is not only a quintessential experience of (post) modernity, as according to Sontag;[10] inducing potential eyewitnesses to watch acts of violence has conceivably become the main offensive weapon in the arsenal of global warfare, equally deployed by Islamic terrorism and Western powers engaged in the war on terror. As Patrick Anderson and Jisha Menon observe, the compelling power of violent images in today's theatres of war is amplified through

> the accumulation of mass audiences who are alternatively moved, sickened, inspired, or repelled by the terrifying images of their effects. Indeed, the spectacle of violence has so dramatically acquired momentum that it has spawned a cognate form of viewership: the seemingly reflexive picture of individual and collective witnessing.[11]

The plays discussed in the following pages acknowledge this loss of innocence by placing the figure of the receiving witness in a deeply problematic light. The ambivalent representation and construction of the war witness becomes the dramatists' particular way of reflecting and reacting to the simultaneous spectacularization and weaponization of witnessing in contemporary conflict: the authors of this new brand of testimonial theatre prove be fully cognizant of the complex questions raised by the practice of bearing witness to war and violence, as well as of the epistemological and political potential of this form of theatrical communication. In the ultimate analysis, their emphasis on witnessing as a type of performance is perhaps best explained as an attempt to reconcile their simultaneous reliance on and suspicion of this particular mode of discourse; the variety of dramatic configurations and formal strategies that this has given rise to is yet another impressive demonstration of the innovative thrust impressed by the representation of war on theatrical language.

The talking cure

As has been observed in the preceding chapter, theatrical responses to the terrorist attacks on the London transport system on 7 July 2005 have been remarkably scarce and slow to appear. Mark Ravenhill's epic cycle *Shoot/Get Treasure/Repeat* was only given full production in April 2008, and Stephens's *Pornography* had to wait until later that autumn for its British premiere after the debut of the German version in 2007. Significantly, the one notable exception to the prevailing reticence is a verbatim collage of testimonies that was presented by documentary theatre company Look Left, Look Right at the Edinburgh Fringe in August 2005, only little more than one month after the attacks took place. *Yesterday Was a Weird Day: Reflections on July 7th 2005* was conceived by its co-authors, Mimi Poskitt and Ben Freedman, as a piece of instant journalism, a selection of interviews made by members of the company with Londoners from all walks of life in the immediate aftermath of the bombings, and then edited into an impressionistic piece of collective witnessing about ways of reacting to, or coping with, a common traumatic experience. While the documentarians' reliance on 'found' words was certainly decisive in enabling an immediate reaction (Lyn Gardner's review of the Edinburgh performance notes that the production is 'so fresh that it isn't even listed in the Fringe programme'[12]), the decision to adopt a factual point of view mainly stemmed from the perception that justice could only be done to such a sensitive topic by steering clear of emotion and drama through the adoption of a 'neutral' stance.[13] At such short distance from a national tragedy, the documentary mode appears to have acted as a strategic safe-conduct to secure the play's acceptance: unlike fictional recreations of the London bombings, which would have been liable to charges of exploiting real and still fresh pain for aesthetic purposes, the verbatim mode with its abdication of authorship to the 'real' witnesses provided the dramatists with a valuable source of discursive entitlement and ethical legitimacy, and enabled their prompt reaction.

Appropriately, then, the Edinburgh production insisted on characterizing the show as 'a news-gathering process'[14] that was modelled by the flux of external events: Claire Spooner's set featured headline boards that changed according to the current day's news. The play, too, continued to evolve: by the time it was revived at London's Battersea Arts Centre, in February 2006, some interviews had been replaced with more recent ones and others had been added, resulting in a broadened spectrum of voices but also bringing about a significant shift in perspective and a new diachronic dimension. At each successive stage, the new materials were chosen according to a principle of relevance and representativeness. The documentarians drew attention self-reflexively to verbatim as a research and textual practice by displaying the content that had not made it into the show: a considerable number of interviews that were left out as well as the full transcripts and audio-recordings of those that were included in edited form were made available to audiences in the foyer.[15] With this form of documentarian transparency towards their sources, Poskitt and Freedman effectively gave an air of open-endedness to the creative process. The script they authored was presented as just one among many possible configurations of the testimonial collage; a much larger mass of 'raw' materials was there for spectators to create their own paths into the story after watching the show: by reading or hearing more about a character they particularly liked, or coming in touch with a new thread that they were then free to pick up or let drop. Similarly, the playwrights' editorial choices are clearly meant to give a distinctly non-hierarchical, kaleidoscopic feel to the script; there is no obvious narrative arrangement in the sequence of testimonies but rather an element of random accumulation, as if the play were simply an open forum for bearing witness, and the writers its unobtrusive moderators.

In keeping with the tenet of neutrality, *Yesterday Was a Weird Day* offers itself as a democratic, undogmatic text, simultaneously polycentric and polyphonic. The process of selection aimed at allowing as broad a variety of voices as possible to be heard on stage, so as to reflect the Babelian multiculturalism of third-millennium London and convey an impression of fair, unbiased reporting. This plurivocality originates from the diversity of speakers' identities (in terms of age, gender, class, ethnicity, profession, education) as much as from their discursive positioning: the view from the street and the comment made in a professional capacity; private citizens and public figures; laymen and experts; individuals and representatives of a community. What is more, the edited fragments alternate between solos, twosomes and ensemble pieces, as when we hear a chorus of Year Six children from Argyle Primary School near King's Cross, or the actors read posts from a discussion forum hosted by the 'Asians in Media' web site. As a result, the coming-to-text of the narrative appears to be regulated by an unmistakably abstract principle of musical orchestration, quite independent from an editorial construction or the imposition of meaning.[16]

The degree of autonomy and unbridled expression that the play appears to grant to 7/7 witnesses was further enhanced through Poskitt and Freedman's decision to edit out the writer/interviewer from their play. Typically for an interview-based verbatim project, *Yesterday Was a Weird Day* adopts the non-mimetic approach which situates the genre apart from the realistic recreation of courtroom proceedings in tribunal drama. Although each time a new character is introduced to the audience a projected slide states his or her name and occupation and the date and location of the interview, the fragments do not reproduce the actual conditions in which the testimony was retrieved. The disjunction between the 'real' setting where the testimony was recorded and the subsequent theatrical performance of witnessing is established from the very onset, when the first slide announces that the words of the anonymous taxi driver were recorded during a journey through Bethnal Green, but the testimony has been reframed as a monologue delivered by an actor standing alone on a bare stage.

Through its reconfiguration of the original dialogic situation as direct audience address and of the players as text-bearers, Poskitt and Freedman take their theatre of witnessing into distinctly postdramatic territory. This transition towards a mode of communication traceable to the post-epic forms of narrative charted by Hans-Thies Lehmann,[17] however, is accomplished by degrees and in a way that makes the dramaturgical operation visible. The original Q&A structure of the moment of retrieval is still occasionally perceptible underneath monologized testimonies. Sometimes characters begin their turn by reacting to a question which can be easily guessed from their words, or resume their monologue after a short break following an implied prompt by an invisible interviewer; in this duologue, the interview situation is even mentioned in a funnily self-conscious moment:

SUSAN & PATRICIA
ART DIRECTOR AND STUDENT
DATE OF INTERVIEW: 23/12/05
LOCATION: CAFÉ NERO, HIGHBURY VILLAGE

SUSAN: /Oh ... age ... I don't want to say how old I am. You know how old I am. If I say I'm a grandmother that could be ... I'm 62/I am

PAT: That was one of the first things she said to me/. And then she said: 'I'm in shock that's why I told you my age.'

SUSAN: I can't remember that.

PAT: Yeah, God … that was one of the first things you said and you said 'I'm 62 and I don't normally tell people my age I must be in shock'. It was really funny.

SUSAN: Well just because of the business I work in, I wouldn't dream of telling anybody how old I was because they immediately pigeonhole you (*pause*) Oh you've got all that on tape already, have you? Ok my name is Susan, I'm originally from South Africa and I'm now living in England and I'm a grandmother and I'm not going to tell you how old I am although you already know.[18]

Later on, Susan answers her mobile phone and explains that she is in the middle of an interview. The prevalent mode, however, is monologic and at times duologic or choral storytelling, especially as the play progresses and the origin of the narrative no longer needs to be established. These remnants of the interview format, moreover, seem deliberately aimed at advertising the emancipation of verbatim presentation from mimetic dialogue: even in Patricia and Susan's testimony the interviewer's presence, while attested in the characters' words, is rendered redundant as the two speakers' joint storytelling proceeds effortlessly of its own accord with no actual need for cues from their interlocutor. What the play ultimately shows, then, is the transition from a more realistic conversational mode during the initial phase of recording witness, to the postdramatic reorganization of the source material into a collective oratorial effort by a communal, polyphonic voice.

The outcome comes very close to Ryan Claycomb's classification of interview-based documentary as 'oral history performance', a genre quite distinct from, on the one hand, history plays in the manner of David Hare's *Stuff Happens*, and on the other, verbatim work based on written records, and having instead strong affinities with the traditions of life writing, biography and autobiography.[19] And it is indeed quite true that from a formal point of view, *Yesterday Was a Weird Day* has much more in common with Simon Stephens's fictional take on the London bombings in *Pornography* than with the signature fact-based genre of the tribunal play, or even Hare's merging of verbatim quotations and dramatic emplotment in *Stuff Happens*. In their dramaturgical handling of the raw material, Poskitt and Freedman have taken a similar course to Stephens's 'method in randomness' (see Chapter Two) in their way of simultaneously suggesting and undercutting a dialogic principle both within the individual stories and in the formal architecture that holds them together. Though each performance of witnessing takes place in a separate, self-enclosed dramatic fragment, repeated words and leitmotifs resonate across the recorded conversations, conveying a sense of strange interrelatedness. The play's title, for example, alerts us to the recurrence of the term 'weird' in both survivors' and secondary witnesses' narratives as they try to account for their experience of 7/7, allowing for the emergence of a shared narrative of trauma underneath the apparently haphazard cacophony of voices. While drained of their original dialectical structure, moreover, the (post-)dramatic reconfiguration of the testimonies infuses them with a new kind of dialogism that no longer emanates from the actual conditions of retrieval, but is rather the effect of an artificial formal construction. The order in which the sequences are arranged is thematic, not chronologic; it is not designed to mimic a real act of witnessing in the past, but rather to establish new relational patterns through symmetry and counterpoint. This is particularly evident in the opening and closing monologues. Both are very near in time to the event: the first interview took place during a taxi ride on 29 July 2005, while the last one was recorded at the Trafalgar Square vigil for the victims of the attack on 14 July. Both speakers react to the events as second-order witnesses who have not been directly exposed to the violence. The comments of the anonymous cockney taxi driver who opens the performance are bathed in xenophobic prejudice towards immigrants and blame Britain's tolerance towards those who bite the hand that feeds; by contrast, the civil servant of Nigerian origin in the closing monologue sees the terrorist attacks as expressly targeting multicultural London's unique model of peaceful cohabitation amongst diversity. At the same time, however, both witnesses give voice to a similar cultural script in their Blitz-spirit display of defiant resilience, as well as in their firm belief that nothing has changed or will change in London, for better or worse. Although neither their real nor their scenic lives intersect, the two framing witnesses answer each other in simultaneous discord and unison.

Elsewhere, the documentarians use interlaced monologues to produce apparent debate among non-communicating members of this community of witness. The effect is sometimes one of concordance, as with the interwoven speeches of former Foreign Secretary, Robin Cook[20] and George Galloway, who was Respect Party MP for Bethnal Green and Bow at the time of the bombings and, like Cook, sees a causal link between the 7/7 attacks and a heightened terrorist threat, on the one hand, and the invasion of Iraq and the 'trigger-happy' (21) foreign policy of the United States and their allies, on the other. More often, however, the interaction of testimonies strikes a dissonant note, as when the moving but subdued monologue of the survivor of one of the train blasts, George, intersects with the perspective of a Sky News executive editor who relates excitedly about the adrenaline rush when the big story of the bombings hit the newsroom.

Taken collectively, the stories point to another element of friction that runs through their shared narrative of trauma. The individual stories of pain and distress told by the witnesses are a response to a seismic event that has bonded them into a community, but this does not automatically entail an enhanced level of solidarity or civic spirit: as another survivor wryly remarks, the tragedy may well have turned some Londoners into a more compassionate breed, but 'there's some other cunts who are carrying on as normal being really rude', such as the 'wankers' who refused to move down in the carriage on his train home on the evening of the bombings (28). Similarly, the other side to the communal act of witnessing recorded in *Yesterday Was a Weird Day* is the irreducible element of individualism in the characters' all too human ways of coping with trauma: in the eyes of a legal secretary, being the survivor of a terrorist attack also means enhanced social opportunities ('The amount of numbers I have in my phone now is amazing', 30); having just come out alive from the Underground, Dave McCarthy amusedly scrounges a cigarette from two office girls who still have not heard about the attack and do not believe he has really been in an explosion. A note of inescapable selfishness, however, also rings in the testimonies of those who generously did their utmost to help the victims or the rescuers, when they insist on the personal reward afforded by that experience.

By muting the realistic interaction of the original testimony and replacing it with a new, artistically-shaped level of intersubjectivity, Poskitt and Freedman provide a subtle formal correlative to the contradictory versions of testimonial truth about the trauma of 7/7. The turning of the monologized testimonies into a choral act of witnessing lends formal support to the Blitz-spirit myth of London's collective response to the violence of terrorism, to the new spirit of solidarity and community which a significant share of the accounts testify to; yet at the same time the model of connectivity provided through the play's structure is deliberately characterized as the result of an artificial, extrinsic artistic construction, not as a formal principle emanating directly from the factual raw material which might authenticate one version of the truth over another.

A further, related strategy whereby the play undermines the factual authority of testimony and implicitly interrogates its epistemological basis is through a self-reflexive focus on witnessing as a type of performance. With four young actors playing about thirty different characters, this production clearly privileged a demonstrative style of acting. Cross-casting was consistently used to maximize the distance between actor and role and thereby estrange the witnesses' presentation of self. For example, the highly formal Mr Wilson, clinical director of Accident & Emergency at London's Royal London Hospital, was played with a posh accent by Nicolle Nzekwe, a young black actress. More in general, the play frequently emphasized the characters' attempt at presenting the public face that they felt was appropriate for a conversation with a stranger who was going to use their words as the raw material for a play. Although the rhetorical effort is more evident in politicians and other public figures, even the unrehearsed comments voiced by the rowdy group of school children, while touching in their naïve spontaneity and also perceptiveness, are clearly marked by a desire to impress an adult audience and show off their cognizance of the subject. The theatricality of the presentation, then, showed the degree to which the original act of witnessing was already in itself a performance designed to produce a particular effect.

As a reflection of its plurivocal quality, moreover, *Yesterday Was a Weird Day* stages a multiplicity of ways of bearing witness, drawing attention to the factors that concur to shape the performances and implicitly inviting us to consider the standards whereby we tend to assess their authenticity. The diversity of interviewees' identities in terms of class, ethnicity, age and profession is only one aspect of this variety. As already mentioned, the witnesses' original performances were also influenced by the conditions of retrieval: whether the interview was arranged or casual; whether it was made in person or over the phone; and whether it occurred in a formal space like an office or an informal one like a city square or a taxi. In addition to this, another important interpretive tool was provided by the projected slides which specify the date when interviews were made and in this way point to the extent to which the passing of time has affected the witnesses' narrative reconfiguration of their experience. Especially in the 2006 BAC version with its enlarged diachronic extent, *Yesterday Was a Weird Day* presents the working-through of trauma as an ongoing, potentially never-ending process. The characters' way of reflecting upon their experience of 7/7 changes as the lived moment recedes in time. One of the survivors, Dave McCarthy, was interviewed twice; in his first testimony, recorded shortly after the attacks, he still manages sufficient ironical detachment to sustain his performance of cool urban ennui, most notably when he informs the audience of how he carried on playing with his videogame console after the train blast; during the second interview, made about four months later, the trauma has started to register and the young software designer sounds far less cocksure as he holds on to the word 'weird' (repeated four times in less than four lines) to connote an experience which he feels painfully unable to share with others. In other cases, we see that temporal distance has enabled a higher degree of narrative processing.

When Dave's first testimony intersects with that of Gracie, an A&E nurse at Royal London Hospital who gave first aid to the wounded and the maimed, the woman's well-wrought narrative of caring and solidarity, delivered several months after the actual moment of witnessing, sounds less believable *vis-à-vis* the glimpse of London's cynical face afforded by the Dave's less meditated and controlled response as a survivor. A too blatant narrative mediation is easily taken as a token of potential insincerity which can undermine the witness's discursive legitimacy. This is paralleled by the different degrees of authoritativeness that are associated with the witnesses' respective physical proximity to the violence of the attacks: in a descending hierarchical order, first come the survivors, then the rescuers and finally the secondary witnesses who were not on site and depended on various forms of mediation for their apprehension of the momentous events on that day.

By foregrounding the factors that affect the transmission and reception of the lived experience of the 7/7 attacks and connecting these variables to the issue of discursive entitlement, Poskitt and Freedman point to a logical impasse at the heart of their theatre of witness: the working-through of trauma by means of verbal performance is shown to be both essential for and detrimental to the discourse of testimony. In this respect, the heightened theatricality of *Yesterday Was a Weird Day* is both a way of acknowledging this contradiction and an attempt to engage with it. By characterizing their verbatim project as the 'fictional' reproduction of a 'real' performance the dramatists effectively collapse the ontological distance between the original act of witnessing and its onstage replica, calling into question fixed discursive hierarchies. In this way, theatricality is astutely turned into a prime validating mechanism for the documentary-makers' take on contemporary conflict—one which, perhaps unexpectedly, seems to outweigh indexicality in its ability to establish a link with reality.

In Robin Soans's interview-based documentary piece, *Talking to Terrorists* the ambivalences surrounding the practice of witnessing are explored with an even sharper focus on the receiving end in the testimonial transaction. A co-production between Out of Joint and the Royal Court, the play stages a collection of testimonies gathered over a year by a 'team of actors-researchers' engaged in a full-ranging documentary investigation into the phenomenon of terrorism.[21] Though it premiered several weeks before the events of 7/7, Soans's work has tended to be read in relation to the terrorist attacks in London, not least because it had just transferred to the Royal Court, after its debut in Bury St Edmunds in Suffolk and a two-month tour through England, when the bombings took place. The unforeseen topicality impacted negatively on the reception of the play: the very notion of entering into a dialogue with terrorists was often criticized by reviewers as inappropriate in the wake of the London bombings, and the phenomenology of terrorism presented in the play was perceived as obsolete and unable to engage with its twenty-first-century manifestations.[22]

It is indeed true that suicide bombers are conspicuously absent from *Talking to Terrorists*: in part, of, course, due to their unavailability to give evidence, but also because this verbatim project was expressly designed to challenge the popular equation of contemporary terrorism with Islamic radicalism and al-Qaeda. If the play fails to meet the expectations raised by its title, this is due to the fact that the documentarians here aimed at a more nuanced, complex understanding of the different forms of organized violence that have come to characterize the global era, and of the specifically political reasons wherefore they come under the common label of 'terrorism'. Neither the former member of the IRA (a thinly disguised Patrick Magee, the executor of the 1984 Brighton bombing) nor the ex-militant within the Ulster Voluntary Force who give evidence in the play would have seen themselves or even the members of the opposed faction as terrorists, although they have both planted bombs in public places and have innocent blood on their hands. The other 'irregular' terrorists featured in the play include a former child soldier drafted into Uganda's National Resistance Army, an ex-member of the PKK Kurdish separatists, and the exiled leader of al-Aqsa Martyrs Brigade in Bethlehem during the Second Intifada. Some witnesses are only potential terrorists, like the Gaza schoolgirl who, by the end of the second act, has traded her painfully waning hopes for a better future with an ominous hunger for revenge; some of them have already been branded as terrorists *in pectore*, like the four British youths in a Luton mosque praising Islamism's superiority to Western life-styles. The witnesses' accounts also testify to forms of state violence which do not usually go by the name of 'terror' but unequivocally qualify as such: we hear for instance about Israeli soldiers planting bombs in the cars of Palestinian leaders, and are aptly reminded of the CIA's systematic use of torture to extract intelligence with the connivance of British Secret Service.

In keeping with the dialogic quality claimed by the title, the range of testimonies presented in *Talking to Terrorists* gives equal weight to the witness as the transmitter of lived experience and the witness as the recipient of mediated experience. For some of the speakers—peace-brokers, psychologists, journalists, relief workers, politicians, army officers—communicating with terrorists is part of their job; others, instead, have been selected as unwilling interlocutors when they have become the target of terrorist violence. While the first act is mainly centred on sketching out 'a universal biography of a "terrorist" that collates very different conflicts',[23] as the play progresses the floor is gradually opened up to an outer circle of 'expert' witnesses, and the dialogue between senders and receivers which results from Soans's editing specifically invites an understanding of terrorism as a distorted or dysfunctional form of communication. A prime example is the long sequence in Act Two where the former IRA member's account of the preparation of the attack on the Grand Hotel in Brighton in 1984 intersects with comments by survivors from the bomb blast: first a Conservative Party delegate who describes the cheerful evening before the explosion, and then Norman Tebbit, a member of Thatcher's cabinet at the time of the IRA strike, flanked by his paralyzed wife. Talking to the terrorist who killed his friends and colleagues and disabled his wife twenty years earlier is still anathema to Tebbit, who would rather 'let him have it from close range' (86). Soans's editing, however, emphatically underscores the political payoff of dialogue by allocating the opening scene to Mo Mowlam, the former Secretary of State for Northern Ireland who brokered the 1998 Good Friday Agreement and continues to hold on to the view that 'talking to terrorists is the only way to beat them' (25). Mowlam's assertion is not only backed up by the historical fact of the end of sectarian hostilities and the dawning of a new era of peaceful relations between opposed factions in the long and bitter Northern Irish conflict; her idea that terrorists are not bloodthirsty psychopaths but rather individuals who are willing and indeed desperate to talk and find 'an ear listening' (28) is also persuasively endorsed by Pat Magee's retrospective analysis of Republican violence as a last resort, the only remaining option for the disenfranchised Ulster Catholics to be heard politically.

The reason why the Northern Irish success story is given particular prominence in the play is that it forcefully supports Soans's overall understanding of terrorism as a form of communicational pathology—to return to Habermas's definition—that can be treated and indeed prevented through a much-needed talking cure. Soans is quite outspoken about the conclusions reached on the basis of the evidence gathered by the creative team:

> What I have learned in the creation of this play is that we are all potential terrorists, but that most of us enjoy a degree of freedom where we don't feel the need to express frustration through violence. We have a variety of means through which we can allow our voices to be heard—and being heard is exceptionally important.[24]

In the play, this political diagnosis finds authoritative confirmation in the professional opinions given by two members of the circle of experts.

Edward, the psychologist who leads the first-act discussion, shaping it as a kind of group therapy for retired terrorists, profiles the potential or actual terrorist as 'someone who's bright but blocked' (36). His theory is backed up by the witnesses' very similar tales of violence, abuse, suffering, humiliation and impossibility to ventilate their grievances other than by embracing violence. Along similar lines, an aid-worker with Save the Children in various parts of Africa, can still 'see hope in individuals' (96) because of the encouraging signs of recovery shown by children who have suffered and often also committed indescribable atrocities once they begin to receive attention as human beings; her words resonate with the 'particularly significant' view of a relief worker, quoted in Soans and Stafford-Clark's note to the published text, whereby 'a huge amount of what we call terrorism comes from no-one listening'.[25]

In accordance with this analysis, Soans's dramaturgy of testimony projects an image of terrorism as an induced, not an innate, disorder which can be cured by removing the conditions that have given rise to it. The collage of terrorists' biographies in the first act underscores environmental factors by pointing to a set of recurring elements and patterns that emerge from the individual stories and cut across geo-historical differences and ideological oppositions: the Ulster unionist and his one-time Republican foe share the recognition that they both could have lived the other's life;[26] their views are corroborated by the British army colonel and counterinsurgency expert who mentions the 'epiphany' he had as a young officer in Northern Ireland during the Troubles, when he realized that if he had been born in County Armagh, he would to all likelihood have become a 'terrorist' (59).

The play's construction of the 'universal' terrorist as a compound yet consistent character was sustained in the Out of Joint production through a cast of eight performers playing up to five roles each in full ensemble mode. The individual portraits of 'terrorists', their victims and their interlocutors were thus presented as interchangeable and gradually merged into a more fluid, composite identity that enabled the perception of an underlying common denominator to the discrete testimonies. Another factor that contributed to the play's unearthing of universals in its multiple narratives of terror was the dramatist's loose application of verbatim as a working method: unlike his more purist colleagues, Soans did not work from recorded conversations but simply from notes taken during interviews which he then edited or even reshaped according to his understanding of the play's informing 'vision'.[27]

The other side to the play's analysis of terrorism as a political and psychological phenomenon is its marked emphasis on the healing power of witnessing and on theatre as an ideal space for the diagnosis, treatment and even prevention of communicational disorders. Following

3. The Out of Joint production of *Talking to Terrorists* (2005): Luton mosque. Photography by John Haynes. © John Haynes/Lebrecht Music & Arts.

his typical editing method, Soans arranges his material in such a way as to foreground thematic interconnectedness and 'create a kind of relay race, with actors passing the baton on to each other'.[28] The overall impression is one of seamless, unconstrained narrative flow, with individual voices effortlessly merging into a collective act of witnessing of considerably amplified resonance. With this ostensible removal of the narrative blockage denounced by the stories, *Talking to Terrorists* enacts formally the political solution for breaking the circle of violence which it advocates thematically. On the scenic level, this is mirrored by the fluid use of stage space prescribed by the text. The characters' performances of witnessing take place in different locations that veer between the realistic settings where the interviews took place—from Mo Mowlam's living room, to 'a bookshop inside a Luton mosque' (30), or 'a coffee-bar in a Dublin shopping-mall' (60)—and a nondescript neutral space when separate testimonies are interwoven into choral scenes. The stage directions describing scene changes stress continuity—a scene '*segues*' (60) into the next one, Edward comes on stage and picks up the coat and scarf dropped by the British colonel who has just exited (59)—and in the Out of Joint production transitions were marked through purely conventional means: mainly, actors' entrances and exits, simple lighting effects, a bare minimum of moveable props, and the shifting

4. The Out of Joint production of *Talking to Terrorists* (2005): ending. Photography by John Haynes. © John Haynes/Lebrecht Music & Arts.

configuration of the rectangular concrete slabs functioning as the set's wings and back wall.

With its anti-illusory quality, Max Stafford-Clark's production brought out the unique duplicity of performance space, its simultaneous capability to signify a potentially infinite number of different scenic situations that are however contained within a single, unchanging physical environment. Though they do not interact as characters, in phenomenal terms the entire community of witnesses featured in *Talking to Terrorists*, including the recipients of testimony in the auditorium, inhabit the same space. The sheer theatricality of the Out of Joint production thus gave prominence to theatre as situation, rather than fiction, and spotlighted its distinctively intersubjective essence.

Structurally, too, Soans's play exploits to the full the theatre's 'bifurcated mode of presence' to build its case for the possibility and necessity of the talking cure as a political solution to violent conflict.[29] Using the same technique employed by the authors of *Yesterday Was a Weird Day*, the writer relies on intercutting monologues to introduce a dialectical element into the characters' storytelling and produce significance through concordance or, more frequently, dissonance. In *Talking to Terrorists*, this ironic interplay is generally achieved by pitting the 'blocked' communication that characterizes the horizontal exchange between characters in scenic space against the inherent intersubjectivity of the theatrical situation. This is particularly evident in the joint performance of witnessing involving Rima, an Associated Press journalist of Lebanese origin, and Terry Waite, the former Special Envoy of the Archbishop of Canterbury who was kidnapped and held captive for four years by Islamic jihadists during the Lebanon hostage crisis. Soans edits their testimonies as intercutting monologues that throw into sharp relief the points of contact between the witnesses' individual experience of the same conflict situation. At exactly the same moment in their parallel narratives, Rima and the envoy mention Terry Anderson, who was Rima's boss at Associated Press before he was kidnapped in Beirut in 1985, and whose release Waite was negotiating when he himself was taken hostage by Hezbollah two years later. Still, while the two characters share the same physical space and, to a remarkable degree, even the same narrative, their performance of witnessing is staged as a split scene: in terms of intra-scenic communication, the two speakers inhabit two separate halves of the acting area which the audience must assume to be non-communicating and ontologically discrete, and each of them remains ostensibly unaware of the other's presence. The same pattern is repeated in Act Two, when Rima discusses the catastrophic situation in present-day Iraq and her words intersect with those of the British Army colonel who, like her, puts down the current escalation of insurgent violence to the 'strategic failure' (78) of American policies in the area. In both cases, the combination of interlaced testimony and split scene throws light on the theatre's capability for activating an unrealized potential for dialogue in the individual acts of witnessing that are reproduced on stage.[30]

Another barrier that is strategically collapsed in *Talking to Terrorists* is the one between the different time frames that are woven into the performance of testimony. Within the dominant mode of representation, which remains that of the witnesses' recollection of past events in the scenic present of the transmission of testimony, the play occasionally features quick, smooth transitions to the enactment of reported episodes and situations. This happens, for instance, in the long sequence of interlaced narrative by the two former Irish 'terrorists' in the second act. As they separately recount their dawning friendship in Long Kesh Prison, the ex UVF paramilitary recalls his offer of a cup of tea to the other man sitting in the library. When he switches to reported speech ('As the morning wore on, I fancied a wee cup of tea; but then I thought it would be very rude to make one for me and not for him. "No, fuck it," I thought, "I won't," ... but then I found myself saying, "Would you like a wee cup of tea?"'), this provides the cue for a restaging of this moment from the past within the scenic present: the Loyalist's question is followed by a long, dramatically-charged silence that is eventually broken by Magee's momentous reply, 'Yes I would, thank you' (87–88).

Elsewhere, the interplay of past and present, mimetic representation and diegetic presentation, points more explicitly to the creative process. In the first-act biographical section, the terrorists' back-stories are given in a format that oscillates between a group therapy, a panel discussion and a lecture addressed to the audience in which Edward, the psychologist, illustrates his findings about the genesis and genealogy of terrorism using live quotes from his patients' testimonies to provide evidential backing for his analysis:

> EDWARD: You can give adolescents the feeling they're shaping history; 'You think you can change the world ... well, yes actually, you can ... I'll show you how.'
>
> I.R.A.: Gun lectures ... an Armalite ... how to strip it ... how to maintain it.
>
> P.K.K.: The older group said to counter violence from the State, there's no alternative but to use violence.
>
> U.V.F.: I had a gun put in my hand at the grand old age of sixteen. I near shot the man who put it there. The only thing I'd ever fired was my finger coming out of the cinema ... here I was at sixteen with this bloody big weirdy weapon. (43)

Throughout the second half of the group presentation led by Edward, the former Ugandan child soldier lies downstage folded in a blanket, following her excruciating recollection of the violence she suffered at the hands of her father and stepmother, her subsequent escape, and how she fell into the hands of National Resistance Army rebels who came out of the bush and gave her two smelly blankets which she pulled up over her head before falling asleep. When the woman wakes, long after the exit of her fellow 'terrorist' witnesses, she resumes her narrative and describes her introduction to military training in the past tense. The stage direction, though, describes her as bathed in a '*bright morning light*' and surrounded by '*sounds of birdsong (African)*' (53); and as she rehearses the excitement of the drill and her childish eagerness to take part, she again shifts into reliving and re-enacting her past gestures. The woman's subsequent turns of speech, in which she narrates the years that followed and the 'total commitment' with which she engaged in acts of murder, torture and dismemberment, are interwoven with the juxtaposed testimonies of the former British ambassador and the British army colonel who jointly report about war crimes committed by child soldiers in Sierra Leone. As in the earlier group session led by Edward, here too the Ugandan woman's recollection of her past actions functions as 'live' documentary evidence to back up the testimony of the two expert witnesses.

On one level, this incorporation of past actions into present narrative comes across as a self-reflexive mirroring of verbatim's typical displacement of war into words. In *Talking to Terrorists*, the reality of war is always located in a past or future elsewhere; the scenic present is entirely taken up by its verbal reconfigurations. On another level, though, the non-referential approach has a more direct bearing on the play's main theme. Especially in the case of the former child soldier, the witness's relapse into the mimetic mode is a sign of the continuing grip of past actions on her present self, of the impossibility to completely dissociate the doer from the deed, the born-again human being from the former terrorist: although she sees herself as 'a very new person', the traumatized Ugandan woman poignantly reveals that 'I'm twenty-eight years old now; sometimes I feel fifteen, sometimes I'm two hundred' (95).

In a more general sense, the replacement of war with words is the very essence of the play's proposed method for breaking deadly cycles of violence. Soans makes a powerful case for the urgency of the talking cure through the bitter parting words of the Bethlehem schoolgirl who closes the performance by reading this entry from her diary:

> This year things are getting worse. Last April … the saddest day; one of the girls in the form below me, Christine, was killed by an Israeli sniper. The Israelis said it was a mistake, but they can't bring her back, can they?
>
> When I first saw the Twin Towers on television, I felt sorry. But now I feel happy that they died. It's their turn to suffer. I could see many thousands of them die. I wouldn't feel a thing. (96–97)

The play's ending effectively throws the problem of the potential for future violence inherent in the girl's despair upon the theatre audience and, by extension, the wider community of citizens they stand for. The Palestinian girl's hardened voice cries out for 'an ear listening', to quote Mo Mowlam's phrase, before her loss of humanity is complete and she turns into just another war machine. An audience's willingness to listen is thus shown to be essential to the play's politics of 'giving voice', and the receiving end accordingly becomes a key concern in the acts of witnessing performed in *Talking to Terrorists*. Throughout the performance, spectators are constructed as the principal interlocutors of testimonial communication; their position, and the responsibilities attached to it, is estranged and critiqued through a self-reflexive focus on different forms of secondary witnessing and the ethical questions they posit.

Talking to Terrorists turns the spotlight onto the audience from its very opening moments. Thwarting the expectations raised by the title, the first person to appear on stage is a woman with a vacuum cleaner—a far less menacing figure than the eponymous terrorists, although she, too, nurses legitimate grievances about the mess on the living-room floor and glowers at the auditorium as soon as she registers the spectators' presence. She is followed after a short while by the lady of the house, Mo Mowlam, and politely dispatched upstairs so that the interview proper can begin. As in *Yesterday Was a Weird Day*, however, the interviewer's voice has been muted in the actual play text, and what we hear is a monologue with interpolated pauses, sometimes to mark abrupt topic shifts, and occasionally interrupted by brief exchanges with the former Secretary of State's husband, John, as he is instructed to make coffee.[31] The first scenic situation thus projects two blank spaces that are there for the audience to fill in: that of the invisible addressee of Mo Mowlam's words and, connectedly, that of the terrorists whom the play claims to be talking to. As the scene develops, the interlocutor's position is deictically determined by the following speaker, Phoebe, who begins her performance of witnessing with 'It's really difficult for me to talk to *you*' (28; emphasis added). Similarly, the vacant role of terrorists is also eventually taken by the group of former militants from various conflict zones; yet the initial ambivalence projected by the opening scene skilfully sets the tone for the problematic identity of the recipients of testimony which emerges from the play as a whole.

The more evident incarnation of the secondary witness on stage is Edward, the psychologist who, by profession, listens to his terrorist-patients and assists them with the therapeutic task of coming to terms with the violence they have suffered and perpetrated. Apart from his professional expertise, Edward's position is very similar to that of the audience: as a belated witness,[32] all he can do is lend a compassionate ear to the unfolding trauma narratives or, at best, act as a facilitator for their emergence. In keeping with the play's theatricalization of testimony, moreover, Edward's role approximates that of a stage-manager who supervises the ongoing performance and sees to its smooth running: when the former child soldier's eyes fill with tears on remembering her father's cruelty, he lends her his handkerchief, and when she mentions her encounter with the Ugandan rebels in the bush, he turns his overcoat into a makeshift prop so she can fold herself in the 'blankets' they gave her; when the ex al-Aqsa combatant remembers the Israeli soldiers who beat him as a child and compared his screams to a donkey's cry, Edward promptly assists with a bray.[33] In this way, the performance connotes this professional listener and, by indirection, his real-life counterparts in the auditorium as belated witnesses with respect to the narrated events, yet active participants in the act of relating them; secondary witnesses are powerless to intervene, but their presence and willingness to contribute to the narrative act is empowering for those who come to testify.

The second half of the play is dominated by another prominent embodiment of the witness as spectator, albeit one who cuts a far more problematic figure than his reliable professional predecessor. A sizeable portion of Soans's second act is allocated to the interview with the former British ambassador to Tashkent, an unnamed but very recognizable Craig Murray. In the company of Nadira, the Uzbek belly-dancer who now shares his London flat, the ambassador gives evidence about the British government's connivance with human rights violations in Uzbekistan and, in particular, with the use of torture to extract intelligence under the sanction of the war on terror. Murray's damning testimony also includes an account, in re-enacted form, of his meeting with a Foreign Office Committee in March 2003, following a telegram with which he had defiantly contravened the rule of silence imposed by Whitehall on its appointed officers. Murray reports the Jesuitical arguments with which the Foreign Office legal advisor denied that the British government's possession and use of intelligence obtained through torture by the CIA would qualify as a material breach of the UN Convention on Torture, and quotes the bewilderingly apodictic view of the Security Services whereby the manifestly false evidence about supposed Uzbek terrorist groups and their links with al-Qaeda should be regarded, on the contrary, as 'high quality intelligence material' playing 'a vital role in the "War on Terror"' (73). After suffering a mental breakdown, and still 'flabbergasted' by the way the government held on to blatant lies simply because they tallied with their notion of a world 'full of Osama bin-Laden groups' (75) and therefore in need of a permanent state of war, the ambassador responds with a second telegram to a circular issued by the Foreign & Commonwealth Office after the Abu Ghraib scandal in 2004, inviting anyone in the Service who might have evidence of torture by UK forces or their allies to report it. As is publicly known, Craig's story ends with the leaking of the incriminating telegram to the press by as yet unknown hands and his instant removal from office.

Unlike Edward, who has only been in touch with former terrorists and witnessed the violence of war from a safe distance, the ex-ambassador found himself 'at the sharp end' (74), as he himself protests, and has paid a high personal price for his decision to act upon the moral obligation to truth-telling that comes with eyewitness status: besides the obvious repercussions on his career, the speaker is now shown as a shaken, ill man bearing the visible signs of vicarious traumatization. In this regard, Murray's physical and emotional proximity to the violence of war would seem to give him a clear advantage in terms of the authoritativeness and accountability of his discourse. On closer inspection, however, we notice that his response-ability as a first-hand witness is actually based on mediated evidence, and that his position is therefore not qualitatively different from that of Edward, the audience's proxy. As he himself recounts, Murray attended a show trial in which the defendant was instrumentally accused of a number of serious common offences (a frequent method with political opponents) as well as of militancy within an al-Qaeda-linked group. The latter accusation was based on a statement signed by the defendant's uncle, an elderly country Uzbek who during the trial broke down and revealed that his children had been tortured before his eyes until he had agreed to give false evidence. Notwithstanding this admission, the accused was sentenced to death. As if in a kind of *mise en abyme*, therefore, the ex-ambassador's present performance of witnessing is based on his role as a silent, powerless spectator to a legal performance that in turn repeated, and corrected, an earlier performance of witnessing recorded in a written statement. In the second episode he relates, Murray's eyewitness account of torture is instead mediated by some photographs handed him by embassy staff, showing the corpse of the member of an Islamic religious sect who was tortured and killed by immersion in boiling water because he had refused to recant his beliefs and denounce his fellow affiliates. Just like in Edward's case, then, here too the witness's reliability as a source of information is considerably reduced by the second-order quality of the evidence he gives.

In addition to casting doubt on his witness status, the ex-ambassador's testimony in *Talking to Terrorists* is also destabilizing as a performance of character. Murray's multilayered, multifaceted identity as a witness is further complicated by the play's uncompromising exposure of his many contradictions and weaknesses as a person, and their potential for seriously detracting from the credibility of his account. For a start, it is hard to reconcile the ambassador's commendable moral outrage and his evident empathy with the victims of torture with the fact that his performance of witnessing takes place in '*a penthouse flat with a view along the Thames to Canary Wharf*' (65), where he gives evidence about inhuman acts of violence perpetrated on helpless innocents while sipping white wine and chewing on a pizza graciously prepared and served by his Oriental ballerina-cum-carer. Similarly, the ambassador's brave denunciation of human rights abuse by the world superpower and its allies sits uncomfortably with the imperialist trope underlying his relationship with the exotic curiosity lifted from a Tashkent nightclub and now showcased in London. This embarrassing side to the Murray story was deliberately amplified in the Royal Court production, where the part of Murray's fiancée was taken by the same actress who played the former Ugandan child soldier whom her self-styled saviours, the rebels, had turned into a sex slave.[34] Further adding to our puzzlement, throughout the quasi-farcical domestic double-act between the ex-ambassador and his belly-dancing girlfriend we also learn about the (white) lies he tells her, and his probable misuse of authority in getting her a visa for Europe.

For the audience, the ultimate effect of this ambivalent characterization of the ex-ambassador is to prompt a questioning of the criteria whereby we, as a judging body, are positioned to assess the witness's performance. At some point, it becomes difficult to tell whether we believe in the truthfulness of Murray's testimony despite his imperfect performance or, rather, because of it. The more we cross-examine the witness, the more we become aware that his blatant inadequacies at once undermine and reinforce the truth-claims of his war narrative: while potentially detrimental to his believability, the ambassador's many faults ultimately humanize his performance of witnessing and give it an aura of authenticity. Even more paradoxically, Murray's morally objectionable behaviour can be interpreted as the symptom of a more compassionate response than Edward's professional aloofness—a tangible proof of his deeper empathic engagement with the pain of others. When retrospectively compared with the more equivocal performance of witnessing offered by the shaken former ambassador to the Uzbek conflict zone, Edward's neat, rational explanation of the psychology of terrorism begins to show its exploitative side, its arguably not so ethical use of other people's tales of suffering to prop up a master narrative of global violence. Even more importantly, perhaps, the sense of narrative closure that ultimately emerges from the latter's performance stands in sharp contrast with the mobility of the witness function which is projected by Murray's case.

In this respect, the ambivalent position of Soans's war witness can be usefully elucidated through reference to Cecilia Parkert's *Witness*, a play about a female interpreter who translates the stories of the survivors of ethnic conflict in the Balkans for a therapist and develops symptoms of vicarious traumatization as a result. A central concern that emerges from Parkert's play is the idea of empathic unsettlement as a by-product of bearing witness to other people's suffering, and the concomitant difficulty of maintaining the required professional detachment when one becomes the depository of deeply disturbing experiences. 'Empathic unsettlement', of course, is a notion made popular by Dominic LaCapra's by now classic study, *Writing History, Writing Trauma*, in which the American intellectual historian famously argued that narratives of trauma lead to the construction of a particular subjectivity for the secondary witness, defined as a capability for 'being responsive to the traumatic experiences of others' while 'resist[ing] full identification with, and appropriation of, the experience of the other'.[35] Due to its translation interest, Parkert's work will be discussed in more detail in Chapter Five; but the assumptions it makes about the transferability of trauma and the witness function are very relevant to the discourse of testimony in *Talking to Terrorists*. In Soans's play, the symptoms of vicarious traumatization that mark out Murray's performance as a secondary witness do more than rehabilitate his ethical credentials; they also function as signs of the real, the indexical evidence of an initial moment of empathic contact with the actual victims of violence and injustice that has generated a mimetic response which both prompts and validates his vicarious act of testimony. In his capacity as a secondary witness, the ex-ambassador is shown to inhabit a zone of mobility, one in which the transition from passive recipient to active bearer of testimony, from spectator to actor is possible and, arguably, also desirable. This mobility clearly also extends to the members of the audience who, as the receiving end of the witnesses' narrative, become directly implicated as a potential further link in the testimonial chain, and are pressed to reflect on their own position within the testimonial transaction, as well as on the different levels and modes of response-ability that are attached to it in the contemporary theatre of war.

The artist is present

In their double capacity as spectators and actors, the figures of secondary witnesses that are juxtaposed, and often contrasted, in verbatim war dramas like *Yesterday Was a Weird Day* and *Talking to Terrorists* provide a mirror image of theatre audiences caught as the recipients of testimony; but they also often function as mimetic analogues of the performers as its carriers and transmitters. The actors' positioning in the plays and the discursive authority ascribed to their role as 'conduits for testimony'[36] are directly related to the problem of mediating witness on stage and of the witness capacity of their expert, professional bodies. As discussed above, the ontological authority of documentary accounts of contemporary conflict is only in part derived from the facticity of their source material; at least equally important is the theatre's capacity for 'making present' before an audience the original act of witnessing. In a kind of epistemological short-circuit, a performance of witnessing in the real past validates its reproduction on stage and, conversely, the phenomenal reality of theatrical performance confers authority on the actuality it stages. As the mediating device upon which the entire mechanism hinges, Carol Martin pointedly remarks, the actor in documentary work gets caught in 'the paradox of a theatre of facts that uses representation to enact a relationship to the real'.[37] A key strategic asset in the creation of presence, the performer's body is at the same time a source of embarrassment because of the way it points to the absence of the real witness whose words and identity it mediates. In Alan Filewod's lucid formulation,

> From the earliest point of theorised practice, the presence of the actor has been a problem for documentary. … The actor embodies the actual, but the actual is perceived only through the effort of the actor's body. The actuality so perceived in the surrogative moment also erases that which the actor does not embody, so that 'reality' collapses into the presence of the actor who stands before us as subject and object, document and documenter, whose authority derives simultaneously from the representation and the erasure of actuality.[38]

The question of authority raised by the actor's surrogate body sits uncomfortably with the epistemological and ethical claims of testimonial theatre. This aporia is vividly denounced in *I've got something to show you* (2005), a documentary project co-ordinated by Alison Jeffers and staged at the University of Manchester in June 2005. The play presents a documentary reconstruction of the painful case of Esrafil Tajaroghi, an Iranian refugee who set himself on fire in Manchester, in 2003, after being denied asylum. In a later article, Jeffers motivates the company's decision not to bring the refugee's body on stage as stemming from the persuasion that 'it would be more respectful to evoke rather than to inadequately embody him'; in the initial part of the play, which focused on Esrafil's experience with British immigration authorities as an asylum-seeker, his absent body was replaced by a rucksack on an empty chair, while different actors spoke his words in order to 'underlin[e] the fact that the one person who might be able to authenticate the story was not able to do so'.[39]

The markedly anti-theatrical performance aesthetics developed by verbatim drama betrays a similar uneasiness about the actor's work in mediating factual material. In the Tricycle's tribunal pieces, the counterpart to the invisibility of the writer-as-editor and of the director-as-chairperson (in Nicolas Kent's own definition) is the tribunal players' 'unwritten pledge' to relinquish acting in favour of a hypernaturalistic reproduction of the real-life characters they stand for. As Kent explains, the trademark Tricycle conventions such as the use of microphones, the fully-lit auditorium and the company's avoidance of the final applause are expressly meant to 'diffuse [sic] the theatricality of the process' and thereby conceal the performers' work in creating this illusion of unmediated verisimilitude.[40] At the other hand of the spectrum from the tribunal plays' aesthetics of transparency, and the paradoxical presence/absence it requires of the actor, we find the enhanced theatricality of the interview-based war dramas discussed above, with their frank acknowledgment of actorly intermediation. By relinquishing all pretences to accurate surrogation, documentary plays in the key of *Talking to Terrorists* or *Yesterday Was a Weird Day* forego impersonation by emphasizing instead the gap between the performers as secondary witnesses and the original performance of witnessing which they make present before a theatre audience. In a seminal theoretical formulation, Attilio Favorini suggested the term *Stellvertreter*, which he borrowed from the title of Rolf Hochhut's semi-documentary Holocaust play, to define the actor's vicarious position as that of a self-conscious deputy or representative. This nomenclature, Favorini argued, is a particularly helpful reminder of the political implications involved in putting oneself into another's place.[41]

Noting the persistence, throughout the history of documentary theatre, of the problems surrounding the actor's presence and the theatre-makers' endeavours to conceal or atone for it, Alan Filewod somewhat provocatively raises the question of 'wherefore?' In the light of the difficulty of mediating the facticity of the original witness, fictional models might seem to be able to provide a more efficient and artistically viable strategy for dealing with the real than documentary. Given that there is no way out of artistic mediation, the critic asks, 'why not complete the act of surrogation by releasing the ethical obligation to actuality source material?'[42] A possibility that is not contemplated in Filewod's discussion is that of bypassing of the actor altogether by bringing on stage directly the primary witness and exhibiting his or her material body of proof: a course of action taken by David Hare in his influential documentary solo *Via Dolorosa*. In this testimonial play about the Israeli-Palestinian conflict, the author opts for a radical solution to the encumbering presence of professional stage mediators by relinquishing his customary invisibility and appearing before the audience in person in order to validate his performance of witnessing.

As he explained in his thought-provoking article 'Why fabulate?', discussed at length at the beginning of Chapter Three, with *Via Dolorosa* Hare was consciously responding to the representational challenges posed by the subject of war by rejecting fictional models and turning to a theatre of facts. His one-man show, however, considerably stretches the formal limits of documentary by including autobiographical memoir within it, and enacts a parallel reorientation of its epistemology by parting with the supposed objectivity of documents or facts as a source of authority, and rooting instead the truth-claims of his take on the Middle East conflict in the wholly subjective, but ontologically authentic, individual voice of the first-hand witness. Drawing on and modifying Peter Weiss's well-known distinction, Derek Paget identifies two main strains in documentary production throughout the twentieth century: a 'recording' tradition that aspires to produce an objective account through the effacement of authorial subjectivity, and a 'reporting' tradition in which, on the contrary, truth is accessed via the subjective apprehension of the testimonial voice.[43] Significantly, Hare's radical embrace of the 'reporting mode' of documentary in *Via Dolorosa* is motivated by his misgivings about actorly intermediation as unfit to fulfil the contract of trust that binds verbatim authors to their audience. In *Acting Up*, his account in diary form of the ten months during which he rehearsed and performed in *Via Dolorosa*, Hare's mistrust of fiction is matched by an equal degree of suspicion raised by the surrogate body of the professional performer:

> I could never write so-called 'scenes' which would one day be played by British actors on a British stage. British-Jewish actors—who in no way resemble Israelis—would seem ridiculous if they tried to enact little dramas opposite, say, a couple of Arabs and the odd light-skinned Pakistani—the only people available in London to play Palestinians. It seemed impossible that it would achieve anything you could call 'authentic'. Or 'real'.[44]

In 'Why fabulate?' Hare similarly dwells on the need to bypass the actor's inadequate body, likening the alternative mode of testimonial presence that he sought to achieve in *Via Dolorosa* to the unmediated presentation of self in performance art:

> As an outsider, a half-informed visitor, I despaired of writing fiction which relied on conventional scenes. I knew that English actors bearing machine guns and challenging each other at guard posts, or wearing yarmulkas, or pressing their wrongly proportioned bodies against the wire of refugee camps, would, almost by definition, introduce an element of falsity which would pollute the subject matter. So I determined to stand—yes, like a Dutch performance artist—making myself the vessel of the show in order better to direct people's attention to the material itself. It was my contention that, in this case, when the subject of a work is so hotly contested, so open to argument, that the audience could best decide whether the witness were honest if the witness were willing to appear before them.[45]

Hare's statement of aesthetics is intriguing for the way it balances subjectivity and objectivity. Like the landmark solo piece by Marina Abramović from which this section borrows its title, *Via Dolorosa* is built around the idea that 'the artist is present'.[46] Like a true performance artist, Hare turns his physical presence on stage into the focus of the show; as he does so, however, he continues to characterize himself as a 'vessel', a transparent conduit for testimonial material that has its own independent existence in the domain of the real. In other words, the testimonial presence that Hare projects in *Via Dolorosa* strategically combines the flaunted subjectivity of the personal voice with the objective gaze of the neutral observer and reporter; in turn, the authenticity that the dramatist seekds to achieve by (not-)playing himself becomes a crucial asset in validating a particular political viewpoint on the Middle East conflict. As is typical of testimonial drama, moreover, the play's truth-claims are reinforced by the principles of individual agency and personal responsibility that are attached to the presentation of witness; yet the type of accountability that is exhibited in *Via Dolorosa* is specifically theatrical, and has to do with the author's willingness to expose his *performative* self before a jury of spectators in order to prove the urgency and sincerity of his report.

The 'sort of fictional character' that Hare admittedly created for his performance of witnessing in *Via Dolorosa* is defined by a double outsider status: the protagonist is a foreigner in the conflict zones he visits, and is likewise out of his element on the Royal Court stage as a novice actor at the age of fifty-one. While bearing the sanction of biographical facticity, these two defining features of the witness-figure in *Via Dolorosa* are in fact the product of a very deliberate artistic construction. The performative self that Hare fashions for himself as the protagonist of his investigative travelogue is, as he frankly acknowledges, 'stupider and more ignorant than I actually was'.[47] In spite of the fact that many of the people he meets on both sides of the barricade know he is a celebrated political playwright (in Tel Aviv, his play *Amy's View* was rehearsing at the Cameri, one of Israel's leading theatres, at the time of his visit), Hare positions himself as the average 'bloke'[48] who starts out on his journey without any specific professional expertise or personal investment. As a witness to the complexities of the Israeli-Palestinian conflict, Hare downplays his public persona and dons the mask of the average representative of the community who goes out to investigate and comes back to report on his findings.

This discursive positioning proves expedient in more than one respect. For a start, it enables the dramatist to shake off the original brief received from the International Department at the Royal Court Theatre that had organized the tour (also supported by the British Council) with a view to producing a play about the period of the British Mandate in Palestine. Hare's change of tack is simultaneously registered and justified at the point in the narrative where Hare meets Benni Begin, the leader of the Likud hardliners, at the Knesset in Jerusalem. Begin has agreed to discuss the period of the British rule in Palestine and is therefore put off by the writer's initial question, which shifts the topic to contemporary politics. The politician's irritated reaction gives Hare a golden opportunity to defend before his audience his right to pursue his own independent line of inquiry into the Israeli-Palestinian conflict. The witness's applaudable fair-mindedness, however, conceals the play's disturbing silence about Britain's colonial legacy in the area and its lasting historical repercussions, as Eitan Bar-Yosef has sharply observed.[49] What is more, the stance of 'passionate neutrality' that replaces the more politicized point of view which might have originated from the Royal Court's commission is itself loaded with political significance, since it is a direct emanation of Hare's persuasion that the only hope for a peaceful settlement of the Israeli-Palestinian conflict rests with 'outside intervention'.[50] When *Via Dolorosa* was revived in 2002, in the wake of the invasion of Afghanistan, and again in 2004, against the backdrop of the Iraq war, the colonial implications embedded in the notion of third-party mediation to which Hare's testimonial act lends backing became disturbingly noticeable. Incidentally, the political recipe that can be evinced from Hare's documentary is also at variance with the view expressed in the closing monologue of *Stuff Happens*, his 2004 Iraq war play: in Hare's subsequent take on the Middle East conflict zone, an exile breaks the up to that point complete silence of Iraqi voices on stage with a passionate cry for his compatriots to take the future of their country in their hands and put an end to war and bloodshed by shaking off the long-standing yoke of external influence.[51]

On stage, Hare's performance as a passionate, yet neutral, eyewitness within the narrative is adroitly confirmed and authenticated by his performatized presence as the renowned political playwright who has embarked on a journey across the foreign territory of professional acting. With its metatheatrical frame, the play creates a strong connection between the writer's visit to Israel and the Palestinian territories in his retrospective account, and the personal voyage of discovery as an actor unfolding in real time before the audience's eyes. Tellingly, the first words that Hare addresses to the audience characterize him as a theatrical eyewitness even before he turns into a historical one:

AUTHOR: Partly, of course, I just want to see what it's like.
That's what I'm doing here. If you are wondering.
The last time I acted I was fifteen, and played
Thomas Cromwell in the school production of *A
Man For All Seasons.* Christopher Hampton played
Richard Rich and the film critic of the *Financial
Times*—as now is—played Thomas More. The

> experience taught me all I needed to know. Since then, I've always tried to get Judi Dench to do this sort of thing. (3)

The reporter's wish to go out and see for himself the reality of the Israeli-Palestinian conflict which originally prompted his tour of the Middle East is thus subsumed into his present venture on a West End stage as a freshman actor. In James Macdonald's original production at the Duke of York's Theatre, Hare's metatheatrical reframing of the testimonial quest was further enhanced through a literalized rendition of the writer's debut into the limelight: having entered from a door at the back of the stage, Hare treaded the boards of the narrow gangway leading to the front 'like a man about to enter a bear-pit'[52] before he tentatively launched into his monologue; the Middle-Eastern minefield traversed by the witness in the past became tantamount to the theatrical Via Dolorosa he was about to travel in the performative present in order to deliver his account.

In the testimonial narrative, Hare's journey across an embattled field of conflicting beliefs, attitudes and cultures aptly culminates in a stroll around the holy sites of Jerusalem, 'the world capital of claim and counter-claim, the acknowledged metropolis of dispute' where 'contention, abrasion and mistrust are scored deep into the subtly pink rock' (36). His pilgrimage to the Middle East has taken him through the stations of the tense political climate of Tel Aviv, the frontier mentality of West Bank settlers, the disturbing squalor, corruption and disillusion of Gaza, the committed artists and intellectuals of Ramallah; now the author decides to repeat the journey in miniature scale by following the Via Dolorosa in the holy city. As he retraces the footsteps of Christ to the cross, he finds himself sharing the other pilgrims' bafflement at the unimpressive stone pavement winding up to Calvary, and comments on the faint impact Christianity has made on the old Arab city. While partaking of the history of contested ownership that troubles Jerusalem's holy sites—as Hare reminds us, the Church of the Holy Sepulchre is 'shared unhappily' (36) by Armenian, Coptic, Latin, Syrian and Ethiopian Christians—Christianity nevertheless holds a strikingly marginal role in the fiery confrontation between Arabs and Jews over the 'most coveted spot in the universe of faith' (37), the Foundation Stone at the heart of the Dome of the Rock.

In the performance, Hare's self-consciousness about his supposed outsider status in Jerusalem as a Western visitor was aptly mirrored and reinforced by the identity he projected as an actor. As one of the most prominent dramatists of the contemporary scene, Hare was hardly a stranger to the theatre world; yet his performance expediently emphasized the awkwardness of the alien and the discomfort he felt at being alone on stage, unshielded by the professional performers he had thus far vicariously relied on to express his views. Through his decision to flaunt the inadequacy of the intermediary's body, Hare managed to turn a potentially burdensome presence into an eloquent embodiment of the grievous state of affairs in Israel and Palestine and of the excruciating task of bearing witness to it—an equation which was then made even more explicit in the title of the filmed version of the Broadway production, available on DVD as *David Hare's Via Dolorosa*.

In addition to naturalizing his particular testimonial stance, the author's performatized presence on stage played a crucial role in establishing the witness's credentials in *Via Dolorosa*. When he decries Hare's 'embarrassingly wooden gestures, badly strained voice, and inability to characterize the people he quoted',[53] Jonathan Kalb fails to recognize the deliberateness, or at any rate expediency, of the performer's evident lack of expertise. Hare's display of non-acting was artfully designed to show the artlessness of his authorial self, his inability to live up to the daunting testimonial task he had set himself. Whether or not they took them at face value, the reviewers of the first production generally agreed that the technical shortcomings of Hare's performance succeeded in conveying his sense of urgency, his genuine commitment to the moral obligations attendant upon first-hand witnessing. Hare's 'enthusiasm as a performer', the strenuousness and 'often comic intensity'[54] with which he undertook the challenge of delivering his report were taken to reflect a commendable readiness, on the part of the recently-knighted playwright, to put himself on the line in order to testify in person before the exacting audience of the Royal Court.

Through this sustained focus on authorial presence, then, *Via Dolorosa* succeeds in turning the manifestly inadequate body of the intermediary into a prime exhibit in the testimonial account, a powerful signifier of both authenticity and facticity.[55] Crucially for my line of argument, the kind of referentiality achieved through Hare's performance of witnessing is one that involves a wholehearted embrace of (meta-)theatricality. If, on the one hand, Hare's display of not-acting is contrived as an ostensible rejection of fictional mediations of the real, on the other the play's self-reflexive focus on the here and now of performance is a key asset in the play's construction of documentary referentiality. By grounding the witness's discursive authority in his material presence on stage as a performer, Hare's documentary solo is marked at one and the same time by a maximum degree of reality and a maximum degree of theatricality; only apparently in conflict, the two dimensions sustain one other and actually overlap in their joint effort to offer a persuasive mediation of the actuality of war.

Technologies of recollection

A recurrent aspect of the forms of testimonial discourse examined so far is their reliance on the theatre's power to create presence and, relatedly, on the phenomenal continuity between the 'fictional' and the 'real' that can be foregrounded through the environmental nature of stage space. This section continues to consider the use of liveness as a sign of the real, adding however a more specific slant on the tensions between live performance and other forms of bearing witness to the truth in documentary versions of contemporary conflict. As already amply evidenced throughout this study, the valorization of the theatre's critical potential as a live art form is one of the distinctive features of recent war plays, almost a default reaction to the utter mediatization of the new wars and their dominant representations in contemporary culture. While clearly touching upon the specificity of theatre as a quintessentially live medium, however, the focus here falls on liveness as an effect, rather than an essence. In the following pages, I look at live performance as a technology of reproduction of the real and underscore the uneasy cohabitation, within current forms of war documentary, of the live and the recorded. This includes the tension between testimony as ephemeral, subjective performance and testimony as permanent, objective knowledge stored in archival records but also, more literally, the co-operation and/or competition between live performance and media technology in the creation and validation of testimonial presence.

My line of argument throughout this chapter is deeply indebted to Philip Auslander's dialectical understanding of the live and the mediatized in his groundbreaking inquiry into the status of live performance in contemporary culture. On this subject, I wholly subscribe to Auslander's rejection of the mystique of liveness, that is to say of the still widely current assumption that 'the live event is "real" and that mediatized events are secondary and somehow artificial reproductions of the real',[56] and I am particularly wary of its potential corollary for a critical examination of theatrical representations of war, which would be to see the simple reversal of the act of mediatization through live performance as constituting in itself a meaningful oppositional/political act. This is something that, for instance, Jeanne Colleran seems to be implying in *Theatre and War* when she locates the political and civic function of the war plays considered in her wide-ranging study within 'the particular power of theatre as a live, embodied, communal art form to raise awareness of complex issues flattened out through hype and spin'.[57] As I hope will become clear, my approach here is less concerned with any purported 'remedial' powers of live communication in the age of simulacra than with liveness as a means for producing significance on stage under the pressure of enabling and enlarging the audience's understanding of the current paradigm of warfare. In addition to providing crucial theoretical backing for my analysis, Auslander's perspective also has a more direct applicability to the authenticating function of liveness in the forms of testimonial discourse examined in this chapter. His insightful observation about performances of witnessing in the legal context and their underlying cultural assumptions about the epistemological authority of liveness is of primary relevance for my discussion of the (re-)production of testimonial presence in the tribunal plays, with their mimesis of legal proceedings; but Auslander's formulations also have an evident bearing on testimonial drama *tout court*, given the more or less explicit juridical rubric that frames this particular *mise-en-forme* of contemporary conflict.

In a paradigmatic chapter of *Liveness* entitled 'Legally live', Auslander dwells at length on the continued centrality of live performance in legal procedure. In comparison to other social domains, the critic notes, the law has offered a striking resistance to the cultural dominance of mediatization by unremittingly holding on to the notion that a trial is 'an ontologically live event'. Examining the failure of the videotape trial to supersede the live performance of witnessing in the American courtroom, notwithstanding the undeniable advantages afforded by technology, Auslander concludes that

> this respect for liveness is ideological and … rooted in an unexamined belief that live confrontation can somehow give rise to truth in ways that recorded representations cannot; the essence of testimony is not the information recalled but the performance of recalling it in the courtroom, before the accused and the jury.[58]

In the discourse of law, that is to say, the witness's capability to elicit truth would appear to depend less on the content of the account given than on an observable performative behaviour in a live situation of face-to-face confrontation—that which in legal parlance goes by the name of 'demeanour'. Charles Spencer follows a similar logic when he qualifies the Tricycle's recreation of the Hutton Inquiry in *Justifying War* as 'a signal public service' because it provided access to the witnesses' body language, a crucial element in the assessment of their credibility that might otherwise have gone unrecorded given that the Hutton hearings were typically not filmed or broadcast.[59]

Auslander's description of testimony as the retrieval of information stored in personal memory and subsequently made present through the witness's 'performance of recalling' in the courtroom appears equally suited to elucidate the mechanism in which testimonial drama grounds its truth-claims. In legal discourse, testimony is a two-fold act involving the 'recordation and recollection' of events as perceived by the witness, that is to say the storage of personal memory and its subsequent retrieval in the live context of a trial.[60] The same dualism inheres verbatim theatre practice, which uses the edited verbal evidence collected through interviews or recorded in inquiry transcripts as a pretext for the live act of testimony before an audience. It is indeed from the co-operation between these two dimensions, from the 'fusion of the live voice and body with texts that have existed in the realm of the real',[61] that verbatim derives its ontological authority. The translation of written evidence into live performance infuses verbatim drama with its distinctive theatrical viability and, by turning verbal record into real presence, reinstates the integrity of the real performance of witnessing from which the verbatim material originates, thereby acting as a powerful guarantor of the latter's authenticity and indexicality.

This isomorphic relationship between the performance of witnessing on stage and the real event it reproduces might easily work to naturalize the use of liveness as a validating mechanism and attenuate some of its embedded contradictions. In the theatrical courtroom, and particularly in plays based on inquiry transcripts, the conversion of stored knowledge into a live experience through the addition of subtextual and extratextual languages does not directly emanate from the actual subjects of testimonial discourse, but is rather the result of actorly and directorial interpretation: as Carol Martin rightly notes, 'what is outside the archive—glances, gesture, body language, the felt experience of space, and the proximity of bodies—is created by actors according to their own rules of admissibility',[62] thereby raising the possibility of falsification. Even more crucially for my argument here, if liveness exerts its authenticating function by restoring the performance elements of testimony that have been erased through recordation, this process ultimately amounts to a reversal, and indeed denial, of the textual mediation it apparently aims to validate. The fact that this reversal is in turn expedient to concealing the simulacral status of staged testimony, its ambition to surrogate the 'real' performance it reproduces, provides further insight into the manipulative aspects of verbatim's exploitation of liveness with its promise of im-mediacy.

The forms of documentary considered in this volume frequently acknowledge the inbuilt duplicity of testimonial practice and its contradictions, seemingly confirming that the representation of contemporary wars has tended to work as a litmus test for the more problematic aspects of witnessing. Richard Norton-Taylor's dramatization of the Saville Inquiry in *Bloody Sunday*, however, is unique for the way it turns this latent split into the focus itself of the drama and systematically taps into its potential for signifying conflict. The playwright's editorial perspective recasts the official investigation about the epitomic episode in the Northern-Irish Troubles as an instance of arrant memory warfare in which documentary evidence and live testimony, recorded and recalled knowledge are pitted against each other to serve the interests of a particular political agenda. As will be argued, the Tricycle documentarians turn the spotlight on testimony as a conflicted practice with the more immediate purpose of extracting contemporary significance from the power struggle informing the Saville Inquiry. But the performance of witnessing in *Bloody Sunday* also implicitly draws attention to the process of intersemiotic translation at the basis of the tribunal play and, in doing so, provokes questions that are relevant to the broader range of testimonial war drama considered in this study, particularly with regard to its reliance on liveness as a sanctioning device that operates side by side with other technologies of reproduction, and sometimes encompasses them.

The Tricycle's recreation of the Bloody Sunday inquiry (2000–2010) begins with a much-abridged version of the opening speech with which the counsel to the inquiry, Christopher Clarke, vibrantly announces the commitment to the truth of the new judicial investigation and its determination to redress past injustice in a changed political climate that would at last allow for the necessary objectivity:

> Whatever happened, whatever the truth of the matter, was a tragedy, the pain of which many have endured down the passage of years. The tribunal's task is to discover as far as humanly possible in the circumstances, the truth. Not the truth as people would like it to be, but the truth, pure and simple, painful or unacceptable to whoever that truth may be. The truth has a light of its own. Although it may be the first casualty of hostility, it has formidable powers of recovery, even after a long interval.[63]

The counsel's rhetoric of justice and reconciliation grounds the pursuit of the truth about the tragic events that unravelled in Derry's Bogside on 30 January 1972 in the act of retrieving the permanent traces they have left in the witnesses' memory; as it does so, however, it also concomitantly raises the question of the limitations of human memory and the potentially disabling factor of temporal distance. In this sense, the drastic editorial selection executed by Norton-Taylor on Clarke's sprawling speech[64] immediately sets the tone for the play's sustained focus on primary witnessing and on the impossibility or unwillingness to perform the live act of recollection. Indeed, while the series of cross-examinations that make up the Tricycle's *Scenes from the Saville Inquiry* (the play's subtitle) all revolve around the crucial political-legal issue of whether British soldiers on Bloody Sunday were shooting at rioters handling weapons or at unarmed civil rights marchers, the topic that actually weaves the individual hearings into a coherent narrative and provides the main source of dramatic tension in the play is that of the authenticating function of live testimony in determining historical truth.

The verbatim editor's resolve to bring centre stage the performances of primary witnesses is already very clear from his choice of dramatis personae. Eminent political figures of the likes of Edward Heath and Lord Carrington, respectively the Prime Minister and the Foreign Secretary back in 1972, were dismissed from the Tricycle's theatrical courtroom even though they had been hauled to give evidence before the Saville tribunal as key players in the Bloody Sunday affair and in the concoction of the state-sanctioned narrative in which the incident rapidly became shrouded. While not departing from the sequence of events in the actual proceedings, Norton-Taylor's pruning of the judicial transcripts results in a markedly bipartite structure which accentuates the demarcation line between two separate and opposed categories of witnesses: the first half of the play presents the testimony of civilian witnesses to the shootings, whose version of the truth is being heard officially for the first time, whereas in the second half the floor is allocated to the representatives of the British Armed Forces, from the high-ranking officials who planned and conducted the calamitous security operations during the march in Derry, down to the soldiers who fired on the victims. With a final twist, the military perspective is complemented by a lone voice from the nationalist side, Reg Tester, who gave evidence in the final stages of the inquiry in response to Lord Saville's appeal to former IRA members to come forward and clarify their role on Bloody Sunday.

The play's exclusive focus on first-hand testimony reflects, on one level, the decisive role of eyewitnesses in triggering the new inquiry after long years of campaigning by survivors and by relatives of the dead and the injured. In the climate of political negotiations surrounding the Good Friday Agreement, Tony Blair's decision to reopen the case in 1998 was significantly prompted by a detailed dossier of evidence submitted by the families of the victims to the UK government. The dossier included new ballistic and medical reports, but also, more importantly, a sizeable corpus of previously neglected eyewitness statements. The campaigners' demands for a fresh independent inquiry were backed by a thorough assessment of the new material by the Irish government which brought into definitively disrepute the hasty conclusions reached by the tribunal of inquiry set up by Prime Minister Heath in 1972 and chaired by Lord Widgery.[65] In this respect, the partition of Norton-Taylor's *Bloody Sunday* into two distinct testimonial factions mirrors the twin (and only partially overlapping) actions which the people of Derry expected from the inquiry: on the one hand, the formal acknowledgment of the innocence of the victims, by allowing their stories to be officially told at last; and on the other, a public admission of military (and governmental) accountability for committing or condoning the cold-blooded murder of civilians.[66]

On the dramaturgical level, the spotlighting of the primary witnesses is a crucial move that enables the verbatim editor to reconfigure the testimonial act as a prime site and mode of conflict. For those who had witnessed the shootings first-hand, the truth about the actions on 30 January 1972 could hardly be a matter of contention: as Eamonn McCann scathingly puts it in his review of the Derry performances of *Bloody Sunday*, 'the killings unfolded over a period of perhaps 17 minutes in a built-up area in broad daylight' and 'every killing and wounding was witnessed, some at very close quarters, from the windows of flats and maisonettes or the nooks and crannies where local people had huddled'.[67] The people of Derry had not campaigned for a new inquiry because they needed to be told the truth, but because they wanted their truth to be officially told and publicly acknowledged; their choral act of testimony thus involved a direct challenge to political power. As a result, the eyewitnesses' position was a deeply ambivalent one: their marginalized voices functioned simultaneously as a source of legitimacy for the new inquiry, which they had been instrumental in triggering, and as a menace to the official discourse of law in its inherent entanglement with the state's interests. This may help explain why, as the voices of the victims entered the legal arena seeking acknowledgment, they were brought under the reach of the repressive mechanisms of control that are mercilessly exposed and critically interrogated in the Tricycle play.[68]

Unlike other legal processes, a public inquiry ought to be strictly inquisitorial; it should aim at ascertaining the truth about a controversial subject by seeking all the relevant evidence, analyzing the collected data and reporting about its findings. The *Scenes* reproduced on the Tricycle stage, however, belie the professed inquisitorial stance of the Bloody Sunday tribunal by bringing to the fore an essentially adversarial quality to the proceedings which is highly questionable not only on legal, but also on ethical and political grounds. In refashioning the Saville courtroom as an outright battlefield, Norton-Taylor shows very clearly that the war being waged there was only superficially one between conflicting versions of the truth, between the victims' and the perpetrators' mutually incompatible accounts, as apparently reflected in the play's bipartite structure; rather bewilderingly, the fiercest opponents of the traumatized eyewitnesses in *Bloody Sunday* turn out to be the very representatives of the law who were purportedly intent on redressing the historical injustice suffered by the people of Derry in order to restore their faith in the rule of law.

Given the degree to which the events on Bloody Sunday had become enmeshed in conflict, the parameters of the Saville Inquiry contemplated the possibility of challenging whatever testimonial evidence would be given before the tribunal. Yet, symptomatically, in the first half of the performance the legal representatives of the soldiers play a very marginal role in the questioning of eyewitnesses, and their presence is arguably made redundant by the steady doubling of the counsel to the inquiry and his assistants as cross-examiners, when not outright prosecutors. Norton-Taylor's editorial selection effectively focuses our attention on the peculiar *modus operandi* of the inquiry's legal team—on legal procedures that seem far more inquisitional than inquisitorial. As he sets about extracting the truth from witnesses on behalf of the tribunal, Christopher Clarke conducts the testimonial hearings as outright interrogations in which the main issue at stake seems to be not so much whatever 'material evidence' about the events of Bloody Sunday might be obtained from their first-hand accounts, but rather the credibility of their performance. In the struggle between truth and power which underpins the legal proceedings, the eyewitnesses are put in the dock and the victims of trauma are tried for the act itself of giving evidence: though no longer able to bar their potentially disruptive voice from the legal stage, the law appears determined to curb its power by expressly targeting its legitimacy and authenticating function.

This emerges very clearly, for example, from Michael Bridge's hearing. On 30 January 1972, Bridge was fired at while frantically shouting abuse and walking towards the soldiers who had just shot in the back, and killed, seventeen-year-old Jackie Duddy. During the hearing, Counsel Clarke duly asks the witness to confirm the detailed account given in his statement to the Saville tribunal, and then proceeds to discredit his evidence by referring to a previous conviction for stabbing a civilian in Bradford: an episode which, though clearly outside the terms of the inquiry, the barrister considers relevant as proof of character. In Bridge's own perceptive framing of the counsel's cross-examination tactic, the tribunal we are being shown on stage 'is not addressing the actions on Bloody Sunday, it is addressing the credibility of people' (23).

Tellingly, however, the main target of Clarke's attacks on the civilian side are the eyewitnesses' memory and the live performance of recalling which is the very essence of their legal testimony. As pointed out above, the inquiry explicitly grounded the possibility of a fair and thorough review of an historically distant episode in the broader and more balanced evidence base that might still be afforded by the archival capacity of human memory. In the Tricycle play, the inquiry's retrospective look is mercilessly exposed as an opportunity for manipulation, a repressive counter-measure aimed at gagging the testimonial voice. The counsel to the inquiry systematically questions the accuracy of the witnesses' memory by comparing and contrasting their present recollection of events with details recorded in statements given thirty years earlier and generally ignored by the first public inquiry conducted by Lord Widgery. To all effects, then, the civilian witnesses' past accounts, unheeded at the time but now objectified into 'hard' documentary evidence, are used by the inquiry to question the reliability of their performance of witnessing in the present. If the law roots the authority of testimony in the presence of the witness, the *Scenes* reproduced on the Tricycle stage are marked by a relentless attempt to undermine that presence by subjugating the live voice to the archival trace, the contingencies of performance to the permanence of texts.

A prime case in point, in this respect, is the testimony rendered by Alice Doherty. Mrs Doherty took part in the march on Bloody Sunday as a volunteer first-aid worker. Amongst the 'large number of different incidents involving various people who were dead or injured' that she reported, one involved a soldier firing into an army vehicle where three civilian victims lay dead or dying. Even before Mrs Doherty is asked to repeat and confirm her eyewitness account of this particular episode, Clarke's assistant, Alan Roxburgh, confronts her with the challenging endeavour of reconstructing the exact chronology of the various events described in her more recent statement to the Saville Inquiry and in those made back in 1972. Unsurprisingly, the witness is brought to admit that in thirty years' time her recollections may have become 'blurred' (40). The factual accuracy of Mrs Doherty's subsequent performance of memory retrieval is thereby pre-empted and this gives weight to the possibility, insinuated in the following cross-examination by the soldiers' barrister, that she may have 'added to her memory unconsciously some images you have seen' (43). In her extended critical analysis of *Bloody Sunday*, Carol-Anne Upton concedes that in their structuring of the play Kent and Norton-Taylor 'clearly recognize the adversarial underpinning of the inquiry as an essential failure of the inquisitorial rhetoric'; yet she concludes that 'instead of deconstructing that process … the dramaturgy of the play simply re-constructs it, and shifts attention away from the process to the content of the hearings'.[69] Upton here neglects to consider that by drawing attention to the counsels' recurrent reference to time as a factor undermining the reliability of testimonial evidence, the Tricycle's recreation of the inquiry actually provides critical insight into the glaring political paradox implied in the inquiry's own truth-seeking method: after being denied official public hearing for almost thirty years, their voices drowned in the paratroopers' state-sanctioned chorus of lies, the witnesses now stand accused for their flawed performances of memory retrieval, as if the blame for the outrageous delay with which the case was reopened rested with the victims of political injustice, rather than the government.[70]

Kent and Norton-Taylor's critical interrogation of the inquiry's ambivalent treatment of the civilian eyewitnesses is further sustained through the play's focus on a blatantly punitive element within the legal process. On the day of the shootings, William Patrick McDonagh looked on impotently at the paratroopers' cold-blooded violence in the Rossville car park from the relative safety of his girlfriend's flat. For him, as for the other eyewitnesses, the act of recollection stirs painful memories, and he nearly breaks down before the tribunal when he is pressed to recall the cries and groans coming from the army tank where sneering soldiers had thrown the bodies of dying civilians. Public inquiries addressing human rights abuses are by definition based on the retrieval of traumatic memories and they inherently involve the possibility of further traumatization for those who have come to seek justice. The perspective afforded by the Tricycle's take on the proceedings, though, leaves the audience wondering whether a method that entails the close questioning of a visibly traumatized eyewitness, followed by cross-examination at the hands of the legal representative of the perpetrators, may not in fact be designed to stymie, rather than facilitate, the live performance of memory retrieval.

In Geraldine McBride's hearing, the procedure followed to extract testimonial information goes beyond the inappropriate or inconsiderate to border on calculated sadism. Mrs McBride was amongst the dismayed onlookers of the army tanks' trespass into the Bogside and the ensuing killing of unarmed and unwarned civilians posing no actual threat to the soldiers. Like the witnesses who have preceded her, the woman is asked to confirm the account given to the inquiry prior to her hearing in court, but she is overcome with emotion and bursts into tears when Christopher Clarke repeats to her the description of Barney McGuigan's head literally exploding when he was shot from the back while waving a white handkerchief and going to the rescue of the dying Patrick Doherty.[71] The forced recollection of this horrifying detail about McGuigan's killing appears totally gratuitous since it is irrelevant to the specific fact that the counsel is trying to ascertain, namely, whether the victim was hit by the first or the second shot fired by the soldier. When Mrs McBride's evidence is again quoted during the hearing of Soldier F, who has been identified as McGuigan's killer, the barrister who cross-examines him refrains from reading out loud the relevant paragraph, arguably out of consideration for the victim's family, and directs instead the witness to the screen where the statement is projected. By contrast, Clarke's brutal interrogation procedure shows how the rendering of testimony may entail not only prosecution but also persecution, the possibility of memory being inflicted on the witness as a form of torture in a perverse dynamic that is both intimidating and retaliatory.

By recasting the Saville Inquiry as yet another episode in the 'war on the people seeking justice in this country' (31), as according to Bernadette McAliskey's words quoted in the play,[72] the documentarians not only provide a scorching critique of the power struggle embedded in the 'truth and reconciliation' rhetoric surrounding the long-overdue official review of the tragic events on Bloody Sunday; they also manage to indirectly address some highly topical issues of legitimacy and legality arising from the war on terror. As already mentioned, *Bloody Sunday* was staged in the interval between the conclusion of the hearings, in November 2004, and the publication of the inquiry's final report, which at the time of the play's debut was thought to be imminent. (As it turned out, Lord Saville's report was only released after the general election, in June 2010, and it therefore rested with the new prime minister, David Cameron, to issue a formal state apology for the British soldiers' 'unjustified and unjustifiable'[73] violence on civilians whose innocence had been unequivocally established.) In the eyes of the Tricycle documentarians, the scheduling of the production looked ideal because of the added topicality achieved by the Saville Inquiry in that particular political climate. Commenting on the play's timeliness, Nicolas Kent pointed to the renewed prominence given by the presence of the British army in Iraq to the thorny issue of how the military is controlled in a democratic society, and to growing public concern over the lawless behaviour of UK troops deployed in the Basra area in light of some recently-documented episodes of civilian killings (see Chapter Three). Though Kent did not push the analogy further, the contemporary relevance of the Saville Inquiry also included its possible political serviceability to the Labour government in the post-Iraq scenario. Back in 1998, the chief political mandate of the inquiry launched by Tony Blair had been to address past wrongs in order to 'close a painful chapter once and for all' and turn a fresh page in British-Irish relations. In his statement to the House of Commons, however, the Prime Minister had also invested the inquiry with a broader impact on Britain's democratic credentials. Bloody Sunday, he had explained, stood out as a special case in the long history of sectarian violence in Northern Ireland because it involved 'the State's own authorities'; hence, the new judicial inquiry would have a crucial bearing on the future credibility and relevance of justice for UK citizens.[74]

By the time *Bloody Sunday* was devised and staged, in April 2005, this second aspect had gained a perhaps unforeseen prominence. Following the disclosure of the illegal machinations surrounding the involvement in Iraq, and amidst mounting public outrage over the UK's connivance with the systematic violation of human rights and international law in the US-led war on terror, the Saville Inquiry could offer a much-needed public demonstration of the Labour government's commitment to the rule of law. It is this particular discourse of public confidence in British democracy that the Tricycle play seems intent on undermining with its critical interrogation of the Bloody Sunday inquiry: Norton-Taylor's editorial choices are skilfully crafted to elicit this contemporary parallel while at the same time revealing its more disturbing—and far less politically expendable—aspects.

This particular re-contextualization of the power struggle underpinning the legal process is corroborated and reinforced by the narrative that emerges from the hearings presented in the second half of the play—or 'the military cover-up', in Nicolas Kent's apposite summary.[75] Summoned to give evidence before the Saville tribunal, the members of the British army join in a collective performance of amnesia, claiming to be unable to recall the actions they have committed, ordered or witnessed on Bloody Sunday. Soldier F, who has been charged with the firing of repeated rounds on terrorized, unarmed civilians, tactically withdraws behind a monotonous refrain of 'I don't remember', his mind conveniently wiped clean of even the broad outlines of the military offensive in which he took part. Soldier S, who shot and killed a teenage boy as he was fleeing from the advancing troops, admits to possible 'inaccuracies' in the statement made to the Royal Military Police back in 1972, but insists on having no present recollection of either the incident or the evidence he gave about it at the time (81). In a legal perspective, the soldiers' common line of defence would appear to be aimed not so much at defending the manifestly dishonest accounts on which Lord Widgery based his verdict of non-culpability, but rather at pre-empting the possibility of future prosecution.[76] But in terms of the power struggle that is shown to inform the legal proceedings, the concerted show of memory loss put on by paratroopers is patently an attempt to continue to secure the protection of the official discourse of law. As they insist on having no recollection whatsoever of the events under scrutiny, the accused invariably cling to statements made in the distant past as the only memorial trace left of those events; at the same time, they are able to disown accountability for the blatant contradictions and falsehoods contained in their earlier statements, pleading a memory blank that effectively exonerates them from the onus and the consequences of testimony in the present.[77]

This mechanism is strikingly illustrated in the bewildering testimonies rendered by Soldier F and General Ford. As he defiantly holds on to the arrant lie that the man he shot dead was handling a gun, the anonymized paratrooper does not seek validation in a live performance of recollection but, more tactically, in the account given at the time of the Widgery inquiry and now permanently fixed in an official transcript: a de-authored and disembodied discursive act whose meaning is no longer bound to the original speaker in his present appearance before the tribunal. When he is questioned about the 'change of gear' in the methods used to restore law and order in Derry, and the possible repercussions of the 'shoot-to-kill' policy on the safety of the civilian population that the British army was allegedly there to protect, General Ford similarly claims to having 'no recollection of this at all, of course' (55). His obliviousness also extends to the dynamics of the shootings on Bloody Sunday: the commander of Land Forces who set the strategy to oversee the civil rights march confirms that he has 'absolutely no independent memory' of the operations and that the account he has been summoned to give before the Saville tribunal will therefore be 'relying entirely on the documents that have been provided' (55). He is echoed by Colonel Wilford, the commander of the 1st Battalion of the Parachute Regiment, whose only present recollection of alleged sniper fire and of personally seeing 'a man with an M1 carbine on the balcony of a flat' (74), as he stated in a radio interview shortly after Bloody Sunday, comes from having just re-read his former evidence to the Widgery Tribunal. Thanks to the official sanction of the Widgery report, the fraudulent account recorded in the written statements of the military witnesses has so far performatively worked as the truth about Bloody Sunday; as the play clearly shows, the refusal to perform the act of recollection in the present is a way to continue to harness the authority emanating from the voice of power—for Wilford and for all those who have historically benefited from this mechanism.

Of course, this display of not-witnessing still qualifies as an observable performative behaviour that ultimately exposes the members of the armed forces to the judgment of their legal and theatrical audiences, often to self-incriminating effect. More than for its doubtful efficacy, the common line of defence adopted by the military side is eloquent in its attempt to surrogate the document for the witness, the objectivity of the written record for the subjectivity of the embodied voice. In this respect, Norton-Taylor's editorial framing underscores the similarities between this strategy and the one deployed by the counsel to the inquiry in the hearings of the civilian eyewitnesses, just as the common narrative that emerges from the military hearings complements and enhances the contemporary relevance of the offensive on the civilian witnesses in the first half of the play. When the Tricycle project was staged, in 2005, the appeal to amply discredited official evidence by those responsible for the violence on Bloody Sunday offered a powerful analogue for the decisive role played by the Blair government's September dossier in Britain's involvement in another bloody and unlawful conflict. The

Widgery report, resulting from an inquiry launched by a British Prime Minister back in 1972, had condoned the massacre of Derry civilians by granting evidentiary status to verbal fictions about the threat posed by supposed terrorists wielding firearms and throwing nail bombs at soldiers. Three decades later, another British Prime Minister promoted unverified intelligence to the rank of documented facts in a dossier that was instrumental in obtaining parliamentary approval for the invasion of Iraq by certifying the major threat posed by Saddam Hussein's weapons of mass destruction. Once again, an official 'truth' based on fabricated evidence had been used to justify illegal state violence in a colonial situation—though preventively, this time.

The revelatory potential of the Bloody Sunday investigation with regard to this new 'painful chapter' in the history of British democracy is even momentarily endorsed by the inquiry transcripts themselves; ironically, the opportunity for a verbatim authentication of parallels between the Widgery report and the September dossier is provided by Christopher Clarke, when he mentions a well-known instance of rhetorical manufacturing of the Iraqi menace in official public discourse. In the closing scene, the tribunal is hearing from Reg Tester, the Official IRA quartermaster who was in charge of weapons on the day of the march. Following Tester's description of the very limited offensive capacity of his unit, the counsel to the inquiry asks the witness whether there might have been other IRA weapons in Derry on Bloody Sunday that had escaped Tester's control. Unwittingly, Clarke introduces his question by conceding that 'what I am about to ask may be a Donald Rumsfeld unknown unknown' (92). This is a reference to the tortuous aphorism with which the US Secretary of Defense, on addressing the lack of evidence connecting Saddam Hussein's weapons of mass destruction to al-Qaeda at a Pentagon press briefing in early 2002, overruled the issue of verifiability by explaining that 'as we know, there are known knowns; there are things we know we know. We also know there are known unknowns; that is to say we know there are some things we do not know. But there are also unknown unknowns—the ones we don't know we don't know.'[78] Clarke's fleeting remark has no detectable impact on the progress of the hearing: the Rumsfeld quotation causes no reaction or change of attitude in the witness. On the extra-scenic axis, however, this sudden appearance of the Iraqi scenario within the Tricycle's verbatim recreation of the Bloody Sunday inquiry gives factual endorsement to the contextual reading that the documentarians are seeking to activate through their dramaturgy of testimony.

This fortuitous pointer apart, it is essentially by playing on the inbuilt duplicity of testimonial discourse that *Bloody Sunday* manages to infuse its verbatim material with an added level of war significance.

Both the civilian hearings during the first half of the performance and the 'military cover-up' that follows revolve around the contrast between the live voice and the archival trace in a legal and political battle over truth and legitimacy which was triggered by a past war but is imbued with contemporary relevance. As typically proves the case with Kent and Norton-Taylor's verbatim projects, this dramaturgical strategy comes with a significant side effect on the self-reflexive front. At the same time as it enables the documentarians to address the Iraqi context through a verbatim rendition of the Saville Inquiry, the play's focalization on testimony as a conflicted practice raises potential questions about the verbatim method itself. Tribunal plays use the transcripts of live performances of witnessing in real courtrooms as a prompt for live performances of witnessing on a theatre stage. *Bloody Sunday* presents the encoding of live performance as a written record in a highly suspicious light, ultimately casting serious doubt on the authenticity of textually-mediated recreations of a live act of witnessing. In its self-reflexive interrogation of testimonial practice, Norton-Taylor's play mercilessly exposes the room for manipulation involved in textual mediation and in the retrospective editing of verbal evidence; even more disruptively, it points to a fundamental incompatibility between the ephemerality of testimony as a live, embodied act and its objectification as permanent archival record: as David Houston Jones puts it in his fascinating study of witnessing in Samuel Beckett's *Krapp's Last Tape*,

> once testimony is achieved, it is no longer testimony in its pure, originary sense. The accession of the document to the archive may guarantee the longevity of testimony, but it is also the sign par excellence of the passing of the witness, of the impossibility of the witness's presence.[79]

In *Bloody Sunday* there is a distinctly Beckettian flavour to the inquiry's offensive on the civilian side, and in the counterpoint of the live and the recorded through which Clarke and his legal team appear intent on demoting the eyewitnesses to marginal status in the truth-seeking process. As happens in *Krapp's Last Tape*, in Norton-Taylor's tribunal play the speakers' past utterances, now permanently fixed as recorded evidence, become a tool for cross-examination and hamper the live act of memory retrieval in the present, rather than assisting with it.

In a further point of contact with Beckett's seminal work on the quagmires of testimony, *Bloody Sunday* juxtaposes and contrasts the live performance of witnessing with forms of testimonial presence that are not only textually, but also technologically mediated. This double dimension was visually prominent in the Tricycle's meticulous reproduction of the inquiry setting as a bureaucratic space packed with office and archive furniture and paper documents but also thoroughly infiltrated by the more immaterial but no less pervasive presence of digital technology. The production's decor has been criticized for its failure to recall architectonically the symbolically-loaded space of the Derry Guildhall,[80] but it undoubtedly managed to capture one of the most striking features of the inquiry, namely, its determination to 'take full advantage'[81] of cutting-edge technology for the recordation, retrieval and reproduction of judicial evidence.

Already in his opening statement, Lord Saville announced that the inquiry would make extensive use of the most advanced information technology available in order to ensure both the public nature and the efficiency of the proceedings. In keeping with its aesthetics of verisimilitude, the Tricycle staging faithfully reproduced the evidence display system that was used during the hearings: the witnesses' statements which were used as a memory prompt or a cross-examination tool appeared simultaneously on the mass of computers placed on the court's and the lawyers' desks and on the large screen hanging at the back of the stage. The interplay between different modes of testimonial presence became particularly poignant when barristers referred witnesses to evidence given at the time of Bloody Sunday, and the verbal record of their past performances of witnessing was displayed on the screens as a typewritten document. By providing access to the original paper documents, the projections functioned as photographic exhibits of the real, thus emphasizing not only historical distance, but also historical authenticity; at the same time (and akin to what happens in *Called to Account*), the indexicality they communicated was undercut by their immaterial status as digitized copies and the successive layers of mediation and remediation they thus betrayed.

A similar mechanism was at work in the opening moments of the performance, where technology, summoned as reliable evidence of past liveness, simultaneously authenticated and undercut the play's construction of testimonial presence. The abridged opening statement of the counsel to the inquiry was introduced and accompanied by the projection of television footage of the civil rights march in Derry in 1972. As a caption explained, this was an exact replica of the way in which the Saville Inquiry had been framed by media evidence, as if to prove that the events under scrutiny had actually happened. On one level, the theatrical reframing of the original screening intensified the discourse of presence it encapsulated, since spectators were presented both with a video recording of real events and with the live reproduction of the real situation in which that media evidence had originally been apprehended; on another, though, the restaging of the scene estranged the multiple layers of mediation through which the real was made present on the Tricycle stage, and exposed its surrogate quality with respect to the original performance of witnessing.

While serving specific thematic purposes, then, the presentation of witnessing as a conflicted practice not only infuses *Bloody Sunday* with metatheatrical resonance, but gives a distinctly dialectical edge to the question of the production and reproduction of liveness on the documentary stage. The play draws attention to the competition between live and mediatized forms as transmitters of the real but also reveals their fundamental imbrications in the performance of witnessing. On the one hand, by reconstructing the Saville courtroom as a high-tech showcase, *Bloody Sunday* provides an implicit commentary on the extensive presence of media in documentary and on the ambivalences it can give rise to. As critics have not failed to point out, contemporary verbatim theatre offers itself as a corrective against excessive mediatization but often relies on technology as an authenticating device: a typical example of this evidential use of technology, already mentioned in Chapter Three, is the home-made video screened at the end of Alan Rickman and Kathy Viner's testimonial solo, *My Name is Rachel Corrie*, and the questionable way in which the video was designed to impress the seal of authenticity onto the individual version of the truth about the Israeli-Palestinian conflict presented in the play. This theatre of witness, it has been observed, taps into the recollection of individual, embodied memories with the declared aim of providing an alternative to totalizing media narratives of war, yet continues to rely on media as a 'sign of the occurrence of the real',[82] turning a record of events into a sanctioning device, a more objective form of witness that can be mobilized to lend backing to the truths expressed by testimonial subjectivity.

There is also a further aspect to the creation of presence on the verbatim stage that has tended to go unnoticed but is helpfully thrown into relief by the multiple dimensions of liveness scrutinized in *Bloody Sunday*. Even when mediatized evidence is not materially present on stage as a visible proxy of the real to authenticate the actors' surrogate bodies, the performance of witnessing in verbatim work is often shaped by media images or recordings. When the real people bodied forth by actors are public characters, as is the case with the well-known political figures appearing in the Tricycle's tribunal plays or the world leaders in *Stuff Happens*, their stage identity is inevitably measured against, and influenced by, their prevalent media-received version. But the reliance of the live on the mediated is pervasive across the whole range of documentary war plays discussed here. With unsuspected frequency, the performers' re-presentation of the primary act of embodied witnessing in verbatim projects is filtered by or actually dependent upon digital technologies of reproduction. Describing her experience of impersonating Clare Short in *Called to Account*, for example, Diane Fletcher explains how she was instructed to base her rendition on a video recording of the former MP's actual hearing at the mock-inquiry set up by the Tricycle documentarians: a practice that, in her view, had little to do with acting, given that her performance was supposed to be the live copy of a mediatized copy and one which, moreover, 'had to be the same every night'.[83] With an interesting self-reflexive twist, the original setting of the hearings that was reproduced on the Tricycle stage, Fletcher notes, also included the video camera used to record the original performances of witnessing.

Rather unexpectedly perhaps, the reliance on recording technologies to produce testimonial presence is even more pervasive in interview-based plays. Unlike tribunal dramas, which are forced to rely on the textual mediation of inquiry transcripts, verbatim projects working from interview material can offer a more direct access to the live performances of witnessing that they reproduce, and as a consequence they often prioritize immediacy as a guarantor of indexicality. Indeed, the term 'verbatim' may be quite misleading when applied to interview-based plays because it tends to characterize them as text-led drama, whereas their promise to deliver a truthful and authentic experience is rather more grounded in the reproduction of an oral performance, a moment of direct contact and face-to-face interaction between the real witnesses and those who have been designated as their theatrical representatives. The working method adopted by Look Left, Look Right during the development of *Yesterday Was a Weird Day* (see also Chapter Three) is a clear instance of this attempt to honour the orality of the sources in order to provide evidence of the moment of intersubjectivity in which the 'contract between performer and performed'[84] was initially established. As Mimi Poskitt explained, the interviews with the survivors and the secondary witnesses of the terrorist attacks in London on 7 July 2005 were initially translated into a written text, but during rehearsals the authoritative 'document' against which the script was checked was the audio recording of the full interview, and the accuracy that the company sought to achieve through repeated re-hearings and textual emendations had to do with the preservation of the original oral language features, the reinstatement of 'all the "ums" and "ers" and bits of detail' that had sometimes been omitted in the drafting of the transcript.[85] Technology thus played a defining role in the shaping of the final text but also, significantly, of the final performance, since the actors worked extensively with the audio of the interviews in order to become attuned to the speakers' cadences and patterns of speech that they would subsequently recreate on stage. To a considerable extent, then, in Poskitt and Freedman's verbatim project the actors' retrieval of the original live experience was made possible by a technologically mediated voice; symptomatically enacting the 'impossible oscillation' which Auslander sees as paradigmatic of the relationship between the live and the mediatized in contemporary culture,[86] in *Yesterday Was a Weird Day* the production of presence and liveness on stage originated and derived authority from a disembodied media recording which, in turn, originated and derived authority from its reference to the live moment of intersubjective encounter between the primary witnesses and their theatrical intermediaries. Ultimately, the theatre-makers' particular method for achieving documentarian authenticity here is in the dramatization of the act of listening, a process in which actors become connoted as secondary witnesses engaged in a performance of recalling; in Poskitt's words,

> because the speech patterns are so authentic, because of that authenticity the audience completely goes into believing that this is that person ... The absolutely endearing thing about this format is that it feels very personal, very intimate, and if we theatre-makers can recreate that really intimate moment that we had with someone who's sharing their really special story, that is a really good go.[87]

This impression of immediacy, however, is to a large extent dependent on presence of recording technology in the interview setting and later on in the rehearsal room. Media reproduction is that which enables the passing on of testimonial status from the real-life witnesses to their onstage representatives: it is on the mediatized traces of that moment of encounter that the transmissibility of the witness function is made dependent. That the intermediation of technology should then become fully obliterated in the subsequent remediation of those traces on a theatre stage is equally symptomatic of, at one and the same time, the ontological authority that continues to be ascribed to liveness in our culture, and the complex and often contradictory ways in which testimonial presence and is produced (and reproduced) in the contemporary theatre of war.

CHAPTER FIVE

Figures of mediation

The conflict dimension of translation is widely acknowledged in the published literature on the subject, and well known to all those who have tried their hand at the demanding job of interlingual and intercultural mediation. An agonistic condition is inherent in the act of translating, often described as a drama of divided loyalties between source text and target audience, an inexorably failed endeavour at settling intractable differences between languages and cultures in order to make communication possible. The commonplace dyad of *traduttore-traditore*—lately condensed in the composite figure of the *transtraitor*[1]—reflects our culturally-rooted awareness of the treachery and treason which haunt translation's promise of mutual understanding in the face of human diversity and language barriers. A classic incarnation of this perception in modern scholarship can be found in George Steiner's landmark study *After Babel*, in which translation is described as the basic principle underlying and enabling human communication and, at the same time, an impossible task entangled in the ultimate incommensurability of languages and cultures and invariably resulting in failure, loss and even violence.[2] The notion of translation as a site of cultural tension and aggressive confrontation has been further pursued, with a more decided slant on political and ideological issues, by the so-called 'cultural turn' that has followed the establishment of Translation Studies as a discipline;[3] more recently, the emphasis laid by translation scholarship on the negotiation of linguistic and cultural differences as a conflict-ridden activity has been taken up by post-colonial approaches to translation, and employed to investigate the role of language mediation in power struggles surrounding the construction and enforcement of identities.[4]

Noting the comparability, and frequent comparisons, between translation and war, Vicente L. Rafael mulls over whether the analogy may not also hold true the other way round, allowing us to regard the war zone as a kind of translation zone.[5] An opportunity to postulate this reversibility is offered, I believe, by Steiner's notion that 'human communication equals translation'[6]—that a mechanism of translation is permanently operative within the interactional deployment of language. In semiotically-oriented strategic studies, war itself has been described as a language, a field of communicational manoeuvre in which 'semiotic weapons' are deployed alongside more conventional ones in order to engage in what can still be considered a form of social interaction, albeit an extreme one.[7] This view of war as language in the field of conflict studies finds a parallel in the stress laid on the strategic/polemical dimension of social and linguistic interaction in semiotic theory from Algirdas J. Greimas onwards, as well as in sociological and sociolinguistic approaches traceable to Erwin Goffman's groundbreaking analysis of conversational exchange as an out-and-out dramaturgy of regulated conflict and negotiation.[8] A prime example of the latter is Jürgen Habermas's theory of a universally-shared 'communicative reason', a common code of pragmatics which guarantees the possibility, however rare, of creating mutually effective dialogue across rival standpoints and beliefs. Habermas's model of communicative action envisages the possibility of conflicts arising from a distortion in communication and their liability to spiral into 'uncontrolled reciprocal mistrust', eventually leading to 'the breakdown of communication'. This possibility does not of itself invalidate the dialogic model: according to the influential German theorist, as long as human communication, or even miscommunication, is governed by a regime of reciprocity, there continues to be room for a rational alternative to violence.[9]

The irredeemably asymmetrical model of warfare that has emerged with—or has been made fully visible by—the events of 9/11 and the ensuing political and military responses has prompted a radical questioning of these assumptions on Habermas's part. As already pointed out in Chapter Two, Habermas sees in the attacks on the Twin Towers and in the subsequent reactions the sign and symptom of a 'communicative pathology' which sets on when mutual perspective-taking is foreclosed by unbridgeable social divisions and complete power imbalance. In this respect, Emily Apter's definition of war as 'a condition of nontranslatability or translation failure at its most violent peak'[10] in her discussion of translation after 9/11 reads as an apposite reformulation of Habermas's notion of defective communication as the root-cause of violence on a global scale: translation, as a form of intercultural dialogue, is irreparably flawed when it occurs in a context where the imbalance of power is so extreme that reciprocity ceases to be a precondition of communicative action, and there is no longer any real or 'rational' need, for the overwhelmingly stronger party, to step into the Other's shoes and engage in a relational definition and redefinition of roles, positions and conceptions.

While similarly laying emphasis on the problem of relationality, Apter continues to see the permanent, boundless war of the twenty-first century as a culmination of the Clausewitzean notion of total warfare, rather than the onset of a new paradigm; her notion that 'war is the continuation of extreme mistranslation or disagreement by other means'[11] is a modified version of the central thesis expressed in Clausewitz's *Vom Kriege*. Though it seems reasonable to argue, as Apter does, that the experience of untranslatability *always* becomes more intense in times of violent strife, there is nevertheless a strong case to be made for the unprecedented overlap of the translation zone and the war zone occasioned by the new forms of belligerence. In contemporary macro-conflict, the geopolitical foundations of the 'old' wars and of the ideologies that fuelled them have given way to new kinds of polarization in which language plays a central role in the construction of the Other as radically different: one need only think of the way in which language divisionism contributed to both justify and rekindle nationalist hatred during the wars in the former Yugoslavia—of the drive towards Babelization that was attendant upon the political and military project of Balkanization.[12] Language difference has functioned as a major battleground—and (mis)translation as a weapon of paramount strategic importance—within the identity-driven confrontations of the new global era, which include not only the organized forms of ethnic violence that flared up in Bosnia, Rwanda, Chechnya and elsewhere at the turn of the millennium, but also the post-9/11 scenario of global warfare with its 'clash of civilizations' rhetoric.

In her introduction to *Nation, Language, and the Ethics of Translation*, one of the first volumes to publish scholarly research on the centrality of translation within ever more globalized patterns of conflict, Sandra Bermann quotes Ilan Stavans's notion of modernity as an experience that is no longer 'lived through nationality ... but through translationality'.[13] The political climate surrounding the launch of the global war on terror and its two largest military campaigns to date, the wars in Afghanistan and Iraq, provides an extensive illustration of this new paradigm. In the immediate aftermath of 9/11, the problem of adequate translation became a matter of unprecedented political as well as military urgency. For the US administration, the shortage of skilled Arabic translators became almost overnight a key national security concern, blatantly exposing the dire consequences of America's traditionally enforced monoglottism. Remarking on this swift rise of translation to a major theme in political, strategic and popular discourse alike following the attacks on the Twin Towers, Emily Apter speaks of 'a growing national language panic subsumed with a general fear of war all around', a 'heightened awareness that something as nano-scaled as a translation error can precipitate catastrophic intelligence failures, and in the worst case scenario, another 9/11'.[14]

Having already become a major component of the war machinery during the intervention in Afghanistan, translation moved centre stage during the Iraqi conflict. Given the dearth of Arabic-speaking military personnel, coalition forces in Iraq were almost entirely dependent on locally hired linguists for communicating with the population they had gone to liberate. Iraqi interpreters effectively functioned as the military's lifeline during the invasion, supplying information on tribal, cultural and religious specificities, deciphering documents, acting as field guides, assisting in the assessment of security risks and also, perhaps even more crucially, providing 'the public face of U.S. occupation'.[15] The translators' indispensability in conducting military operations turned them into strategic targets for the Iraqi insurgency while simultaneously exposing them to allegations of treacherous duplicity on the part of their Western employers. As had already happened to interpreters working for international peacekeeping forces in the former Yugoslavia, Iraqi linguists were murdered by the dozen and even publicly executed on television because of their collaboration with the occupiers;[16] at the same time, their reliability and trustworthiness was widely doubted by the political and military establishment of the US-led coalition, which viewed them as potential enemies, 'necessary evils'[17] to be put up with. As a result, Iraqi language workers were denied proper protection—in most cases, ironically, in the name of security reasons—and left at the mercy of their persecutors; meanwhile, on the home front of the war on terror, their colleagues working for suspect jihadists held in Guantanamo Bay were being accused of sabotaging interrogations and stood charges as al-Qaeda spies and infiltrators.[18]

While the solution envisaged by the occupying forces in Iraq to counter the menace of native language brokers was to launch programmes to train their own 'combat linguists'[19] to be deployed amongst troops, the shaping influence exerted by interlingual and intercultural mediators on the construction of the public narrative of the war was too pervasive to be contained. As Jerry Palmer observes, Iraqi 'fixers' or 'slingers' who worked for Western media wielded considerable control over their employers' access to and elaboration of information. Interpreters were entrusted with an active role in the information gathering process, for instance through the selection of potential interviewees, and were granted an equal degree of freedom in sorting out by relevance what they communicated about the utterances made by participants in the conversation. The forms of gate-keeping they exercised may have often gone unacknowledged, but local language workers acted in every respect as proxy journalists and indeed as prime 'chroniclers of the war':

> Both military staff and journalists come and go, spending relatively short periods in a war zone, but the local interpreters remain there throughout the war and provide the continuity of narration that ultimately makes it possible for others to write a history, a chronicle of the events and relationships that define the war. It is local translators and interpreters who help piece the narrative together for the next group of military personnel, journalists, charity workers or peace keepers.[20]

In Iraq, then, translators played a major part in the management of conflict through their direct and massive recruitment into the ranks of the armed forces but also, and arguably more decisively, because their ubiquitous mediation deeply affected the unfolding narrative of the war and, with it, the moral and intellectual climate which sustained it. Mona Baker comments for example on the importance sometimes ascribed by Iraqi fixers to the Sunni/Shi'a sectarian divide in their assessment of security risks, and she aptly raises the question of how this perception may have helped to corroborate the depiction, in Western political discourse and mainstream media, of the sectarian problem as a further legitimizing factor for the occupation.[21]

While the integration of translation into the institution of war goes a long way back in time, there can be no doubt that the Iraqi campaign has dealt a final and fatal blow to the traditional notion of translation as the transfer of semantic content and of the translator as a neutral conduit. A clear indication in this regard is offered by the considerable share of innovative thinking in contemporary translation scholarship that has been produced in response to the war in Iraq, and the glaring evidence it has provided about the profound entanglement of language mediation and violent conflict. In accounting for the enlarged role taken on by language workers in the war zone and their conflict-ridden predicament, several recent studies have advocated a broadening of the concept of translation in a context of globalized political violence and have exposed the limits of the models that currently guide the teaching, practice and conceptualization of language mediation.[22] These new developments in translation studies have been paralleled by a gradual but steady coming into the fore of the issue of translation in contemporary accounts of war, whether originating in historical or journalistic contexts, or in the broader cultural realm of literature, drama, film and popular media. Whereas this move into the cultural mainstream of the topic of translation is mainly a post-Iraq phenomenon,[23] the theatre must be credited with remarkable foresight in turning to translation as a signifier of violent conflict before the developments traced above had become apparent. A significant share of the works I have selected for discussion in this chapter were written before the Iraq war, and sometimes even before 9/11, yet they prefigure in a perceptive and clear-eyed way the translation turn in contemporary warfare as well as the degree to which this emerging feature of the new paradigm has intensified our awareness of both the conflicts embedded in the practice of translation and the contradictory narratives that surround it.

The translation turn

Translators and interpreters have featured regularly as the characters and sometimes the protagonists of British war drama over the past two decades, with the operations of translation, and particularly its failures, compromises and contradictions, functioning both as a metaphor and as a formal embodiment of violent conflict. The trilogy of plays about post-Cold War Europe written by David Edgar during the 1990s offers an exemplary illustration of the progressive emergence of the translation theme and trope in concomitance with the escalation and increasing globalization of conflict across the decade. *The Shape of the Table,* staged in 1990 at the National Theatre, dramatizes the fall of East European communism through a fictionalized narrative that attempts to demonstrate a common process whereby the collapse of the old order brings about extraordinary opportunities but also formidable dangers, particularly the resurgence of nationalism and racism. Entirely set around a negotiating table, the play charts the tense confrontations between the political old guard and the pro-democracy forces, creating a sustained parallel between the building of a new country and the building of the New Europe, through a series of dialogues that are still firmly rooted in English monolingualism.

Four years later, in *Pentecost*, the possibility of mutual understanding in the face of linguistic and cultural differences is portrayed as a short-lived utopia, with post-Wall Europe falling headlong into the grips of ethnic hatred and East/West animosity. The second play in Edgar's trilogy is set in an unnamed country in the South East of the Continent and features a multiethnic group of desperate asylum-seekers who break into a church and take hostage a local art curator while she is intent on demonstrating to her two foreign colleagues, one British and the other American, that the medieval fresco newly exposed on the crumbling wall of the building actually inspired Giotto's *Lamentation*. Between the refugees' arrival and the tragic epilogue, with armed commandos storming the church and shooting nearly everyone on sight, *Pentecost* exposes the audience to a multilingual cacophony of voices—Polish, Russian, Bulgarian, Arabic, Sinhalese, German, French and Italian, as well as different varieties of 'broken' English—and to repeated attempts at bridging language difference through translation. In this second 'New Europe' play, the Pentecostal dream of human communication beyond language barriers is placed alongside the Babelian narrative of multilingualism as both deriving from and leading to violent conflict. The play's heightened polyglottism is effectively used by the dramatist to accentuate his political argument: breaking with the convention of accessibility, *Pentecost* leaves several chunks of dialogue in foreign language untranslated, thus positioning its English-speaking audiences as the recipients of a linguistic hotchpotch that seems deliberately meant to evoke the meaningless babble which typifies the outsider according to the Greek etymon 'barbaros'. Through the paradox of prospective EU countries forcefully shutting their doors on the new 'barbarians', the play indirectly points to the violent policing of borders that underpins European identity at large.[24]

Emily Apter's post-Clausewitzean definition of war as 'the continuation of extreme mistranslation or disagreement by other means'[25] seems particularly fit to describe the mechanics of conflict at work in the third and final play in Edgar's post-Wall trilogy. In *The Prisoner's Dilemma* (2001), adequate translation becomes no less than a matter of war and peace as foreign mediators attempt to avoid the outbreak of hostilities first, and to broker an agreement later, between the invented countries of Kavkhazia and Drozhdania. In a fictionalized situation which conflates an impressive collection of contemporary theatres of war—Palestine, Chechnya, Bosnia, Northern Ireland, Kosovo and Afghanistan among others—the two conflicting parties refuse to communicate using the other's idiom notwithstanding their geopolitical and linguistic proximity or rather, more exactly, because of it; hence their forced reliance not only on Western peace-brokers, but also on the mediation of English as a lingua franca. Following the method inaugurated with *Pentecost*, in *The Prisoner's Dilemma* Edgar plunges the audience into a fictional world where a multitude of languages, both real and invented,[26] are heard and where mutual intelligibility is a matter of the utmost difficulty and urgency. When speaking in their native tongues, Kavkhazians and Drozhdans remain utterly incomprehensible to the audience, who must grasp the general meaning of their lines basing their guesses on context and on actors' gestures and inflections. It is only when characters switch to English or their lines are translated by interpreters that spectators are relieved from this demanding effort. The play's multilingualism is thus geared to foster the audience's awareness of the vital role played by translation in a truly Babelian global village, and particularly in the conflict situation portrayed in *The Prisoner's Dilemma*, where the prevention of the outbreak of hostilities and the ensuing bloodshed rests on the possibility of effective language mediation. Holding their breath, audiences witness the tense climate of peace negotiations, the mediators' efforts to find a patch of common ground between opposed factions, and the way these efforts are ultimately wrecked by power imbalance, the West's economic interests and, connectedly, the failure of the world's *lingua franca* to truly operate as a neutral intermediary.[27]

The critical response to Edgar's third play is in itself a telling indicator of the coming into the mainstream of the translation topic after the events of 11 September. During its initial run at Stratford's The Other Place, in July 2001, *The Prisoner's Dilemma* received mixed reviews: critics were in the main appreciative of the play's political erudition and intellectual complexity, but some found the fictional conflict too abstract to produce any real emotional engagement. When the RSC revived the play at the Barbican's Pit in London, in January 2002, Edgar's state-of-the-world play met with a considerably warmer reception. As *Guardian* critic, Lyn Gardner was ready to admit, 'It seems unlikely that the play has changed greatly since its July 2001 premiere. The world, however, has, and … we all have a greater emotional investment in the settlement of conflicts around the world, particularly at those hot spots where the west and the Islamic world meet.'[28] It is probably fair to add that after the 'translation turn' brought about by 9/11 and the onset of the war on terror, audiences were readier to connect with a play that ascribes massive firepower to language, and credits something as apparently irrelevant as a discussion on semantic minutiae with the liability to either prevent or precipitate a human catastrophe of momentous proportions.

The progressive Babelization of Edgar's trilogy about contemporary conflict and the concomitant sharpening of the focus on the war/translation nexus reflects a more general trend within British war drama produced over the past two decades or so. A more or less overt multilingual dimension features in a considerable number of the war plays considered thus far, usually in conjunction with the presence of translation as a theme, a mode of interaction, and in some cases also a cornerstone of formal construction. Significantly, this heightened awareness of the language dimension to the new wars is already discernible in Trevor Griffiths's *The Gulf Between Us*. As already noted in Chapter Two, Griffiths's First Gulf War play opens with the monologic, monolingual voice of the narrator giving way to a Babelian medley of disparate and dissonant discourses in Arabic and English, a cacophonic verbal turmoil in which one language breeds another and is swallowed by it in turn, whilst human voices morph into mechanical sounds:

> *A coil of Arab voices in quotidian discourse: souk, bazaar, schoolroom, state-radio, tea-shop, mosque. Threads of English start up, within the coil: an endless lexicon of words invisibly ingested from the Arabic; a discontinuous mesh of readings detailing the Near East origins of our alphabet; commercial jingles; a moral litany from first world leaders justifying the punitive use of force against Third World intransigents.*
>
> *The light has gradually thickened to pre-dawn. The voice-coil eventually gives way to a muezzin calling the faithful to first prayer. The call holds, grave and pure, for some moments; becomes, almost seamlessly, a city siren wailing the raid to come. The siren builds, grows harsh, violent; cuts abruptly as the raid begins.* (2)

The brawling dissonance of Griffiths's Iraq is eventually stilled and replaced by the signature '*mute cock-pit videos*' (2) through which the air campaign of Operation Desert Storm in 1991 was dished-up to the global media public in the shape of a sanitized video game. Almost two decades later, a kindred Babelian soundscape erupts in the very heart of London, in the cacophony of mutually uncomprehending voices that form the dramatic texture of Simon Stephens's *Pornography.* As has been illustrated in Chapter Two, in Stephens's theatrical response to the terrorist attacks in London on 7 July 2005 the postmodern metropolis conjured up by the voices of its inhabitants comes across both as a Western reincarnation of the ancient Babylon, the city that once rose in Iraqi territory, and as a present-day Babel in which the curse of incommunicability simultaneously reflects an age-long history of conflict and, as in Griffiths's play, foreshadows the impending havoc of war—a parallel which the original German production poignantly evoked through the crumbling mosaic of Brueghel's *Tower of Babel* that formed the backdrop to the characters' narrative descent into hell. On the structural level, too, the formal construction of *Pornography* implicitly hints at translation's promise of effective intersubjective communication while at the same time exposing it as a myth, a Pentecostal longing triggered by the heightened awareness of untranslatability in times of war. Stephens, as we have seen, relies on a web of recurring narrative and linguistic elements to create an uncanny sense of connectedness between the disjointed narratives that make up the play; but the possibility of finding a pattern in chaos, or digging out the remnants of a common language underneath the Babelian confusion, is held up as a purely arbitrary gesture, a form of intellectual closure that the play imposes on the radical non-translatability of the experience it seeks to mediate.

The translation dimension is equally pervasive in Martin Crimp's polyphonic play *Attempts on her Life*, itself an evident formal antecedent for Stephens's *Pornography*. Setting an influential template for the ban on mimetic representation in new war drama, Crimp's work is entirely built on the attempts by its anonymous speakers at translating into words the absent central character of the performance. As mentioned in Chapter Two, the incoherent versions of the female protagonist that are produced by her onstage interpreters are at once comical and sinister, and as the play proceeds we become increasingly aware of the degree of arbitrariness involved in each subsequent attempt at imposing a particular identity onto the woman's protean self. Across the plurality of discourses and speech situations that animate Crimp's scenarios, the speakers typically tend to reduce to comprehension in their own terms the invisible target of their 'attempts'. This results in a foregrounding of the exploitative, consumerist subtext of translation: with scorching irony, the absent human subject is objectified as the make of a car ('The new Anny', as announced by the title of the seventh scenario), turned into a work of art (in the critics' panel discussion about Anne, the suicidal artist), or imagined as a saleable piece of atrocitainment (Anya, the survivor of ethnic slaughter, in the narrative spun by media producers in 'Faith in ourselves'). Prefiguring Stephens's analysis of the violence of terrorism in *Pornography*, Crimp's play associates the erasure of the subject's humanity with her apprehension across different media and media formats: film scripts, television programmes, commercials, photographs. In *Attempts on her Life*, as in Stephens's 7/7 drama, the recurrent verbal references to pornography sharpen our perception of the fundamentally voyeuristic quality of Anne's media versions and of the kind of commodification they both imply and induce.

Even as he gestures towards the violent underside to Anne's multiple translations, however, Crimp seems to warn us against a simplistic reading of the speakers' 'attempts' as a forthright critique of mediatization: this discourse is patently articulated by the dialogues but also deftly undermined through parody and playful self-consciousness. To give but a couple of examples, in the scenario which constructs Anne as a suicidal performance artist, a bunch of critics debate over the value and meaning of the spectacularization of her 'broken and abused body' and self-inflicted death. Rebutting all allegations of narcissism or cynical pretence on the artist's part, one of the voices enthuses about Anne's deliberate objectification of her body, qualifying this gesture as a sublimely post-modern and truly subversive form of 'radical *pornography*' (51; original emphasis). In the story in which 'Annie' is described as the radiant Arian mother in a family of American survivalists, the 'degenerate images' of pornographers are listed among the evils they have set about to eradicate, alongside with 'abortionists', 'faggots', 'crack dealers and the Blacks', the inevitable 'conspiring Jews' and 'all those who would deny our right to bear arms' (42–43). At a deeper level, the whole opposition between the real and the mediated is significantly undermined through Crimp's radical narrativization of the drama form: not only Anne as a character but her mediatized images, too, are everywhere in the play but never 'there' on stage, since they only exist as narrative reconstructions in the speakers' dialogues. Language is the all-encompassing medium which creates the real in the world of Crimp's *Attempts*; and this is reflected in the elevation of translation to its structuring principle, a process that is made even more manifest in two symmetrical scenarios where language mediation is actually staged, and a direct correspondence is suggested between the violence of ethnic cleansing and the potential for violence that inheres the act of translating.

In the seventh scenario, modelled as a TV commercial, the seemingly countless qualities of 'The new Anny' are extolled through lines of dialogue spoken in a foreign language with consecutive translation into English. The initial stage direction in the published play text prescribes 'an African or Eastern European language' (30), perhaps with the intention of evoking Rwanda or the former Yugoslavia; in the first production at the Royal Court, in 1997, the lines were spoken in Serbo-Croatian by a Bosnian actress, Etela Pardo, with Howard Ward translating.[29] The associations with the signature ethnic conflicts of the 1990s are corroborated by the increasingly surreal promises of exclusive beauty, safety, comfort and performance advertised by the speakers: as their narrative unfolds, we learn that there is no room, in the clean, environment-friendly Anny and in the charming Mediterranean landscapes she cruises for 'filthy gypsies … the degenerate races … the mentally deficient … the physically imperfect … Arabs, Jews, Turks, Kurds, Blacks or any of that human scum' (32–33).

The second instance of interlingual translation stages the reverse process. The sixteenth scenario, entitled 'Pornó', features '*a very young woman*' who speaks her lines in English while her words are translated into a foreign language to be chosen among a range of '*African, South American or Eastern European*' possible varieties (65). In the first production, the lines of the principal speaker were translated into Portuguese by Danny Cerqueira in the '*dispassionate*' (65) tone prescribed by the stage direction; meanwhile, the naïve, fragile girl launched in an apology of the porn industry which she described as a land of professional opportunity for a young woman and also as a way of 'taking control' over traditional patterns of spectatorship by becoming the producer, rather than the passive consumer, of images (67). Already in itself dubious, this show of assurance was placed in ironic counterpoint to the girl's faltering control over her performance and her growing dependence on prompts to proceed with the speech. According to the script, the speaker's evident confusion and her ever more frequent hesitations '*imply a distress that is never allowed to surface*' (68). Even when she eventually breaks down and her role is momentarily taken over by another member of the company while she is being revived with a drink of water, Crimp's stage directions continue to prescribe ambiguity about whether the girl's poor performance is simply due to stage fright or to the actual distress caused by the story she is telling and its resonance with her personal situation. If we take the latter to be the case, further interpretive possibilities open up. Maybe the actress is only empathizing with the sex worker within the narrative on account of their shared youth and professional use of their bodies; but she might as well be the actual protagonist of the narrative, her true identity only thinly disguised under the anonymity of the third-person form. A similar ambivalence surrounds the other speakers' prompts, which can be decoded as either a gesture of solidarity with the girl, or a form of coercion; and the girl's response to these prompts is equally liable to be read as a straightforward request to repeat words she cannot hear clearly enough, or as an expression of mounting dissent:

– She has an inner light.
– [translation]

– She responds sensitively to the world.
– [translation]

– The scenario in fact of the drugged and desensitized child …
– [translation]

– … humiliated …
– [translation]

– and then photographed or filmed without her knowledge …
– [translation]

– … is a ludicrous caricature.
– [translation]

Again a pause. Again she looks for a prompt.
– Yes?
– (*prompt*) Everything is provided.

– What?
– (*more emphatic prompt*) Everything is provided for her needs.

Pause.

– I can't.
– [translation of 'I can't']

Pause.

– I can't.
– [translation of 'I can't'] (68–69)

Whatever the meaning we decide to attach to the performer's default, it is significant that the principal speaker's breakdown should occur in concomitance with the relinquishing of the third person as she utters an unscripted 'I can't'. Yet even in this case it is by no means clear whether the young woman's inability to proceed stems from a momentary refusal to collude with the symbolic violence perpetrated through the story she has been appointed to deliver, or simply from her lack of the emotional poise and memory ability required of a public performer. Moreover, even if we (arbitrarily) construe this moment in the performance as a gesture of resistance,[30] the young woman's refusal to comply spectacularly misfires: Anne's success story actually gathers momentum through the replacement of the main speaker's individual voice with an enthusiastic chorus that glorifies the absent woman as a role model, an astonishing achiever and, finally, a true heroine of global capitalism who will one day 'change the world' and 'distribute the world's resources evenly across the earth … while guaranteeing not to erode the privileges of the middle class' (70–71), a new messiah whose reported exploits include the personal endorsement of 'a brand of imported lager' (72), a Christ-like crucifixion and resurrection, as well as the by now routine go at exterminating the gypsies. During this rhetorical crescendo, complete with climactic violin score, the chorus splits into two simultaneous strands of discourse, each of which is translated into a different foreign language. In sharp contrast with the increasingly ecstatic tone and content of the speakers' narrative, however, the consecutive translation never strains from the impassive tone prescribed for interpreters throughout the entire scenario. This evidently mimics, and parodies, the neutrality and detachment that are generally held to be the norm for the translator, at the same time querying what actually constitutes ethical behaviour in a situation in which language mediation is shown to potentially abet pornography, oppression, and symbolic as well as physical violence.

Crimp's script makes it clear that the translator's impassivity should become particularly conspicuous at the point in the performance when the principal speaker collapses: a moment of potential intersubjectivity that is blocked by the translator's (self-)imposed detachment *vis-à-vis* the young woman's visible agony, whatever its actual causes. Compared with the girl's inability to keep her cool throughout her performance, the translator's unwavering adherence to the norm of neutrality and impersonality comes across as, at once, a sign of superior professional skills and a callous lack of response-ability: the code of professional ethics that instructs the language mediator to act as a mere conduit is shown to foreclose the exercise of moral subjectivity, with ultimately dehumanizing effects. In acting as a vehicle of reification, the translator becomes in turn reified, thus adding up to the sizeable collection of translation's human casualties displayed in *Attempts on her Life*.

The references to contemporary conflict that periodically surface in Crimp's scenarios contribute to illuminate the violent underside to translation both as a form of human interaction taking place on stage, and as the formal principle through which reality is apprehended and reconfigured in the (post-)dramatic universe of the play. Whereas in *Attempts* these references are intermittent and unmoored from a referential context, in the plays examined in the rest of this chapter the acts of translating and being translated are firmly located in a more or less recognizable war zone. Consciously reflecting the 'translation turn' in contemporary conflict, these works present language mediation as a key aspect of the new forms of belligerence and also, in parallel, as an embodiment of its mechanics. In showing the degree to which language difference and its management or mismanagement have become integral to the new wars of our times, their authors systematically rely on translation as a means and model of inter-subjective communication that can be strategically mobilized in order to signify war on stage. In this respect, they offer a more manifest illustration of the tendency, discussed above, to tie the representation of translation *in* the war zone to the representation of translation *as* a war zone, a conflict-ridden practice that is invested with hermeneutic value with respect to the situations of belligerence in which it is performed. Whether as an intended effect or an unwitting corollary, moreover, the thematization of interlingual (and often also intralingual) translation in these war plays draws attention to the more covert forms of verbal and cultural mediation that are implicated in their own genesis and structuring, thus turning the spotlight, self-reflexively, onto the discursive limitations and ideological underpinnings of the particular form of drama which they inhabit.

In the pages that follow, I illustrate these processes by focusing on three distinct incarnations of the wartime translator, privileging one particular thread of analysis for each typology. The section on 'The translator's invisibility' examines Gregory Burke's *Black Watch* and George Packer's *Betrayed*, two plays that deal with the fate of locally-hired linguists during the Iraq war from a shared documentary angle, but choose diametrically opposed ways of constructing the translators' onstage presence. By reading the portrayal of wartime interpreters in *Betrayed* in parallel with the utter invisibility to which the figure of the Iraqi interpreter is polemically consigned in Burke's play, I point to some eloquent gaps and silences in Packer's way of spotlighting the plight of Iraqi mediators and engaging with the conflicting discourses they have elicited. In 'The combat linguist' I consider another meta-translation piece that has been connected with the Iraqi scenario, David Greig's *The American Pilot*. Through the figure of a truly multi-tasking military translator who also serves as political advisor, *aide-de-camp*, interrogator, deputy torturer and putative successor to the leader of a rebel army, Greig's play exposes the full weaponization of language mediation in contemporary warfare, offering yet another counterpoint to the image conveyed by Packer's *Betrayed* of wartime interpreters as well-meaning but tragically misunderstood facilitators. Finally, in 'Uncanny bodies' I focus on Tony Kushner's *Homebody/Kabul*, a precursor of the translation turn in both the military and the dramatic field and its most archetypical incarnation so far. In sharp contrast to the fundamentally monoglot quality of the other plays examined below, *Homebody/Kabul* embraces an extreme form of multilingualism in order to embody textually the multiple and conflicting narratives surrounding the wartime translator. In Kushner's truly Babelian work, various forms of translation proliferate and infiltrate dramatic language and structure, becoming at once the main mode of (mis)communication used by characters to relate to each other and the world they inhabit, and the unifying principle holding together the play's formal framework.

The translator's invisibility

As a non-Arabic-speaking foreign journalist covering the Iraq war for the *New Yorker* magazine, George Packer shared with the majority of news media personnel on the ground a history of protracted professional and human contact with local language mediators, and was therefore a perfectly valid candidate to report about their position as influential actors in the conflict arena. He did so through a fifteen-thousand-word article published in the *New Yorker* in 2007, entitled 'Betrayed: The Iraqis who trusted America the most', and through a subsequent stage adaptation produced by Manhattan-based theatre company, Culture Project. With the shortened title of *Betrayed*, the play opened in New York City on

4 February 2008 and saw its British premiere two years later, when a production directed by Leann O'Kasi was staged in Glasgow as part of the Tron Theatre's newly-launched festival of political theatre, Mayfesto.

Like the journalistic piece from which it originated, Packer's debut play does more than simply document the role of Iraqi wartime translators, thereby countering the invisibility to which they were generally consigned by mainstream narratives of the war.[31] *Betrayed* is a moving tribute to the bravery, loyalty and helpfulness of interpreters working for the American government in Iraq, and a scathing indictment of the callous indifference or outright hostility with which they were treated by the institutions that employed them. It is also a very effective attempt at turning the plight of local linguists into a telltale case of the politically inept and ethically untenable way in which the Bush administration handled the reconstruction phase in Iraq, thereby jeopardizing any chance of success at fostering democracy, security and economic recovery in the country it had purported to liberate.

Resolved to reinstate translators in their rightful place and role within the narrative of the war, throughout January 2007 Packer interviewed some forty Iraqi linguists who had worked for Americans during and after the invasion; while some conversations took place in a by then spectral Baghdad, several others had to be arranged outside Iraq, either for security reasons or because of the painful diaspora forced upon Iraqi collaborators by their former employers' refusal to take responsibility for their protection against retaliatory violence at the hands of the insurgents. As stated in the author's introduction to the play text, out of these disparate voices 'a single overwhelming story emerged':[32] a shared narrative of many-sided betrayal suffered, rather than perpetrated, by the ill-famed breed of *traduttori-traditori*. In a deliberate attempt at reversing this cliché, *Betrayed* endorses a counter-narrative in which language brokers come across as the prime victims of war's mistranslations: they perceive themselves as well-meaning interlingual and intercultural facilitators but are invariably misconstrued as treacherous double agents in both camps; they are treated as betrayers of their country and religion by their fellow Iraqis, and as potential terrorists by their American allies; and because of their commendable ability and willingness to move between languages and societies, they become exiled from both communities and are reduced to 'social pariahs—an outcast group perceived by many Americans and Iraqis alike as the enemy within'.[33]

Akin to his fellow reporter-cum-playwright Richard Norton-Taylor at London's Tricycle Theatre, Packer turned to theatre because he viewed it as an opportunity to improve on journalism; unlike the British tribunal dramatist, however, Packer mainly saw the broadening of perspective afforded by a dramatization of the stories he had collected and transcribed in his long journalistic report as an opportunity to foreground the human interest element or, as he put it in an interview, of 'go[ing] deeper in the experience of the Iraqis' and 'explor[ing] them as human beings in this incredibly complicated and heartbreaking situation'.[34] The stage version of *Betrayed* allows Iraqi translators to appear in person before an audience and gives them freedom to speak for themselves, in their own terms, about their experience of the war. Packer himself, in his introduction to the printed text, identifies the key difference between the article and the play in the shift from the diegetic mediation of the journalist to the directness of verbatim quotation. The writer's determination to hand over narrative control to the protagonists of the story is clearly signalled in the scenes of the play which still reproduce the interview situation: here, characters are engaged in a conversation in which one of the participants, '*an unseen interviewer situated ostensibly among the audience*' (7), has been purposefully muted and rendered invisible.

The solution adopted by Packer to give voice to the Iraqi perspective deviates under many respects from strict verbatim orthodoxy, and not only because the play features invented scenes that re-enact episodes reported in the interviews. Like Robin Soans in *Talking to Terrorists*, Packer creates composite characters who become, in a sense, a mouthpiece for the larger community of linguists who gave him their words, as gratefully acknowledged on the dedication page of *Betrayed*. The Iraqis' stories are conflated in the figures of three interpreters, two male and one female, and the verbatim material that forms about half of the dialogue is split among them and Bill Prescott, their boss in the US Embassy office.[35] While arguably detracting from the integrity of the witness, this technique is implicitly justified by the writer's claim that all the people he interviewed were basically telling the same consistent tale, one that invariably traced

> a trajectory from suffering to hope—the kind of dazzling, outsize hope that comes when, as several Iraqis put it, your world is a prison and someone suddenly opens the door—through a slow, reluctant, increasingly brutal process of disillusionment to a sense of abandonment and betrayal. (viii)

On the personal level, the individual stories of misplaced trust and brutal disillusionment gathered in *Betrayed* speak of a sadly missed opportunity to build a mutual relationship. The Iraqis mistake the readiness with which they are welcomed into the ranks of coalition forces and the status of 'fictive equals' that they are temporarily granted in day-to-day interaction for a true bond of friendship;[36] consequently, they are appalled to find out that the risks they take and the hardships they daily suffer in order to go to work in the Green Zone are treated with flippancy by their Western employers, and that the majority of their adoptive kin in fact perceive them as a menace. When he identifies this downward course as 'the essential experience of the Iraq war' (viii), Packer is thinking about both sides in the conflict; his own 'terrible sense of loss' (ix), as a US citizen who had initially supported the invasion and believed in the possibility of bringing peace and stability to Iraq, is writ large across *Betrayed* and the way it depicts 'how the small window of opportunity, when America could have helped to stabilize the country and acquire a durable ally in the Middle East, closed, perhaps permanently'.[37]

If, on the one hand, the unanimous account that emerges from the play serves to authenticate the dramatist's rather loose application of the verbatim method, on the other the re-creation of testimonial presence through performance is used to lend authenticity as well as authority to the account itself. When he observes that the Iraqis in his article can only 'speak indirectly through a journalist' (x), Packer is not being entirely accurate, since direct verbatim quotations from the interviews are also frequent in his feature for the *New Yorker*; what is missing there is, rather, the aura of authenticity produced through the witnesses' presence on stage, as well as the testimonial positioning of the audience with respect to both their verbal account of the experience of war and the representation of the most significant episodes from their stories in scenes of dramatic re-enactment. It is one thing to read in Packer's article that Othman and Laith 'before the war … had both longed for the arrival of the Americans, expecting them to change their lives';[38] it is a quite different thing to hear their onstage representatives testify to this in person, thereby acknowledging direct authorship over the narrative of a disenfranchised group of bright, brave, civilized young Iraqis awaiting salvation from the West and enthusiastically welcoming their American liberators. Similarly, Packer translates part of his reportage into realistically recreated scenes that lend factual backing to the interpreters' account of their experience, and in this way strengthen the audience's empathic response towards it. We witness first-hand the unscheduled polygraph session in which Laith is intimidated and humiliated by the security officer who wants him to fail: a scene providing damning evidence that 'All the sacrifices, all the work, all the devotion mean nothing to you. We are still terrorists in your eyes' (88), as his colleague Adnan observes in rage. More compellingly still, the disparate stories and words collected in the journalistic piece become physically concentrated in a trio of fully-rounded characters whom we actually see striving to hold on to their hopes, dreams and ideals long after these have been shattered by the indifference and mistrust of their American friends.

The third member of Packer's close-knit group of friends and translators, Intisar, offers the best illustration of the way in which the 'wide latitude to invent' (xi) that the writer admittedly allowed himself was deployed to provide live, embodied evidence of the veracity of the interpreters' communal narrative of betrayal and disillusionment. The only female voice quoted in the *New Yorker* article is that of a nameless Iraqi woman working at an American base who decided to report the death threats she had received to Titan corporation, the infamous defence company contracted by the Pentagon for the employment of interpreters in Iraq, only to be dismissively informed that the safety of contract workers was not their business. A person named Intisar features on the dedication page of *Betrayed* among the list of Iraqis who gave their words to the dramatist. On stage, these two brief references are fleshed out in the memorable character of a courageous, educated, independent-minded young woman who saw the fall of Saddam as heralding a new era of female emancipation and still defiantly refuses to cover her head despite the fact that in post-war Iraq it has become ever more dangerous to do so. The play charts Intisar's returning despair as her hopes for a better future are quickly and painfully stifled: we see her being harassed in the street by an acquaintance who works as an informer for the militia, and witness her rage and dejection when she is forced to give in to wearing hijab; shortly afterwards, we are taken to the Embassy office where Bill Prescott breaks to Adnan and Laith the heartrending news that Intisar's girlhood dream, of riding a bicycle through the streets of Baghdad like her brothers, will never come true because she has been brutally killed by the insurgents in retaliation for her collaboration with the American occupiers. This tragic epilogue obviously does not belong to the real-life Intisar who was interviewed by Packer during his research, and neither the episode nor its gruesome details—the shaving off of the young woman's hair, the shooting, the wounded body dumped on the street and then picked up by a taxi and left to bleed to death on the back seat—are mentioned in the journalistic report or attributed to a different source there.

The counterpart to this enlargement of the interpreters' individual stories and psychology, in the translation of *Betrayed* from journalism to drama, is the muting or at least mitigation of some more disturbing aspects pertaining to their role in the unfolding conflict. Before he got a more respectable (and less risky) job at the Embassy, Laith had been hired as a military interpreter by Alpha Company, the anti-terrorist US Marine corps also known as 'the Assassins'. Laith admits to having enjoyed his job with a combat unit and explains that his duties included assisting during interrogations and going on military raids; yet his ethics are never questioned and the troubling issue of the wartime translator as a direct or indirect perpetrator of violence is tactfully skirted.

The work of translation scholar Moira Inghilleri provides insight into the questionable ethical position of Iraqi translators working with combat units. In addition to participating in 'combat foot patrols, vehicle patrols, ambushes, bomb-clearing and base security missions', interpreters often accompanied so-called 'cordon-and-search' raids: a neighbourhood would be surrounded with tanks while armed units burst down the doors of Iraqi households in search of insurgents and/or weapons. More often than not, these operations were based on flawed intelligence and only resulted in further traumatization of the civilian population; for many Iraqis, the raids 'came to define the occupation', and the interpreters' symbolic identification with these acts of unlawful violence was intensified by the fact that they, too, 'dressed in army fatigues, wore body armour, travelled in Humvees and sometimes carried weapons'.[39]

By 2007, when Packer wrote his play, the complicity of Arabic-speaking translators in the violence of war had been amply established; the official military inquiry launched after the Abu Ghraib scandal, in particular, confirmed suspicions that translators contracted by Titan corporation had witnessed numerous episodes of prisoner abuse, that they had functioned as a conduit for violence by transmitting the torturers' orders and, in one ascertained case, had directly perpetrated sexual abuse on a teenage detainee.[40] Though no Iraqi nationals were identified among the contract linguists associated with human rights violations inside Abu Ghraib prison, the possibility could not be entirely ruled out; as an American lawyer gathering testimony from former detainees explained, it was very hard for his witnesses to tell whether the perpetrators of abuse were 'US military, mercenaries, Iraqis, private translators or others', because 'the line was so blurred, and they were [sic] crossed all the time'.[41] Emily Apter also fittingly reminds us of another way in which translators functioned as the relayers of psychological violence during the Second Gulf War, when she mentions the leaflet-bombing campaign carried out by coalition forces through which quasi-terroristic messages such as 'We Can See Everything' or 'Take an Offensive Posture and You Will be Destroyed' were conveyed in Arabic to Iraqi civilians.[42]

Both as a verbatim editor and as a dramatist with a license to invent, then, Packer includes in *Betrayed* only those aspects of translation activity that are compatible with his sympathetic and somewhat romanticized portrayal of the wartime interpreters as innocent victims and misunderstood facilitators.[43] This self-imposed no-go area also extends to the problematic implications of the interpreters' potential role as local knowledge specialists, an aspect of their profession that the play does indeed touch upon, without however excavating its more disturbing aspects. In the scene where Laith is recruited by a chummy US soldier at the Assassin's Gate, Packer shows that local linguists came equipped with added cultural skills, and that these represented a very valuable asset for their military employers. Throughout the play, Packer's characters are ever ready to share with their American friends a wealth of logistic advice, useful contacts and, more in general, cultural expertise; they do this out of professional loyalty but also because they are eager to contribute to the pacification and reconstruction of their country. And indeed, the Americans' unwillingness to trust their devoted allies and capitalize on the strategic resources they had to offer is exposed by Packer as a clear proof of the 'bunker mentality'[44] that turned Operation Iraqi Freedom into a colossal failure.

In the *New Yorker* article, where America's gross mistranslation and culpable betrayal of its closest friends in Iraq is glossed as 'a small drama that contains the larger history of defeat' (5), Packer provides further insight into the reasons behind this squandered opportunity: in the words of Jeffrey Beals, a young political counsellor in the foreign service, the high turnover rate of American personnel in Iraq entailed a *de facto* inversion of status between US officials and their local employees, who ended up being 'the real institutional memory and repository of expertise' (9) and were therefore perceived as a threat to professional and social hierarchies. By framing the problem of trust within a wider net of power relations, Packer adds yet another layer to his thorough and thoughtful account of the American mindset and its detrimental effects on the outcome of the Iraqi campaign. Compared with this nuanced analysis, however, the silence that surrounds the moral and political standpoint of the interpreters as cultural informants, in both the article and its stage adaptation, is rather surprising, especially when one considers Packer's stated intention to turn the light on the Iraqis' experience of the war. When Packer carried out his interviews, four years into the war, the 'cultural turn' in the management of operations was well underway. The initial belief that the Iraq war would be won through overwhelming force and superior technology—and the 'Shock and Awe' they were able to produce—had soon proved flawed. As early as June 2004, US Congress hearings were held with the aim of 'determining corrective actions that might be undertaken to regain the confidence and cooperation (hearts and minds) of the Iraqi people', following the emerging consensus that victory depended on winning the Iraqi people's support against the insurgents, and on removing the 'curtain of cultural ignorance' that continued to 'separate the good intentions of the American soldier from Iraqis of good will'.[45] Unable to deal with a thriving insurgency, faced with mounting sectarian violence and growing hostility amongst the civilian population at large, the US administration could no longer dismiss the strategic relevance of cultural intelligence, as had been done in the early stages of the invasion. As President Bush put it rather more coarsely, speaking before an assembly of university presidents in 2006, 'in order to convince [Iraqi] people we care about them, we've got to understand their culture and show them we care about their culture';[46] only a few months later, a team of US military experts, scholars and practitioners published the still highly influential *The U.S. Army/Marine Corps Counterinsurgency Field Manual*, wherein a new model of 'culture-centric warfare' is advocated as a timely antidote to the serious military vulnerabilities brought on by America's inadequate knowledge of the political, social and cultural environment of Iraq.[47]

With its insistence on missed chances for the American side, Packer's analysis of the Iraqi fiasco is singularly aligned with this new military and political orthodoxy. As it charts the 'larger history of defeat' contained in the interpreters' human drama, *Betrayed* stresses the willingness of Iraqi linguists to double as cultural informants for their employers, and berates the US administration for its failure to recognize the tactical value of the cultural knowledge they might have supplied. In order to further underscore the crass ineptitude of US military and political leaders, the play goes as far as showing that the interpreters themselves were indeed aware of the possible weaponization of their interlingual and intercultural skills in the battle for control over the territory and population of Iraq. While he is being escorted out of the embassy after the injustice of the polygraph test, Laith takes a rushed leave from his mentor Prescott, who has been powerless to defend him, and bitterly warns him that 'the U.S. is still in a war. I don't think you're going to win this war if you don't win the hearts of your allies' (89). In this verbatim remark one can hear distinct echoes of President Johnson's 'Hearts and Minds' campaign in Vietnam and a rather straightforward allusion to its more recent application to the Iraqi context;[48] but the implications of this parallel are not pursued and Laith's grievances in the following scene are once more exclusively focused on his dismal fate as an outcast within both camps, American and Iraqi.

There is no room, in Packer's reportage, for a questioning of the possible instrumental and moral connivance of interpreters with what is, to all effects, a war of aggression: *Betrayed* is equally silent about the legitimacy of the war under international law and about the ethical and professional legitimacy of the translators' involvement in it. While these omissions are characteristic of wartime interpreters' narratives,[49] the hybrid documentary mode adopted in *Betrayed* might have allowed sufficient leeway to raise these issues; yet Packer chose to second the interpreters' silence both as a dramatist, by refraining from exercising his 'latitude to invent' in order to enlarge the scope of the inquiry, and also, more revealingly, as a journalist and a documentarian, by keeping from putting the relevant questions to his interviewees, and/or muting them in his report. The only possible exception to this questionable reticence could be the interview scene at the Palestine Hotel at the play's opening, when Laith utters the potentially judgmental term 'invasion' and Othman cuts in with the specification that he was 'totally against' this word (10). However, neither statement appears to have been prompted by a specific question from the invisible interviewer, nor do we sense any attempt at delving further into slippery ground.

Still on this point, it is worth remarking that Packer's room for manoeuvre was significantly greater than the one customarily granted to the verbatim playwright. The evidence base of his investigation was not predetermined by the terms of reference of an official inquiry, or dependent on the existence and availability of legal records, as is the case with the editors of tribunal plays. Moreover, Packer's inquisitorial practice was not even tied to a particular protocol—legal or otherwise—for the extraction of information: the Q&A format of the original conversations, which the play still in part retains, shows no traces of the ethical reservations underpinning Victoria Brittain and Gillian Slovo's verbatim project on Guantanamo Bay prison, and their decision to stand back and leave the floor to their traumatized witnesses in order to spare them another round of interrogation (see Chapter Three). Packer's acquiescence in the narrative horizon formed by his sources is not motivated by objective constraints or methodological considerations; it is, rather, the result of a deliberate narrowing of focus which the play subsequently naturalizes through its erasure of the authorial figure from the picture. By apparently entitling the Iraqi interpreters to be the sole mediators of their experience of the war, and attributing to them full responsibility for the narrative and its epistemological limitations, *Betrayed* ultimately shades the presence of Packer's editorial gaze and his crucial role in the shaping of the story.

Though not envisaged as such, it is tempting to see Gregory Burke's *Black Watch* as a response to the portrayal of the wartime translator in *Betrayed*. Like Packer's semi-documentary project, Burke's 'unauthorised biography'[50] of the time-honoured Scottish Regiment deployed in southern Iraq is also a tale of betrayal that involves mediator figures; here, however, the fate of the wartime translator is tackled from the point of view of the coalition troops, with the dialectic between the visible and invisible interpreters of war becoming completely reversed.

At the end of 2004, shortly after her appointment as the first artistic director of the National Theatre of Scotland, Vicky Featherstone asked Gregory Burke to look into the story of the Royal Highland Regiment, known as the Black Watch, following its return from Camp Dogwood in Iraq. Programmed as the highlight of the NTS's inaugural season in 2006, and entrusted to John Tiffany's direction, the piece was meant to honour the typically Scottish tradition of 'highly physical',[51] visually creative and vigorously demotic political drama. *Black Watch* premiered in August at the Edinburgh Fringe, taking audiences by storm, and subsequently embarked on a Scottish and then world tour, where it met with huge acclaim. When Tiffany's production was revived in 2010, with an entirely new cast, *Black Watch* had long since achieved iconic status as '*the* Scottish play about Iraq', a 'cultural landmark' of the Scottish way to war-making and theatre-making alike.[52]

Burke's play taps into the political controversy surrounding the UK government's decision to comply with the US Forces' request to relocate the Black Watch outside of the British-controlled zone, in an area south of Baghdad later dubbed the 'triangle of death', in order to relieve American troops temporarily redeployed for the second offensive on Fallujah. As was to be expected, this move did not go down well with Scottish public opinion. The Black Watch regiment, it was claimed, lacked adequate training for the specific theatre of operations; and the suspiciously vague 'support' task they were being sent to perform was seen as a further factor that might contribute to turning them into soft targets for the Iraqi insurgency. These fears were sadly confirmed in November 2004, when three Black Watch soldiers and their local interpreter died in a car bomb blast at a checkpoint. It was amidst growing public outrage at Whitehall's apparent lack of concern for the safety of Scottish troops—adding up to the nation-wide indignation aroused by the proven inconsistency of the *casus belli* for the invasion of Iraq and the recent scandal of Abu Ghraib—that the British government, with appalling timing, proceeded to discharge its own round of friendly fire against the most senior and representative regiment of Highlanders, officially confirming that the Black Watch would be amalgamated into the Royal Regiment of Scotland and downgraded to a battalion. This final act of 'betrayal' was accomplished in March 2006, just a few months before Burke's play premiered in Edinburgh.

In tackling the story of this flagship military institution and its embedded symbolical and cultural meanings, Burke casts a critical glance on the Western intervention in Iraq but also, perhaps less predictably, on the centuries-long record of Scotland's support to Britain's imperialist ventures. This is particularly evident in the highly sardonic scene called 'Fashion', in which one of the squaddies, Cammy, is 'dress[ed] in and out of significant and distinct uniforms from the regiment's history' by his comrades-in-arms, in what looks like an absurdist visual crossover between a catwalk show and the assembling and disassembling of a military cannon, while he narrates the countless battles fought throughout the regiment's long and honoured service as Britain's hired 'warriors' (30–31). Still, although the prevalent mood throughout scenes is unsentimental and often scathingly ironical, the portrayal of the military offered in *Black Watch* is far from unsympathetic: like Packer, Burke relies on the human interest component to create documentary authenticity. While predictably sexist, invariably foul-mouthed, and capable of gratuitous violence, the soldiers are not depicted as an indistinct mass of like-minded thugs, but rather as individualized human beings, each with their own story and personality. Burke's warriors are presented as willing participants in the war game, not mere cogs in the machine; yet their statutory bravado barely hides their emotional frailty and almost childlike vulnerability, their psychological and often also professional unpreparedness for a high-risk assignment. By the same token, underneath the macho camaraderie we recognize genuine affective bonds and a strong sense of solidarity amongst the members of this select 'tribe'. Finally, while the squaddies' language is rough and their communication skills are definitely limited, the dialogue bristles with gallows humour and a clear-eyed grasp of rhetoric's mystificatory power. This, for example, is how the troops react to their first taste of insurgent fire upon arrival at Camp Dogwood:

FRAZ: Welcome to Camp Dogwood.
GRANTY: In beautiful Babil province.
CAMMY: Ancient home ay Babylon.
ROSSCO: Birthplace ay civilisation.

Another mortar lands. This time very close, making them all dive for cover.

CAMMY: Twenty-four-hour beach facilities.
GRANTY: A scorpion in every tent.
FRAZ: Friendly locals.
ROSSCO: Your home for the next six months.
MACCA: Six fucking months?
NASBY: I thought they said we were gonnay be home by Christmas? (10–11)

Nasby's ironic allusion to First World War propaganda is expanded later on in the play when Lord Elgin, in kilt and tartan, breaks into a scene set in a Scottish pub in the present to start his recruiting session. Wielding the sword of his glorious ancestor Robert the Bruce, Elgin depicts trench warfare as a leisurely break from the miners' dreary life in the pit, a golden opportunity to enjoy the 'fresh air, the meadows, the rivers' (27) of the charming Somme region with the added bonus of 'shoot[ing] a few Germans'. He then closes his peroration by throwing in the routine humbug that 'it would all be over by Christmas' (28).

In the first NTS production, historical continuity in politicians' war narratives was visually underscored by having the same actor play Lord Elgin and the Scottish National Party Leader, Alex Salmond. Just like the First World War recruits who do not buy into Elgin's rhetoric of Scottish military heroism and his promise of glory in lieu of pay, their present-day counterparts are open-eyed about the fact that they have been sent to fight in a war which is both unheroic and illegal. In the third pub scene, they comment thus on the utter imbalance between coalition and Iraqi troops in terms of equipment and firepower:

> CAMMY: ... After a while it's more bullying than fighting ay.
> STEWARTY: You dinnay join up tay bully cunts day you.
> ROSSCO: Bullying's the job.
> GRANTY: It's no the reason you want tay be in the army, though.
> CAMMY: It's a buzz, you're in a war ay, but you're no really doing the job you're trained for but it's no like they're a massive threat tay you or tay your country, you're no defending your country. We're invading their country and fucking their day up. (48–49)

In an earlier scene set in the Iraqi desert, as the Scottish soldiers watch the massive air strike on the city of Fallujah, Rossco subscribes to Cammy's definition of the Western military offensive as 'plain old-fashioned bullying', quickly adding that in the present circumstances 'it's good to be the bully' (40).

Even if his method for humanizing characters relies on irony more than emotion, Burke essentially shares the sympathetic posture adopted by Packer in his documentary. On the methodological level, too, Burke's approach has some important points of contact with Packer's war dramaturgy. Exactly like *Betrayed*, *Black Watch* is a hybrid play that mixes verbatim quotation and fictional recreation. Following John Tiffany's suggestion that the piece should attempt to 'tell the "real" stories of the soldiers in their own words' (x), Burke talked to several former Black Watch servicemen who had fought in Iraq. The interviews took place over a two-month period in Fife, one of Black Watch's main recruiting areas. When the creative team set about workshopping the play, the writer also delivered a number of unsolicited fictional scenes set in Camp Dogwood that he had 'secretly' developed while collecting and editing the verbatim testimonies. The company welcomed this possibility for counterpoint and as a result the final version of the play travels back and forth between a recreation of the original testimonial sessions, set in a pub in present-day Scotland, and the mimetic re-enactment of the soldiers' past experiences in Iraq. These oscillations are attuned to the polyphonic mode that is operative at various other levels in *Black Watch*, a play that juxtaposes, and sometimes interweaves, voices that are dissonant in terms of accent and register (the soldiers' demotic Scottish vernacular versus the standard English spoken by officers and politicians), format (dialogue/email/song), speech economy (homosocial male banter/media discourse/political rhetoric) and communication modality (verbal/nonverbal). Further to shaping the play's architecture, Burke's unprompted reintroduction of fiction into the formal model of verbatim also served the purpose of shielding the soldiers who had agreed to share sensitive information about their service in Iraq: as remarked by John Tiffany, this was a case in which the 'welfare and anonymity' of the interviewees was a matter of serious concern.[53]

Even more than in *Betrayed*, then, in *Black Watch* the verbatim method remains largely confined to the gathering of primary material which is then freely reworked to suit the production's particular needs and aims. Still, the writer exercises his license to invent sparingly, and the play's overall adherence to the soldiers' perspective also results, as in Packer's case, in some potentially disturbing gaps in the narrative that have not gone unnoticed in the critical literature. According to Trish Reid, for example, by allowing Black Watch soldiers to be represented in their own terms the play ultimately fails to call into question the 'totalising narrative of continuity through heroism' that they articulate throughout the performance, particularly in the section where Cammy offers his digest of the regiment's three-hundred-year-long history. Although Reid is right in pointing out that Burke's overview remains silent about Black Watch's involvement in Ireland, thereby failing to fully disclose 'how heavily the regiment, and Scotland in general, was implicated in, and benefited from, British colonial violence',[54] on the other hand Cammy's account includes ample evidence of Scotland's active role in British imperial wars past and present; and at any rate, the blatantly parodistic style of presentation of the scene alone is sufficient to place the soldier's history lesson in inverted commas and erode its claims to objectivity.

An arguably more disturbing omission, likewise resulting from Burke's adoption of the troops' perspective, concerns instead the Iraqi interpreter who was also killed in the attack but never appears on stage. In striking contrast to what happens in Packer's Iraq play, in *Black Watch* the figure of the wartime translator is completely banished from the picture. Through a skilful use of repetition and verbalization, however, the dramatist is able to make this testimonial lacuna conspicuous, and therefore highly eloquent.

The poignant episode of the suicide bombing is accounted for at three different moments in the play. Each time, it is rendered from

5. Fraz (Andrew Fraser) and Kenzie (Scott Fletcher) emerging from the pool table in the National Theatre of Scotland's production of *Black Watch* (2013 international tour). Photography by Manuel Harlan. © Manuel Harlan.

a different point of view and presented in a different format, thereby disrupting all illusion of transparency and pointing instead to the particular slant informing each of these mediations of the experience of war, an awareness that is also fostered by the play's overt dramatization of the creative process. The first reproduction of the attack is diegetic and occurs at the beginning of the play, after the soldiers' first testimonial session. The sound of gunfire signals the transition from Fife pub to Iraqi war zone: the interview setting disappears, the cloth of the pool table is ripped open by a knife and Fraz, dressed in full Black Watch gear, emerges from the table, soon to be followed by Kenzie, the other soldier killed in the explosion. As the ghosts from the past are let loose through this symbolical gateway to and from Iraq,[55] we hear John Humphrys's report of the killings on the BBC Radio 4 *Today* programme. This works as a prelude to the subsequent live recreation of an on-air confrontation between the UK Defence Secretary, Geoff Hoon, and Alex Salmond, the leader of the Scottish National Party. In the apparently factual account of the deadly ambush delivered by the presenter, the interpreter is tellingly left out of the body count; in this way, when the Iraqi victim is eventually mentioned by Hoon in the heated discussion that follows, we are instantly reminded of what bodies count in news media discourse. It is highly ironic, however, that the local linguist's body should achieve grievability, and with it human individuality,[56] only to be immediately overwritten by factitious political discourse:

ALEX SALMOND: I think [grief] will give way to a wave of anger as Scotland and the Black Watch families compare and contrast the bravery of our Scottish soldiers with the duplicity and chicanery of the politicians who sent them in this deployment.
JOHN HUMPHRYS: Is that anger justified, Mr Hoon?
GEOFF HOON: No, it's not, and I'm afraid the leader of the Scottish Nationalists' comments demonstrate very clearly there are no depths to which he will not sink to seek—and I can't think why he does this, I cannot understand why someone should seek to take political advantage about the tragic deaths of three brave men and one interpreter. (8)

The second reconstruction of the suicide bombing is presented in the form of a retrospective account collectively spun by the survivors in the fourth and final pub scene. The military eyewitnesses mention the death of an Iraqi translator in the attack but are unable to produce his name when solicited by the character of the Writer because, as Granty and Cammy explain, 'They didnay use their real names … Tay protect their families from getting in the shite. For working for us' (63–64). The namelessness of the 'Iraqi boy' (63) and the reasons behind it are all we ever hear in the play about the translator's identity. The fact that not even a patrol linguist, for all his physical and experiential proximity to troops, should figure as a full human being in the soldiers' narratives is a compelling indication of the tremendous distance between the British contingent and the local population—as is also provocatively acknowledged in this exchange during the third Q&A session:

WRITER: Did you have much contact with the Iraqis?
STEWARTY: What the fuck have the Iraqis got tay fucking day way anything? (46)

The translator's invisibility is thus adroitly turned into a sign and symptom of the one-sidedness of the West's humanitarian intervention in Iraq, a damning proof of the overwhelming preoccupation of the self-styled liberators with their own interests and safety.

It is only upon the third reprise that the playwright takes direct responsibility for the telling of the episode of the terrorist attack; frustratingly, however, even this fictional recreation remains firmly anchored within the cognitive horizon formed by Burke's sources. The climactic bomb blast is staged as a spectacular slow-motion in which Fraz, Kenzie and the Sergeant, covered in blood, float in mid-air and then hit the ground one after the other while a voice-over calls out their personal identification number and triage code. This overexposure of the soldiers' corporeal presence in the war zone works to forcefully offset the utter invisibility which envelops the body of the interpreter, a condition that the latter significantly shares with the other ghosted Iraqis who haunt the picture, the equally nameless and faceless authors of the terrorist attack. This is a representational default that the dramatist openly denounces through the soldiers' banter prefacing the 'Casualties' sequence. As they observe the fateful car approach and stop at the checkpoint, the soldiers who have remained inside the wagon crack a few jokes about Fraz's patter and then mention the translator's posting at the checkpoint to assist with communication. In this way, the audience is verbally alerted to the presence of another character in the scene they are witnessing, of another actor in the Iraqi theatre of war whose body has been erased from the visual representation of that scene.

The exhibited invisibility of the interlingual translator in *Black Watch* stands in close connection with the whole issue of the writer's intralingual translation of the soldiers' testimonial account. Burke's decision to subordinate his dramatization of the scene to the limited gaze of his primary witnesses is mainly aimed at bringing fictional recreation under the rubric of documentary authenticity. But this move also produces the apparently opposed effect of drawing attention to the mediated nature of the source material the playwright is working from. The translator's erasure from scenic space in *Black Watch* is thereby revealed as originating in an act of mistranslation performed by the real-life interviewees, an act that the writer, in turn, has chosen to bear witness to, rather than rectify through the exercise of authorial license; somewhat paradoxically, then, testimonial accuracy is here shown to be dependent on the playwright's seconding of an act of translational infidelity.

The problematic connection between testimony and translation that is established in *Black Watch* through the invisibility of the interpreter within the story is further emphasized by the play's sustained focus on the playwright as the recipient and transmitter of the soldiers' narrative

6. 'Casualties': Kenzie (Scott Fletcher), Fraz (Andrew Fraser) and The Sergeant (Robert Jack) in the National Theatre of Scotland's production of *Black Watch* (2013 international tour). Photography by Manuel Harlan. © Manuel Harlan.

in the interview scenes set in the Scottish pub, where Burke's testimonial investiture is thematized and openly questioned. This, again, invites comparison with the silence surrounding Packer's editorial mediation in *Betrayed*. In the opening scene of Packer's documentary, a small recorder on the table of the Baghdad hotel room has replaced the writer's physical presence in the original interview setting; the technology that surrogates his subjective mediation constructs the verbatim playwright as a neutral conduit, and the Iraqi interpreters never challenge the transparency of his recordation and reproduction of their stories. Conversely, while the Iraqi translator becomes virtually transparent in their eyes, Burke's soldiers are very much aware of the act of translation that the writer is going to perform upon their words and experiences in order to turn them into a play, and equally wary of the possibility for treachery, distortion and manipulation inherent in this process. These Black Watch veterans have fought in an unpopular, inglorious war that has further widened the gap between civilians and returning soldiers, thereby increasing the risk of misperception and, consequently, the soldiers' reluctance to 'explain myself tay people' (3), as Cammy informs the audience in the prologue. During their deployment in Iraq, Burke's interviewees were instructed to exercise self-censorship before the cameras of news media crews in order to 'reassure the great British public that you are happy in your job' (36) and avoid further damage to the troops' already battered public image. Though we smile at Granty's present preoccupation with the looks of the actor who will be playing his character and at his suggestion of Ewan McGregor as a likely candidate, the soldiers' playful attempt to take control over the casting process reveals their common concern about the act of surrogation and a heightened sensitivity about the whole issue of representation. In their eyes the digital recorder with which the verbatim playwright also comes armed in *Black Watch* has long lost its innocence, and the human subject who operates it is viewed with suspicion and sometimes genuine hostility by the witnesses whose stories he has come to collect. The high-testosterone regulars of the Fife pool hall may well outnumber and even outsmart Burke's nerdish, somewhat dumbed-down and visibly ill-at-ease onstage representative; yet even this apparently harmless 'poof' (5) is immediately perceived by the interviewees as a potential menace to their integrity and identity.

The figure of the dramatist as a secondary witness that emerges from *Black Watch* is at the other extreme from Packer's portrayal of the interviewer as an unobtrusive, neutral technology of recordation in *Betrayed*. A closer match for Burke's spotlighting of the intermediary would be David Hare's construction of his stage persona in *Via Dolorosa*, not least on account of the latter's intellectually unflattering characterization of himself in his testimonial solo. As has been argued in Chapter Four, however, Hare turned himself into a 'stupider and more ignorant'[57] character for the purpose of consolidating his credentials as an impartial witness to the Israeli-Palestinian conflict, rather than subjecting them to criticism. In *Black Watch*, instead, the passing on of testimony acquires a distinctly dialectical edge, with the writer's visibility as a professional interpreter turning him into a soft target for the soldiers' offensive on his trustworthiness as a second-order witness.

The twin and complementary topics of translational accuracy and discursive entitlement are raised as early as the first pub scene, when the terms of the soldiers' contribution to the documentary project are still subject to negotiation, and continue to be picked up, with intensifying vehemence, through to the final testimonial session. From the very opening moments of their conversation, the soldiers react with scepticism to the assumption underpinning the Writer's testimonial project, namely, the idea that vicarious witnessing might constitute a valid cognitive position:

CAMMY: What day you want tay know?
WRITER: What it was like in Iraq.

CAMMY: What it was fucking like?
STEWARTY: Go to fucking Baghdad if you want tay ken what it's like. (7)

Towards the end of the play, Stewarty mounts another attack on the Writer's presumption that he will be able to gain insight into the reality of the Iraq war through the soldiers' retrospective account; this time, however, the cognitive shortcomings ascribed to the Writer's position are more directly related to the risk of mistranslation inhering the subsequent act of passing on their lived experience:

WRITER: What was it like to be fired at?
STEWARTY: It fucks people up. Big time.
Beat.
Rips them apart.
Beat.
You seen the size ay the bullets we use in a chain gun?
Beat.
You seen what happens when a bullet that size hits somebody?
WRITER: Well … no … I haven't.
STEWARTY: So how the fuck are you gonnay explain it tay folk, then? (59)

The connection between testimonial fallacy and translational inaccuracy is fully articulated in Stewarty's final, violent assault on the Writer's credentials and prerogatives. After the soldiers have collectively shared their recollection of the suicide bombing episode and the death of their comrades, Stewarty reveals that he broke an arm in the explosion, and then kept breaking it when it got better. The Writer's promise to perform his testimonial duty with respect to Stewarty's story is not sufficient to overcome the soldier's hostility—on the contrary, it triggers an outburst of violence:

STEWARTY: … Write that down.
WRITER: I will.
STEWARTY: Write it down with a broken arm though.
Stewarty grabs the Writer's arm.
CAMMY: Come on, Stewarty, leave the boy alone.
STEWARTY: Let me break your arm and see if you can write it down way a broken arm.
CAMMY: Stewarty, come on tay fuck.

STEWARTY: If he wants tay ken about Iraq, he has tay feel some pain? (64–65)

The others promptly come to the rescue, shuffling Stewarty out of the room; once they are left alone, Cammy explains his comrade's aggressive behaviour to the Writer, revealing that Stewarty was sent back to Iraq for a second tour of duty despite being diagnosed with Post-Traumatic Stress Disorder after his first deployment there.

When placed in the context of the play's overall discourse on visible/invisible translators, Stewarty's gesture becomes loaded with self-reflexive meaning. On one level, at the same time as it subordinates the possibility of knowledge to direct experience, the soldier's attack on the self-appointed bearer of wartime testimony points to the inevitability of surrogation: mistranslation thus becomes a symbol of the irreducible foreignness of witnessing. Underneath its crude retaliatory logic, moreover, Stewarty's violent reaction against the Writer also reads as a literalized version of the notion of vicarious traumatization and an implicit comment on the function that is often attributed to it in testimonial war drama. The logical corollary to Stewarty's mystique of first-hand experience is the idea of the Writer's broken arm as the tangible proof of a moment of empathic contact with the real which would then enable the transmissibility of the testimonial function and validate his vicarious narrative. It is the same mechanism which is described through the character of the traumatized former UK Ambassador to Uzbekistan in Robin Soans's *Talking to Terrorists* (see Chapter Four) and, with a more decided slant on translation in times of war, in Cecilia Parkert's *Witness*. Based on a real story and originally written in 1995, Parkert's one-woman play was performed at London's Gate Theatre in July 2002 in a translation from the Swedish by Kevin Halliwell. It features a long monologue delivered to the audience by 'The Interpreter', an unnamed woman who translates the testimony of survivors of the war in the former Yugoslavia for a Swedish therapist. As she listens to the patients' stories, the interpreter finds it increasingly impossible to be 'just an echo'[58] that mechanically repeats their unspeakable and unbearable tales of violence; responding empathically to the victims' deeply unsettling experiences, the woman develops symptoms of vicarious traumatization and risks both her job and her sanity when she finally breaks down the barrier set up by professional ethics to form a bond with one of the participants in the therapy sessions. By becoming a witness, Parkert's protagonist ceases to be a translator; yet it is the act of translating that has turned her into a witness in the first place, exposing the untenability of the professional stance required of the translator as a neutral, transparent conduit for other people's words.

In a very interesting study on the translators of testimonies during the war in Croatia, Zrinka Stahlujak deals with a similar conflict between the translators' desire to bear witness before the international community and the self-effacing dogma of linguistic neutrality. Pointing to the paradoxical position in which these wartime interpreters found themselves on account of the deep imbrications between translating and witnessing, Stahlujak invites a reconsideration of both the theory of translation and the theory of testimony insofar as they continue to misleadingly construe these two fields as mutually exclusive.[59] However coarsely expressed, Stewarty's critique of the mediation of the fictional writer in *Black Watch* is rooted in a similar conflation of the translator with the witness. The self-reflexive implications of this questioning of the translator's testimonial function are best explored in connection with the problematics of in/visibility that are foregrounded in the play. In more than one respect, the stark opposition between visible and invisible translators established in *Black Watch* functions as an illustration, and concomitantly as an interrogation, of the act of witnessing performed by Burke though his play. In a meta-dramatic perspective, the playwright's response to Stewarty's delegitimizing attacks on the discursive entitlement of his onstage proxy is in the very act of showing these attacks and, more in general, in the full visibility which the play confers on the human agent behind the transmission of the soldiers' traumatic experience. From this point of view, the problematic invisibility of the other mediator figure in the play, that of the Iraqi interpreter, also reads as a self-reflexive comment on the customary erasure of subjective agency in the verbatim author's translation of reality onto the stage, and a pointed allusion to its questionable ethical undersides. At the same time, however, the emphatic exposure of the intralingual translator sharpens our awareness of the obliterated presence of the wartime translator and turns the light on the translational dilemma this poses to the dramatist.

Burke's testimonial impasse becomes particularly evident in the fraught moment in the performance when Stewarty grabs hold of the Writer's arm and threatens to break it before the others intervene to stop him. The corporeality of the intralingual translator, his physical vulnerability, immediately invites comparison with the disembodied presence of the interlingual translator who died in the attack. The Iraqi interpreter is a primary witness who has been blotted out twice, once in the actual explosion and then again in the lack of acknowledgment as a victim. His missing body places a heavy ethical burden upon the dramatist: the linguist's unspoken testimony demands to be accounted for but the very act of reinstating his presence within the representational field would obfuscate its problematic foreignness. Faced with the challenge of exercising his ethical right to bear witness to the violent effacement of the Iraqi victim while keeping his imaginative recreation of the scene firmly set within a testimonial horizon, Burke navigates this translational dilemma by employing dramatic invention in a truly testimonial way: not to fill a gaping void in the narrative but, on the contrary, to testify to it by using stage space in order to turn the invisible presence of the translator into a visible absence that interrogates us all.

The combat linguist

The deep entanglement between war and translation that the Iraqi conflict has revealed, and that both *Betrayed* and *Black Watch* document *ex post facto* through their antithetical configurations of the interpreters' in/visibility, is presented as a fait accompli in David Greig's forward-looking *The American Pilot*, a provocative fictional take on the new wars written in February 2003, when the invasion of Iraq could still be regarded as a major disaster to be averted, rather than a disgraceful reality to be reckoned with.

Greig's play is set in the remote village of an imaginary Third World country where a rebel army is waging a 'terrorist' guerrilla warfare against a brutal military regime instated and supported by the USA. The plot is set in motion by the fateful arrival of the titular American pilot who has crash-landed into a nearby hillside. As the farmer who found him and took him into his shed debates with the village counsellor about the wisest way to deal with the pilot's troubling presence, the leader of the armed resistance, the anonymous Captain, arrives on site accompanied by his interpreter. Speech prefixes define him as a 'Translator', but impartial linguistic mediation is not even an issue for Matthew: the very first task he is ordered to perform is to search the wounded prisoner, and throughout the first interview he unperturbedly partakes in the Captain's standard methods for 'enhanced interrogation', to borrow the infamous euphemism for torture made current by the war on terror.

As we soon gather, Matthew is no novice to operations of this kind; he has fought and killed for the cause and after years of loyal service he is now on the upper echelon in the insurgents' military-political hierarchy: though he may still routinely stoop to polish the Captain's boots, in his capacity as combat linguist he effectively acts as the rebel leader's chief political advisor and has already been designated to succeed him in command.[60] Akin to the Trader, who assesses the situation with a keen eye for profit, the Translator, too, is quick to detect an opportunity where others only see an impending calamity for the village now that 'America has happened to you',[61] as the Captain puts it to a bewildered Farmer. Matthew's plan is to record the prisoner's execution and broadcast the video internationally via a satellite station. Though wary of the possible consequences of global-scale media refraction—'At the moment our cause is misunderstood by a handful of diplomats. Now we have the chance to be misunderstood by the entire population of the world.' (34)—the Captain initially backs Matthew's go at image warfare, having himself lost all hope in the rebels' lopsided struggle against the mighty American colossus; but he is eventually convinced by the Farmer's teenage daughter, Evie, to spare the captive's life and send out an entirely different message to the world. The young and innocent girl who believes the Pilot is a saviour 'sent here to test us' (60) will become the new icon of the resistance; when the released airman carries back the video of 'a saint, a visionary' (64) leading the rebel army into the valley to meet government troops, and recruiting more and more followers with each town she passes, the American government will have no choice but support their struggle before the international community.

Unfortunately, there is no time to find out which communication strategy works better—the promise of retaliatory violence or a suicidal gesture of trust—because even before they can begin recording their message the villagers are mercilessly crushed under the giant foot of the American superpower. Helicopter-borne assault forces storm into the barn from a hole blown in the shed roof, killing nearly everyone on sight in order to save one of their own who, by then, has already been released and is about to be taken over to the border by his original rescuer, the Farmer, generously equipped with food, drink and warm clothes. With the bombing and gunfire continuing after the American saviours have left, Greig's finale suggests that the civil war and conflict in which this unnamed country has been mired for many years has finally escalated into a state of permanent war.

David Greig wrote *The American Pilot* in two days before Operation Iraqi Freedom started, driven by the rage he felt at the senselessness of the forthcoming war: at the obvious lack of any rational military, political or even economic justification for invading Iraq, as well as at the maddening prospect of the human cost that would have to be paid for the 'monstrous vanity' of world leaders. As a Scottish playwright, Greig had friends with sons in the Black Watch and was sharply aware of how they were about to 'be sent to kill and die for no reason'.[62] Still, for all his keen perception of the closeness of the war and its dire consequences, Greig did not expressly envisage *The American Pilot* as a play about Iraq. The story takes place in an unspecified setting which he imagined could be 'Tadjikistan, or Darfur'; the vaguely Afghan costumes of the first production, at the RSC's The Other Place in Stratford-upon-Avon, appeared to corroborate the first possibility.[63] The dialogue, however, also evokes other scenarios: for instance, when the Captain fondly reminisces about his happy time in civilized Oslo, away from the brutal reality of his war-torn country, we are instantly reminded of the secret negotiations between Israel and the PLO in the Norwegian capital during the 1990s. In the two years that it took to get this uncommissioned piece to the stage, moreover, *The American Pilot* inevitably turned into a post-Iraq play, and most reviewers of the Stratford performances read Greig's crude, bitter parable as a commentary upon the US-led intervention and its disastrous aftermath.

By April 2005, when the play opened at The Other Place, the Translator's abandoned plan to launch an airwave attack through the videoed execution of the American prisoner had become standard combat practice in the asymmetrical warfare fought by the Iraqi resistance. Similarly, the *deus ex machina* intervention of the assault forces in the final scene automatically called to mind the spectacular evacuation of Private Jessica Lynch on a Black Hawk helicopter from the Nassiriya hospital where she lay wounded. According to the Pentagon-licensed version of Lynch's story, on 23 March 2003 the army maintenance vehicle in which she was riding was ambushed by the insurgents; the nineteen-year-old servicewoman allegedly fought to the death before she was taken hostage and transported to Saddam Hospital, where she remained at the mercy of militia brutality until American forces came to the rescue in a high-risk nighttime raid. The operation was filmed by the military and the dramatic video footage was endlessly replayed on television following the announcement of Lynch's deliverance. This official narrative swamped the airwaves and the press for weeks before a quite different version of 'Saving Private Lynch'[64] gradually began to emerge. Not only was the assessment of Lynch's injuries found to be at variance with the original story of her capture and fierce resistance on the battlefield; the daring helicopter rescue itself was exposed as a colossal hoax, most notably in 'War Spin', a programme aired by the BBC on 18 May 2003 and narrated by BBC correspondent John Kampfner. Several sources testified that Jessica Lynch was treated with kindness and received special care while in hospital, and that the US Special Forces met with no resistance when they stormed the ward at the cry of 'go, go, go', smashing down doors and firing rounds in a carefully-scripted imitation of a Hollywood action movie. In her first public pronouncements, months after the rescue, Lynch largely concurred with the version given by Iraqi doctors of her time in hospital and even confirmed that her captors had actually tried to hand her over to US forces, only recoiling when their ambulance came under American fire.[65]

To the audiences of the original Stratford run in 2005, of the 2006 revival at London's Soho Theatre, and of the three American versions produced at close distance between 2006 and 2008, the parallels between the fictional war depicted in *The American Pilot* and the ongoing conflict in Iraq were evident and were generally interpreted as a token of the play's urgent topicality, although reactions varied with each specific context of reception.[66] As I write this chapter, it is undoubtedly through its open-ended conclusion that Greig's imagined war continues to retain its power to engage proleptically with a future reality: more than one decade after the Iraq war was officially declared over, the play's final picture of a country in the grips of never-ending conflict feels like a very accurate guess as we witness Iraq's day-by-day descent into a hell of escalating internecine conflagration. At the same time, because of the indefinite location of Greig's conflict zone, the bitter finale could just as easily apply to Afghanistan, where the West's promise of 'Enduring Freedom' has similarly resulted in a fully-fledged war with no end in sight and, more in general, to the lasting legacy of the war on terror and its proven proactive capability for fuelling violence on a global scale.

To a large extent, the anticipatory gaze that has been ascribed to *The American Pilot* is a result of Greig's ambition to investigate the mechanics of power underpinning the new paradigm of warfare, rather than reflect their actual manifestations in a particular conflict zone. Through the abstract quality of the setting, the representative characters, the moments of direct audience address which interrupt the flow of the action, Greig's war drama shows its close affiliations with the genre of the Brechtian parable play and its allegorical method of inquiry into the deep structures of socio-political conflict. But whereas Greig's debt to the Brechtian model has been frequently acknowledged, the way in which his dramaturgy of war relies on the translation trope as a heuristic device deserves more in-depth consideration. In Greig's endeavour to provide an explanatory model for the wars of the twenty-first century, and the kind of world order they express, translation becomes a prime conceptual tool through which patterns of conflict can be estranged and held up for scrutiny. In formal terms, this results in a paradoxical dramaturgy of translation in which language mediation is as at once ubiquitous and non-existent in the contemporary field of operations.

Even before Greig's combat linguist, Matthew, steps on stage sanctioning the full and definitive integration of language mediation in the institution of war, translation figures in the play as the principal mode of dramatic interaction between characters, as the villagers strive to come to terms with the disruptive presence of the heaven-sent American alien. To the Farmer and his family, the duty of hospitality and a varying mixture of curiosity and fascination for the stranger are a strong incentive to crossing language barriers. Similarly, for the wounded, helpless Pilot the possibility of effective interlingual communication with the local community is his only hope of survival. Mime may come to the rescue when it comes to asking for a drink of water, but the message that the Pilot depends upon for his release can only be put across verbally:

EVIE: My name is Evie. What is your name? I speak English.
PILOT: You speak English? My name is Jason Reinhardt. I am an officer of the United States Air Force. Do you understand? OK?
EVIE: OK.
PILOT: If you arrange for me to be safely transported to the nearest telephone or radio I will personally ensure that you and your family are well rewarded by the United States government. OK?
EVIE: OK.
FARMER: What did he say?
EVIE: I don't know. (*She speaks to the Pilot again.*) My name is Evie. What is your name? I speak English.
PILOT: Miss. My name is Jason Reinhardt. Do you understand?
EVIE: This is hopeless. He doesn't understand. (16–17)

It would be reductive to see Greig's conventional rendition of the foreign language spoken by the local people into English as simply driven by a desire to maximize accessibility. Akin to Brian Friel's epitomic play about the Troubles, *Translations* (1980), English monoglottism provides the dramatist with a formal device whereby he is able to tackle the problematics of untranslatability from a distinctly political angle. Though the Pilot's visitation is an exceptional and unprecedented event for the villagers, their world shows clear signs of protracted contact with an American or Americanized world. As is to be expected, not even the secluded, almost primitive mountain community of the play has been immune from the global reach of media; underneath an appearance of complete separateness, the Western outsider and his local interlocutors actually share a patch of linguistic and cultural common ground, however small it may look. Even if access to technology is very limited and even television sets are still an unaffordable luxury for most of the villagers, young people like Evie have made the best of their forays into the contact zone created by the global media, and have come back loaded with pop songs, images of America, and scraps of the world's lingua franca; but even for Evie's more traditional parents, Disney cartoon characters are part of the household's lexicon, although their American guest comically fails to realize this:

The Pilot reaches into a pocket of his flying suit and takes out a small wallet. In the wallet is a photograph. He holds the photograph out to Sarah.

PILOT: Here. My wife. Francesca. My kid. Carl. Carl. This is the Georgia State Show. See? That's Carl with Daffy Duck. Daffy Duck?

She doesn't take the picture. He puts it on the ground in front of her.

I guess you guys don't get Daffy Duck.

Sarah picks it up. She shows it to the Farmer.

FARMER: Looks like Daffy Duck. (11–12)

Greig's Pilot seems equally blind to the surprising—almost suspicious—resemblance between these non-Western others and our own Western selves. All the local characters, except for the anonymous Farmer, Trader and Captain, have English names or diminutives; during the interrogation scene, Evie enters carrying tea and cake on a tray, and towards the end of the play her father celebrates the American pilot's imminent release by offering him whisky. In the light of the accomplished fact of this cultural annexation, the strenuous military resistance that the rebels are opposing to American imperialism becomes loaded with irony, and this paradox is cleverly underscored by Greig's anglicization of the natives' foreign language. Evie's efforts at interlingual negotiation, which we must assume to be actually happening within the world of scenic fiction, are completely redundant on the extra-scenic axis of communication. Though the participants in the conversation are blind to this, language difference has already vanished from the picture and the global spread of English has made translation obsolete. The ultimate effect of Greig's monolingual representation of intercultural exchange is to root translation failure in sameness, rather than difference; more precisely, in a unilateral, non-dialectical process of assimilation that has never involved a reciprocal negotiation of meanings and identities.

Once the translation effort is taken over by the play's official language worker, Matthew, this condition of communicative pathology is more explicitly placed in the context of the new forms of war and diagnosed as a symptom of their 'totalitarian dramaturgy', to again quote Virilio's definition. When he acts in his alleged capacity, Matthew produces translations that are flauntingly perfunctory: as he knows well, mutual understanding is simply beside the point in a situation of utter power imbalance, in a war so asymmetrical that antagonism (and the potential for dialectic and negotiation it entails) has been replaced by the 'Shock and Awe' inflicted upon the powerless by the overwhelmingly powerful. Similarly, from the interrogation scene it is quite clear that the Captain avails himself of Matthew's services out of homage to routine, rather than faith in any possible strategic advantages to be gained by communicating with the American prisoner. The war-weary rebel leader has long ago realized that their cause is doomed and that 'Nothing we can do will make any difference to our fate' (32); to him, effective interlingual communication is not an unattainable goal in itself as much as a pointless endeavour under current arrangements:

TRANSLATOR: He won't talk.
CAPTAIN: Of course he won't talk.
TRANSLATOR: Maybe we should torture him. Make him talk.
CAPTAIN: What could he possibly say?
TRANSLATOR: I don't know. What he's doing here. What they're up to.
CAPTAIN: We wouldn't understand.
TRANSLATOR: We're not fools.
CAPTAIN: Whatever information he has will make no sense to us. Because it doesn't refer to us. The information he has is about another world.
He wouldn't even understand our questions. We may as well interrogate a word about the meaning of a sentence. (31)

Through the Captain's metalinguistic commentary, the problem of the non-dialogical, non-conflictive nature of the current model of belligerence is reframed as a condition of radical nontranslatability. The incommensurability between the conflicting parties does not so much preclude the transfer of meaning across linguistic barriers as render it void, since the process fails to produce a mutually transformative intersubjective relation. Later on in the scene, when the Captain contemplates the possibility of at least negotiating a ransom for the hostage, it becomes Matthew's turn to promptly remind him that 'America never negotiates … It is not rational for an elephant to bargain with an ant' (33). The Captain's residual belief in the 'communicative rationality' that Habermas sees as a universal pragmatic feature of human interaction ('Everyone in the world makes bargains. It's rational to make bargains', 33) is voiced only to be instantly belied by the total lack of reciprocity that governs their exchange.

In this context, the violence that Greig's combat translator inflicts upon the helpless American prisoner loses its more immediate retaliatory meaning to become instead a plea for mutual perspective-taking, something approaching the 'call to interdependency' and the 'move towards the recognition of a generalized condition of precariousness' advocated by Judith Butler in *Frames of War*.[67] In a monologue addressed to the audience, Matthew admits that hurting the pilot afforded him a momentary release from the clutches of grief because, through the violence perpetrated on the body of the helpless hostage, a connection was suddenly established with Belle, his beloved bride-to-be who 'evaporated' (44) when an American missile hit their wedding party. When we actually watch the Translator stab the Pilot's wounded leg, in preparation for the intended beheading—'I wanted to see if I could bring myself to do it' (56), he explains when the Captain re-enters—this act of gratuitous cruelty is preceded by a frantic entreaty that his American interlocutor may for once relinquish his stubborn monoglottism so they can swap positions and contribute in equal measure to the translation effort: 'You try translating these thoughts. I have to translate your thoughts into my language. I would like you to translate my thoughts into your language.' (55) In this way, Greig's obliteration of interlingual negotiation from his dramaturgy of translation does more than provide an eloquent formal analogue for asymmetrical warfare; it also ironically denaturalizes the notion of nontranslatability as deriving from intractable differences between languages and cultures, pointing instead to its rootedness in power relations and the political violence that sustains them.

The historically-contingent nature of the communicative pathology denounced in Greig's war play is further underscored through the particular vantage point from which the Self/Other opposition is articulated. At the same time as it is exposed as unfeasible in the domain of the real, the reversibility of standpoints that Matthew longs for is peremptorily effected by Greig through an exercise of authorial sovereignty over the fictive conflict dramatized in the play and the formal construction that mediates it. As in Packer's *Betrayed*, in *The American Pilot* we look at contemporary conflict from the point of view of its non-Western actors; unlike what happens in Packer's semi-documentary account of the Iraq war, however, the reversal of perspective here is also embedded in the construction and presentation of the characters' identities. In *Betrayed* the promotion of the Iraqi interpreters to the rank of fully-rounded characters does not detract from the complexity and depth of their American co-protagonist, the humane, sympathetic Embassy officer Bill Prescott; by contrast, in *The American Pilot* the adoption of a non-Western vantage point involves a parallel downgrading of the Western subject to the status of a flattened, reified Other. Greig expressly denotes this radical shift in perspective as a reaction to a prior and prevailing form of mistranslation typified by our perception of the Iraq war:

> Americans are allowed to have stories and lives and complex characters whereas the three thousand Iraqis dying every month in that horrible war are presented as numbers or, at best, uncomplex ciphers 'SUNNI' or 'INSURGENT' or 'VICTIM'

> or 'WARLORD'. All my play tried to do was restore to those people we routinely label their stories, and to place the American in the position of 'THE AMERICAN'. I do not do this to punish the American character, or even to make some easy point about 'see how you like it'. I do it because labeling is what we do to THE OTHER. I wanted to examine that process and see how complex it is.[68]

The principal device whereby Greig returns to the villagers their individuality is by allotting them a diegetic space for direct communication with the audience, a privilege which is instead resolutely denied to the Pilot. The play opens with a monologue by the Farmer and every now and then the action is suspended to allow all of the main characters to take turns at sharing their thoughts, impressions and back-stories with the offstage witnesses to their predicament. As we gradually realize that with the exception of Sarah, the Farmer's wife, and Evie, his daughter, the other speakers are looking back upon the dramatized events from a post-mortem elsewhere, their monologues acquire an added emotional edge that further intensifies the intimacy created through the heightening of the extra-scenic axis of communication. Clare Wallace observes that in the RSC production at Stratford's The Other Place, the rupture of naturalism was further accentuated by the lack of scenery and the fact that the entire cast remained on stage throughout the performance.[69]

But even when the local characters interact in the mimetic mode, their dialogues grant us access to a depth of motive and feeling that we hardly ever glimpse about the Pilot. For once in charge of the narrative, the rebels are able to tell us about the political antecedents of their armed struggle—the usual pattern of a democratic experiment in socialism brutally crushed by a US-orchestrated regime change—and we become acquainted with their personal history of suffering and loss. We learn for instance that the Captain's entire family, including his daughter Belle, was exterminated by an American missile: the bonds of comradeship and trust between himself and the Translator have been cemented by a shared burden of pain. We understand that Matthew's resentment towards America is rooted in unrequited love: as he explains to the Farmer's assembled family, the melancholic, bespectacled poetry-lover who doubles as a reluctant torturer was awarded a scholarship to travel to the United States as a young student, and he still has to overcome his infatuation with 'the most perfect society in the world' (48). The Translator in *The American Pilot*, then, shares with Packer's 'Iraqis who trusted America the most' the sense of betrayal of the disenfranchised; the anger of these 'terrorists' (33), Greig further suggests, stems from a position that is to some extent shared by the rest of the non-American world:

> I am like the villagers in the play, not American but steeped in the culture of America ... This land is our land. This is particularly true in the Middle East, by the way. Which is why, of course, young men feel so particularly humiliated by America's rejection of them. This is the predicament of the Translator in *The American Pilot*.[70]

By contrast, the Pilot's deliberate othering inhibits our imaginative adoption of his perspective. Apart from the little we can infer from his observable behaviour, the character of 'the American' is presented through the eyes and words of others and thereby systematically subjected to a process of translation. The majority of the villagers agree about the Pilot's almost extraterrestrial beauty, but apart from this shared impression each one of them attaches a different meaning to his presence there, arbitrarily moulding his identity according to their individual needs and wishes. Though not entirely ghosted like the Iraqi interpreter in *Black Watch*, or the ineffable Anne in Crimp's *Attempts on her Life*, the human subjectivity of Greig's Pilot emanates less from the character's own words and actions than from a prism of exogenous impressions and refractions which escape his control.

With this tactical reversal of standpoints, *The American Pilot* estranges the metaphorical translatedness that defines the condition of the Other in the fictional world of the play. The dehumanizing effects of this process of othering are then placed in parallel with the more literal forms of mistranslation that are widely employed in the contemporary theatre of war in order to justify and legitimize political violence. When the leader of the resistance expresses his misgivings about the potential association with terrorists if they go ahead with the gruesome execution of the hostage, the Translator replies that in the world's eyes their translation into the category of 'terrorists' is already an accomplished fact; hence, though the Captain may still like to think of himself as a soldier rather than a terrorist, it is no longer in his power to determine his own identity (33). This linguistic shaping of the insurgents' identity powerfully resonates with the Jessica Lynch trope that is evoked through the Pilot's story: a tale of heroism in which a select group of Special Operations troops face a vastly outnumbering, faceless enemy in order to rescue a young and brave servicewoman from her Iraqi captors, and therefore a narrative whereby an illegal war of aggression against Iraq becomes reconfigured as defensive response.

The interrogation scene, too, draws attention to the central role assumed in the post-9/11 political arena by the 'discursive disposition of the terms adopted in the public sphere to describe terrorism and political violence',[71] and to the dire material consequences attendant upon the definition and redefinition of these semantic contours. One of the arguments that the Pilot resorts to in his attempt to convince the Captain to release him is the warning that 'he will be regarded as an enemy combatant of the United States of America and he will be treated as such if there is any contact between our forces' (30). With one of his typical breaches of professional duty, Matthew does not bother to translate the threat because, as he explains to the American prisoner, his commander has already been dubbed an 'enemy combatant' and thereby linguistically consigned to the permanent state of exception of the war on terror. In the new world order, as *The American Pilot* eloquently reminds us, a unilateral act of lexical transfer can arbitrarily conjure up a space of legalized lawlessness in which individuals are stripped of their fundamental human rights: the overlap between asymmetrical warfare and asymmetrical translation could not be more complete.

Uncanny bodies

I cannot think of a better way of concluding this account of the translation turn in contemporary war drama than through a discussion of Tony Kushner's *Homebody/Kabul*, a play that exploits to the full the meaning-making potential of translation as a metaphorical and formal equivalent of contemporary conflict, and at the same time seizes on the epistemological possibilities of war as a limit-situation in which fundamental questions can be raised about the contradictory, and possibly irreconcilable, drives that inhere all human endeavours at bridging interpersonal and intercultural divides. Translation in its multiple facets and manifestations provides Kushner with the main conceptual lens through which the experience of war is apprehended and embodied on stage; yet the various forms of translation that permeate each and every level of the play—from the thematic to the formal and dramaturgical—are invariably marked by failure and haunted and the ever-present counterpoint of radical incommensurability and untranslatability. As will be shown, this scepticism concerning the capability of translation to provide authentic and transformative contact with difference also extends to author's reliability as an intercultural mediator and to theatre as a medium for addressing and understanding conflict.

Issues of translation, war and conflict are already woven into the production history of *Homebody/Kabul*, a work marked by an outstanding record of subsequent retranslations and reconfigurations with each different context of reception. The play was originally written by the New York-based dramatist as a solo piece for British actress, Kika Markham. This shorter version, directed by David Esbjorson and featuring Markham in the title role, premiered at London's Chelsea

Centre in July 1999. In an uninterrupted monologue lasting over one hour, the self-styled 'Homebody', sitting in an ornate high-backed chair near a lamp-lit table in her cosy London home, alternates between reading and commenting excerpts from an outdated historical guide to Afghanistan, and sharing with the audience the meandering, digressive, intimate tale of her own personal encounter with Eastern Otherness. The connections between the two narratives begin to emerge only as this unhappily married, middle-class housewife and book addict eventually gets round to recounting the jagged story of her trip to an Afghan junk shop in search of hats for a party. In the story, the shocking sight of the shopkeeper's mutilated hand, which bears an uncanny resemblance to the map of Afghanistan,[72] sparks off the woman's fantasy of being led by the stranger on a guided tour through the ruins of modern-day Kabul and making love with him in the gardens of Babur Shah. The Homebody's daydream of a mutually transformative, regenerative intercourse between East and West, London and Kabul ('We kiss, his breath is very bitter, he places his hand inside me, it seems to me his whole hand inside me, and it seems to me a whole hand'), is then abruptly and bathetically interrupted by the grim reality of the transaction—the signing of the credit card receipt, the handing of the carrier-bag stuffed with the purchased goods. The narrative ends with the woman hurrying back to the safe haven of her home, to her 'culpable shore' of passive and vicarious witnessing to other people's suffering (26–27).

The Homebody's monologue was subsequently expanded by Kushner into a full-length play through the addition of a Kabul part (Act One, Scene Two, and the whole of Acts Two and Three), where the light turns onto the Homebody's baffled husband, Milton, and her estranged daughter Priscilla. When Kushner's protagonist goes missing in Afghanistan, Priscilla angrily refuses to believe the Taliban authorities' story of her brutal killing at the hands of an infuriated mob and begins to roam the dangerous streets of Kabul in order to find her mother. Priscilla's suspicions seem confirmed when Khwaja, who acts as her local guide and interpreter, introduces her to a hat seller called Zai Garshi, who tells her that the Homebody has converted to Islam and is about to marry a wealthy Afghan man. According to the message he carries, is it the Homebody's wish to swap places with Mahala, the man's first wife. Mahala, he explains, has been driven crazy by the endless succession of wars and by the hardships imposed on Afghan women by the Taliban, and the Homebody is now entrusting Priscilla and Milton to take her back to London with them. Whereas the truth about the Homebody's fate will remain shrouded in mystery, the final scene shows Mahala dressed like a modern English woman and looking quite at home in the exact same London interior of the opening monologue.

This expanded version of *Homebody/Kabul* premiered at New York's Theatre Workshop in December 2001, under Declan Donnellan's direction and with Linda Emond in the role of the Homebody. Though written before the attacks on the World Trade Center and explicitly set in 1998, at the time of President Clinton's bombing of suspected terrorist training camps in Afghanistan, the new context of reception immediately turned Kushner's work into a paradoxical 'post-September 11 play written before September 11'.[73] Remarks about the prophetic quality of Mahala's line on the Taliban's imminent storming of New York (83) featured in almost every review of the play—as Kushner amusedly observes in the Afterword, the phrase 'eerily prescient' was 'repeated so often that my boyfriend Mark suggested I adopt it as a drag name: Eara Lee Prescient' (146). While it is hard to disagree with the author's remark that no extraordinary powers of divination were needed to foresee an imminent retaliation for America's foreign policy in the Middle East, it is all the same undeniable that after 9/11 the connection made in the play between the West's proclivity for mistranslating the East and the risk of a formidable retort had been forcefully proven. The timeliness of Kushner's take on the war/translation nexus became again apparent when a heavily revised version of *Homebody/Kabul* premiered at the Brooklyn Academy of Music in May 2004, amidst the still ongoing war in Afghanistan, the recent occupation of Iraq, and the worldwide circulation of the chilling images of the violence and humiliation inflicted on Iraqi detainees at Abu Ghraib by the Western champions of democracy.[74]

When Donnellan's 2001 New York production transferred to London in May 2002, with Kika Markham resuming the Homebody's role, another dimension of conflict came to the fore, one that this time more directly concerned Kushner's legitimacy and competence as a cultural translator addressing 'a British audience watching an American writer writing British characters'.[75] This anxiety about cross-oceanic translation and translatability is to some extent self-ironically woven into the Kabul part of the play, where the English characters are constantly in danger of being mistaken for Americans, with potentially deadly consequences. While the Afghan characters' tendency to conflate America and Britain is expressly presented as a consequence of the latter's political subservience to its overmighty transatlantic cousin, the parallel inability displayed by Kushner's stage Westerners to discriminate between the different languages spoken in Afghanistan and the correspondent ethnic groups is ascribed to ignorance concerning the country's history and culture. For its part, this glaring informational deficit also inevitably casts doubt on the accuracy of the play's own account of Eastern difference.

But Kushner's debatable credentials as a cultural interpreter are also foregrounded through the way the play advertises its author's forced reliance on a number of other translators, both linguistic and cultural, to compensate for his limited base of knowledge. The published text acknowledges the collaboration of a number of linguists who turned the dramatist's monoglot text into the Babel of languages resonating on stage—Dari, Pashtu, Russian, French, German, Arabic and Esperanto, often coexisting within the same turn of speech—and likewise credits an assortment of other intermediaries who assisted with their terminological expertise in medicine and computer engineering, or shared their first-hand knowledge of Afghan matters, thereby supplementing the historical and cultural wisdom drawn from the books listed in the credit information. By openly declaring his dependence upon secondary sources, Kushner aligns himself with his fictional cultural translator, the Homebody, for whom books are the only point of contact with Otherness, and with whom he confesses to share a passion for the obsolete and unashamedly Orientalist *Historical Guide to Kabul*. To this particular book, written by Nancy Hatch Dupree in the 1960s, the play owes not only a considerable amount of lines but also, admittedly, its initial inspiration.[76] Akin to what happens to the Homebody, the guide triggered in Kushner a sharp desire for a more intimate contact with Eastern difference, while at the same time heightening his awareness of the attendant snares of 'narcissism and self-referentiality' (144); through this invited identification with the Homebody, the author of *Homebody/Kabul* lays bare his questionable competence, as a New York-born-and-bred Jewish-American who admittedly never set foot in Afghanistan, to offer an accurate cultural interpretation of Eastern foreignness through his fictional recreation.

The ironic counterpart to this self-deconstructing plea of guilty on the part of the playwright as a cultural translator is his unashamed reliance on translation as a structuring formal principle. As signalled by the slash in the title, Kushner's *Homebody/Kabul* is structured around division, disjunction, dichotomy. The Kabul sequel to the Homebody's monologue does not show, as one might expect, the woman's journey to a much-coveted Orient, but opens instead with a minute and ghastly description of the Homebody's mangled body by the doctor who allegedly performed the autopsy before her corpse went missing over a long row of hospital transfers amidst the chaos of war-ravaged Afghanistan. After holding the scene for a good hour and a half, Kushner's protagonist has quite literally gone lost in translation, her dismemberment and disappearance bearing witness to the violence and intensity of the dislocation she has experienced.

The vanishing of the play's central character up to that point is counterbalanced by the crucial mediating function that translation performs at the dramaturgical level. Both as a theme and as an activity carried out on stage, translation creates a strong link between the two otherwise disjointed parts of *Homebody/Kabul*. Though this may not be immediately apparent, the Homebody's monologue prefigures the forms and modes of translation—whether interlingual, intralingual, or intersemiotic—that are practiced or discussed in the subsequent Kabul part. Already inside the initial London section, moreover, translation provides the *trait d'union* between the two ostensibly discrete, and to some extent competing, discourses that are alternatively delivered across the Homebody's monologic and monolingual solo performance.

The bipartite nature of the Homebody's narrative is established since the very onset of her monologue, which constantly veers between the public, socio-political, factual history of Afghanistan taken from Dupree's guidebook, and the speaker's confessional life story in the subjective mode. The Homebody's autobiographical account fails to translate her thoughts into a linear narrative, and develops circuitously and digressively towards its long-delayed resolution; by contrast, Dupree's short history of Afghanistan proceeds at a steadfast pace, moving teleologically from 'the very dawn of history, circa 3,000 B.C.' (9) up to the present, through an orderly succession of invasions, wars, violent dislocations. The language used by the Homebody to tell the tale of her personal encounter with Afghanistan tumbles over itself as it strives for accuracy, piling gloss upon gloss, detail upon detail, synonym upon synonym; Dupree's historical overview, on the contrary, is related in the objective tone of positivist grand narratives, firmly rooting its accuracy in a solid architecture of facts, dates, places and names. The difference and dissonance between the two voices is further enhanced by the fact that narrative shifts are governed by no discernible causal link, whether logical or even merely associative.

The connections underneath the seemingly conflicting yarns begin to emerge only gradually, as it becomes clear that the Homebody, too, is acting as a cultural translator for a Western audience just like the guidebook she is reading from, and that her approach is only deceitfully antithetical to the one adopted by her predecessor. On more than one occasion during the monologue Kushner has the Homebody comment on the dubious accuracy of Dupree's history of Afghanistan, thereby inviting comparison with her own strategies of translation. Initially ascribed to its obsoleteness, the fallacy—and with it the enduring appeal—of Dupree's history of Afghanistan is eventually traced to the Orientalism implied in its domesticating stance. The guidebook's tendency to 'translat[e] a strange terrain in familiar language to make it legible for the curious traveller embarking on a voyage to Kabul'[77] would appear to be quite the opposite of the Homebody's elusive, convoluted, idiosyncratic manner of storytelling. On closer scrutiny, however, her translation practice turns out to be just as mired in self-referentiality. Obsessed with accurate intersemiotic translation, unremittingly bent on making her thoughts, impressions, insights and fantasies accessible to her audience, the Homebody struggles to pin down meaning by clarifying, specifying, paraphrasing, synonymising; yet as she does so, words breed more words, meanings proliferate, and language almost takes on a life of its own. In a kind of vicious circle, the Homebody's awareness of being in dire need of interpretation, testified by her repeated apologies and recurrent metalinguistic comments, turns her narrative performance into a feat of intralingual translation that further increases the narrative drift of the text and the Babelian quality of its language.

In its attempt at bridging the gap between the foreign and the familiar, translation is systematically shown to breed discordance, rather than appease it. This contradiction is best epitomized by the Homebody's imagined performance as an interpreter for the Afghan shopkeeper. Moved by her empathy for his maimed hand, the narrator translates the man's silence into a long harangue in which the story of his mutilated limb and the story of his conflict-ridden country are told through a cacophony of antinomies:

> I was with the Mujahideen, and the Russians did this. I was with the Mujahideen, and an enemy faction of Mujahideen did this. I was with the Russians, I was known to have assisted the Russians. [...] *Look, look at my country, look at my Kabul, my city, what is left of my city? The streets are as bare as the mountains now, the buildings are as ragged as mountains and as bare and empty of life, there is no life here only fear, we do not live in the buildings now, we live in terror in the cellars in the caves in the mountains, only God can save us now, only order can save us now, only God's Law harsh and strictly administered can save us now, only the Department for the Promotion of Virtue and the Prevention of Vice can save us now, only terror can save us from ruin, only neverending war, save us from terror and neverending war, save my wife they are stoning my wife, they are chasing her with sticks, save my wife save my daughter from punishment by God, save us from God, from war, from exile, from oil exploration, from no oil exploration, from the West, from the children with rifles, carrying stones, only children with rifles, carrying stones, can save us now.* You will never understand ... (23; original emphasis)

By presenting cultural differences as not only irreducible, but also intractable, the embedded monologue of the Afghan shopkeeper seems to rule out the possibility that translation may open up a space for meaningful dialogue and mutual understanding. With a further ironic twist, however, even the radically foreignizing stance of the fictional translator who delivers the monologue is ultimately inscribed within a discourse of Orientalism. The Homebody's feat of ventriloquism reads as just another instance of the West's deep-ingrained habit of fabricating the Eastern subject in its own image: though the vicarious speech is allegedly triggered by the narrator's Pentecostal claim that all of a sudden she is 'able to speak perfect Pushtu' (23), the silent Other is typically rendered through an English voice; hence, the radical aporia that informs the Afghan man's language is as much a symptom of the Homebody's genuine desire for a more authentic encounter with alterity as a projection of her own wounded, disjointed psyche.

The inadequacies of the Homebody's translation strategy are made manifest in the rude awakening from the romantic reverie that follows the shopkeeper's imagined monologue. From the flocks of pigeons and festive kites 'on the heights of Bemaru' (23), sanctioning the consummation of a remedial intimacy between East and West, we are abruptly brought back to the grim reality of the mutilated hand passing over the receipt of the Homebody's 'Master' Card in the London ethnic shop. Unsurprisingly, the Homebody's translation has failed to make the healing real, and East/West relations are back to business as usual. Still, it is the ensuing frustration that triggers the Homebody's decision to leave the safety zone of her own home, nation and culture in order to encounter Afghanistan on its own ground and on its own terms. The radical, irreversible transformation that the protagonist's unhoming entails is anticipated, in the monologue, by the narrative shift to the third person: for all its narcissistic premises, impersonation has allowed the translator to see herself from the standpoint of the Other, and now her own identity has become, as it were, foreign to itself. As far as the Homebody's stance is concerned, then, domestication and foreignization, self-referentiality and self-effacement, are presented not so much as alternative strategies, but rather as two concomitant, clashing drives that are inherent in every act of translation. In the Kabul part of the play, where the conflictive nature of intercultural and interlingual negotiation is explored against a background of fully-blown violence and war, this fundamental paradox acquires a distinctly political relevance—one which arguably became all the more evident in the post-9/11 context of reception, when the struggle to find a model of intercultural communication that would enable contact without erasing difference had taken on a special urgency.

With its focus on the disruptive consequences of the Homebody's translation to Afghanistan, and on the actual interlingual negotiations performed by the other displaced Westerners in war-torn Kabul, the second part of Kushner's play establishes a more direct connection between translation and various forms of violent conflict. The shocking transition from the sensuous, evocative description of Kabul by the Persian poet Sa'ib-I-Tabrizi, recited by the Homebody as she prepares to depart, to the chilling scientific rigour of Doctor Qari Shah's post-mortem that leads us into the following scene, is a powerful way of alerting the audience to the fact that translation can be a dangerous affair, especially when it occurs in a war zone. Whether the Homebody has actually been torn to pieces by fundamentalists while seeking to locate the grave of Cain unshielded by a burqa, or whether she has willingly shed her former Western self in order to become a submissive Afghan wife, this radical effacement of the translating/translated subject is a far cry from the protagonist's earlier fantasy of cross-fertilization. This ambivalence is sustained through to the 'Periplum' scene which closes the play, at once evoking and subverting the familiar literary motif of the journey of self-discovery through contact with the Other, a 'trip to a far-away place in order to come "home"'[78] such as the one articulated, most evidently, in David Hare's testimonial play *Via Dolorosa*. As we have seen, Hare's pilgrimage to the Holy Land confers maximum visibility on his authorial and performative persona, and this in turn provides a powerful validating mechanism for the writer's particular political interpretation of the Israeli-Palestinian conflict. By contrast, in *Homebody/Kabul* the encounter with alterity entails a complete and irreversible loss of self on the translator's part, and therefore a resolute denial of the testimonial status to which she might aspire through her unhoming.

The opening moments of the Kabul section are a brilliant illustration of the violent subtext of translation and its liability to backfire. On the one hand, the text motivates the shocking—and, according to the Mullah, unprecedented—violence perpetrated upon the imprudent visitor as a consequence of growing anti-Western hatred among the population of Kabul after the civilian bloodshed caused by President Clinton's bombings in 1998. On a more symbolic level, the alleged lynching could be seen as a nemesis of sorts for the Homebody's unauthorized reconstruction of the silent shopkeeper's story, considering that her imagined biography likewise featured a wife being chased with sticks and stoned to death. At the same time, however, this eerie coincidence subtracts from the credibility of both accounts of the Homebody's fate—death by lynching or metamorphosis into an observant Muslim wife. In the end, the one single piece of reliable evidence that is allowed to emerge from this cognitive muddle is that as soon as she is transferred to Afghanistan, Kushner's translator vanishes and becomes instantly reincarnated into verbal representations that erase the woman's self through the very act of rendering it. In the autopsy monologue, Doctor Qari Shah's accurate but admittedly 'impenetrable' (35) technical jargon—ironically acquired in his days as a medical student in Edinburgh—obfuscates the material evidence of the woman's dismembered body through the objectifying and distancing effect of the scientist's gaze:

> The conoid tubercle of the left clavicle was found to have been traumatically separated from the conacoid process of the left scapula following severe damage to the conoid ligament, and also the infra spinous fossa quite, ah, shattered by a heavy blow, most probably as the woman was dragged—your wife—by her upper limb, arm that is to say, up and down rubble-strewn streets over piles of bomb debris. After dislocation of the humerus from the glenohumeral joint, there was separation and consequent calamitous exsanguinations from the humeral stump. The flexori digitori sublimus and profundis of the middle three phalanges are absent and indicate ... trauma also, perhaps occurring as the wife attempted self-defense ... (31)

If it is true, as the Mullah eventually reveals, that the doctor is in fact Mahala's husband, and that the Homebody is now his new wife, then we can retrospectively construe his mistranslation as a deliberate attempt at persuading the Englishwoman's family to give up the search. It is however equally possible that the doctor in the opening scene is simply appealing to the authority of Latinate words and technical jargon in order to cover up the sheer brutality of Islamic fundamentalism and the embarrassing fact that the victim's remains have gone missing. In a more metaphorical reading, the language of autopsy could be seen as carrying associations with the work of the biographer, also a process of posthumous scrutiny with marked forensic overtones, a post-hoc attempt at intellectual closure that is strikingly at odds with the live experience it aims to capture.[79] In this respect, Kushner's dramaturgy of translation reveals an important affinity with the documentary war plays addressed earlier on in the book: by counterpointing the warmth and liveliness of the Homebody's personal, embodied testimony in the first part of the play and the rigor mortis of the doctor's presentation of her body as an exhibit, *Homebody/Kabul* similarly draws attention to the problem of the mediation of testimony, and in particular to the tension between the live and the recorded, the subjective and the objective that haunts the performance of witnessing and the 'technologies of recollection' it mobilizes.

From the point of view of the audience, the abrupt disappearance of the play's protagonist is particularly unsettling not only because Kushner, with his extraordinary gift for language, has deftly ensured that we grow fond of the Homebody's penetrating humour, witty eccentricity, and endearing frailty; even more disturbingly, the Homebody's communication strategy is obviously designed to call forth complicit empathy in her listeners: her public confessional mode, steady recourse to direct audience address, and inclusive use of 'we' all conspire to draw the audience into a secret compact with the narrator, with the occasional metadramatic commentary further underscoring the shared assumptions and conventions that regulate their conversation.

This sense of closeness, already prefigured by the guidebook's own familiarizing incipit, is established from the very beginning of the Homebody's account of her momentous trip to the hat shop:

> I am reading from an outdated guidebook about the city of Kabul. In Afghanistan. In the valleys of the Hindu Kush mountains. A guidebook to a city which as we all know, has ... undergone change ... Several months ago I was feeling low and decided to throw a party and a party needs festive hats. So I took the tube to ___________, (*She gestures; see prefatory 'Notes' above*) where there are shops full of merchandise from exotic locales, wonderful things made by people who believe, as I do not, as we do not, in magic ... (9–10)

Kushner's textual note specifies that '[w]hen the Homebody, in Act One, Scene One, refers to the street on which she found the hat shop, she doesn't mention its name; instead, where the name would fall in the sentence, she makes a wide, sweeping gesture in the air with her right hand, almost as if to say: "I know the name but I will not tell you." It is the same gesture each time.' (5) The intentional omission works throughout the monologue to heighten a sense of shared space and location between narrator and audience because the referent implied by the Homebody's ostensive gesture is a double one: their shared London habitat and the concrete scenic space in which they have gathered to listen to her story. In the second part of *Homebody/Kabul*, therefore, spectators are not only abruptly bereft of the Homebody's presence and the comfort of her diegetic mediation; through the violent opening of the first Kabul scene, the play also sends out an indirect warning to those who have collaborated, and colluded, in the Homebody's attempt at deciphering the cultural and political complexity of present-day Afghanistan.

The audience's sudden disorientation is mirrored in the predicament of the Western characters in Kabul, groping about in the dark in a country that is for them linguistically impenetrable, let alone culturally alien, and where they are completely dependent on the services of local translators and on guides of doubtable reliability. The radical reversal of the foreign/native polarities in the second part of Kushner's play makes a clean sweep of the atmosphere of cosy intimacy and commonality of values in which the Homebody has up till then performed as a cultural translator. Once the play moves to Kabul, the Afghan Other ceases to speak the same language as the Self. Moreover, if Kushner's English-speaking characters share the audience's outsider status with respect to the ethnic and linguistic diversity of their new environment, this is only in part a consequence of the dramatist's decision to flout the convention of accessibility and leave a good share of the lines in Dari, Pashtun and Arabic untranslated in performance. Interlingual translation does occasionally take place on stage—either through the mediation of an interpreter, or when Afghan speakers switch to English in order to communicate with their Western interlocutors—but it just makes things more confusing for Milton and Priscilla, who return to London still entirely ignorant about the Homebody's fate, as well as about the real intentions and identities of the Afghan people whom they have met on their quest.[80] At the end of the journey, a number of questions continue to ring in their (and the audience's) minds. Is Khwaja—Priscilla's fatherly 'fixer' and genial guide about town—really a poet, or do the papers that he has entreated her to deliver to a fellow Esperantist in Maida Vale actually contain coded military intelligence for the Northern Alliance, as according to the Taliban's allegations? Were Khwaja and Zai Garshi really trying to help Priscilla find out the truth about her mother, or were they simply exploiting her emotional vulnerability to smuggle Mahala and the 'poems' out of the country? Is Mahala an ethnic Dari, or a Pashtun like the Taliban occupiers whom she accuses of ethnic cleansing? When she first ventures out of her hotel room, at beginning of Act Two, Priscilla quickly realizes that her mother's guidebook, which she has taken along on the perilous streets of Kabul, is not only completely unreliable, but has also become difficult to read through the grille of the burqa she is now forced to wear. The symbolical opacity of the only intercultural mediator to have survived the transition from London to Kabul is complemented by the discovery that every other alternative linguistic and/or cultural guide available on site is liable to misguide: far from facilitating understanding, translation actually works to put up a smoke screen between the displaced Westerners and the intricacies of present-day Afghanistan.

Both the mystifying agency of translation and the myth of the interpreter's neutrality are blatantly exposed through the transactions performed by the other language intermediaries in the field. Through several instances of deliberate mistranslation, or selective non-translation, Kushner's dialogues direct our attention to the vested interests involved in interlingual transfer. During Priscilla's first encounter with Mahala, for example, Khwaja's real trouble in keeping pace with the woman's torrent of words forces him to provide an abridged translation which betrays his desire to mitigate the woman's invective against the Taliban regime and its one-time American supporters, arguably with a view to presenting a more acceptable picture of Afghanistan and Afghans to her Western client and potential ally. Even overwhelmingly outspoken Mahala shows a comparable reticence to translate Afghanistan's internecine conflicts once Milton has agreed to help her leave the country, as is apparent from the exchange with the Taliban guard who is detaining them:

THE GUARD: (*In Pashtun*) T'bayaday ekhpul chahdaree pah sar klay. (*You should put on your burqa.*)
MAHALA: (*In Pashtun, fierce hiss*) Moolsah! T'dah chardare pah sar kah! Kalakhar! (*Drop dead! Put on your own burqa, you shit head!*)
(*Little pause.*)
MILTON: What did he say?
MAHALA: He ask if I shall like a glass of water. I tell him I did not. He is so polite boy.
THE GUARD: (*In Pashtun*) Tamawmay mardhawyay Inglees kooneeastand. Ekhpul mah shookatah dah woowayah. (*All British men are homosexuals. Tell your boyfriend that.*)
MAHALA: (*Overlapping, in Dari*) Birow-woo dohborah saray kish'zorat day konay Pakistanee. (*Go back to the farm, Pakistani peasant.*) (120)

While the exact matter of contention remains obscure to the audience—Kushner's English translations in brackets are only accessible to the reader—Mahala's deliberate infidelities still manage to come across in performance, mostly to comic effect. But her amusing manipulation of language takes on more suspicious overtones when we find out, at the end of Act Three, that Mahala might actually be responsible for the sudden disappearance of Khwaja's 'strange language papers' (123) from Priscilla's suitcase, just before the Taliban search her belongings, and we therefore get a glimpse of the possible hidden agenda under her apparently well-meaning mitigations. In spite of the remarkable amount of translation activity being performed on stage, and indeed to a great extent *because* of it, Afghanistan remains on the whole unreadable to Western eyes. In David Greig's *The American Pilot*, language mediation is made redundant by having ostensibly interlingual communication take place within the same code; in *Homebody/Kabul*, conversely, translation proves so flawed that it becomes ultimately irrelevant and therefore equally redundant, albeit for opposed reasons.

Delving further into the war and/as translation trope, this untranslatability of Afghanistan is repeatedly associated with the country's history of violent translations: wave upon wave of migration, conquest and colonization breeding a state of permanent, endless war. Kushner explicitly defines the ensuing political chaos in linguistic terms, for instance through Milton's realization that in today's tangle of 'armies, and, and gas pipelines, licit and illicit markets, and even Islam, communism, tribes, the incommensurable interests of the West and the East, heroin, missiles, refugees', each of these conflict factors is best understood as 'a language, moving chaotically' (127). If war results from a metaphorical Babelian condition, the play argues that the reverse is also true, presenting the linguistic chaos that reigns in end-of-millennium Kabul as a *consequence* of war. This notion is brilliantly condensed in one of the prefatory quotes to the published text, a statement reported in a *New York Times* article dated 13 October 2001: amidst the rubble of a Kabul neighbourhood that had just been hit by a two-thousand-pound US bomb, while the other residents wept or wandered about in a daze, an unnamed woman revealed to the interviewer that the members of her community were 'so afraid of the attacks we have forgotten our own names and can't even understand what we are saying to each other' (8). Along the same lines, in Kushner's dialogues the shattering effect of war on subjectivity and collectivity alike is eloquently reproduced through Mahala's crazed and crazy polyglottism, an almost surreal conflation of English, French, German, Dari and Arabic mingling, and clashing, within the same turn of speech:

> The CIA posylaiet sredstva etim ubliudkam cherez Pakistan, gdie vooruzhionnyie vlasti, c'est tout les Pashtuni-wallah, sumasshedshikh i terroristov, auf die eine oder andere Art warden sie an den Tueren alle ihrer Herren erscheinen, but still Se She Ah platit im den'gi, posylaiet im oruzhiie (*The CIA sends these bastards funding through Pakistan, where the military high command, it's all Pashtuni-wallahs, these madmen and terrorists, they'll turn on their masters sooner or later, and still the U.S. pays them money and sends them guns.*) (82)

Mahala, whose former job as a librarian involved arranging and ordering linguistic artefacts, is now possessed by a language that has been infiltrated by the havoc of war; like the Homebody in the first part of the play, she has become foreign to herself, as well as to others. By the same token, Afghanistan, a translated land and hence a land of multiple conflicts, is found to be in need of translation, internally as much as externally.

The urgency of translation, and the attendant reality of translation failure, are recurrently thematized in the dialogues of the Kabul part, where a number of cross-cultural communication models are advocated only to be exposed as either irremediably utopian or intrinsically violent. This is true, for instance, of Esperanto, envisaged, as Khwaja explains, as a truly cosmopolitan idiom with 'no history, and hence no history of oppression' (65) by a Polish Jew 'who believed that until we could speak to one another in a mother tongue which draws from us our common humanity, peace will never be attained' (67). Ironically, upon his first encounter with Priscilla Khwaja tries to address her in Esperanto, but is soon forced to give up and switch to English, the only real lingua franca of the new world order. Towards the end of the play, in the scene where they are held captive by the Taliban, Milton and Mahala strive without much success to find some conversational common ground; the sudden, unexpected breakthrough in communication comes when Milton half-heartedly attempts an explanation of binary code sequencing in computer science and Mahala reacts by pointing out the similarities with the Dewey System of classification she knows so well. The paradox, of course, is that these two universal languages are based on a principle of intersemiotic translation whose efficacy fundamentally rests upon the erasure of difference—either by 'digitally reducing the unmediated slovenly complexities which exist ... analogically in space', as Milton puts it, or by changing 'knowledge ... to les fiches de reference, to numerals which ... metaphor, represent' (124), in Mahala's description of the international library classification system. Like the Homebody's Pentecostal fantasy when she ventriloquizes the Afghan shopkeeper, the universalistic assumption underlying these systems of representation is exposed as a form of linguistic and cultural cannibalism that is unable to establish a truly interactive form of contact with the Other. Each and every successful attempt at 'banish[ing] confusion' (126) by overcoming linguistic and cultural difference in *Homebody/Kabul* invariably turns out to be a one-sided affair, a way of silencing, but not transforming, conflicts.

If the author offers no easy solution to the dilemmas of interlingual and intercultural communication, the play does however seem to point to an alternative model of engaging with the 'foreign', one which would rest on a sharp awareness of difference and on the valorization of its transformative power, rather than on the belief in deep-seated structural similarities underneath surface incompatibilities, as presupposed by traditional notions of equivalence or correspondence. In *Homebody/Kabul*, this inquiry into the limits and possibilities of translation is taken onto distinctly metatheatrical ground. In its probing scrutiny of linguistic transactions as a site and metaphor of cultural and political conflict, *Homebody/Kabul* systematically foregrounds the close affinities between translation and performance as activities that involve imagining and inhabiting an alien self. This metatheatrical subtext is forcefully brought to the fore in the Homebody's narrative, where the cognitive strength of translation as a form of contact with otherness is expressly located in the corporeal experience of play-acting: more specifically, in the playful gesture of putting on a different hat, and in the tangible evidence of incommensurability that this embodied activity is able to produce.

'A party needs hats': it is this axiomatic truth, repeated like a mantra with each attempt at resuming her personal narrative, that prompts the Homebody to leave her room and set out for the Afghan junk shop. These apparently trivial gadgets she sees as crucial to another dream of conflict transformation, one which, contrary to her expectations, is eventually fulfilled:

> ... in my mind's eye I remembered quite remarkable hats, not as tall as fezzes nor yet as closely cleaving to the curve of the skull as a skullcap, but really rather pillboxy as ladies wore hats in the early '60s ... I could see these hats perched on top of the heads of the family members and friends who usually appear at my parties, lovely lovely people all of them but when we assemble we rather ... affect one another, one might even say *afflict* one another, in baleful ways and tend to dampen one another's festive spirits, there's no ... I suppose one would like something combustible at a party, something catalytic, some fizz, each element triggering transformation in all the other elements till all elements, which is to say, *guests*, are ... surprising to themselves and return home feeling less ... less certain of ... those certainties which ... *Because* of which, for example, powerful antidepressants are consumed. (14–15; original emphasis)

Hats are what a good party needs in order to become a truly interactive experience; these exotic props destabilize identities and, by so doing, facilitate contact with others with lasting beneficial effects for all those involved. Later on in the monologue, the Homebody dons one of the ten hats she has removed from the shopping bag and displayed on the table, and keeps it on until she finishes her tale of transformation—a transformation prompted, it is worth reminding, by a hat seller whose ruined hand beckons to her from a parted 'curtain' at the back of the shop (28).

The theatrical associations of hats become even more explicit in the Kabul section, where Zai Garshi, the go-between whose mediation is instrumental in the Homebody and Mahala's swapping of identities, is introduced by Khwaja as a former actor who, following the fundamentalist ban on all forms of representation, has fallen back on selling hats. Moreover, the two relics that the Taliban Mullah offers to the Homebody's bewildered family in place of the woman's vanished remains are, tellingly, three *'rough wool berets'* (36)—maybe a purchase from Zai Garshi's shop?—and Dupree's guidebook. The Homebody's legacy to her husband and daughter thus consists of these two related emblems of impersonation and translation which duly succeed in prompting sudden, unexpected transformations in their new owners: straight, rational Milton is wearing one of the Pakol hats when he reluctantly takes the first of many eager puffs at the opium pipe offered him by the British government's contact person in Kabul; while Priscilla, shortly after picking up the guidebook, begins to eerily morph into her mother, both physically and linguistically, as she embarks on retracing the Homebody's route through the city's war-torn streets.

Towards the end of her narrative, the Homebody illustrates the actual effect of the Afghan hats upon her guests:

> The hats at the party are a brilliant success. My guests adore them. They are hard to keep on the head, made for smaller people than the people we are and so they slip off, which generates amusement, and the guests exchange them while dancing, kaleidoscopic and self-effacing and I think perhaps to our surprise in some small way meltingly intimate, someone else's hat atop your head, making your scalp stiffen at the imagined strangeness ... (28)

The encounter with difference enabled by the hats would seem to replicate the same pattern that informed the Homebody's earlier translation of the Afghan shopkeeper: a fundamentally narcissistic, consumerist relationship with a tame simulacrum of Otherness. Unlike the narrator's ventriloquial fantasy, however, the material quality of the hats here turns the contact with the absent foreign subject into an embodied experience. The tangible contours of the Eastern scalps for which the hats were originally designed provoke in their Western stand-ins a physical reaction of discomfort at the perceived difference that frames the 'meltingly intimate' pleasure of self-effacement and mutual exchange. If all translation is inescapably domesticating, this form of cohabitation *in absentia* would at least seem to counter the illusion of easy relationality: the hats' intractable corporeality produces a friction that compels their new occupants to register the presence of former tenants with their competing claims to ownership; in their materially recalcitrant facticity, these props foster the perception of the inevitable and irreducible remainder in every act of cultural translation/transaction.

The epilogue to the play offers a second image of cross-cultural cohabitation, a kind of symmetrical counterpart to the Afghan hats worn by the Homebody and the party guests in the monologue section. In the closing scene, a much-changed Mahala, in Western attire, has taken abode in the Homebody's room where she is shown reading a book—the Quran in English translation, as she explains to Priscilla. The final outcome of the violent erasure of the Homebody's identity following her transfer from West to East is this visual metaphor of the doubly translated self: a foreign body in familiar clothes, attitudes, and surroundings, the reverse image of the native bodies in exotic apparel at the party. The protagonist's experience of inhabiting the space of the Other has resulted in her own space being inhabited by the Other, and the two women now co-exist in a condition that recalls Homi K. Bhabha's notion of hybridity: not 'a third term that resolves the tensions between two cultures … in a dialectical play of "recognition"' but 'always the split screen of the self and its doubling'.[81]

An embodied counterpart to the Homebody's earlier narrative of 'someone else's hat atop your head', this final image of joint tenancy also intriguingly chimes with Paul Ricoeur's view of translation as a form of 'linguistic hospitality'; indeed, it reads almost as a physicalized version of Ricoeur's notion of translation as 'the act of inhabiting the word of the Other paralleled by the act of receiving the word of the Other into one's own home'.[82] According to Ricoeur's philosophy of language, the way out of the quagmires of translation lies in embracing, rather than seeking to overcome, the irreducibility of the Self/Other pair; indeed, the very conflictive dimension that renders the task of the translator dramatic can be turned into a positive through the recognition of 'the dialogicality of the act of translating as the reasonable horizon of the desire to translate'.[83] Translators, in other words, find their reward when they give up on the adequacy of the transformed product in order to revel in the transformative relationality of the process.

The title of Kushner's epilogue seems to ascribe a precise cognitive value to the experience of 'correspondence without adhesion' theorized by Ricoeur and actualized in the play's parting image of the uncanny body of the re-translated translator. 'Periplum', a prefatory quotes informs us, is 'Pound's shorthand for a tour which takes you round then back again', a tour which is 'by definition profitable, if not in coins then in knowledge' (n.p.). At the same time, through the idyllic mood of the finale—complete with nightingales singing in the English garden that Mahala is now fondly tending—Kushner continues to remind us with scathing irony of the possibility that the only knowledge to be gained, at the end of the journey, is the knowledge of the irredeemably exploitative underside to our encounters with the Other.

The unresolved ambivalence on which the play closes reads as an epitomic attestation of the self-reflexive strain that runs through the dramaturgy of war and/as translation. Taking a similar posture to the other writers discussed above, Kushner credits translation with hermeneutic power with respect to the new modes and patterns of conflict that have come to characterize the global age, while at the same time casting his exacting critical gaze on the ethical underpinnings and actual cognitive import of this fundamental human activity. On another level, though, *Homebody/Kabul* is unique among the theatre pieces examined in this chapter because of the radical metatheatrical corollary to the dramatist's self-reflexive scrutiny of his formal conceit of choice, an added dimension that lends it a special paradigmatic value with respect to the whole body of work considered in this volume. Kushner's inquiry into the new forms of political violence is based on an understanding of the field of translation and the field of performance as essentially coterminous; as a result, the aura of suspicion that surrounds the act of crossing personal, linguistic and cultural barriers in *Homebody/Kabul* ultimately invests the very root and basis of the theatre experience: the deep-planted, insuppressible human need to put on a different hat, and the cognitive wager that drama continues to place on this unsettling contact with strangeness.

Conclusion

In an article written in 1960, more than one decade before her professional debut at the Royal Court, Caryl Churchill unabashedly voiced her discontent with the state of post-war British drama, urging her contemporaries to forgo the safety of convention and explore new formal possibilities in order to be able to address the pressing topics of their time. Theatre-makers, she reminded her future colleagues, are not bound by the limitations of science or factual knowledge and therefore stand under no obligation to 'feel, visualize and imagine cautiously'.[1] The plays considered in this book—several of them penned by Churchill herself—are a testament to the readiness of British drama to acknowledge and react to the novelty of twenty-first century warfare, and especially to the propulsive force of new, complex and seemingly intractable subjects in pushing the world of contemporary theatre forward. An exciting lack of caution is evident behind the whole range of dramatic responses to the frightening landscape of global permanent warfare charted in *Forms of Conflict*. With their steadfast commitment to explore, interrogate and stretch the boundaries of the theatrical medium, the authors discussed in this book appear to have consciously premised their endeavour to tackle the present crisis on a determination not to play it safe.

According to Churchill's early manifesto piece—one of the few explicit aesthetic statements she has given during the course of her formidable career—the theatre's political viability, its role and agency in the public sphere, are dependent on practitioners' ability and willingness to renew its formal landscape. It is beyond doubt that the new forms of conflict, especially the war on terror and Iraqi campaign, have acted as a prime motor for political drama in Britain and elsewhere, as has been generally observed in the critical literature produced over the past decade or so. To take but the more obvious case in point, the reinvention of documentary theatre in Britain and the widespread currency achieved by the new dramaturgies of the real at the turn of the millennium have been rightly hailed as a powerful demonstration of the ability of the stage to react promptly to contemporary events of crucial collective import. These new forms of documentary, 'verbatim' or testimonial drama are seen to provide a much-needed forum for public debate and—perhaps most importantly—to counter the depoliticization that has affected Western societies by rekindling theatre audiences' confidence in their individual and especially collective agency as citizens at this troubled historical juncture. More generally, major critical studies such as Jeanne Colleran's *Theatre and War* and Jenny Spencer's edited collection *Political and Protest Theatre after 9/11* bear witness to the wealth and variety of theatrical acts of 'patriotic dissent'—to borrow the latter's subtitle—that cropped up on both sides of the Atlantic in response to the political and military developments following the al-Qaeda attacks on America. In her comprehensive analysis, Colleran specifically traces this renewed political militancy to changes in the public sphere installed by the all-encompassing sweep of media, and credits the live, embodied and communal experience provided by theatre with a unique power to counter a worrying process of disenfranchisement. Even as she puts the case for the specificity of drama's critical power, however, Colleran's close reading of the plays tends to locate their political bite at the level of theme and content, rather than in the kind of theatre experience they afford and their particular terms of engagement with their audience. On the whole, Colleran's assessment of the critical and pedagogical (her own term) value of drama rests on an understanding of the stage as an accurate source of information about individual situations of conflict; accordingly, dramatists are prized for their ability to provide a nuanced, in-depth analysis of the complex issues which surround each of these situations.

While not wishing to play down the information value of the political critique enacted by contemporary war drama, this study examines the political ambitions and response capacity of new war plays from a different perspective. It gives primacy to the theatre-makers' cognitive investment in form, and looks at their contribution to an epistemology of contemporary warfare as primarily articulated through the mediating frame, more than the mediated content. The main accent, in *Forms of Conflict*, falls on the special suitability of dramatic structures and performance practices to provide a valid conceptual framework for understanding the patterns and mechanisms of today's global conflict, and on the range of formal strategies that have been expressly devised by the British stage in order to rise to this cognitive challenge. As has been argued, it is first and foremost through the formal landscapes they have envisaged that the dramatists discussed above have been able to capture with striking precision—and often with eerie prescience—the disparate facets of a shapeshifting war, while at the same time managing to bring out its underlying structural features. In sum, their utilization of dramatic construction as a heuristic device is what makes their portrayal of global permanent conflict at once symptomatic and paradigmatic.

With its focus on the correlation and reciprocity between forms of drama and the defining structural features of the new modes of warfare, the thinking presented in this book shares some theoretical ground with Julia Boll's *The New War Plays*, as is also apparent from the central role assumed by new war theory as a point of reference for our respective discussions of tendencies and developments taking place within the field of drama. But although we approach the subject from a similar angle, our accounts take diverging paths. Boll mounts an argument about the trans-historical nature of modes and models of warfare, and follows its dramaturgical reflections in the timeless characters and recursive conflict mechanisms which she sees as haunting the new war plays. The endpoint of the trajectory drawn by Boll is the discovery of ancient tropes underwriting dramatists' take on contemporary conflict, and her book appositely closes with a chapter on present-day adaptations of classical plays as providing the fullest illustration of the essentially palimpsestic structures of the new wars. By contrast, in *Forms of Conflict* I emphasize change over continuity, pursuing structural similarities along the synchronic axis rather than the diachronic one, and refocusing attention on the dialectical and even confrontational edge to the playwrights' dialogue with existing dramaturgical templates.

In order to chart the innovative artistic answers provided by the British stage to a number of concrete aesthetic problems raised by the representation of the new wars I have adopted a critical posture that consciously replicates the playwrights' rendition of global permanent warfare as, at once, phenomenally polymorphous and conceptually consistent. Accordingly, throughout my account of the diverse formal configurations engendered by the writers' engagement with a common subject I have sought to dig out some structural concerns, patterns and strategies that can be related to the paradigm shift that has been described by new war theorists. This approach has led me to register a number of significant convergences between different and sometimes apparently opposed formal approaches that are not usually acknowledged in current critical surveys of British new writing. An outstanding example in this respect is the embargo on the scenic representation of war that likewise informs dystopian fictional scenarios in the key of Caryl Churchill's *Far Away* or Sarah Kane's *Blasted* and the supposed hardline realism of the Tricycle Theatre's verbatim recreations of official inquiries; but several other not-so-evident connections have emerged from my research, such as for instance the widespread mistrust in the suitability of verbal interaction as a formal embodiment of postmodern conflict and the attendant shift towards the post-dialogic. As this study shows, this tendency is equally discernible across the entire spectrum of documentary, in the diegetic drift of postdramatic forms and—with conspicuous self-consciousness—in the plays on language mediation discussed in the final part of the book.

But the distinctive formal feature to have emerged from this account of new war drama, the common denominator that animates the whole gamut of trends, currents and approaches explored in the book, is the vibrant metatheatrical vein that runs through the considerable diversity of scenic landscapes and dramaturgical practices I have sought to catalogue, infiltrating even the strict realist orthodoxy of some documentary forms. As they have set about exploring and exploiting the cognitive and ethico-political advantages afforded by theatricality as a critical tool for understanding the recent mutations of violent conflict, British playwrights have regularly turned their gaze onto the boundaries and the strengths of theatre as an art form. In *Forms of Conflict* I do not claim that this stance is unique to the body of work examined above, or indeed limited to the field of drama: as an extreme experience that defies conceptualization and representation alike, war has historically worked to put a strain on artistic languages and conventions, prompting more or less conscious efforts to reconsider and renew the representational resources at hand. Still, it has been one of my central contentions throughout this study that the heightened self-reflexivity which connotes the new generation of British war plays should be specifically related to the 'performance turn' in contemporary warfare—to the new aesthetic challenges and ethical issues raised by the weaponization of performance in the age of global terror, and also, at the same time, to the new critical spaces that this development has opened up for the languages of the stage. Through the broad range of case studies offered for discussion I have tried to provide ample—and I hope conclusive—evidence of the process whereby the extensive overlap of the constituents of war and the constituents of performance within the current paradigm of belligerence has consistently resulted in a dramaturgy of war in which representational conflicts take primacy over the representation of conflict.

This discursive friction manifests itself, on one level, as an antagonistic stance towards mainstream narratives of war, usually taking the shape of a critical scrutiny of media-induced frames of perception and of their political and ethical underpinnings. Theatricality thus becomes a strategic vantage point from which the spectacle of contemporary warfare can be defamiliarized and held up for scrutiny, thereby enacting a form of political resistance to the regimes of visibility and invisibility that define the theatre of operations under current arrangements. But it was one of my aims in *Forms of Conflict* to move beyond this widely acknowledged aspect of the cognitive weaponry mobilized by theatre, turning the spotlight instead onto the dialectical processes instigated by the subject of war *within* the formal constructions that have been devised to mediate it. Though this process of internal contradiction may occasionally emerge as an unwitting corollary to a particular dramaturgical strategy, or as a result of the conversation that develops among the plays once they are understood as a corpus, in most cases this heightened critical self-reflexivity is an intended effect and indeed constitutes the playwrights' signature ethical and political gesture, their prime tool for positioning their addressees as the active co-participants in a pressing interpretive endeavour. Whether through an all-out problematization of the mimetic basis of stage-craft, the foregrounding of the manipulative dimension to verbatim processes, the disclosure of the simulacral status and inherent paradoxes of testimonial discourse, the radical doubts cast on the theatre's epistemological credentials as a live and embodied art form and on its ability to induce authentic and truly transformative relationality, the dramatists' distinctive way of honouring the cognitive firepower of the theatre experience has been shown to reside in an act of recognition of the inherent tensions, latent contradictions, and also potential defaults of the medium they work with.

APPENDIX

Contemporary wars on the British stage, 1991–2011: the plays

The plays are listed in chronological order by date of UK premiere. Unless otherwise indicated, this is also the date of the world premiere. Uncertain dates are given in square brackets.

This list includes both original plays and rewritings, but not restagings. For a survey and discussion of contemporary productions and adaptations of classical and Shakespearean plays, see the following: J. Boll, 'Palimpsests', in *The New War Plays: From Kane to Harris* (Basingstoke: Palgrave Macmillan, 2013); S. Soncini, 'Shakespeare va alla guerra. Conflitti contemporanei in alcune rivisitazioni sceniche del canone', in R. Ferrari and L. Giovannelli (eds), *The Complete Consort. Saggi di Anglistica in onore di Francesco Gozzi* (Pisa: Plus/Pisa University Press, 2005); S. Soncini, 'War Images/War of Images: Looking at Contemporary Conflict Through Shakespeare', *Stratagemmi—Prospettive teatrali* 24/25 (2013), pp. 85–113.

Author/Title	Date and venue of UK premiere	Warscape(s)	Notes
Harold Pinter, *The New World Order*	9 July 1991, London, Royal Court Theatre	An unspecified repressive regime; references to the First Gulf War	
Harold Pinter, *Party Time*	6 November 1991, London, Almeida Theatre	An unspecified repressive regime; references to the First Gulf War	Double billed with a revival of *Mountain Language*
Trevor Griffiths, *The Gulf Between Us*	16 January 1992, Leeds, West Yorkshire Playhouse	First Gulf War	
Howard Barker, *The Europeans: Struggles to Love*	2 February 1993, Glasgow, Tramway	Vienna in the aftermath of the 1683 Ottoman siege (references to identitarian conflict, ethnic rape)	Commissioned in 1984 by the RSC, which then turned it down; world premiere: April 1990, du Maurier Theatre Centre, Toronto, Canada
Michel Azama, *Crossfire*	24 August 1993, Edinburgh, Traverse Theatre	War atrocities, from Hiroshima to Bosnia	Original French title: *Croisades*; world premiere: Dijon, CDN, 1989
Richard Norton-Taylor and John McGrath, *Half the Picture*	15 June 1994, London, Tricycle Theatre	First Gulf War	Transcripts of the Scott Arms-to-Iraq Inquiry edited by Norton-Taylor, interpolated monologues written by John McGrath
Naomi Wallace, *In the Heart of America*	3 August 1994, London, Bush Theatre	First Gulf War	
David Greig, *Europe*	22 October 1994, Edinburgh, Traverse Theatre	New Europe, breakup of former Yugoslavia	
David Edgar, *Pentecost*	26 October 1994, Stratford, RSC (The Other Place)	New Europe, resurgence of ethnic hatred, asylum-seekers	

Author/Title	Date and venue of UK premiere	Warscape(s)	Notes
Sarah Kane, *Blasted*	17 January 1995, London, Royal Court Theatre	A hotel room in Leeds turns into a Balkan-like scenario of ethnic slaughter	
Howard Barker, *Ego in Arcadia*	[??] 1996, Huddersfield, Lawrence Batley Theatre	An Arcadian landscape infiltrated by the violence of European wars past and present (Balkan conflict)	World premiere: 10 June 1992, Siena, Dionysia World Theatre Festival
Richard Norton-Taylor (ed.), *Nuremberg*	8 May 1996, London, Tricycle Theatre	Extracts from the 1945–46 trials of leading Nazis (parallels with 1990s ethnic genocide)	Main production flanked by three 'Responses' by different writers about recent atrocities: Femi Osofisan, *Rwanda*; Keith Reddin, *Haiti;* Goran Stefanovski, *Ex-Yu*
Nicolas Kent, *Srebrenica*	10 October 1996, London, Tricycle Theatre	Bosnia (edited proceedings from the UN War Crimes Tribunal at the Hague)	
Martin Crimp, *Attempts on her Life*	7 March 1997, London, Royal Court Theatre	Ethnic cleansing, global terrorism	
Caryl Churchill, *This Is a Chair*	25 June 1997, London, Royal Court Theatre	Evokes (but does not show) the war in Bosnia	
Sarah Kane, *Cleansed*	30 April 1998, London, Royal Court Theatre	Bosnian war, ethnic cleansing	
David Hare, *Via Dolorosa*	3 September 1998, London, Royal Court Theatre	Israeli-Palestinian Conflict	
Tariq Ali, Howard Brenton, Andy de la Tour, *Collateral Damage*	19 May 1999, London, Tricycle Theatre	Kosovo, NATO bombing of Serbia	

Author/Title	Date and venue of UK premiere	Warscape(s)	Notes
Abi Morgan, *Splendour*	3 August 2000, Edinburgh, Traverse Theatre	Civil war in Eastern Europe	
Kay Adshead, *The Bogus Woman*	4 August 2000, Edinburgh, Traverse Theatre	Asylum seekers (Africa)	
Chris Thorpe, *Static*	[9] August 2000, Edinburgh, Pleasance Theatre	Balkan wars, role of media	Unpublished
Roy Smiles, *Bombing People*	24 August 2000, London, Jermyn Street Theatre	NATO bombing of Serbia	Unpublished
Caryl Churchill, *Far Away*	24 November 2000, London, Royal Court Theatre	Permanent global warfare	
Timberlake Wertenbaker, *Credible Witness*	8 February 2001, London, Royal Court Theatre	Victims of ethnic persecution seeking asylum in Britain	
Peter Whelan, *A Russian in the Woods*	21 March 2001, Stratford, RSC (The Other Place)	Cold War and resurgence of violent conflict in the New Europe	
Martin McDonagh, *The Lieutenant of Inishmore*	11 April 2001, Stratford, RSC (The Other Place)	Northern Irish conflict, global terrorism	
David Edgar, *The Prisoner's Dilemma*	11 July 2001, Stratford, RSC (The Other Place)	A composite civil war (Bosnia, Kosovo, Chechnya, Palestine, Afghanistan, Northern Ireland)	
Tony Kushner, *Homebody/Kabul*	22 May 2002, London, Young Vic	Afghanistan	World premiere: New York Theatre Workshop, 19 December 2001; an earlier one-act version premiered in London, Chelsea Centre, on 15 July 1999

Author/Title	Date and venue of UK premiere	Warscape(s)	Notes
Cecilia Parkert, *Witness*	18 July 2002, London, Gate Theatre	Survivors of ethnic conflict in the Balkans	Original Swedish title: *Vittne*; first performed in Gothenburg, Backa Teater, on 18 April 1997
Tanika Gupta, *Sanctuary*	29 July 2002, London, National Theatre Loft	Refugees (Kashmir and Rwanda)	
Gary Owen, *The Drowned World*	1 August 2002, Edinburgh, Traverse Theatre	Post-9/11 dystopia, genocide	
Chris Thorpe, *Safety*	1 August 2002, Edinburgh, Traverse Theatre	Balkan wars (role of media)	
Anne Nelson, *The Guys*	14 August 2002, Edinburgh, Lyceum	9/11 (firefighters)	First performed in New York, Flea Theatre, 4 December 2001
John McGrath, *Hyperlynx*	14 August 2002, Edinburgh, Pleasance Dome	Suicide bombing, anti-globalization movement	First performed as a one-act rehearsed reading at the 2001 Edinburgh Festival; the second act was added after 9/11
Steven Berkoff, *Requiem for Ground Zero*	17 August 2002, Edinburgh, Scotsman Assembly	9/11	
Justin Butcher, *The Madness of George Dubya*	14 January 2003, London, Theatro Technis	Iraq war (satire based on Kubrick's *Doctor Strangelove*)	Unpublished
Presnyakov Brothers, *Terrorism*	10 March 2003, London, Royal Court Theatre	Contemporary Russia, violence as the 'New Normal'	First performed in Moscow, Arts Theatre, November 2002
Naomi Wallace, *The Retreating World*	13 March 2003, London, Latchmere Theatre	Iraq war (ghost play)	Double billed with *Gifts of War*

Author/Title	Date and venue of UK premiere	Warscape(s)	Notes
Frazer Grace, *Gifts of War*	13 March 2003, London, Latchmere Theatre	Iraq war (retelling of Trojan war)	Double billed with *The Retreating World*
Julia Pascal, *Crossing Jerusalem*	13 March 2003, London, Tricycle Theatre	Israeli-Palestinian conflict (Second Intifada)	
Amber Lone, *Paradise*	20 March 2003, Birmingham, The Door (Birmingham Rep)	Recruitment of British Muslims by al-Qaeda	Unpublished
David Williams, *Warcrime*	26 March 2003, London, Theatre Underground	NATO bombing of Serbia	Unpublished
War Correspondence	7 April 2003, London, Royal Court Theatre	Iraq war	A series of short plays by Caryl Churchill (*Iraq.doc*), Martin Crimp (*Advice to Iraqi Women*), Rebecca Pritchard (*Delirium*), April De Angelis, Elyse Dodgson and Indhu Rubasingham (*Voices from Within*)
Vanessa Badham, *Capital*	22 April 2003, London, Old Red Lion Theatre	War on terror (Afghanistan, image warfare)	Part Three of *Bedtime for Bastards*, a triple bill of short plays by V. Badham
Steve Waters, *World Music*	28 May 2003, Sheffield, Crucible Theatre	Rwandan genocide	
Tariq Ali, *The Illustrious Corpse*	12 June 2003, Leicester, Haymarket Theatre	Post-9/11 British politics, war on terror	Later double-billed with *Animal* at London's Soho Theatre, September 2003
Sonja Linden, *I Have Before Me a Remarkable Document Given to Me by a Young Lady from Rwanda*	17 June 2003, London, Finborough Theatre	Refugees from Rwandan genocide	

Author/Title	Date and venue of UK premiere	Warscape(s)	Notes
Henry Adam, *The People Next Door*	11 July 2003, Edinburgh, Traverse Theatre	Post-9/11 Britain, war on terror	
Heather Raffo, *Nine Parts of Desire*	31 July 2003, Edinburgh, Traverse Theatre	Iraq war (female viewpoint)	
Adriano Shaplin, *Pugilist Specialist*	1 August 2003, Edinburgh, Pleasance Theatre	War on terror (Middle East)	
Gregory Burke, *The Straits*	1 August 2003, Edinburgh, Traverse Theatre	Falkands war (parallels with Iraq)	
Kay Adshead, *Animal*	4 September 2003, London, Soho Theatre	Post-9/11 Britain, war on terror	Double-billed with *The Illustrious Corpse*
Richard Norton-Taylor (ed.), *Justifying War: Scenes from the Hutton Inquiry*	30 October 2003, London, Tricycle Theatre	Iraq war (WMD hoax)	
Neil Labute, *The Mercy Seat*	30 October 2003, London, Almeida Theatre	9/11	First performed in New York, Theatre Row Studios, on 18 December 2002
A Royal Welcome	19 November 2003, London, Royal Court Theatre	Iraq war	Lunchtime readings of short anti-war plays on the occasion of G.W. Bush's visit to the UK: Tony Kushner, *Only We Who Guard the Mystery Shall Be Unhappy*; Caryl Churchill, *Iraq.doc*; Martin Crimp, *Advice to Iraqi Women*
Richard Bean, *The God Botherers*	21 November 2003, London, Bush Theatre	Western aid workers in a fictional African country	

Author/Title	Date and venue of UK premiere	Warscape(s)	Notes
Justin Butcher, *A Weapons Inspector Calls*	11 December 2003, London, Theatro Technis	Iraq war, WMD (satire based on J.B. Priestley's 1946 thriller)	Unpublished sequel to *The Madness of George Dubya*
Alistair Beaton, *Follow My Leader*	26 March 2004, Birmingham, Birmingham Rep	War on terror (musical satire)	
David Eldridge, *M.A.D.*	23 April 2004, London, Bush Theatre	Nuclear threat during Cold War (connected with run-up to Iraq war)	
Dennis Kelly, *Osama the Hero*	11 May 2004, London, Young Vic	Post-9/11 Britain, terror scare	Staged as part of the *Wild Lunch* series at the Young Vic Theatre; first full production: London, Hampstead Theatre, May 2005
Martin Crimp, *Cruel and Tender*	14 May 2004, London, Young Vic	War on terror (a reworking of Sophocles's *The Women of Trachis*)	
Victoria Brittain and Gillian Slovo (eds), *Guantanamo: 'Honor Bound to Defend Freedom'*	20 May 2004, London, Tricycle Theatre	War on terror (verbatim)	
Robin Soans, *The Arab-Israeli Cookbook*	10 June 2004, London, Gate Theatre	Israeli-Palestinian conflict (verbatim)	
Jonathan Lichtenstein, *The Pull of Negative Gravity*	5 August 2004, Edinburgh, Traverse Theatre	Iraq war (returning soldier)	
David Hare, *Stuff Happens*	1 September 2004, London, National Theatre (Olivier)	Iraq war (political machinations)	

Author/Title	Date and venue of UK premiere	Warscape(s)	Notes
Tim Robbins, *Embedded*	9 September 2004, London, Riverside Studios	Iraq war (complicity of American journalism)	World premiere: New York, Public Theater, 24 February 2004; unpublished
Kaite O'Reilly, *Henhouse*	21 September 2004, London, Arcola Theatre	A composite civil war (former Yugoslavia, Chechnya, Palestine and future scenarios)	
Zinnie Harris, *Midwinter*	5 October 2004, Stratford, RSC (Swan)	An unspecified never-ending war	Part of the *Midwinter—Solstice—Fall* war trilogy
Justin Butcher, *Guantanamo Baywatch*	19 October 2004, London, New Players Theatre	War on terror (satire)	Unpublished; third play in the *Dubya* trilogy
Kay Adshead, *Bites*	14 January 2005, London, Bush Theatre	War on terror (multiple locations)	
Zinnie Harris, *Solstice*	30 March 2005, Stratford, RSC (The Other Place)	Civil war, terrorism (unspecified location)	Part of the *Midwinter—Solstice—Fall* trilogy
debbie tucker green, *Stoning Mary*	1 April 2005, London, Royal Court Theatre	Child soldiers	
Richard Norton-Taylor (ed.), *Bloody Sunday: Scenes from the Saville Inquiry*	7 April 2005, London, Tricycle Theatre	Northern Ireland (relevance to the post-Iraq context)	
Alan Rickman and Katharine Viner (eds), *My Name is Rachel Corrie*	7 April 2005, London, Royal Court Theatre	Israeli-Palestinian conflict (verbatim)	
Thomas Crowe, *Photos of Religion*	21 April 2005, London, Theatre 503	Iraq (prisoner abuse, photos of torture)	In double bill with *A State of Innocence*; unpublished

Author/Title	Date and venue of UK premiere	Warscape(s)	Notes
Naomi Wallace, *A State of Innocence*	21 April 2005, London, Theatre 503	Israeli-Palestinian conflict	In double bill with *Photos of Religion*
Robin Soans, *Talking to Terrorists*	21 April 2005, Bury St Edmunds, Theatre Royal	A documentary investigation into the phenomenon of terrorism	
David Greig, *The American Pilot*	27 April 2005, Stratford, RSC (The Other Place)	An unnamed country mired in civil war (references to Afghanistan, Iraq)	
Nick Dear, *Lunch in Venice*	9 July 2005, London, National Theatre (Cottesloe)	Post-9/11 'clash of civilizations'	
Dennis Kelly, *After the End*	5 August 2005, Edinburgh, Traverse Theatre	Post-9/11 Britain, terror scare	
Davey Anderson, *Snuff*	5 August 2005, Edinburgh, Traverse Theatre	Iraq war (returning soldier)	Unpublished
Peter Morris, *Guardians*	7 August 2005, Edinburgh, Pleasance Cavern	Iraq war, weaponization of images	
Look Left, Look Right, *Yesterday Was a Weird Day*	[15] August 2005, Edinburgh, Sweet on the Grassmarket	7/7 London bombings (a collage of interviews)	Unpublished; an expanded version with added testimonies ran at London's Battersea Arts Centre during February 2006
Mark Ravenhill, *Product*	17 August 2005, Edinburgh, Traverse Theatre	Islamist terror (media narratives)	An enlarged 'World Remix' version was presented at London's Bush Theatre in January 2007

Author/Title	Date and venue of UK premiere	Warscape(s)	Notes
Edward Kemp, *5/11*	18 August 2005, Chichester, Chichester Festival Theatre	Gunpowder Plot (parallels with 7/7)	
Sonja Linden, *Crocodile Seeking Refuge*	20 September 2005, London, Lyric Hammersmith	Asylum seekers in Britain	
Ryan Craig, *What We Did to Weinstein*	21 September 2005, London, Menier Chocolate Factory	Israeli-Palestinian conflict	
Frank McGuinness, *Speaking like Magpies*	29 September 2005, Stratford, RSC (Swan)	Gunpowder Plot (parallels with 7/7)	
Nirjay Mahindru, *The Hot Zone: Individual Truth versus the Global War on Terror*	11 October 2005, London, Lyric Hammersmith	War on terror (detention of suspect terrorists)	
Stella Feehily, *O Go My Man*	12 January 2006, London, Royal Court Theatre	Darfur (returning reporter)	
Simon Stephens, *Motortown*	21 April 2006, London, Royal Court Theatre	Iraq war (returning soldier)	
J.T. Rogers, *The Overwhelming*	9 May 2006, London, National Theatre (Cottesloe)	Rwandan genocide	
Henry Adam, *Petrol Jesus Nightmare #5 (In the Time of the Messiah)*	28 July 2006, Edinburgh, Traverse Theatre	Israeli-Palestinian conflict, post-9/11 global politics	
Gregory Burke, *Black Watch*	1 August 2006, Edinburgh, Drill Hall	Iraq war	

Author/Title	Date and venue of UK premiere	Warscape(s)	Notes
Simon Levy, *What I Heard About Iraq*	2 August 2006, Edinburgh, Pleasance Courtyard	Iraq war (collage of politicians' statements)	Adapted from Eliot Weinberger's 2005 article of the same title; world premiere: Los Angeles, Fountain Theatre, 2005; unpublished
Colin Teevan, *How Many Miles to Basra?*	28 September 2006, Leeds, West Yorkshire Playhouse	Iraq war (embedded journalist)	An earlier version was broadcast on BBC Radio 3
How Long is Never? Darfur—A Response	24 October 2006, London, Tricycle Theatre	Darfur	An evening of short plays: *words words words* by Jennifer Farmer, *Silhouette* by Carlo Gebler, *Give, again?* by Lynn Nottage, *IDP* by Winsome Pinnock, *Distant Violence* by Michael Bhim, *Many Men's Wife* by Amy Evans, *Bilad al-Sudan* by Juliet Gilkes
Caryl Churchill, *Drunk Enough to Say I Love You?*	10 November 2006, London, Royal Court Theatre	Global permanent war (American militarism and the Special Relationship)	
Roy Williams, *Days of Significance*	10 January 2007, Stratford, RSC (Swan)	Iraq war (based on *Much Ado About Nothing*)	
Richard Norton-Taylor (ed.), *Called to Account: The indictment of Anthony Charles Lynton Blair for the crime of aggression against Iraq—a hearing*	19 April 2007, London, Tricycle Theatre	Iraq war (verbatim)	

Author/Title	Date and venue of UK premiere	Warscape(s)	Notes
Jonathan Holmes, *Fallujah*	1 May 2007, London, Old Truman Brewery	Iraq war (verbatim)	Unpublished
Ron Hutchinson, *Topless Mums*	23 May 2007, Bristol, Tobacco Factory	Afghanistan (media, manipulation of images)	
Hassan Abdulrazzak, *Baghdad Wedding*	21 June 2007, London, Soho Theatre	Alternates between London and war-ravaged Iraq, 1998–2005	
David Greig, *Damascus*	27 July 2007, Edinburgh, Traverse Theatre	Syria (terrorism, East vs. West)	
Clare Bayley, *The Container*	3 August 2007, Edinburgh, a container lorry	Asylum-seekers on a shipping container bound for the UK	
David Hare, *The Vertical Hour*	17 January 2008, London, Royal Court Theatre	Iraq war (conflict between pro- and anti-interventionist positions)	World premiere: 30 November 2006, New York, Music Box
Mike Bartlett, *Artefacts*	25 February 2008, London, Bush Theatre	Iraq (through the eyes of a British–Iraqi teenage girl)	
Steven Hevey, *In My Name*	25 March 2008, London, Old Red Lion Theatre	Life in a squalid East London basement on the day of the 7/7 attacks	Unpublished
Mark Ravenhill, *Shoot/Get Treasure/Repeat*	3 April 2008, London, various venues	Disparate war zones (Iraq, Afghanistan, contemporary Britain) in an epic cycle of short plays	Originally presented as a series of readings at the 2007 Edinburgh Festival Fringe ('Ravenhill for Breakfast')
Adam Brace, *Stovepipe*	1 May 2008, Halesworth, HighTide Festival (The Cut)	Post-war Iraq	

Author/Title	Date and venue of UK premiere	Warscape(s)	Notes
Stella Feehily, *Think Global, Fuck Local*	11 July 2008, London, Royal Court Theatre	Afghanistan (UN/NGO workers)	Unpublished
Zinnie Harris, *Fall*	24 July 2008, Edinburgh, Traverse Theatre	The difficult aftermath of a bloody war	Final play in the *Midwinter—Solstice—Fall* trilogy
Simon Stephens, *Pornography*	28 July 2008, Edinburgh, Traverse Theatre	7/7 terrorist attacks	World premiere: 15 June 2007, Hanover, Schauspiel Hannover
Steve Gilroy, *Motherland*	2 August 2008, Edinburgh, Underbelly	Female relatives and lovers of British soldiers sent to Iraq (verbatim)	
Sam Holcroft, *Cockroach*	23 October 2008, Edinburgh, Traverse Theatre	Schoolboys mobilizing for an unnamed, ongoing military conflict	
Caryl Churchill, *Seven Jewish Children: A Play for Gaza*	6 February 2009, London, Royal Court Theatre	Israeli-Palestinian conflict (bombing of Gaza)	
Justin Butcher and Ahmed Masoud, *Go to Gaza, Drink the Sea*	17 February 2009, London, Theatro Technis	Israeli-Palestinian conflict (bombing of Gaza)	Unpublished
David Hare, *Wall*	14 April 2009, London, Royal Court Theatre	Israeli-Palestinian conflict (building of the Israel/Palestine separation barrier)	A companion piece, *Berlin*, played at the National Theatre through March
The Great Game: Afghanistan	17 April 2009, London, Tricycle Theatre	Afghanistan (Part 1: Nineteenth-century Anglo-Afghan wars; Part 2: Soviet invasion; Part 3: post-9/11 US-led war)	Twelve short plays by different writers presented in three instalments

Author/Title	Date and venue of UK premiere	Warscape(s)	Notes
Dennis Kelly, *Orphans*	31 July 2009, Edinburgh, Traverse Theatre	War on terror (use of torture by Western democracies)	
David Greig, *Dunsinane*	10 February 2010, London, Hampstead Theatre	Invasion, regime change and peacekeeping in a sequel to *Macbeth* (parallels with Afghanistan, Iraq)	
George Packer, *Betrayed*	7 May 2010, Glasgow, Tron Theatre	Iraq war (interpreters)	World premiere: 4 February 2008, New York, Culture Project
David Greig, *Ramallah*	7 May 2010, Glasgow, Tron Theatre	Israeli-Palestinian conflict	First part of 'From the West Bank: Three Short Plays'
Moira Buffini, *Welcome to Thebes*	15 June 2010, London, National Theatre (Olivier)	A twentieth-century Thebes in the aftermath of a civil war	
Jessica Blank and Erik Jensen, *Aftermath*	8 July 2010, London, Old Vic Tunnels	Iraqi refugees in Jordan	World premiere: 15 September 2009, New York, New York Theatre Workshop
Judith Thompson, *Palace of the End*	26 October 2010, London, Arcola Theatre	Iraq war	World premiere: 12 June 2006, Los Angeles, NOHO Arts Center
Morgan Lloyd Malcolm, *Belongings*	19 May 2011, London, Hampstead Theatre	Afghanistan (returning female soldier)	
Richard Norton-Taylor (ed.), *Tactical Questioning: Scenes from the Baha Mousa Inquiry*	6 June 2011, London, Tricycle Theatre	Iraq war (treatment of suspect insurgents in detention; verbatim)	

Author/Title	Date and venue of UK premiere	Warscape(s)	Notes
Andrew Keatley, *Go to Your God Like a Soldier*	17 July 2011, London, Old Vic Tunnels	Afghanistan (working lives of British soldiers)	Unpublished
Zinnie Harris, *The Wheel*	7 August 2011, Edinburgh, Traverse Theatre	An epic journey through the warscapes of the twentieth and twenty-first centuries, up to present-day Iraq.	
Various Authors, *Our Days of Rage*	19 August 2011, London, Old Vic Tunnels	Arab spring, NATO bombing of Libya, London riots	Penned by a team of young writers for National Youth Theatre
debbie tucker green, *truth and reconciliation*	1 September 2011, London, Royal Court Theatre	The aftermath of ethnic conflict (South Africa, Rwanda, Northern Ireland, Bosnia, Zimbabwe)	
Stella Feehily, *Bang Bang Bang*	5 September 2011, Bolton, Octagon Theatre	Congolese civil war (humanitarian workers)	
Mike Bartlett, *13*	18 October 2011, London, National Theatre (Olivier)	Preventive war on Iran (protesters in London)	

Notes

Preface

1 This distinction was authoritatively argued by Mary Kaldor in her highly influential book, *New and Old Wars*, originally published in 1999 and gone through four editions in little more than a decade.

2 J. Hughes, *Performance in a Time of Terror: Critical Mimesis and the Age of Uncertainty* (Manchester: Manchester University Press, 2011), p. 15.

3 See D. Freedman and D.K. Thussu, 'Introduction: Dynamics of Media and Terrorism', in D. Freedman and D.K. Thussu (eds), *Media and Terrorism: Global Perspectives* (London: Sage, 2012).

4 Quoted in M. Schiavenza, 'France declares its own "War on Terror"', *The Atlantic*, 10 January 2015 <http://www.theatlantic.com/international/archive/2015/01/france-declares-its-own-war-on-terror/384409> [accessed 13 February 2015].

5 A. Appadurai, *Fear of Small Numbers: An Essay on the Geography of Anger* (Durham, NC: Duke University Press, 2006), p. 31.

Chapter 1: Introduction: mapping the terrain

1 A. de Benoist, 'The 20th Century Ended September 11', trans. by K. Ackermann, *Telos* 121 (2001), pp. 113–33 (p. 113).

2 M. Kaldor, *New and Old Wars: Organized Violence in a Global Era* (Cambridge: Polity Press, 1999), p. 2.

3 M. Kaldor, 'Beyond Militarism, Arms Races and Arms Control', *Social Science Research Council/After Sept. 11* (2001) <http://essays.ssrc.org/sept11/essays/kaldor_text_only.htm> [accessed 13 February 2014] (repr. in C. Calhoun,

P. Price and A. Timmer (eds), *Understanding September 11* (New York: The New Press, 2002), pp. 159–76).

4 See e.g. Retort, *Afflicted Powers: Capital and Spectacle in a New Age of War* (London and New York: Verso, 2005).

5 M. Kaldor, 'In Defence of New Wars', *Stability* 2(1):4 (2013), pp. 1–16 <http://dx.doi.org/10.5334/sta.at>.

6 No official count of Iraqi deaths between the two wars is available, but the figure has been estimated around one million people. Hunger and disease were the main cause of 'collateral damage' during the ten-year embargo, but it is worth remembering that the bombings never really ceased: Retort reports that 'between July 1997 and January 1999 alone, American aircraft flew 36,000 sorties over Iraq' (Retort, *Afflicted Powers*, p. 98).

7 De Benoist, 'September 11', p. 120.

8 Appadurai, *Fear of Small Numbers*, pp. 31–32.

9 R. Blackhurst, 'The air force men who fly drones in Afghanistan by remote control', *The Telegraph*, 24 September 2012 <http://www.telegraph.co.uk/news/uknews/defence/9552547/The-air-force-men-who-fly-drones-in-Afghanistan-by-remote-control.html> [accessed 18 February 2015].

10 'Autoimmunity: Real and Symbolic Suicides—A Dialogue with Jacques Derrida', in G. Borradori, *Philosophy in a Time of Terror: Dialogues with Jürgen Habermas and Jacques Derrida* (Chicago: University of Chicago Press, 2003), pp. 85–136 (p. 101).

11 These definitions are mentioned, along with several others, in Kaldor, *New and Old Wars*.

12 A. Asor Rosa, *La guerra. Sulle forme attuali della convivenza umana* (Turin: Einaudi, 2002), p. 67 (translation mine).

13 P. Rau, 'Introduction: Between Absence and Ubiquity—on the Meanings of the Body-at-War', in P. Rau (ed.), *Conflict, Nationhood and Corporeality in Modern Literature* (Basingstoke: Palgrave Macmillan, 2010), pp. 12–13.

14 M. Ignatieff, *Virtual War: Kosovo and Beyond* (London: Vintage, 2001), pp. 5, 163.

15 Retort, *Afflicted Powers*, p. 98. The authors are quoting from Sven Lindqvist's *A History of Bombing*.

16 T. Barkawi, *Globalization and War* (Lanham, MD: Rowman & Littlefield, 2006), p. 141.

17 The image of Islamic militancy as a disease was first used by the British Premier on 3 October 2014 during a visit to Afghanistan. While addressing troops stationed in Camp Bastion, he voiced his belief that the 'disease' of Islamic extremism would 'threaten Britain for a generation'. Since then, the characterization of fundamentalist terror as an epidemiological hazard has become a staple of Cameron's public pronouncements about the current state of affairs.

18 Barkawi, *Globalization and War*, p. 140.

19 J. Baudrillard, 'The Spirit of Terrorism', in *The Spirit of Terrorism and Other Essays*, trans. by C. Turner (London: Verso, 2003), p. 11 (original emphasis). Baudrillard's essay was written in October 2001 and originally published as 'L'esprit du terrorisme' in *Le Monde* on 2 November 2001.

20 Barkawi, *Globalization and War*, p. 142.

21 Kaldor, 'Beyond Militarism'.
22 Kaldor, 'In Defence of New Wars', p. 2.
23 Ibid., p. 13.
24 Ibid., p. 3.
25 P. Virilio, *War and Cinema: The Logistics of Perception*, trans. by Patrick Camiller (London: Verso, [1984] 2000), p. 6.
26 J. Butler, *Frames of War: When is Life Grievable?* (London: Verso, 2009), p. 1.
27 E. Scarry, *The Body in Pain: The Making and Unmaking of the World* (Oxford: Oxford University Press, 1985), p. 137. Like Butler, Scarry draws attention to the 'framing language' that manages meaning and generates legitimacy in war and remarks on its typically 'unanchored' character, i.e. its tendency to elide the material reality of physical injury and actual suffering by subsuming them into ideologically-charged abstractions.
28 'Hypertelia' is a term used by Federico Montanari in his study on war as a semiotic system: see F. Montanari, *Linguaggi della guerra* (Rome: Meltemi, 2004). Montanari connects this hypertrophic narrative dimension to Alain Joxe's denunciation of the 'chrematistics' of permanent global war, an economic analogy that draws on the Aristotelian distinction between the management of resources to satisfy natural wants (*oikonomia*), and the speculative, artificial economy when money produces money. See A. Joxe, *Empire of Disorder* (Cambridge, MA: MIT Press, 2002).
29 J. Derrida, *The Politics of Friendship* (1997), quoted in A. Feldman, 'The Structuring Enemy and Archival War', *PMLA* 124:5 (2009), Special Issue on 'War', pp. 1704–13 (pp. 1704–05). In an earlier contribution on the Cold War, Derrida tackled the process whereby the irrationality or impossibility of war in the nuclear age turned armed combat into an utterly narrative activity: 'Nuclear weaponry depends, more than any weaponry in the past, it seems, upon structures of information and communication, structures of language, including non-vocalizable language, structures of codes and graphic decoding. But the phenomenon is fabulously textual also to the extent that, for the moment, nuclear war has not taken place; one can only talk and write about it.' J. Derrida, 'No Apocalypse, Not Now (Full Speed Ahead, Seven Missiles, Seven Missives)', *Diacritics* 14:2 (1984), pp. 20–31 (p. 23).
30 N. Roger, *Image Warfare in the War on Terror* (Basingstoke: Palgrave Macmillan, 2013).
31 In *Comments on the Society of the Spectacle* (1988), Guy Debord updated his scathing critique of the mechanisms of social control in *The Society of the Spectacle* (1967) to the age of global media, pointing to the close interconnection of spectacular domination and generalized secrecy as an essential feature of the workings of power. Drawing on and partly revising Debord's perspective, Jack Bratich further developed the concept of 'spectacular secrecy' with specific reference to the post-9/11 landscape in 'Cultural Studies, Immanent War, Everyday Life', in N.K. Denzin and Y.S. Lincoln (eds), *9/11 in American Culture* (Oxford: Altamira, 2003), pp. 41–43 and then, more extensively, in 'Public Secrecy and Immanent Security: A Strategic Analysis', *Cultural Studies* 20:4–5 (2006), pp. 493–511.
32 William Leiss famously exposed the paradox whereby 'on the great issues of

society and politics, the role of knowledge in the composition of informed judgment very well may decline in proportion to the increase of available information': see W. Leiss, 'The Myth of the Information Society', in I. Angus and S. Jhally (eds), *Cultural Politics in Contemporary America* (New York: Routledge, 1989), p. 282–98 (p. 297). For some early critical analyses of the First Gulf war as a media event, see D. Kellner, *The Persian Gulf TV War* (Boulder, CO: Westview Press, 1992) and S. Jeffords and L. Rabinovitz (eds), *Seeing Through the Media: The Persian Gulf War* (New Brunswick, NJ: Rutgers University Press, 1994).

33 L. Finnegan, *No Questions Asked: News Coverage since 9/11* (Westport, CT: Praeger, 2007), p. 71.

34 The existence of the Office and the nature of its appointment were disclosed in February 2002 by the *New York Times*. According to Pentagon sources quoted in the *NYT* reportage, the tasks envisaged for the newly-created Office included the provision of 'news items, possibly even false ones, to foreign media organizations as part of a new effort to influence public sentiment and policy makers in both friendly and unfriendly countries': see J. Dao and E. Schmitt, 'A nation challenged: Hearts and minds; Pentagon readies efforts to sway sentiment abroad', *New York Times*, 19 February 2002 <http://www.nytimes.com/2001/10/07/us/a-nation-challenged-the-weapons-in-80-s-afghan-militias-used-us-rifles.html> [accessed 12 March 2015]. In 2009, the Rendon Group received a new no-bid contract from the Obama administration for the screening of journalists prior to their embedment with US troops.

35 This expression, first made popular by former US Vice President Dick Cheney in 2001, is used in the post-9/11 context to denote the condition of permanent instability installed by the threat of terrorism, systemic economic crises and global epidemics. As Bratich notes, 'The emergence of permanent and infinite war, with its unspecified enemy and immanentization of terror into everyday life, is constitutive of this New Normal' ('Public Secrecy', p. 493).

36 The exclusion of photojournalists from proximity to the front during the First Gulf War involved a sea change in the imagery of war. Whereas old conventions of photojournalism had stressed closeness to traumatic events, the aerial shots of the Kuwaiti desert in the aftermath of military operations typified a new iconography that focused instead on 'fragments, melted metal and blasted remains' as the only 'residual evidence' left of the violence of war: see Mark Holborn quoted in J. Walsh, 'Introduction: The Legacy of the Gulf War', in J. Walsh (ed.), *The Gulf War Did not Happen: Politics, Culture and Warfare post-Vietnam* (Aldershot: Arena, 1995), pp. 1–20 (p. 16).

37 G. Agamben, *State of Exception*, trans. by K. Attell (Chicago: University of Chicago Press, [2003] 2005). 'Antidemography of the discounted' is a definition I have borrowed from Feldman, 'Structuring Enemy', p. 1712.

38 Butler, *Frames of War*.

39 J. Der Derian, 'Imaging Terror: Logos, Pathos and Ethos', *Third World Quartely* 26:1 (2005), pp. 23–47 (p. 23).

40 R. Schechner, '9/11 as Avant-Garde Art?', *PMLA* 124:5 (2009), Special Issue on 'War', pp. 1820–29 (p. 1824).

41 Freedman and Thussu, 'Dynamics of Media and Terrorism', p. 10.
42 Retort, *Afflicted Powers*, p. 26.
43 As according to the description of the scene made by a correspondent reporting live from Baghdad on 9 April 2003 during Tg1, the newscast of the main channel of Italian state television. See F. Tonello, 'War of Images, Images of War', in C. Dente and S. Soncini (eds), *Conflict Zones: Actions Languages Mediations* (Pisa: ETS, 2004), pp. 103–13 (p. 107).
44 M. Ignatieff, 'The Terrorist as Auteur', *New York Times*, 14 November 2004 <http://www.nytimes.com/2004/11/14/movies/14TERROR.html?_r=0> [accessed 17 March 2015].
45 I have borrowed these observations from Branislav Jakovlievic's very helpful essay on de Jomini's classical theory and its supersession in the contemporary theatre of war (with particular reference to Bosnia): 'Theater of Atrocities: Toward a Disreality Principle', *PMLA* 124:5 (2009), Special Issue on 'War', pp. 1813–19.
46 J. Mieszkowski, 'Watching War', *PMLA* 124:5 (2009), Special Issue on 'War', pp. 1648–61 (p. 1650).
47 Mieszkowski, 'Watching War', p. 1651.
48 Rau, 'Body-at-War', p. 17.
49 R. Emig, 'A Double Disappearance Act: War and the Media', in W. Görtschacher and H. Klein (eds), *Modern War on Stage and Screen/Der moderne Krieg auf der Bühne* (Lewiston: E. Mellen, 1997), pp. 219–36 (p. 227).
50 G. Borradori, 'Fundamentalism and Terror—A Dialogue with Jürgen Habermas', in *Philosophy in a Time of Terror*, pp. 25–44 (p. 28).
51 Hughes, *Performance in a Time of Terror*, p. 9.
52 J. Colleran, *Theatre and War: Theatrical Responses since 1991* (New York: Palgrave Macmillan, 2012), pp. 17–18.
53 Stockhausen made this shocking comment at a press conference during the Hamburg music festival only six days after the attacks took place.
54 Schechner, '9/11', p. 1825.
55 For a concise overview, see S. Soncini, 'Conflict Zones: A Transdisciplinary (Battle)field', in Dente and Soncini, *Conflict Zones*, pp. 21–27. David Edgar's essay in the same collection ('Making Drama out of Conflict', pp. 31–38) focuses on drama as a metaphor and means for conflict resolution with particular regard to his 2001 play, *The Prisoner's Dilemma*.
56 D. Taylor, 'Afterword: War Play', *PMLA* 124:5 (2009), Special Issue on 'War', pp. 1886–95.
57 S. Magelssen, 'Rehearsing the "Warrior Ethos": "Theatre Immersion" and the Simulation of Theatres of War', *TRD: The Drama Review* 53:1 (2009), pp. 47–72 (pp. 63, 55). Magelssen's article provides a comprehensive survey of the performance practices employed at Fort Irwin and a probing investigation of the issues they raise. On the same subject, Carol Martin's recent book, *Theatre of the Real* (Basingstoke: Palgrave Macmillan, 2013) has an engaging chapter on war games where the case of immersive training at Fort Irwin is also considered.
58 Taylor, 'War Play', 1890.
59 J. Bell, 'Performance Studies in an Age of Terror', *TDR: The Drama Review* 47:2 (2003), pp. 6–8 (p. 7).

60 J. Baudrillard, 'The Precession of Simulacra', in *Simulacra and Simulations*, trans. by S. Faria Glaser (Ann Arbor: University of Michigan Press, [1981] 1994), pp. 1–42 (p. 31).

Chapter 2: This is not a war

1 For a very accurate survey of post-1945 war drama in Britain and a discussion of its experimental quality the reader is referred to T. Howard and J. Stokes (eds), *Acts of War. The Representation of Military Conflict on the British Stage and Television since 1945* (Aldershot: Scolar Press, 1996).

2 W. Shakespeare, *Henry V*, in *The Complete Works*, Oxford Shakespeare Series, ed. by S. Wells and G. Taylor (Oxford: Clarendon Press, 1988), Prologue, vv. 11–14.

3 K. McLoughlin, 'War and words', in K. McLoughlin (ed.), *The Cambridge Companion to War Writing* (Cambridge: Cambridge University Press, 2009), pp. 15–24 (p. 15).

4 Baudrillard, 'Precession of Simulacra', p. 31.

5 T. Englehart, 'The Gulf War as Total Television', in Jeffords and Rabinovitz, *Seeing Through the Media*, pp. 81–96 (p. 82).

6 Baudrillard, 'Spirit of Terrorism', p. 34.

7 Edgar made this remark in an article discussing the new wave of documentary drama: D. Edgar, 'Doc and Dram', *Guardian*, 27 September 2008 <http://www.theguardian.com/stage/2008/sep/27/theatre.davidedgar> [accessed 13 May 2012].

8 This cursory mention cannot even remotely claim to render justice to Kane's contemporary classic and its importance as a cornerstone of new war drama. For a protracted and insightful critical engagement with *Blasted* the reader is referred to J. Boll, *New War Plays: From Kane to Harris* (Basingstoke: Palgrave Macmillan, 2013). Steve Waters's chapter on 'Sarah Kane from Terror to Trauma', in M. Luckhurst (ed.), *A Companion to Modern British Drama 1880–2005* (Oxford: Blackwell, 2006), pp. 371–82 offers a persuasive reading of Kane's Bosnian war play as a striking prefiguration of the age of global terror. I have written about the heightened theatricality of Kane's staging of violence and its continuous slippages between reference and representation in S. Soncini, '"A horror so deep only ritual can contain it": The art of dying in the theatre of Sarah Kane', *Altre Modernità* 4 (2010), pp. 116–31 < DOI: 10.13130/2035-7680/695>.

9 I owe the distinction between a 'world-reflecting' and a 'world-creating' understanding of mimesis to Stephen Halliwell's well-known historical account of the concept in *The Aesthetics of Mimesis: Ancient Texts and Modern Problems* (Princeton: Princeton University Press, 2002). The characterization of the world-reflecting model as a way of creating presence and authenticity through metonymy is instead modelled on the mimicry/mimesis dichotomy established by Homi Bhabha's essay 'On mimicry and man: The ambivalence of colonial discourse', in *The Location of Culture* (London: Routledge, 1994), pp. 85–92.

10 For a survey of the critical literature that has been responsible for this repositioning of Aristotle's definition see C. Dente, 'Intersemiotic Complexities:

The Word of Drama', in M. Bertuccelli Papi, G. Cappelli, and S. Masi (eds), *Lexical Complexity: Theoretical Assessment and Translational Perspectives* (Pisa: Plus/Pisa University Press, 2007), pp. 261–69.

11 C. von Clausewitz, *On War*, trans. by M. Howard and P. Paret (London: David Campbell, 1993), p. 83.

12 G.W.F. Hegel, *Aesthetics. Lectures on Fine Arts*, trans. by T.M. Knox, 2 vols (Oxford: Clarendon Press, 1998), ii, p. 1159 (original emphasis).

13 See in particular *On War*, Book VI, Chapter VII ('Interaction Between Attack and Defence').

14 J. Baudrillard, *The Gulf War did not Take Place*, trans. by P. Patton (Bloomington: Indiana University Press, [1991] 1995), pp. 44–45.

15 G. Borradori, 'Dialogue with Jürgen Habermas', p. 64.

16 Borradori, *Philosophy in a Time of Terror*, p. xi.

17 K. Jürs-Munby, 'Introduction', in H.-T. Lehmann, *Postdramatic Theatre*, trans. by K. Jürs-Munby (London: Routledge, [1999] 2006), pp. 1–15 (p. 6). Jürs-Munby is paraphrasing Lyotard's exegesis of the 'post' in postmodernism.

18 The only other exception in this respect is Richard Norton-Taylor and John McGrath's documentary piece on the Arms-to-Iraq affair, *Half the Picture* (London, Tricycle Theatre, 1994).

19 T. Griffiths, *The Gulf Between Us, or, The Truth and Other Fictions* (London: Faber, 1992), p. 2. Further references to this edition are given after quotations in the text.

20 J. Colleran, 'Disposable Wars, Disappearing Acts: Theatrical Responses to the 1991 Gulf War', *Theatre Journal* 55 (2003), pp. 613–32 (p. 624).

21 N. Wallace, *In the Heart of America*, in *In the Heart of America and Other Plays* (New York: Theatre Communications Group, 2001), pp. 77–142 (p. 123). Further references to this edition are given after quotations in the text.

22 Churchill's preoccupation with international affairs is detailed in P. Roberts, *About Churchill: The Playwright and the Work* (London: Faber and Faber, 2008).

23 C. Churchill, *Seven Jewish Children: A Play for Gaza* (London: Nick Hern, 2009), p. 1. Copies of the play were made available for free download from, among others, the Royal Court web site. Performances were licensed gratis worldwide provided that no admission fee was charged and that a collection was taken at each performance for the London-based NGO Medical Aid for Palestinians.

24 In his recent survey of the British theatre scene of the 2000s, Aleks Sierz describes *Far Away* as a 'prescient' work and quotes Simon Stephens's definition of Churchill's play as 'the strongest theatrical response to 9/11': see A. Sierz, *Rewriting the Nation: British Theatre Today* (London: Methuen, 2011), p. 75. Sierz's and Stephens's perception is generally shared by reviewers of post-9/11 productions of *Far Away*: see e.g. Paul Taylor's comments on Peter Brook's revival in Paris, at the Bouffes du Nord, in January 2002: 'Peter Brook: an open brook', *The Independent*, 30 January 2002 <http://www.independent.co.uk/arts-entertainment/theatre-dance/features/peter-brook-an-open-brook-9161992.html> [accessed 23 April 2015].

25 C. Churchill, *Far Away* (London: Nick Hern, 2000), p. 14. Further references to this edition are given after quotations in the text.

26 Incidentally, hats play a prominent role in *Homebody/Kabul* (2000), Tony Kushner's equally prophetic text on the wars of the new millennium, which will be discussed in Chapter Five. Kushner's and Churchill's hats are insightfully compared in U. Chaudhury, 'Different Hats', *Theater* 33:3 (2003), pp. 132–34.

27 E. Diamond, 'On Churchill and Terror', in E. Aston and E. Diamond (eds), *The Cambridge Companion to Caryl Churchill* (Cambridge: Cambridge University Press, 2009), pp. 125–43 (p. 139).

28 Ibid., p. 141.

29 Tozer had been expressly instructed not to deliver the final sentence as if it actually were the last line of the play: see Roberts, *About Churchill*, p. 261.

30 The only exception in this respect could be Todd, who exhibits a scar from a wound to prove that he is well aware of the offensive potential of deer. However, when Harper asks him if he was attacked by a deer, Todd admits: 'In fact it was a bear. I don't like being doubted.' (34) The circumstances of the alleged attack, moreover, are left completely unspecified.

31 The statement was made during the 12 May 1996 showing of CBS's newsmagazine television programme *60 minutes*. When the host, Leslie Stahl, remarked that more children had died in Iraq because of UN sanctions than in Hiroshima, and asked her whether she considered those casualties justifiable, the US Secretary of State replied: 'I think this is a very hard choice, but the price—we think the price is worth it'. See de Benoist, 'September 11', p. 3.

32 See J. Stauber and R. Sheldon, *Toxic Sludge is Good for You! Lies, Damn Lies and the Public Relations Industry* (Monroe, ME: Common Courage Press, 1995), pp. 172–74.

33 R. Robertson, *Globalization: Social Theory and Global Culture* (London: Sage, 1992).

34 The stories featured, respectively, in *La Repubblica*, Italy's second largest-circulation daily newspaper (G. Romagnoli, 'I piccioni kamikaze del Cairo', 10 January 2003); on the Midday News of *Raidue*, the second channel of Italian state television (31 January 2003); and again in *La Repubblica* ('è scomparso Tacoma il delfino "sminatore"', 1 April 2003).

35 The terms appear respectively in the reviews of the Royal Court performance by C. Woddis in the *Herald* (6 December 2000) and R. Koenig in *The Independent* (2 December 2000), both reprinted in *Theatre Record* 20 (2000), pp. 1577–78, 1576.

36 Sierz, *Rewriting the Nation*, p. 75.

37 Baudrillard, *The Gulf War Did not Take Place*, p. 58.

38 The propagandistic and political uses of representations of the English countryside during the First World War is the subject of C. Berberich's chapter, '"Isn't This Worth Fighting For?" The First World War and the (Ab)Uses of the Pastoral Tradition', in Rau, *Conflict, Nationhood and Corporeality*, pp. 26–45.

39 C. Churchill, *Drunk Enough to Say I Love You?* (London: Nick Hern, 2006), p. 4. Further references to this edition are given after quotations in the text.

40 Roberts, *About Churchill*, pp. 269–70.

41 No stage directions are given in the published play text. My descriptions are based on press reviews of the Royal Court production and on information gathered from Roberts, *About Churchill*. A. Howe Kritzer's extended review in *Theatre Journal* 59:30 (2007), pp. 516–17 has also been extremely helpful.

42 Colleran, *Theatre and War*, p. 16.

43 A. Hoskins and B. O'Loughlin's widely-read *War and Media: The Emergence of Diffused War* (London: Polity Press, 2010) focuses on the concomitant ubiquity and intangibility of a war that is predominantly waged in and through the electronic and digital media.

44 See Diamond, 'On Churchill and Terror', pp. 126–27. Diamond sees this method for invoking the affect of terror as being operative throughout the whole of Churchill's production, where it comprises 'terror in the mundane, the swings from there to here, the proximal yet noncausal relation of desire and violence, linguistic interruption and disjunctive form' (p. 135).

45 A. Howe Kritzer, 'America as Rogue State: Caryl Churchill's *Drunk Enough to Say I Love You?*', in J. Spencer (ed.), *Political and Protest Theatre after 9/11: Patriotic Dissent* (New York: Routledge, 2012), pp. 53–62 (p. 57).

46 P. Virilio, *Strategy of Deception*, trans. by C. Turner (London: Verso, [1999] 2000), p. 77.

47 Howe Kritzer is critical of *Drunk Enough to Say I Love You?* on account of its break with the polyphony and multiplicity of perspectives that has come to be identified as the trademark of Churchill's drama: 'Throughout the play only one viewpoint is voiced—that of Sam. Guy either agrees or differs with what Sam says, but does not suggest alternatives.' ('America as Rogue State', p. 59). I see this instead as a very accurate formal embodiment of the central point the play is trying to make, about the fundamentally non-dialogical quality of contemporary warfare.

48 Caryl Churchill explained this to actors during rehearsals: see Roberts, *About Churchill*, p. 251.

49 D. Lane, *Contemporary British Drama* (Edinburgh: Edinburgh University Press, 2010), p. 49.

50 M. Crimp, *Attempts on her Life* (London: Faber and Faber, 1997), p. 60. Further references to this edition are given after quotations in the text.

51 M. Crimp, *Attempts on Her Life*, in *Plays: Two: No One Sees the Video, The Misanthrope, Attempts on Her Life, The Country* (London: Faber & Faber, 2005), p. 198. The quotation is taken from J. Baudrillard, *The Transparency of Evil. Essays on Extreme Phenomena*, trans. by J. Benedict (London and New York: Verso, [1990] 1993), p. 80.

52 See Tim Albery's description of the production in Sierz, *Theatre of Martin Crimp*, pp. 192–97.

53 Sierz, *Theatre of Martin Crimp*, p. 198.

54 In the 2005 revised script the original initial scene ('All Messages Deleted') has been cut and the play now begins with scenario '2. Tragedy of Love and Ideology'.

55 M. Ravenhill, *Product*, in *Plays 2: Mother Clap's Molly House, Product, The Cut, Citizenship, Pool (No Water)* (London: Methuen, 2008), pp. 153–78

(p. 155). Further references taken from this expanded version are given after quotations in the text.

56 P. Billingham, *At the Sharp End: Uncovering the Work of Five Contemporary Dramatists* (London: Methuen, 2007), p. 153.

57 S. Connor, *Postmodernist Culture: An Introduction to Theories of the Contemporary* (London: Basil Blackwell, 1989), p. 170.

58 A. Stanley, 'A Nation at War: The TV Watch, Lengthy Hours Magnify Strengths and Foibles', *New York Times*, 26 March 2003, Section B, p. 14.

59 M. Ravenhill quoted in M. Sawyer, 'Think of it as Bridget Jones goes Jihad', *Observer*, 31 July 2005 <http://www.theguardian.com/stage/2005/jul/31/theatre.edinburghfestival2005> [accessed 23 April 2015].

60 Billingham, *At the Sharp End*, p. 130.

61 My observations are based on the video recording of the 31 January 2007 evening performance at London's Bush Theatre, held in the V&A National Video Archive of Performance.

62 'National Theatre Education Workpack: *Attempts on Her Life*', p. 12 <http://www.nationaltheatre.org.uk/sites/all/libraries/files/documents/Attempts_bkpk.pdf> [accessed 23 April 2015].

63 I have borrowed this term from Larry Bogad's article on activist performance during the Bush administration: 'Patriot Acts: All-American Tactical Performance in the Age of Permawar', in Spencer, *Political and Protest Theatre*, pp. 191–207 (p. 204).

64 Dennis Kelly made this remark during a pre-performance talk on the occasion of the Italian premiere of the play at Milan's Teatro i on 26 April 2007.

65 D. Kelly, *After the End* (London: Oberon, 2005), p. 15.

66 B. Logan, 'One Day in July', *Guardian*, 19 June 2007 <http://www.theguardian.com/stage/2007/jun/19/theatre> [accessed 23 April 2015].

67 S. Stephens, 'Introduction', in *Plays 2: One Minute, Country Music, Motortown, Pornography, Sea Wall* (London: Methuen, 2009), p. xviii. Further references to this edition are given after quotations in the text.

68 'Playwright Simon Stephens on Pornography, 20th October 2008' (podcast), *TheatreVOICE*, <http://www.theatrevoice.com/2307/playwright-simon-stephens-on-pornography/> [accessed 19 December 2012].

69 S. Sontag, *Regarding the Pain of Others* (New York: Farrar, Straus & Giroux, 2003), p. 18.

70 'Playwright Simon Stephens on Pornography' (podcast).

71 Personal communication to author, 5 November 2012. The obituaries have now been updated and the original version which Stephens drew upon is no longer available.

72 'Playwright Simon Stephens on Pornography' (podcast).

73 Lehmann, *Postdramatic Theatre*, p. 21.

74 'Playwright Simon Stephens on Pornography' (podcast).

75 In her study on the 'no longer dramatic theatre text', Gerda Poschmann suggests the replacement of the term 'characters' with 'text bearers' for postdramatic performances in which the actors are not required to interpret the text but simply to deliver it. See *Der nicht mehr dramatische Theatertext. Aktuelle Bühnentexte und ihre dramaturgische Analyse* (1997), quoted in D. Barnett, 'When is a Play not a Drama? Two Examples of

Postdramatic Theatre Texts', *New Theatre Quarterly* 24:1 (February 2008), pp. 14–23 (p. 18).

76 The writer himself hints at this potential shrinking from dialogue to monologue when he explains, in the Introduction to his first volume of collected plays, that 'in all of the plays I've been drawn to the duologue as a means of distilling worlds. In three of them this has been distilled further into the monologue.' (xxi)

77 See E. Kuti, 'Tragic Plots from Bootle to Baghdad', *Contemporary Theatre Review* 18:4 (2008), pp. 457–69. The plays examined are Mark Ravenhill's *Shopping and Fucking*, Sarah Kane's *Blasted* and David Hare's *Stuff Happens*, and the main thrust of Kuti's argument is a deconstruction of neat categorizations such as 'in-yer-face' or 'verbatim' drama in light of the dramatists' fundamentally tragic way of ordering of events and thereby creating meaning out of them.

78 Discussing the marked disruption of linear temporality in 1990s cinema, Roger Luckhurst points to the disarticulation of the traditional linear plot of narrative film into the loop or mosaic as a typical strategy used to convey the experience of traumatized subjectivity. See R. Luckhurst, *The Trauma Question* (London: Routledge, 2008).

79 A. Cavarero, *Orrorismo, ovvero della violenza sull'inerme* (Milan: Feltrinelli, 2007).

80 D. Cavendish, review of *Pornography*, *Daily Telegraph*, 5 August 2009, in *Theatre Record* 29 (2009), Edinburgh Festival and Fringe Supplement, p. 1519. This is a review of the London transfer (Tricycle Theatre, 6–29 August 2009) of the original Edinburgh production.

81 W. Shakespeare, *As You Like It*, in *The Complete Works*, II.vii.165, 153–56.

82 'Playwright Simon Stephens on Pornography' (podcast).

Chapter 3: 'Why fabulate?'

1 D. Hare, 'Why Fabulate?', *Guardian*, 2 February 2002, Saturday Review, p. 3 (repr. in D. Hare, *Obedience, Struggle and Revolt: Lectures on Theatre* (London: Faber, 2005), pp. 64–86).

2 See on this E. Bar-Yosef, '"I'm just a pen': Travel, Performance, and Orientalism in David Hare's *Via Dolorosa* and *Acting Up*', *Theatre Journal* 59 (2007), pp. 259–77.

3 C. Marowitz, 'Let's Not Forgo Imagination for Voyeurism', *New York Times*, 29 October 2000 <http://www.nytimes.com/2000/10/29/arts/29MARO.html> [accessed 7 February 2013].

4 J. Baudrillard, 'Precession of Simulacra', pp. 6–7.

5 D. Paget, 'The "Broken Tradition" of Documentary Theatre and Its Continued Power of Endurance', in A. Forsyth and C. Megson (eds), *Get Real: Documentary Theatre Past and Present* (Basingstoke: Palgrave Macmillan, 2009), pp. 224–38.

6 D. Paget, 'Verbatim Theatre: Oral History and Documentary Techniques', *New Theatre Quarterly* 3:12 (1987), pp. 317–36. On the 'Stoke method' see P. Cheeseman, '... *on documentary theatre*', in R. Soans, *Talking to Terrorists* (London: Oberon, 2005), pp. 104–07. A helpful genealogy of documentary

theatre, charting its European as well as American ramifications, is provided in A. Favorini, 'Representation and Reality: The Case of Documentary Theatre', *Theatre Survey* 35:2 (1994), pp. 31–42.

7 J. Reinelt, 'The Promise of Documentary', in Forsyth and Megson, *Get Real*, pp. 6–23 (pp. 13–14). For the views mentioned above, see respectively S. Bottoms, 'Putting the Document into Documentary: An Unwelcome Corrective?', *TDR: The Drama Review* 50:3 (2006), pp. 56–68 and W. Hammond and D. Steward, 'Introduction', in W. Hammond and D. Steward (eds), *Verbatim Verbatim: Contemporary documentary theatre* (London: Oberon, 2008), pp. 7–13 (p. 9).

8 See C. Innes, 'Towards a Post-Millennial Mainstream? Documents of the Times', *Modern Drama* 50 (2007), pp. 435–52 (p. 436), and 'David Hare & Max Stafford-Clark', in Hammond and Steward, *Verbatim Verbatim*, pp. 45–75. Elsewhere Hare claimed to have been 'involved, as a producer or writer, in such [verbatim] projects for over thirty years': see D. Hare, '*… on factual theatre*', in Soans, *Talking to Terrorists*, pp. 111–13 (p. 111).

9 See for instance Colleran, *Theatre and War*, p. 136, and J. Reinelt, 'Toward a Poetics of Theatre and Public Events: In the Case of Stephen Lawrence', *TDR: The Drama Review* 50:3 (2006), pp. 69–87.

10 Paget, 'Broken Tradition', p. 225.

11 Hughes, *Performance in a Time of Terror*, p. 9.

12 C. Martin, 'Bodies of Evidence', *TDR: The Drama Review* 50:3 (2006), pp. 9–15.

13 'Richard Norton-Taylor', in Hammond and Steward, *Verbatim Verbatim*, pp. 103–31 (p. 114).

14 'Nicolas Kent', in Hammond and Steward, *Verbatim Verbatim*, pp. 133–68 (p. 152).

15 D. Hare, *Via Dolorosa*, in *Via Dolorosa & When Shall We Live?* (London: Faber, 1998), pp. 1–43 (p. 41). Further references to this edition are given after quotations in the text.

16 All of the verbatim texts produced by Richard Norton-Taylor for the Tricycle stage—*Nuremberg: The War Crimes Trial* (1997), *Justifying War: Scenes from the Hutton Inquiry* (2003), *Bloody Sunday: Scenes from the Saville Inquiry* (2005), *Called to Account: The indictment of Anthony Charles Lynton Blair for the crime of aggression against Iraq—a hearing* (2007), *Tactical Questioning: Scenes from the Baha Mousa Inquiry* (2011)—bear the indication 'edited by Richard Norton-Taylor' on the front page. The only exception in this respect is Norton-Taylor's first experiment with the verbatim method, *Half the Picture* (1994), also directed by Nicolas Kent at the Tricycle. While important in establishing the genre, this dramatic re-enactment of the Scott Arms-to-Iraq inquiry, investigating the alleged violation by members of the British government of the embargo on the sale of arms to Iraq after the First Gulf War, is not a strictly orthodox tribunal play in that the play complements the transcripts of the inquiry edited by Norton-Taylor with interpolated monologues written by John McGrath, who is named in the published script as the co-author of the text. Apart from *The Colour of Justice*—a rendering of the public inquiry concerning the British police force's attempt to derail investigations into the murder of a seventeen-year-old black boy, Stephen

Lawrence, by a group of white racist thugs—the verbatim projects born out of the partnership between Kent and Norton-Taylor all deal with wars (and war crimes) past and present.

17 'I just thought the story [of *The Permanent Way*] was so shocking that I didn't want to get in the way. And it is an illusion. It's craft. Actually I'm all over it, but I don't want to be seen.' D. Hare quoted in P. Preston, 'Extra! Extra!', *Guardian*, 17 March 2004 <http://www.theguardian.com/stage/2004/mar/17/theatre.pressandpublishing> [accessed 24 April 2015].

18 'Nicolas Kent', p. 150.

19 Hare, 'Why Fabulate?'

20 This is wholly consonant with the three propositions set forth by Janelle Reinelt as a premise to her penetrating analysis of the status of the document and of documentary in contemporary theatre:

'1. The value of the document is predicated on a realist epistemology, but the experience of documentary is dependent on a phenomenological engagement.
2. The documentary is not in the object but in the relationship between the object, its mediators (artists, historians, authors) and its audiences.
3. The experience of documentary is connected to reality but is not transparent, and is in fact constitutive of the reality it seeks.'

J. Reinelt, 'The Promise of Documentary', in Forsyth and Megson, *Get Real*, pp. 6–23 (p. 7).

21 'Nicolas Kent', pp. 152–53.

22 Ibid., p. 135.

23 'Richard Norton-Taylor', p. 122.

24 'Robin Soans', in Hammond and Steward, *Verbatim Verbatim*, pp. 15–44 (p. 32).

25 'Nicolas Kent', p. 165.

26 'We do these inquiries because they're not televised, which I think is shocking in the 21st century. [The Bloody Sunday inquiry] is called a "public inquiry" and yet we don't use the main media of TV and radio. So we're forced to do it with actors. But I'm pleased to see that more and more inquiries are starting to be televised. So I hope we'll be put out of business eventually.' Quoted in L. Hoggard, 'Out of crises, a drama', *Observer*, 27 March 2005 <http://www.theguardian.com/stage/2005/mar/27/theatre> [accessed 24 April 2015].

27 The publication of the inquiry's findings was actually delayed by four more years, and Lord Saville's report was only released after the 2010 general election.

28 The inquiry's official website provides the following description of the scale of information dealt with by the tribunal: 'Approximately 2,500 witness statements were received by the Inquiry and 33 bundles of evidence comprising about 160 volumes, including 13 volumes of photographs, were sent to representatives of the interested parties. It is estimated that these bundles contain 20–30 million words. In addition, the bundles contain 121 audiotapes and 110 videotapes.' <http://archive.is/VQ7S> [accessed 26 March 2013].

29 Hoggard, 'Out of crises'.

30 'Nicolas Kent', p. 154.

31 Ibid., p. 139.

32 R. Norton-Taylor quoted in M. Luckhurst, 'Verbatim Theatre, Media Relations and Ethics', in N. Holdsworth and M. Luckhurst (eds), *A Concise Companion to Contemporary British and Irish Drama* (Oxford: Blackwell, 2008), pp. 200–22 (p. 209).

33 See Aristotle, *Poetics*, trans. by M. Heath (London: Penguin, 1996), Chapter Six.

34 In her analysis of Norton-Taylor's *Justifying War*, Jeanne Colleran describes the dramatic model that emerges from the play as a version of Ibsen's and Miller's social drama inflected with a Chekhovian vein (*Theatre and War*, pp. 147–48).

35 'Richard Norton-Taylor', p. 122.

36 'I suppose there is a slight tension between us, with me looking for slightly more dramatic material and Richard always hoeing the path of truth and non-bias. But that tension is useful.' 'Nicolas Kent', p. 142.

37 R. Norton-Taylor quoted in Lane, *Contemporary British Drama*, p. 69.

38 R. Norton-Taylor (ed.), *Justifying War: Scenes from the Hutton Inquiry* (London: Oberon, 2003), p. 7.

39 'Richard Norton-Taylor', pp. 113–14.

40 Hegel, *Aesthetics*, ii, p. 1159 (original emphasis).

41 I. Shuttleworth, 'Prompt Corner', *Theatre Record* 25 (2005) <http://www.theatrerecord.org/Archives/2005/archive08–2005.html> [accessed 8 April 2013]. For a penetrating analysis of the crucial role played by the two recorded extracts in the construction of Corrie's dramatic persona and the simplification and sentimentalization of her narrative, see Martin, 'Bodies of Evidence'.

42 Kuti, 'Tragic Plots'.

43 R. Cook, review of *Stuff Happens*, *Guardian*, 3 September 2004, in *Theatre Record* 24 (2004), p. 1160.

44 D. Hare, 'Author's Note', *Stuff Happens* (London: Faber, 2004), [n.p.]. The note also featured in the play's programme. Further references to this edition are given after quotations in the text.

45 D. Soto-Morettini, 'Trouble in the House: David Hare's *Stuff Happens*', *Contemporary Theatre Review* 15:3 (2005), pp. 309–19 (p. 309).

46 Edgar, 'Doc and Dram'.

47 Reinelt, 'Promise of Documentary', p. 18.

48 Hughes, *Performance in a Time of Terror*, p. 104.

49 Ibid., p. 103.

50 J. Peter, review of *Guantanamo: 'Honor Bound to Defend Freedom'*, *Sunday Times*, 30 May 2004, in *Theatre Record* 24 (2004), p. 684.

51 V. Brittain and G. Slovo, *Guantanamo: 'Honor Bound to Defend Freedom'* (London: Oberon, 2004), p. 5. Further references to this edition are given after quotations in the text.

52 This was the twenty-seventh F. Mann Lecture, 'Guantanamo Bay: The Legal Black Hole', given by Lord Steyn on 25 November 2003 at the British Institute of International and Comparative Law in London. In the text, the lecture is mistakenly dated 23 November.

53 R. Claycomb, 'Voices of the Other: Documentary and Oral History Performance in Post-9/11 British Theatre', in Spencer, *Political and Protest Theatre*, pp. 93–107 (p. 103).

54 Rumsfeld made this statement in January 2002 to deny that American-held detainees of the war on terror, most of them arrested in or around Afghanistan, were being mistreated and tortured in Guantanamo; as is well known, he also rebutted charges of patent violation of the Geneva convention regulations regarding prisoner treatment by classifying the detainees as illegal enemy combatants to whom international humanitarian law did not apply. The first group of prisoners had arrived at what was then still Camp X-Ray in January 2002. The infamous images of the detainees in their cages were released by the Associated Press later that month, following a Red Cross visit, ironically with the intention of reassuring Western public opinion about the prompt and effective measures taken by the US against the threat of Islamic terrorism.

55 A note appended to the list of characters in the printed text specifies that 'The interviews for the play were conducted at the end of March and beginning of April 2004. Numerous attempts were made to get the viewpoint of members of the government (both in the Lords and the Commons) for this play, but no one was prepared to be interviewed' (3).

56 Luckhurst, 'Verbatim Theatre', p. 214. As a political journalist with a strong interest in foreign politics and human rights issues, Brittain in particular would have been familiar with legal procedures for the recording of testimony and the question of how, in any given interview setting, conditions of retrieval may influence content.

57 V. Brittain, 'Questions and lies', *Guardian*, 24 May 2004 <http://www.theguardian.com/stage/2004/may/24/theatre.guantanamo> [accessed 24 April 2015].

58 Ruhel Ahmed, Shafiq Rasul and Asif Iqbal were British citizens from Tipton (England). They were all in their twenties when they were captured by Afghan paramilitaries in 2001 and then handed over to American forces. They were held in detention in Guantanamo for two years and eventually released without charge.

59 R. Norton-Taylor, *Called to Account: The indictment of Anthony Charles Lynton Blair for the crime of aggression against Iraq—a hearing* (London: Oberon, 2007), p. 9. Further references to this edition are given after quotations in the text.

60 R. Norton-Taylor, 'Blair in the dock', *Guardian*, 16 April 2007 <http://www.theguardian.com/politics/2007/apr/16/politicsandthearts.theatre> [accessed 24 April 2015].

61 The official Iraq inquiry was launched on 30 July 2009. It was entrusted to a committee of five Privy Counsellors chosen by Prime Minister Gordon Brown and chaired by Sir John Chilcot. The hearings were only partially held in public and ended in February 2011; the committee's final report has yet to be delivered; in January 2015, Chilcot announced that the publication would be delayed until after the general election, sparking a public outcry. A process of declassification is currently underway but not all the evidence given will be made public due to national security reasons.

62 'Diane Fletcher', in T. Cantrell and M. Luckhurst (eds), *Playing for Real: Actors on Playing Real People* (Basingstoke: Palgrave Macmillan, 2010), pp. 68–72.

63 Norton-Taylor, 'Blair in the dock'.

64 The publication of Sir Greenstock's war memoirs was announced in 2005 but immediately halted at the request of the Foreign & Commonwealth Office; in the play, Sands refers to an extract which briefly appeared on the publisher's website. In 2008, during an interview for the *Charlie Rose Show* on PBS, the former ambassador disclosed some of the book's contents and publicly declared that the British and the American government knew that Saddam Hussein had no weapons of mass destruction. To date, his memoir is still unpublished (though it misleadingly figures as available on some bookselling websites).

65 Philippe Sands QC, legal counsel for the prosecution in the Tricycle inquiry, later responded to the official inquiry's invitation to international lawyers to share their analysis of the arguments drawn upon by the British government to justify military intervention in Iraq through a submission in which he firmly reasserted that there was no legal basis for the war, and unfavourably compared the lack of legal expertise of the committee members in the Chilcot Inquiry to the high legal standing of an independent Dutch inquiry which had just reached the conclusion that the Iraq war was not justified under international law. Sands's submission, dated 10 September 2010, was later published in the *Guardian*: see P. Sands, 'Submission to Iraq inquiry from Philippe Sands QC', *Guardian*, 4 October 2010 <http://www.theguardian.com/law/interactive/2010/oct/04/iraq-inquiry-submissions-philippe-sands> [accessed 29 April 2013].

66 When he testified at the official Iraq inquiry, in January 2010, Lord Goldsmith denied that pressure had been put on him to curtail his legal opinion in order to bolster up the case for war in Cabinet. In the recently-published full version of his diaries, Alastair Campbell tells a quite different story: according to Blair's former spin doctor, during a meeting on 11 March Blair and his closest aides blocked Lord Goldsmith from presenting to Cabinet his full legal advice, fearing it would be seized upon by ministerial opposition to prove that the war was illegal. As a consequence, the Attorney General produced the shorter and more Blair-friendly version of his legal opinion which was put before Cabinet and then used in Parliament to justify military intervention. See J. Merrick and M. Chorley, 'Blair blocked Cabinet from hearing legal advice on Iraq', *The Independent*, 24 June 2012 <http://www.independent.co.uk/news/uk/politics/blair-blocked-cabinet-from-hearing-legal-advice-on-iraq-7878737.html> [accessed 31 May 2013].

67 Hare, 'Author's Note'.

68 D. McManus, 'Great Souls, Big Wheels, and Other Words: Experiments with Truth and Representation in Verbatim Theatre', in K. Gounaridou (ed.), *Text and Presentation 2009* (Jefferson, NC: McFarland, 2010), pp. 141–53 (p. 149). See also Bottoms, 'Putting the Document into Documentary'.

69 Claycomb, 'Voices of the Other', p. 95.

70 This expression was coined by Michael Frayn to describe the use of fictional speech in *Democracy*, his 2003 quasi-documentary play about the Guillaume

affair in Cold War Germany: see Hughes, *Performance in a Time of Terror*, p. 114.

71 A video recording of the performance is available for viewing at the National Theatre archive.

72 Bottoms, 'Putting the Document into Documentary', p. 59.

73 Reinelt, 'Promise of Documentary', p. 10.

74 Claycomb, 'Voices of the Other', p. 96. Christopher Innes hears distinct echoes of Brecht's Lehrstück *The Exception and the Rule* in the opening speech of Hare's play: see Innes, 'Documents of the Times', p. 443.

75 Rice's statement was made on CNN on 8 September 2012 and immediately hit the world headlines. The smoking gun/mushroom cloud metaphor was apparently coined by Michael Gerson, G.W. Bush's top speechwriter and a key figure within the White House Iraq Group (WHIG), a propaganda team formed with the precise task of selling the invasion to American public opinion. See on this M. Isikoff and D. Corn, *Hubris: The Inside Story of Spin, Scandal, and the Iraq War* (New York: Crown Publishers, 2006).

76 Levy's unpublished play is based on Eliot Weinberger's essay of the same title published in the *London Review on Books* in February 2005. It premiered at the Fountain Theatre in Los Angeles in 2005 and was then presented at the Edinburgh festival in August 2006.

Chapter 4: The performance of witnessing

1 The influence of the oral history movement on the development of early verbatim theatre is traced by Derek Paget in his seminal 1987 article, 'Verbatim Theatre'.

2 Aeschylus, *Persians* in P. Burian and A. Shapiro (eds), *The Complete Aeschylus, Volume II: Persians and Other Plays*, trans. by J. Lembke and C.J. Herington (New York: Oxford UP, 2009), p. 46, vv. 436–37.

3 McManus, 'Truth and Representation in Verbatim Theatre', p. 143.

4 P. Rosen, *Theorizing Documentary* (1993), quoted in Reinelt, 'In the Case of Stephen Lawrence', p. 83. In a later contribution Reinelt sees the minimal claim of postmodern documentary as 'simple facticity', that is to say 'the indexical value of documents [as] the corroboration that something happened, that events took place' ('Promise of Documentary', p. 10).

5 Paget, 'Broken Tradition', pp. 235–36.

6 Ibid.

7 Colleran, *Theatre and War*, p. 24. In Colleran's analysis, this phrase is specifically related to the ambivalence of popular and political discourse when it comes to the indexicality of war images: quoting Donald Rumsfeld's appalling denial that media images of the looting of Baghdad told the truth about what was happening in liberated Iraq, Colleran remarks that 'much popular and political discourse … veers between asserting that the body or scene, as photographed and televised, is a verifiable historical and material referent and suggesting that the body or scene has been staged or mediated' (ibid.). Colleran's observations about the public sphere chime with Stanton B. Garner's description of the field of performance as constitutionally duplicitous on account of the fact that spectators' perception of

all theatrical objects, including the performers' bodies, constantly oscillates between sign and substance, scenic fiction and environmental actuality: see S.B. Garner, *Bodied Spaces: Phenomenology and Performance in Contemporary Drama* (Ithaca, NY: Cornell University Press, 1994), pp. 39–45.

8 N. Rogers, 'The Play of Law: Comparing Performances in Law and Theatre', *Queensland University of Technology Law Journal* 8:2 (2008), pp. 429–43 (p. 438). Rogers is here applying to the Tricycle tribunal plays Victor Turner's view, expressed in *From Ritual to Theatre* (1982), that legal performances are the 'generative source' of theatrical and other forms of cultural performances.

9 This remark was made by Robin Soans with reference to his play *Talking to Terrorists*: see 'Robin Soans', in Hammond and Steward, *Verbatim Verbatim*, p. 21.

10 Sontag, *Regarding the Pain of Others*, p. 18.

11 P. Anderson and J. Menon, 'Introduction: Violence Performed', in P. Anderson and J. Menon (eds), *Violence Performed: Local Roots and Global Routes of Conflict* (Basingstoke: Palgrave Macmillan, 2009), pp. 1–14 (p. 4).

12 L. Gardner, review of *Yesterday Was a Weird Day*, *Guardian*, 17 August 2005 <http://www.theguardian.com/stage/2005/aug/17/theatre.edinburgh-festival20051> [accessed 24 April 2015].

13 Ben Freedman quoted in N. Calvi, 'Ben Freedman & Mimi Poskitt', *The Stage*, 10 February 2006. Freedman shares responsibility for artistic direction at Look Left, Look Right with its co-founder, Mimi Poskitt.

14 Calvi, 'Freedman & Poskitt'.

15 Author's conversation with Mimi Poskitt, London, 3 February 2011.

16 During our conversation, Poskitt indicated pace as a prime factor driving editorial decisions.

17 Lehmann, *Postdramatic Theatre*, pp. 125–29.

18 Look Left, Look Right, *Yesterday Was a Weird Day*, unpublished typescript of the Battersea Arts Centre production, p. 10. I am extremely grateful to Mimi Poskitt for providing me with a copy of the script and allowing me to quote from it. Further references are given after quotations in the text.

19 Claycomb, 'Voices of the Other', p. 100.

20 Robin Cook was interviewed over the phone by Ruaridh Arrow, one of the members of the cast, on 28 July 2005. It was one of Cook's last interviews before his sudden death on 6 August.

21 R. Soans and M. Stafford-Clark, untitled note, in Soans, *Talking to Terrorists*, [n.p.]. Further details about the company's role in researching and devising the play can be found in Chipo Chung's interview with Tom Cantrell in Cantrell and Luckhurst, *Playing for Real*, pp. 53–58. Further references to this edition of *Talking to Terrorists* are given after quotations in the text.

22 The reviews of the London performances are collected in *Theatre Record* 25 (2005), pp. 913–19.

23 Hughes, *Performance in a Time of Terror*, p. 111.

24 R. Soans, 'It Could be You', *Guardian*, 20 April 2005 <http://www.theguardian.com/stage/2005/apr/20/theatre.terrorism> [accessed 24 April 2015].

25 The discussion group in Act One and the play in general owe a lot to the work of Nobel Prize nominee Scilla Elworthy, the founder of the conflict

resolution organization Peace Direct and director of the Oxford Research Group for nuclear disarmament. Dr Elworthy's methods for developing dialogue in order to prevent or transform deadly conflicts were a major influence on the form taken by Soans and Stafford-Clark's verbatim project, not least because the former terrorists who were interviewed by the company were Elworthy's own contacts. See Cantrell and Luckhurst, *Playing for Real*, pp. 53–55.

26 As the former UVF militant acknowledges, 'We were both working-class men from Belfast; we had both put cardboard into our shoes when it rained; by and large, I could have lived his life.' (88)

27 See 'Robin Soans', pp. 34–35. Soans is open about conflating the words of more than one source within one speech or occasionally writing representative dialogue from his notes and from memory. His verbatim practice has many affinities with the Joint Stock method devised in the 1970s and '80s to research and develop fact-based plays and more recently applied by Max Stafford-Clark and David Hare in their renewed collaboration on *The Permanent Way*. See on this 'David Hare & Max Stafford-Clark' in Hammond and Steward, *Verbatim Verbatim*, pp. 45–75 and Paget, 'Broken Tradition', pp. 230–31. In the case of *Talking to Terrorists*, the script was generated within a workshop in which the people who eventually became the play's characters were brought into the rehearsal room to talk to the company or were approached by actors who then shared with the rest of the team both a report and a re-enactment of the interview: for a description of the performers' role in the creative process, see Cantrell and Luckhurst, *Playing for Real*, pp. 54–55.

28 'Robin Soans', p. 35.

29 The seemingly 'universal' recipe for the prevention and cure of terrorism put forward by the play was often the target of hostile reviewers. For a more rounded critique of Soans's liberal-humanist approach see Bottoms, 'Putting the Document into Documentary', and Hughes, *Performance in a Time of Terror*, pp. 106–13.

30 Unless otherwise specified, my observations are based on the video recording of the 29 July 2005 evening performance, held in the V&A National Video Archive of Performance.

31 The text uses double spacing to mark the short conversational gaps corresponding to the interviewer's muted turns of speech.

32 The phrase 'belated witnesses' is used by Wendy Hesford to describe the position assigned to the audience by Brittain and Slovo's testimonial play, *Guantanamo*: W.S. Hesford, 'Staging Terror', *TDR: The Drama Review* 50:3 (2006), pp. 29–41 (p. 37).

33 None of these actions are noted in the published script.

34 When interviewed about her doubling in *Talking to Terrorists*, Chipo Chung expressed her belief that Craig Murray's partner had been underrepresented, when not misrepresented, in Soans's rendition of the interview. See Cantrell and Luckhurst, *Playing for Real*, p. 57.

35 D. LaCapra, *Writing History, Writing Trauma* (Baltimore: Johns Hopkins University Press, 2001), pp. 41, 79.

36 This expression is used by Jonathan Kalb while discussing the documentary

work of American solo performers Anna Deavere Smith and Marc Wolf: see J. Kalb, 'Documentary Solo Performance: The Politics of the Mirrored Self', *Theater* 31:3 (2001), pp. 13–29 (p. 9).

37 Martin, 'Bodies of Evidence', p. 13.

38 A. Filewod, 'The Documentary Body: Theatre Workshop to Banner Theatre', in Forsyth and Megson, *Get Real*, pp. 55–73 (p. 62).

39 A. Jeffers, 'Looking for Esrafil: Witnessing "Refugitive" Bodies in *I've got something to show you*', in Forsyth and Megson, *Get Real*, pp. 91–106 (pp. 97, 101).

40 'Nicolas Kent', pp. 155–56.

41 Favorini, 'Representation and Reality', p. 38. For an account of the difficult and unrewarding experience of acting in verbatim plays, see Chipo Chung's and Diane Fletcher's interviews in Cantrell and Luckhurst, *Playing for Real*.

42 Filewod, 'Documentary Body', p. 61.

43 D. Paget, *True Stories? Documentary Drama on Radio, Screen and Stage* (Manchester: Manchester University Press, 1990), pp. 39–41. Paget's perception of the 'liberal/conservative' recording mode as the dominant one, and of the reporting tradition as its 'radical/revolutionary' alternative has been revised in his more recent contribution to the collection *Get Real* ('Broken Tradition'), where he registers the rise to prominence of the figure of the witness in turn-of-the-millennium verbatim drama.

44 D. Hare, *Acting Up* (London: Faber and Faber, 1999), p. 15.

45 Hare, 'Why Fabulate?'

46 *The Artist is Present* is the title of the landmark solo performance presented by Abramović in 2010 on the occasion of a major retrospective of her work at the Museum of Modern Art in New York. It is also the title of the documentary film (released in 2012) that records the preparatory phases of the retrospective and the three-month-long performance in which the iconic Serbian artist sat all day in complete silence at a table placed in the museum's atrium, exchanging gazes with the countless members of the audience who, one after the other, came to sit across from her.

47 'David Hare & Max Stafford-Clark', p. 68.

48 D. Hare interviewed in A. Sierz, 'To each his Via Dolorosa', *Al-Ahram Weekly*, 5 February 2001 <http://weekly.ahram.org.eg/1998/1948/396_via.htm> [accessed 18 January 2011].

49 Bar-Yosef, 'Just a Pen'.

50 'Sierz interview'.

51 Hare, *Stuff Happens*, p. 120.

52 M. Billington, review of *Via Dolorosa*, *Guardian*, 9 September 1998, in *Theatre Record* 18 (1998), p. 1558.

53 Kalb, 'Documentary Solo Performance', p. 23.

54 R. Butler, review of *Via Dolorosa*, *The Independent on Sunday*, 13 September, and P. Taylor, review of *Via Dolorosa*, *The Independent*, 10 September 1998, in *Theatre Record* 18 (1998), pp. 1555, 1557.

55 While still praising the play's unabated topicality, Michael Billington's review of the 2002 revival in London regrets the witness's 'growing actorly assurance': M. Billington, review of *Via Dolorosa*, *Guardian*, 19 July 2002 <http://www.theguardian.com/stage/2002/jul/19/theatre.artsfeatures> [accessed 24 April

2015]. Suzi Feay likewise hints at the short shelf life of Hare's display of unconstructedness when she remarks that 'his original experiences must have been worn smooth and polished by now: they've become his party piece': S. Feay, review of *Via Dolorosa*, *The Independent*, 28 July 2002 <http://www.independent.co.uk/arts-entertainment/theatre-dance/reviews/alive-from-palestine-young-vic-london-brbrvia-dolorosa-duchess-london-brbrwitness-gate-theatre-london-186387.html> [accessed 24 April 2015].

56 Auslander, *Liveness*, p. 3.

57 Colleran, *Theatre and War*, p. 6. In his critique Auslander quotes as a representative example of the 'ontological' position within contemporary performance studies Peggy Phelan's view that 'performance's independence from mass reproduction, technologically, economically, and linguistically, is its greatest strength'; rebutting this opposition, he advocates instead a relational notion of liveness and insists on the fundamental 'dependence and imbrication' between live and mediatized forms in contemporary culture: see Auslander, *Liveness*, pp. 44, 46.

58 Auslander, *Liveness*, pp. 129, 144–45.

59 C. Spencer, review of *Justifying War*, *Daily Telegraph*, 6 November 2003, in *Theatre Record* 23 (2003), p. 1480. Nicolas Kent and some members of the company attended the proceedings, and the Tricycle production strove for maximum accuracy in its minutely detailed reconstruction of the original performances of witnessing.

60 Auslander, *Liveness*, p. 144.

61 J. Hughes, 'Theatre, Performance and the "War on Terror": Ethical and Political Questions Arising from British Theatrical Responses to War and Terrorism', *Contemporary Theatre Review* 17:2 (2007), pp. 149–64 (p. 152).

62 Martin, 'Bodies of Evidence', p. 11.

63 Richard Norton-Taylor (ed.), *Bloody Sunday: Scenes from the Saville Inquiry* (London: Oberon, 2005), p. 7. Further references to this edition are given after quotations in the text.

64 As already mentioned in Chapter Three, Clarke's opening statement was the longest ever in British legal history, lasting forty-two days.

65 The terms of reference of the new inquiry explicitly mentioned 'taking account of any new information relevant to events on that day', and Lord Saville's opening address accordingly urged 'those who consider that they have material evidence to give (or who know of people they consider are likely to be able to give such evidence) … to contact the Inquiry Secretary as soon as possible'. See Lord Saville, 'Opening Statement of Bloody Sunday Inquiry', 3 April 1998 <http://cain.ulst.ac.uk/events/bsunday/ms030498.htm> [accessed 23 December 2013]. For a thorough review of the Widgery Report and its shortcomings, see D. Walsh, *Bloody Sunday and the Rule of Law in Northern Ireland* (Basingstoke: Palgrave Macmillan, 2000).

66 The two other goals that the families had been long campaigning for, namely, the direct repudiation of Lord Widgery's conclusions and the prosecution of those responsible for the killings and the woundings, fell outside the inquiry's terms of reference, as Lord Saville made clear in his opening statement.

67 E. McCann, 'Why isn't this shown on the BBC?', *Guardian*, 19 September

2005. <http://www.theguardian.com/stage/2005/sep/19/theatre.northernireland> [accessed 24 April 2015]. Herron and Lynch further note that while it became entangled in multiple and conflicting narratives, 'on the face of it, Bloody Sunday was not an ungraspably complex event', but rather one that had been 'captured comprehensively in multiple media formats' and was on the whole well documented: see T. Herron and J. Lynch, *After Bloody Sunday: Representation, Ethics, Justice* (Cork: Cork University Press, 2007), p. 4.

68 Strong reservations about public inquiries as state-sponsored and state-managed truth-seeking processes have been expressed by a considerable number of scholars in the legal field: for the relevant bibliography the reader is referred to Elizabeth Ball's highly informed article, 'Truth, Power and Inquiry', *Quest* 4 (2007) <http://www.qub.ac.uk/sites/QUEST/JournalIssues/> [accessed 24 April 2015], which deals at length with the Bloody Sunday inquiry.

69 C.-A. Upton, 'The Performance of Truth and Justice in Northern Ireland', in Forsyth and Megson, *Get Real*, pp. 179–94 (p. 190).

70 I equally disagree with Upton's assessment of *Bloody Sunday* as 'more a memory play about the victims of Bloody Sunday than a critique of the contemporary inquiry's capacity to manage the consequences of remembering' ('Performance of Truth and Justice', p. 187); to me the retrospective look, far from making this a 'reactionary' play, is a theatrically effective way of directing attention towards the repressive uses of memory in legal performance. In a very recent article, Aoife Monks follows Upton in assuming that 'while the production critiqued the injustice that led to the Inquiry, the status of the law itself was protected carefully'. This proposition, however, is largely at variance with Monks's own conclusions about the play's meta-theatrical quality and its unsettling effects upon the play's alleged intent to protect the status of the law: see A. Monks, '"This Painful Chapter": Performing the Law in *Bloody Sunday: Scenes from the Saville Inquiry*', *Contemporary Theatre Review* 23:3 (2013), pp. 345–56.

71 Geraldine McBride's breakdown is not noted in the stage directions; unless otherwise specified, my observations about the Tricycle production are based on the video recording of the 6 October 2005 evening performance, held in the V&A National Video Archive of Performance.

72 Bernadette McAliskey (née Devlin) was a speaker at the anti-internment march on Bloody Sunday and later, as an MP for Mid-Ulster, was persistently denied the floor in Westminster and prevented from reporting about the Derry incidents. In her hearing before the Saville Inquiry she is scathingly outspoken about the irregularity of an investigation generating from and run by representatives the main accused party.

73 See 'Statement by David Cameron to the House of Commons following the publication of the Saville Report', 15 June 2010 <http://cain.ulst.ac.uk/issues/politics/docs/pmo/dc150610.htm> [accessed 3 December 2013].

74 See 'Statement by Tony Blair on new Bloody Sunday Inquiry, 29 January 1998' <http://cain.ulst.ac.uk/events/bsunday/tb29198.htm> [accessed 18 September 2013].

75 Hoggard, 'Out of crises'.

76 The inquiry's provisions for 'encourag[ing] people to come forward and speak freely with no inhibitions' (Saville, 'Opening Statement') included some form of protection for the members of the armed forces facing allegations of serious criminal offences: rather controversially, given the flauntedly open and public nature of the investigation, some military witnesses were granted anonymity, and some were allowed to testify behind screens; Lord Saville's opening statement, however, had ruled out the possibility of a 'blanket recommendation' to the Attorney General for immunity from prosecution for all those who came to testify. Though not within the scope of the inquiry, then, criminal liability might be inferred from it and the evidence gathered by the Saville tribunal could provide the basis for a further police investigation.

77 A similar interpretation of the wilful amnesia of the military witnesses at the inquiry is provided in G.D. White, '"Quite a Profound Day": The Public Performance of Memory by Military Witnesses at the Bloody Sunday Tribunal', *Theatre Research International* 31:2 (2006), pp. 174–87.

78 US Department of Defense, 'News Transcript: DoD News Briefing—Secretary Rumsfeld and Gen. Myers, 12 February 2002' <http://www.defense.gov/transcripts/transcript.aspx?transcriptid=2636> [accessed 27 September 2013]. Rumsfeld went on to add that 'if one looks throughout the history of our country and other free countries, it is the latter category that tend to be the difficult ones', and concluded with a warning to 'people who have the omniscience that they can say with high certainty that something has not happened or is not being tried'.

79 D.H. Jones, *Samuel Beckett and Testimony* (Basingstoke: Palgrave Macmillan, 2011), p. 169.

80 Monks, 'Painful Chapter'.

81 Saville, 'Opening Statement'. The Lord Justice announced the setting up of a dedicated web site and illustrated the advantages of real-time transcription in enabling the instant digitization of the witnesses' oral performances. Another cutting-edge digital technology that was employed during almost all testimonial hearings, though it is not mentioned in Saville's speech, was an award-winning software called Virtual Derry which allowed witnesses to navigate a 3D reconstruction of the city at the time of the events. Herron and Lynch comment on the frequent use of this software as a 'memory jogging' tool but also as a way of testing eyewitness evidence: see Herron and Lynch, *After Bloody Sunday*, pp. 61–62.

82 C. Martin, 'Living Simulations: The Use of Media in Documentary in the UK, Lebanon and Israel', in Forsyth and Megson, *Get Real*, pp. 74–90 (p. 74).

83 Cantrell and Luckhurst, *Playing for Real*, pp. 71–72. For an in-depth analysis of *Called to Account*, see Chapter Three.

84 Claycomb, 'Voices of the Other', p. 102.

85 Author's conversation with Mimi Poskitt.

86 Auslander, *Liveness*, p. 42. Auslander invokes the Baudrillardian notion of simulation as particularly apt to describe the current paradigm: 'nothing separates one pole from the other, the initial from the terminal: there is just a sort of contraction into each other, a fantastic telescoping, a collapsing

of the two traditional poles into one another: an implosion … *this is where simulation begins*' (pp. 42–43; original emphasis).

87 Author's conversation with Mimi Poskitt.

Chapter 5: Figures of mediation

1 This coinage is put forward by T.O. Beebee in 'Shoot The Transtraitor! The Translator as *Homo Sacer* in Fiction and Reality', *The Translator* 16:2 (2010), Special Issue on 'Translation and Violent Conflict', pp. 295–313.

2 G. Steiner, *After Babel: Aspects of Language and Translation* (Oxford: Oxford University Press, 1975).

3 That of translation as an embattled field is a pervasive notion throughout the cornerstones of the 'cultural turn' in translation scholarship: see S. Bassnett and A. Lefevere (eds), *Translation, History and Culture* (London: Pinter, 1990); S. Bassnett and A. Lefevere (eds), *Constructing Cultures: Essays on Literary Translation* (Clevedon: Cromwell Press, 1998); L. Venuti (ed.), *Rethinking Translation: Discourse, Subjectivity, Ideology* (London: Routledge, 1992); L. Venuti, *The Translator's Invisibility. A History of Translation* (London: Routledge, 1995).

4 See for instance S. Bermann and M. Wood (eds), *Nation, Language, and the Ethics of Translation* (Princeton: Princeton University Press, 2005); M. Cronin, *Translation and Identity* (London: Routledge, 2006).

5 V.L. Rafael, 'Translation in Wartime', *Public Culture* 19:2 (2007), pp. 239–46 (p. 246).

6 Steiner, *After Babel*, p. 49.

7 Montanari, *Linguaggi della guerra*, p. 121. Montanari's communicative model of war is based on Alain Joxe's and Lucien Poirier's semiotic approach to strategic studies: see A. Joxe, *Le cycle de la dissuasion, 1945–1990: Essai de stratégie critique* (Paris: La Découverte, 1990), and L. Poirier, *Le chantier stratégique* (Paris: Hachette, 1997).

8 See in particular E. Goffman, *Strategic Interaction* (Philadelphia: University of Pennsylvania Press, 1969).

9 Borradori, 'Dialogue with Jürgen Habermas', p. 35

10 E. Apter, *The Translation Zone: A New Comparative Literature* (Princeton: Princeton University Press, 2006), p. 16.

11 Ibid.

12 On the instrumental use of language divisionism in the Balkan context, see R.D. Greenberg, *Language and Identity in the Balkans* (Oxford: Oxford University Press, 2004). In *The Translation Zone* Apter devotes a chapter to the language wars in the former Yugoslavia ('Balkan Babel: Language Zones, Military Zones', pp. 129–38), where she also deals with their representation in contemporary fiction.

13 Bermann and Wood, *Ethics of Translation*, p. 1. The Mexican-American writer, translator and sociolinguist originally made this remark during an interview in 2002.

14 E. Apter, 'Translation—9/11: Terrorism, Immigration, Language Politics', in E. Bielsa and C.W. Hughes (eds), *Globalization, Political Violence and Translation* (Basingstoke: Palgrave Macmillan, 2009), pp. 195–206 (p. 195).

15 This is according to the spokesman for the American Translators Association, quoted in Rafael, 'Translation in Wartime', p. 243.

16 M. Friel, 'Human Problems Facing Translators and Interpreters Worldwide Today', *Translation Ireland*, 16:1 (2005), pp. 4–6. Friel draws attention to the fact that 'translators and interpreters have always been killed or injured on the job, but usually for being in the wrong place or with the wrong people at the wrong time. This is no longer the case and linguists are being specifically targeted because of the work they do.' (p. 4) According to official sources, 360 locally hired interpreters were killed in Iraq between 2003 and 2008: see Council of Europe Parliamentary Assembly, 'We should protect interpreters in conflict zones!', Doc. 12239, Written Declaration No 442, 29 April 2010 <http://assembly.coe.int/nw/xml/XRef/X2H-Xref-ViewPDF.asp?FileID=12805&lang=en> [accessed 5 September 2014]. More recently, The List Project for the Resettlement of Iraqi Allies, a US non-profit organization providing *pro bono* legal assistance to US-affiliated asylum-seeking Iraqis, has reset the casualty figure at about one thousand. Maya Hess, to whom I am grateful for directing me to this source, offers the following explanations for the difficulty in coming by an authoritative estimate: first, 'U.S. private employers are not mandated to publicly report employee/subcontractor fatalities'; secondly, 'these figures are frequently subsumed under private contractor deaths'; and finally, 'interpreters who were killed after their assignments ended and/or after troop withdrawal most likely remain uncounted'. See M. Hess, 'Translator, traitor: A critical ethnography of a U.S. terrorism trial', (unpublished dissertation, The Graduate Center, CUNY, 2014) <http://works.gc.cuny.edu/etd/226/> [accessed 17 September 2014], p. 153n.

17 Joshua Foust quoted in M. Baker, 'Interpreters and Translators in the War Zone: Narrated and Narrators', *The Translator* 16:2 (2010), Special Issue on 'Translation and Violent Conflict', pp. 197–222 (p. 210).

18 See Apter, 'Translation—9/11', Beebee, 'Shoot the Transtraitor!', as well as the cases mentioned in M.L. Pratt, 'Harm's Way: Language and the Contemporary Arts of War', *PMLA* 124:5 (2009), Special Issue on 'War', pp. 1515–31.

19 J.M. Glionna and A. Khalil, '"Combat Linguists" Battle on Two Fronts', *Los Angeles Times*, 5 June 2005 <http://articles.latimes.com/2005/jun/05/world/fg-interpret5> [accessed 25 April 2015].

20 Baker, 'Interpreters and Translators in the War Zone', p. 213.

21 Ibid., pp. 216–17.

22 See Baker, 'Interpreters and Translators in the War Zone', for a comprehensive survey of the published literature in the field. Since the publication of Baker's essay, a number of new titles have appeared within the recently launched 'Palgrave Studies in Languages at War' series: among these, of particular relevance for the subject of this book are H. Footitt and M. Kelly (eds), *Languages at War: Policies and Practices of Language Contacts in Conflict* (Basingstoke: Palgrave Macmillan, 2012); H. Footitt and M. Kelly (eds), *Languages and the Military: Alliances, Occupation and Peace Building* (Basingstoke: Palgrave Macmillan, 2012); M. Kelly and C. Baker, *Interpreting the Peace: Peace Operations, Conflict and Language in*

Bosnia-Herzegovina (Basingstoke: Palgrave Macmillan, 2012). The case for the need to rethink the translator's task is convincingly put in M. Tymoczko, 'Translation, Ethics and Ideology in a Violent Globalizing World', in Bielsa and Hughes (eds), *Globalization, Political Violence and Translation*, pp. 171–94. Over a number of successive contributions on language workers in Iraq, Moira Inghilleri has offered a far-ranging critique of the code of ethics that currently guides linguists' training and practice; in her more recent monograph study, *Interpreting Justice: Ethics, Politics, and Language* (New York: Routledge, 2012), she has broadened the scope of her research to include also interpreting in the legal field and in the UK asylum system.

23 The films and books listed in Apter's 'Translation—9/11' to substantiate her argument about the rise to prominence of the translation theme all date from the mid-2000s onwards, and the same holds true for the translators' memoirs considered in Inghilleri's *Interpreting Justice* and in Marija Todorova's essay 'Interpreting Conflict: Memories of an Interpreter', in K. Kaindl and K. Spitzl (eds), *Transfiction: Research into the Realities of Translation Fiction* (Amsterdam: John Benjamins, 2014), pp. 221–32. This edited volume provides a wide-ranging diachronic survey of the presence of translation as theme and of translators and interpreters as characters in literature and film, though not in drama.

24 I have addressed this topic and its treatment in contemporary British drama in 'New Order, New Borders: Post-Cold War Europe on the British stage', in R. Littlejohns and S. Soncini (eds), *Myths of Europe* (Amsterdam: Rodopi, 2007), pp. 247–61. For an in-depth analysis of the translation theme in *Pentecost* as an expression of the play's politics, see J. Spencer, 'Performing Translation in Contemporary Anglo-American Drama', *Theatre Journal* 59 (2007), pp. 389–410.

25 Apter, *Translation Zone*, p. 16.

26 In addition to the fictional Kavkhar and Drozhdani languages—the first largely based on Bulgarian, the second a hybrid mix of Azerbaijani and other Western Turkic languages—characters in the play speak French, German, Italian, as well as different variants of English as a native or second language.

27 For a detailed discussion of the politics of untranslatability in *The Prisoner's Dilemma* see S. Soncini, '"A Job for the Go-Between": Dramatising Translation in Brian Friel and David Edgar', in S. Coelsch-Foisner and H. Klein (eds), *Drama Translation and Theatre Practice* (Frankfurt am Main: Peter Lang, 2004), pp. 489–507.

28 L. Gardner, review of *The Prisoner's Dilemma*, *Guardian*, 31 January 2002, in *Theatre Record* 22 (2002), pp. 102–04.

29 For a detailed description of the original production see A. Sierz, *The Theatre of Martin Crimp* (London: Methuen, 2006), pp. 50–51.

30 This view is held by C. Escoda Agustí in *Martin Crimp's Theatre: Collapse as Resistance to Late Capitalist Society* (Berlin: de Gruyter, 2013). In Escoda Agustí's analysis of *Attempts*, the young woman's question, 'What?' is univocally interpreted as a refusal to participate in 'late capitalist exploitative relationships', and the female speaker is seen as a mouthpiece for the author's 'radical disagreement' with the oppressive parameters of the society of the spectacle (p. 133). I see a problem with these neat identifications given the

suspicion that surrounds each and every attempt at pinning down the play's central character.

31 Until not very long ago, this silence also extended to translation scholarship (see Baker, 'Interpreters and Translators in the War Zone'). Moira Inghilleri has underscored the paradox whereby in the critical literature, 'the problem of the unacknowledged visibility of the translator of written texts has received more critical attention than the questionable insistence on the invisibility of the highly visible interpreter of spoken utterances'. Inghilleri, *Interpreting Justice*, p. ix.

32 G. Packer, *Betrayed: A Play* (New York: Faber and Faber, 2008), p. vii. Further references to this edition are given after quotations in the text.

33 M. Inghilleri, 'Translators in War Zones: Ethics under Fire in Iraq', in Bielsa and Hughes (eds), *Globalization, Political Violence and Translation*, pp. 207–21 (p. 212).

34 D. Filkins, 'A Reporter Finds Drama in Iraqis' Heartbreak', *New York Times*, 3 February 2008 <http://www.nytimes.com/2008/02/03/theater/03filk.html?ref=topics&_r=0> [accessed 25 April 2015].

35 Prescott, too, is a mixed character. Described in the characters list as 'A junior foreign service officer from Missouri, posted at the U.S. Embassy in Baghdad' (5), Prescott is an amalgam of the Embassy's political counsellor, Robert Ford, and of a handful of more enlightened members of embassy staff who were sympathetic to the Iraqis' predicament and outraged by the indifference and insensitivity of their colleagues and seniors. He is also a very recognizable version of Kirk Johnson, a young information officer with the United States Agency for International Development (USAID) in Baghdad who holds a special place among the Americans mentioned in the *New Yorker* article for his strenuous campaigning in support of visa requests by Iraqi foreign-service personnel whom the US administration had callously left behind, although their safety was severely imperilled by their former association with the occupying forces. Johnson's story made its way into a documentary film, *The List*, released in 2012.

36 In her study on wartime interpreting, Inghilleri likewise stresses the bitter disappointment attendant upon this misunderstanding. Because 'the bond that develops between interpreters and their units is equivalent in many cases to the affective bond which develops among the soldiers of a platoon where safety and survival depend on mutual trust', at interactional level this often results in 'temporarily granting interpreters the status of fictive equals—like fictive kin—within their group'. Language workers, however, are not legitimate members of the military, as they are unmistakably reminded when they are denied their right to protection or asylum as soon as they relinquish their professional role. See M. Inghilleri, '"You Don't Make War without Knowing Why": the Decision to Interpret in Iraq', *The Translator* 16:2 (2010), Special Issue on 'Translation and Violent Conflict', pp. 175–96 (p. 179).

37 Colleran, *Theatre and War*, p. 157.

38 G. Packer, 'Betrayed: The Iraqis who trusted America the most', *The New Yorker*, 26 March 2007 <http://www.newyorker.com/magazine/2007/03/26/betrayed–2> [accessed 7 January 2015].

39 Inghilleri, 'You Don't Make War without Knowing Why', p. 182.

40 The classified report compiled by Major General Antonio Taguba, who was in charge of the investigation, was leaked to the press in May 2004. It is currently available on several web sites; see e.g. <http://news.findlaw.com/hdocs/docs/iraq/tagubarpt.html> [accessed 21 May 2014].

41 L. Ashkenaz Croke, 'American Lawyer Finds New Evidence of Recent Torture in Iraq', *New Standard*, 30 August 2004 < http://www.information-clearinghouse.info/article6820.htm> [accessed 21 May 2014].

42 Apter, 'Translation—9/11', p. 200.

43 My views are shared by Mona Baker in her discussion of Packer's narrative of victimhood as typical of media reports: 'Interpreters and Translators in the War Zone', p. 205.

44 The 'bunker mentality, administrative incompetence and the unwillingness of many Americans working in the CPA to solicit Iraqis' knowledge of the cultural and political landscape of pre- and post-invasion Iraq in the earlier stages of the reconstruction effort' have been indicated by many as 'significant factors in a growing mistrust among Iraqi citizens of the US occupying forces': Inghilleri, 'Translators in War Zones', pp. 212–13.

45 The two quotations are taken, respectively, from 'Iraq: Winning Hearts and Minds', Hearing before the Subcommittee on National Security, Emerging Threats and International Relations, US House of Representatives, 108th Congress, Second Session, June 15, 2004 <https://house.resource.org/108/org.c-span.182290-1.pdf> [accessed 9 September 2014]; and 'Efforts to Improve the Department of Defense's Language and Cultural Awareness Capabilities', Report to US Senate (2007), quoted in Inghilleri, *Interpreting Justice*, p. 113.

46 Quoted in Rafael, 'Translation in Wartime', p. 239.

47 Inghilleri, *Interpreting Justice*, p. 114.

48 For a probing analysis of the historical links between the Vietnam experience and the Second Gulf War see Barkawi, *Globalization and War*, pp. 109–26.

49 See Inghilleri, 'You Don't Make War without Knowing Why', p. 178.

50 As advertised on the National Theatre of Scotland's web site <http://www.nationaltheatrescotland.com/content/default.asp?page=home_BlackWatchEdinburgh2006> [accessed 10 June 2013].

51 G. Burke, *The National Theatre of Scotland's Black Watch*, 2nd rev. edn (London: Faber and Faber, 2010), p. x. Further references to this edition are given after quotations in the text.

52 D. Archibald, '"We're just big bullies ...": Gregory Burke's *Black Watch*', *The Drouth* 26 (2008) <http://eprints.gla.ac.uk/3896/1/The_Drouth3896.pdf> [accessed 30 June 2014], and M. Blumberg, 'Unraveling the "Golden Thread": Performing the Politics of Black Watch', in *Political and Protest Theatre*, pp. 79–92 (p. 79).

53 M. Posner, 'The many shades of Black Watch', *Globe and Mail*, 7 June 2008 <http://www.theglobeandmail.com/arts/the-many-shades-of-black-watch/article674229/> [accessed 17 June 2014]. It must be observed, in partial disconfirmation of this claim, that no such cautiousness is used in the BBC Scotland documentary *Black Watch: A Soldier's Story* included in the DVD of the BBC TV production of the play. Here, the soldiers who inspired

Burke's characters express their views openly, showing no apparent fear of repercussions.

54 T. Reid, 'Post-Devolutionary Drama', in I. Brown (ed.), *The Edinburgh Companion to Scottish Drama* (Edinburgh: Edinburgh University Press, 2011), pp. 188–99 (pp. 195–96). A similar view of the play's allegedly lenient treatment of Scotland's bad conscience can be found in Archibald, 'We're just big bullies' (to whom Reid also refers) and in Boll, *New War Plays*, pp. 105–06.

55 Later on in the play, the pool table doubles as the 'Warrior', the armoured wagon in which Black Watch soldiers lived crammed for weeks on end during their tour of duty in the Iraqi desert. In order to account for the non-verbal elements of the performance, the published version supplements the dramatist's stage directions with a very helpful set of production notes, authored by John Tiffany, and numerous photographs. Unless otherwise specified, my descriptions are based on the BBC TV version of the original production, filmed in Dingwall during the 2007 Scottish tour and released on DVD in 2008, and may sometimes differ from those reported in the text.

56 Butler's argument in *Frames of War* about the varying levels of grievability accorded to Western and non-Western casualties in contemporary conflicts, and the different entitlement to personhood they imply, has been detailed in Chapter One.

57 'David Hare & Max Stafford-Clark', p. 68.

58 C. Parkert, *Witness*, trans. K. Halliwell (London: Oberon, 2002), p. 50.

59 Z. Stahlujak, 'Violent Distortions: Bearing Witness to the Task of Wartime Translators', *TTR: traduction, terminologie, rédaction* 13:1 (2000), pp. 37–51 <http://id.erudit.org/iderudit/037392ar> [accessed 25 April 2015]. Stahlujak grounds her argument in a preliminary review of the invisibility of the interlingual translator in the narratives of the Shoah and the enduring hold of the tenet of linguistic transparency over the theory of testimony that has moved from these narratives.

60 If his story had been known to David Greig at the time of writing, Matthew's career would read as a poignant reference to Sadi Othman's surprising rise to power and prominence within the military and political ranks of the American-led coalition in Iraq. A US-naturalized Palestinian born in Brazil and raised in Jordan, Othman moved quickly from driving a taxi in New York to being one of the most influential players in the Iraqi conflict and beyond. He signed up as a contract linguist in Iraq after the attacks on the Twin Towers, ashamed at the behaviour of his fellow Muslims and determined to place his linguistic and cultural knowledge at the service of world peace; in this capacity, he served as advisor to General David Petreaus during the latter's leadership of Multi-National Security Transition Command-Iraq, and was eventually promoted to the status of senior advisor when Petraeus became Commanding General of Multi-National Force-Iraq in January 2007. In her study on the role of interpreters in culture-centric warfare, Moira Inghilleri has some insightful observations about the figure of a neutral, impartial, pacifist language broker that emerges from official accounts, and the concomitant silence that surrounds Othman's possible moral and political implication in the violence of war: see Inghilleri,

Interpreting Justice, pp. 117–19. This may well be purely coincidental but it is worth noting that the Sunni interpreter in Packer's *Betrayed* is also called Othman.

61 D. Greig, *The American Pilot* (London: Faber and Faber, 2005), p. 24. Further references to this edition are given after quotations in the text.

62 D. Greig quoted in Billingham, *At the Sharp End*, p. 90, and C. Svich, 'Physical Poetry: David Greig in Conversation with Caridad Svich', *PAJ: A Journal of Performance and Art* 29:2 (2007), pp. 51–58 (p. 56).

63 Svich, 'Physical Poetry', p. 56. See also C. Wallace, *The Theatre of David Greig* (London: Bloomsbury, 2013), p. 141.

64 The calque from Steven Spielberg's epic film about Second World War heroism, *Saving Private Ryan* (1998), was exploited *ad nauseam* in triumphalist media reports of the rescue.

65 A very useful reconstruction of the Jessica Lynch saga and its media reverberations is provided in the Harvard Kennedy School of Government Case Program, '"Reporting in the Fog of War": the Story of Jessica Lynch' <http://shorensteincenter.org/wp-content/uploads/2012/03/1773_0_scott.pdf> [accessed 14 July 2014]. In November 2003, Lynch's account of her vicissitudes was delivered through the intermediation of Rick Bragg's pen in a book called *I Am a Soldier, Too: The Jessica Lynch Story*.

66 A concise account of differences between UK and US reviews of the play is provided in Wallace, *David Greig*, p. 145.

67 Butler, *Frames of War*, p. 48.

68 Svich, 'Physical Poetry', p. 56.

69 Wallace, *David Greig*, p. 142.

70 Svich, 'Physical Poetry', pp. 54–55.

71 M. Montgomery, 'Semantic Asymmetries and the "War on Terror"', in Bielsa and Hughes (eds), *Globalization, Political Violence and Translation*, pp. 117–34 (p. 117).

72 The first epigraph to the published text, taken from a book about Ahmad Shah Durrani, the eighteenth-century father to the Afghan nation, reminds the reader that 'the shape of the map of present-day Afghanistan resembles a left-hand fist with the thumb open'. T. Kushner, *Homebody/Kabul* (London: Nick Hern, 2002), n.p.; further references to this edition are given in the text after quotations. In the performance, Kika Markham reproduced the shopkeeper's hand while describing it.

73 From J. Nathan's review of the London production, *Jewish Chronicle*, 1 June 2002, in *Theatre Record* 22 (2002), p. 688.

74 A detailed account of the changing shape of Kushner's play with each subsequent revival is provided in P. Dickinson, 'Travels with Tony Kushner and David Beckham, 2002–2004', *Theatre Journal* 57:3 (2005), pp. 429–50.

75 C. Miller, 'Goodbye Cats … hello Kabul', *Observer*, 5 May 2002 <http://www.theguardian.com/theobserver/2002/may/05/featuresreview.review2> [accessed 25 April 2015].

76 Kushner explained in an interview that apart from Kika Markham's plea to write a monologue for her, the other factor that helped him bring the play into focus after a long gestation was the encounter with Dupree's guide: 'There were all these other books with photos of everything she was

describing in ruins. That's where the idea started: describing a city that doesn't exist any longer.' S. Fanshawe, 'America on the line', *The Times*, 5 May 2002, p. 16.

77 F. Minwalla, 'Tony Kushner's *Homebody/Kabul*: Staging History in a Post-Colonial World', *Theater* 33:1 (2003), pp. 29–43 (p. 31). This in-depth discussion of Kushner's critique of cultural translation was written while the Kabul part of the play was still a work in progress, and therefore considers only the Homebody's monologue. For a penetrating analysis of the full-length version see Spencer, 'Performing Translation'. Colleran devotes some pages to Kushner's work in her chapter on Afghanistan in *Theatre and War*, but unlike Spencer and Minwalla she does not engage with the meta-translation aspect of the play.

78 J. Miller, 'New Forms for New Conflicts: Thinking about Tony Kushner's *Homebody/Kabul* and the Theatre du Soleil's *Le dernier caravanserail*', *Contemporary Theatre Review* 16:2 (2006), pp. 212–19 (p. 261).

79 For a discussion of the autopsy metaphor and its use to characterize biography as a forensic process of sorts, see H. Lee, *Biography: A Very Short Introduction* (Oxford: Oxford University Press, 2009), p. 2.

80 Elizabeth S. Anker suggests that Milton and Priscilla's misadventures lend themselves to be read as 'a parody of various dynamics of Western involvement in Afghanistan'; in particular, she points to the self-interest that guides their rescue operation as a reference to the legacy of empire underpinning the rhetoric of humanitarian intervention. See E.S. Anker, '"The Spectacle of Our Suffering": Staging the International Human Rights Imaginary in Tony Kushner's *Homebody/Kabul*', in F.N. Becker, P.S. Hernández, and B. Werth (eds), *Imagining Human Rights in Twenty-First-Century Theater: Global Perspectives* (New York: Palgrave Macmillan, 2013), pp. 209–25 (p. 210).

81 Bhabha, *The Location of Culture*, p. 162.

82 R. Kearney, 'Introduction: Ricoeur's Philosophy of Translation', in P. Ricoeur, *On Translation,* trans. by E. Brennan (London: Routledge, [2004] 2006), pp. vii–xx (p. xvi). This is Kearney's translation of the passage from the French in his introduction; Eileen Brennan's rendition in the main body text is slightly different.

83 Ricoeur, *On Translation*, p. 10.

Conclusion

1 Caryl Churchill, 'Not Ordinary, Not Safe: A Direction for Drama?', *The Twentieth Century* 168 (1960), pp. 443–51 (446).

Bibliography

Abdulrazzak, H., *Baghdad Wedding* (London: Oberon, 2007).

Adam, H., *The People Next Door* (London: Nick Hern, 2003).

Adam, H., *Petrol Jesus Nightmare #5 (In the Time of the Messiah)* (London: Nick Hern, 2006).

Adshead, K., *Animal* (London: Oberon, 2003).

Adshead, K., *Bites* (London: Oberon, 2005).

Adshead, K., *The Bogus Woman* (London: Oberon, 2001).

Aeschylus, *Persians*, trans. by J. Lembke and C.J. Herington, in P. Burian and A. Shapiro (eds), *The Complete Aeschylus, Volume II: Persians and Other Plays* (New York: Oxford University Press, 2009).

Agamben, G., *State of Exception*, trans. by K. Attell (Chicago: University of Chicago Press, [2003] 2005).

Ali, T., *The Illustrious Corpse* (London: Oberon, 2003).

Ali, T., H. Brenton, and A. de la Tour, *Collateral Damage* (London: Oberon, 1999).

Anderson, D., *Snuff*, in P. Howard (ed.), *Scottish Shorts* (London: Nick Hern, 2010).

Anderson, P., and J. Menon (eds), *Violence Performed: Local Roots and Global Routes of Conflict* (Basingstoke: Palgrave Macmillan, 2009).

Appadurai, A., *Fear of Small Numbers: An Essay on the Geography of Anger* (Durham, NC: Duke University Press, 2006).

Apter, E., *The Translation Zone: A New Comparative Literature* (Princeton: Princeton University Press, 2006).

Aristotle, *Poetics*, trans. by M. Heath (London: Penguin, 1996).

Ashkenaz Croke, L., 'American Lawyer Finds New Evidence of Recent Torture in Iraq', *New Standard*, 30 August 2004 <http://www.informationclearinghouse.info/article6820.htm> [accessed 21 May 2014].

Asor Rosa, A., *La guerra. Sulle forme attuali della convivenza umana* (Turin: Einaudi, 2002).

Aston E., and E. Diamond (eds), *The Cambridge Companion to Caryl Churchill* (Cambridge: Cambridge University Press, 2009).

Azama, M., *Crossfire* (London: Oberon, [1993] 2003).

Badham, V., *Capital* (Hobart: The Australian Script Centre, 2003).

Ball, E., 'Truth, Power and Inquiry', *Quest* 4 (2007) <http://www.qub.ac.uk/sites/QUEST/JournalIssues/> [accessed 24 April 2015].

Baker, M., 'Interpreters and Translators in the War Zone: Narrated and Narrators', *The Translator* 16:2 (2010), Special Issue on 'Translation and Violent Conflict', pp. 197–222.

Bar-Yosef, E., '"I'm just a pen": Travel, Performance, and Orientalism in David Hare's *Via Dolorosa* and *Acting Up*', *Theatre Journal* 59 (2007), pp. 259–77.

Barkawi, T., *Globalization and War* (Lanham, MD: Rowman & Littlefield, 2006).

Barker, H., *Collected Plays, Volume Three (The Power of the Dog, The Europeans, Women Beware Women, Minna, Judith, Ego in Arcadia)* (London: Calder, 1996).

Barnett, D., 'When is a Play not a Drama? Two Examples of Postdramatic Theatre Texts', *New Theatre Quarterly* 24:1 (February 2008), pp. 14–23.

Bartlett, M., *13* (London: Methuen, 2011).

Bartlett, M., *Artefacts*, in *Plays: 1 (Not Talking; My Child; Artefacts; Contractions; Cock)* (London: Methuen, 2011).

Bassnett, S., and A. Lefevere (eds), *Constructing Cultures: Essays on Literary Translation* (Clevedon: Cromwell Press, 1998).

Bassnett, S., and A. Lefevere (eds), *Translation, History and Culture* (London: Pinter, 1990).

Baudrillard, J., *The Gulf War did not Take Place*, trans. by P. Patton (Bloomington: Indiana University Press, [1991] 1995).

Baudrillard, J., *Simulacra and Simulations*, trans. by S. Faria Glaser (Ann Arbor: University of Michigan Press, [1981] 1994).

Baudrillard, J., *The Spirit of Terrorism and Other Essays*, trans. by C. Turner (London: Verso, 2003).

Baudrillard, J., *The Transparency of Evil. Essays on Extreme Phenomena*, trans. by James Benedict (London: Verso, [1990] 1993).

Bayley, C., *The Container* (London: Nick Hern, 2007).

Bean, R., *The God Botherers* (London: Oberon, 2003).

Beaton, A., *Follow My Leader* (London: Methuen, 2004).

Becker, F.N., P.S. Hernández, and B. Werth (eds), *Imagining Human Rights in Twenty-First-Century Theater: Global Perspectives* (New York: Palgrave Macmillan, 2013).

Beebee, T.O., 'Shoot The Transtraitor! The Translator as *Homo Sacer* in Fiction and Reality', *The Translator* 16:2 (2010), Special Issue on 'Translation and Violent Conflict', pp. 295–313.

Bell, J., 'Performance Studies in an Age of Terror', *TDR: The Drama Review* 47:2 (2003), pp. 6–8.

Benoist, A. de, 'The 20th Century Ended September 11', trans. by K. Ackermann, *Telos* 121 (2001) pp. 113–33.

Berkoff, S., *Requiem for Ground Zero* (Charlbury: Amber Lane Press, 2002).

Bermann, S., and M. Wood (eds), *Nation, Language, and the Ethics of Translation* (Princeton: Princeton University Press, 2005).

Bhabha, H., *The Location of Culture* (London: Routledge, 1994).

Bielsa, E., and C.W. Hughes (eds), *Globalization, Political Violence and Translation* (Basingstoke: Palgrave Macmillan, 2009).

Billingham, P., *At the Sharp End: Uncovering the Work of Five Contemporary Dramatists* (London: Methuen, 2007).

Blackhurst, R., 'The air force men who fly drones in Afghanistan by remote control', *The Telegraph*, 24 September 2012 <http://www.telegraph.co.uk/news/uknews/defence/9552547/The-air-force-men-who-fly-drones-in-Afghanistan-by-remote-control.html> [accessed 18 February 2015].

Blank, J., and E. Jensen, *Aftermath* (New York: Dramatists Play Service, 2010).

Boll, J., *The New War Plays: From Kane to Harris* (Basingstoke: Palgrave Macmillan, 2013).

Borradori, G., *Philosophy in a Time of Terror: Dialogues with Jürgen Habermas and Jacques Derrida* (Chicago: University of Chicago Press, 2003).

Borowski, M., and M. Sugiera (eds), *Fictional Realities / Real Fictions* (Newcastle: Cambridge Scholars, 2007).

Bottoms, S., 'Putting the Document into Documentary: An Unwelcome Corrective?', *TDR: The Drama Review* 50:3 (2006).

Brace, A., *Stovepipe* (London: Faber and Faber, 2009).

Brady, S., *Performance, Politics, and the War on Terror: 'Whatever it Takes'* (Basingstoke: Palgrave Macmillan, 2012).

Bratich, J., 'Cultural Studies, Immanent War, Everyday Life', in N.K. Denzin and Y.S. Lincoln (eds), *9/11 in American Culture* (Oxford: Altamira, 2003), pp. 41–43.

Bratich, J., 'Public Secrecy and Immanent Security: A Strategic Analysis', *Cultural Studies* 20:4–5 (2006), pp. 493–511.

Brittain, V., 'Questions and lies', *Guardian*, 24 May 2004 <http://www.theguardian.com/stage/2004/may/24/theatre.guantanamo> [accessed 24 April 2015].

Brittain, V., and G. Slovo, *Guantanamo: 'Honor Bound to Defend Freedom'* (London: Oberon, 2004).

Brown I. (ed.), *The Edinburgh Companion to Scottish Drama* (Edinburgh: Edinburgh University Press, 2011).

Buffini, M., *Welcome to Thebes* (London: Faber and Faber, 2010).

Burke, G., *The National Theatre of Scotland's Black Watch*, 2nd rev. edn (London: Faber and Faber, 2010).

Burke, G., *The Straits* (London: Faber and Faber, 2003).

Butler, J., *Frames of War: When is Life Grievable?* (London: Verso, 2009).

Cantrell T., and M. Luckhurst (eds), *Playing for Real: Actors on Playing Real People* (Basingstoke: Palgrave Macmillan, 2010).

Carlson, M., *Speaking in Tongues: Languages at Play in the Theatre* (Ann Arbor: University of Michigan Press, 2009).

Cavarero, A., *Orrorismo, ovvero della violenza sull'inerme* (Milan: Feltrinelli, 2007).

Chaudhury, U., 'Different Hats', *Theater* 33:3 (2003), pp. 132–34.

Churchill, C., *Drunk Enough to Say I Love You?* (London: Nick Hern, 2006).

Churchill, C., *Far Away* (London: Nick Hern, 2000).

Churchill, C., 'Not Ordinary, Not Safe: A Direction for Drama?', *The Twentieth Century* 168 (1960), pp. 443–51.

Churchill, C., *Seven Jewish Children: A Play for Gaza* (London: Nick Hern, 2009).

Churchill, C., *This is a Chair* (London: Nick Hern, 1999).

Clausewitz, C. von, *On War*, trans. by M. Howard and P. Paret (London: David Campbell, 1993).

Colleran, J., 'Disposable Wars, Disappearing Acts: Theatrical Responses to the 1991 Gulf War', *Theatre Journal* 55 (2003), pp. 613–32.

Colleran, J., *Theatre and War: Theatrical Responses since 1991* (New York: Palgrave Macmillan, 2012).

Connor, S., *Postmodernist Culture: An Introduction to Theories of the Contemporary* (London: Basil Blackwell, 1989).

Craig, R., *What We Did to Weinstein* (London: Oberon, 2005).

Crimp, M., *Attempts on her Life* (London: Faber and Faber, 1997).

Crimp, M., *Cruel and Tender* (London: Faber and Faber, 2004).

Cronin, M., *Translation and Identity* (London: Routledge, 2006).

Dao, J., and E. Schmitt, 'A nation challenged: Hearts and minds; Pentagon readies efforts to sway sentiment abroad', *New York Times*, 19 February 2002 <http://www.nytimes.com/2001/10/07/us/a-nation-challenged-the-weapons-in-80-s-afghan-militias-used-us-rifles.html> [accessed 12 March 2015].

Dear, N., *Lunch in Venice*, in S. Graham-Adriani (ed.), *Shell Connections 2005: New Plays for Young People* (London: Faber and Faber, 2005).

Debord, G., *Comments on the Society of the Spectacle*, trans. by M. Imrie (London: Verso, [1988] 1990).

Debord, G., *Society of the Spectacle*, trans. by D. Nicholson-Smith, 3rd edn (New York: Zone Books, [1967] 1994).

Dente, C., 'Intersemiotic Complexities: The Word of Drama', in M. Bertuccelli Papi, G. Cappelli, and S. Masi (eds), *Lexical Complexity: Theoretical Assessment and Translational Perspectives* (Pisa: Plus/Pisa University Press, 2007).

Dente, C., and S. Soncini (eds), *Conflict Zones: Actions Languages Mediations* (Pisa: ETS, 2004).

Der Derian, J., 'Imaging Terror: Logos, Pathos and Ethos', *Third World Quartely* 26:1 (2005), pp. 23–47.

Derrida, J., 'No Apocalypse, Not Now (Full Speed Ahead, Seven Missiles, Seven Missives)', *Diacritics* 14:2 (1984), pp. 20–31.

Dickinson, P., 'Travels with Tony Kushner and David Beckham, 2002–2004', *Theatre Journal* 57:3 (2005), pp. 429–50.

Edgar, D., 'Doc and Dram', *Guardian*, 27 September 2008 <http://www.theguardian.com/stage/2008/sep/27/theatre.davidedgar> [accessed 13 May 2012].

Edgar, D., *Pentecost* (London: Nick Hern, 1995).

Edgar, D., *The Prisoner's Dilemma*, 2nd rev. edn (London: Nick Hern, 2002).

Edgar, D., *The Shape of the Table* (London: Nick Hern, 1990).

Eldridge, D., *M.A.D.*, in *Plays 1: Serving It Up, Summer Begins, Under the Blue Sky, M.A.D.* (London: Methuen, 2005).

Elliott, D., and M. McGuinness, 'Public Inquiry: Panacea or Placebo?', *Journal of Contingencies and Crisis Management* 10:1 (2002), pp. 14–25.

Escoda Agustí, C., *Martin Crimp's Theatre: Collapse as Resistance to Late Capitalist Society* (Berlin: de Gruyter, 2013).

Favorini, A., 'Representation and Reality: The Case of Documentary Theatre', *Theatre Survey* 35:2 (1994), pp. 31–42.

Feehily, S., *Bang, Bang, Bang* (London: Nick Hern, 2006).

Feehily, S., *O Go My Man* (London: Nick Hern, 2006).

Feldman, A., 'The Structuring Enemy and Archival War', *PMLA* 124:5 (2009), Special Issue on 'War', pp. 1704–13.

Finnegan, L., *No Questions Asked: News Coverage since 9/11* (Westport, CT: Praeger, 2007).

Footitt, H., and M. Kelly (eds), *Languages and the Military: Alliances, Occupation and Peace Building* (Basingstoke: Palgrave Macmillan, 2012).

Footitt, H., and M. Kelly (eds), *Languages at War: Policies and Practices of Language Contacts in Conflict* (Basingstoke: Palgrave Macmillan, 2012).

Forsyth, A., and C. Megson (eds), *Get Real: Documentary Theatre Past and Present* (Basingstoke: Palgrave Macmillan, 2009).

Freedman, D., and D.K. Thussu (eds), *Media and Terrorism: Global Perspectives* (London: Sage, 2012).

Friel, B., *Translations* (London: Faber and Faber, 1981).

Friel, M., 'Human Problems Facing Translators and Interpreters Worldwide Today', *Translation Ireland* 16:1 (2005), pp. 4–6.

Fussell, P., *The Great War and Modern Memory* (Oxford: Oxford University Press, 1977).

Garner, S.B., *Bodied Spaces: Phenomenology and Performance in Contemporary Drama* (Ithaca, NY: Cornell University Press, 1994).

Gilroy, S., *Motherland* (London: Oberon, 2009).

Glionna, J.M., and A. Khalil, '"Combat Linguists" Battle on Two Fronts', *Los Angeles Times*, 5 June 2005 <http://articles.latimes.com/2005/jun/05/world/fg-interpret5> [accessed 25 April 2015].

Goffman, E., *Strategic Interaction* (Philadelphia: University of Pennsylvania Press, 1969).

Görtschacher, W., and H. Klein (eds), *Modern War on Stage and Screen/Der moderne Krieg auf der Bühne* (Lewiston, NY: E. Mellen, 1997).

Grace, F., *Gifts of War*, in F. Grace and N. Wallace, *Two Into War* (London: Oberon Books, 2005).

Greenberg, R.D., *Language and Identity in the Balkans* (Oxford: Oxford University Press, 2004).

Greig, D., *The American Pilot* (London: Faber and Faber, 2005).

Greig, D., *Damascus* (London: Faber and Faber, 2007).

Greig, D., *Dunsinane* (London: Faber and Faber, 2010).

Greig, D., *Europe*, in *Plays 1: Europe; The Architect; The Cosmonaut's Last Message to the Woman he Once Loved in the Soviet Union* (London: Methuen, 2002).

Greig, D., *Ramallah*, in P. Howard (ed.), *Scottish Shorts* (London: Nick Hern, 2010).

Griffiths, T., *The Gulf Between Us, or, The Truth and Other Fictions* (London: Faber and Faber, 1992).

Gupta, T., *Sanctuary* (London: Oberon, 2002).

Habermas, J., *The Theory of Communicative Action*, trans. by T. McCarthy, 2 vols (Boston: Beacon Press, 1995 [1981]).

Halliwell, S., *The Aesthetics of Mimesis: Ancient Texts and Modern Problems* (Princeton: Princeton University Press, 2002).
Hammond W., and D. Steward (eds), *Verbatim Verbatim: Contemporary Documentary Theatre* (London: Oberon, 2008).
Hare, D., *Acting Up* (London: Faber and Faber, 1999).
Hare, D., *Berlin/Wall* (London: Faber and Faber, 2009).
Hare, D., *Stuff Happens* (London: Faber and Faber, 2004).
Hare, D., *The Vertical Hour* (London: Faber and Faber, 2008).
Hare, D., *Via Dolorosa & When Shall We Live?* (London: Faber and Faber, 1998).
Hare, D., 'Why Fabulate?', *Guardian*, 2 February 2002, Saturday Review, p. 3 (repr. in D. Hare, *Obedience, Struggle and Revolt: Lectures on Theatre* (London: Faber and Faber, 2005)).
Harris, Z., *Fall* (London: Faber and Faber, 2008).
Harris, Z., *Midwinter* (London: Faber and Faber, 2004).
Harris, Z., *Solstice* (London: Faber and Faber, 2005).
Harris, Z., *The Wheel* (London: Faber and Faber, 2011).
Harvard Kennedy School of Government Case Program, '"Reporting in the Fog of War": the Story of Jessica Lynch' <http://shorensteincenter.org/wp-content/uploads/2012/03/1773_0_scott.pdf> [accessed 14 July 2014].
Hegarty, A., 'Truth, Law and Official Denial: The Case of Bloody Sunday', *Criminal Law Forum* 15 (2004), pp. 199–246.
Hegel, G.W.F., *Aesthetics. Lectures on Fine Arts*, trans. by T.M. Knox, 2 vols, (Oxford: Clarendon Press, 1998).
Herron, T., and J. Lynch, *After Bloody Sunday: Representation, Ethics, Justice* (Cork: Cork University Press, 2007).
Hesford, W.S., 'Staging Terror', *TDR: The Drama Review* 50:3 (2006), pp. 29–41.
Hess, M., 'Translator, traitor: A critical ethnography of a U.S. terrorism trial' (unpublished dissertation, The Graduate Center, CUNY, 2014), <http://works.gc.cuny.edu/etd/226/> [accessed 17 September 2014].
Holcroft, S., *Cockroach* (London: Nick Hern, 2008).
Holdsworth, N., and M. Luckhurst (eds), *A Concise Companion to Contemporary British and Irish Drama* (Oxford: Blackwell, 2008).
Hoskins, A., and B. O'Loughlin, *War and Media: The Emergence of Diffused War* (London: Polity Press, 2010).
Howard, T., and J. Stokes (eds), *Acts of War. The Representation of Military Conflict on the British Stage and Television since 1945* (Aldershot: Scolar Press, 1996).
Howe Kritzer, A., '*Drunk Enough to Say I Love You?* (Review)', *Theatre Journal* 59:30 (2007), pp. 516–17.
Hughes, J., *Performance in a Time of Terror: Critical Mimesis and the Age of Uncertainty* (Manchester: Manchester University Press, 2011).
Hughes, J., 'Theatre, Performance and the "War on Terror": Ethical and Political Questions Arising from British Theatrical Responses to War and Terrorism', *Contemporary Theatre Review* 17:2 (2007), pp. 149–64.
Hutchinson, R., *Topless Mum* (London: Oberon, 2008).
Ignatieff, M., 'The Terrorist as Auteur', *New York Times*, 14 November 2004 <http://www.nytimes.com/2004/11/14/movies/14TERROR.html?_r=0> [accessed 17 March 2015].

Ignatieff, M., *Virtual War: Kosovo and Beyond* (London: Vintage, 2001).

Inghilleri, M., *Interpreting Justice: Ethics, Politics, and Language* (New York: Routledge, 2012).

Inghilleri, M., '"You Don't Make War without Knowing Why": the Decision to Interpret in Iraq', *The Translator* 16:2 (2010), Special Issue on 'Translation and Violent Conflict', pp. 175–96.

Innes, C., 'Towards a Post-Millennial Mainstream? Documents of the Times', *Modern Drama* 50 (2007), pp. 435–52.

Isikoff, M., and D. Corn, *Hubris: The Inside Story of Spin, Scandal, and the Iraq War* (New York: Crown Publishers, 2006).

Jakovlievic, B., 'Theater of Atrocities: Toward a Disreality Principle', *PMLA* 124:5 (2009), Special Issue on 'War', pp. 1813–19.

Jeffers, A., *Refugees, Theatre and Crisis: Performing Global Identities* (Basingstoke: Palgrave Macmillan, 2012).

Jeffords, S., and L. Rabinovitz (eds), *Seeing Through the Media: The Persian Gulf War* (New Brunswick, NJ: Rutgers University Press, 1994).

Jones, D.H., *Samuel Beckett and Testimony* (Basingstoke: Palgrave Macmillan, 2011).

Joxe, A., *Le cycle de la dissuasion, 1945–1990: Essai de stratégie critique* (Paris: La Découverte, 1990).

Joxe, A., *Empire of Disorder* (Cambridge, MA: MIT Press, 2002).

Kaindl, K., and K. Spitzl (eds), *Transfiction: Research into the Realities of Translation Fiction* (Amsterdam: John Benjamins, 2014).

Kalb, J., 'Documentary Solo Performance: The Politics of the Mirrored Self', *Theater* 31:3 (2001), pp. 13–29.

Kaldor, M., 'Beyond Militarism, Arms Races and Arms Control', *Social Science Research Council/After Sept. 11* (2001) <http://essays.ssrc.org/sept11/essays/kaldor_text_only.htm> [accessed 13 February 2014] (repr. in C. Calhoun, P. Price and A. Timmer (eds), *Understanding September 11* (New York: The New Press, 2002)).

Kaldor, M., 'In Defence of New Wars', *Stability* 2(1):4 (2013), pp. 1–16 <DOI: http://dx.doi.org/10.5334/sta.at>.

Kaldor, M., *New and Old Wars: Organized Violence in a Global Era*, 2nd edn (Cambridge: Polity Press, 1999).

Kane, S., *Complete Plays: Blasted, Phaedra's Love, Cleansed, Crave, 4.48 Psychosis, Skin* (London: Methuen, 2001).

Kellner, D., *The Persian Gulf TV War* (Boulder, CO: Westview Press, 1992).

Kelly, D., *After the End* (London: Oberon, 2005).

Kelly, D., *Orphans* (London: Oberon, 2009).

Kelly, D., *Osama the Hero* (London: Oberon, 2005).

Kelly, M., and C. Baker, *Interpreting the Peace: Peace Operations, Conflict and Language in Bosnia-Herzegovina* (Basingstoke: Palgrave Macmillan, 2012).

Kemp, E., *5/11* (London: Nick Hern, 2005).

Kent, N., *Srebrenica* (London: Oberon, 2005).

Kushner, T., *Homebody/Kabul* (London: Nick Hern, 2002).

Kuti, E., 'Tragic Plots from Bootle to Baghdad', *Contemporary Theatre Review* 18:4 (2008), pp. 457–69.

LaBute, N., *The Mercy Seat* (New York: Faber and Faber, 2003).

LaCapra, D., *Writing History, Writing Trauma* (Baltimore: Johns Hopkins University Press, 2001).

Lane, D., *Contemporary British Drama* (Edinburgh: Edinburgh University Press, 2010).

Lee, H., *Biography: A Very Short Introduction* (Oxford: Oxford University Press, 2009).

Lehmann, H.-T., *Postdramatic Theatre*, trans. by K. Jürs-Munby (London: Routledge, [1999] 2006).

Leiss, W., 'The Myth of the Information Society', in I. Angus and S. Jhally (eds), *Cultural Politics in Contemporary America* (New York: Routledge, 1989).

Lichtenstein, J., *The Pull of Negative Gravity* (London: Nick Hern, 2004).

Linden, S., *Crocodile Seeking Refuge* (London: Aurora Metro Publications, 2005).

Linden, S., *I Have Before Me a Remarkable Document Given to Me by a Young Lady from Rwanda* (London: Ice and Fire, 2003).

Lloyd Malcolm, M., *Belongings* (London: Oberon, 2011).

Luckhurst, R., *The Trauma Question* (London: Routledge, 2008).

Magelssen, S., 'Rehearsing the "Warrior Ethos": "Theatre Immersion" and the Simulation of Theatres of War', *TRD: The Drama Review* 53:1 (2009), pp. 47–72.

Mahindru, N., *The Hot Zone: Individual Truth versus the Global War on Terror* (London: Oberon, 2005).

Marowitz, C., 'Let's Not Forgo Imagination for Voyeurism', *New York Times*, 29 October 2000 <http://www.nytimes.com/2000/10/29/arts/29MARO.html> [accessed 7 February 2013].

Martin, C., 'Bodies of Evidence', *TDR: The Drama Review* 50:3 (2006), pp. 9–15.

Martin, C. (ed.), *Dramaturgy of the Real on the World Stage* (Basingstoke: Palgrave Macmillan, 2010).

Martin, C., *Theatre of the Real* (Basingstoke: Palgrave Macmillan, 2013).

McDonagh, M., *The Lieutenant of Inishmore* (London: Methuen, 2001).

McGrath, J., *Hyperlynx* (London: Oberon, 2002).

McGuinness, F., *Speaking like Magpies* (London: Faber and Faber, 2005).

McLoughlin, K. (ed.), *The Cambridge Companion to War Writing* (Cambridge: Cambridge University Press, 2009).

McManus, D., 'Great Souls, Big Wheels, and Other Words: Experiments with Truth and Representation in Verbatim Theatre', in K. Gounaridou (ed.), *Text and Presentation 2009* (Jefferson, NC: McFarland, 2010).

Mieszkowski, J., 'Watching War', *PMLA* 124:5 (2009), Special Issue on 'War', pp. 1648–61.

Miller, J., 'New Forms for New Conflicts: Thinking about Tony Kushner's *Homebody/Kabul* and the Theatre du Soleil's *Le dernier caravanserail*', *Contemporary Theatre Review* 16:2 (2006), pp. 212–19.

Minwalla, F., 'Tony Kushner's *Homebody/Kabul*: Staging History in a Post-Colonial World', *Theater* 33:1 (2003), pp. 29–43.

Monks, A., '"This Painful Chapter": Performing the Law in *Bloody Sunday: Scenes from the Saville Inquiry*', *Contemporary Theatre Review* 23:3 (2013), pp. 345–56.

Montanari, F., *Linguaggi della guerra* (Rome: Meltemi, 2004).

Morgan, A., *Splendour* (London: Oberon, 2000).
Morris, P., *Guardians* (London: Oberon, 2005).
Nelson, A., *The Guys*, in A Havis (ed.), *American Political Plays after 9/11* (Carbondale: Southern Illinois University Press, 2010).
Norton-Taylor, R. (ed.), *Bloody Sunday: Scenes from the Saville Inquiry* (London: Oberon, 2005).
Norton-Taylor, R. (ed.), *Called to Account: The indictment of Anthony Charles Lynton Blair for the crime of aggression against Iraq—a hearing* (London: Oberon, 2007).
Norton-Taylor, R. (ed.), *The Colour of Justice: Based on the Transcripts of the Stephen Lawrence Inquiry* (London: Oberon, 1999).
Norton-Taylor, R. (ed.), *Justifying War: Scenes from the Hutton Inquiry* (London: Oberon, 2003).
Norton-Taylor, R. (ed.), *Nuremberg: The War Crimes Trial* (London: Nick Hern, 1997).
Norton-Taylor, R. (ed.), *Tactical Questioning: Scenes from the Baha Mousa Inquiry* (London: Oberon, 2011).
Norton-Taylor, R., and J. McGrath, *Half the Picture*, in R. Norton-Taylor and M. Lloyd, *Truth is a Difficult Concept: Inside the Scott Inquiry* (London: Fourth Estate, 1995).
O'Reilly, K., *Henhouse* (London: Oberon, 2004).
Owen, G., *The Drowned World* (London: Methuen, 2002).
Packer, G., *Betrayed: A Play* (New York: Faber and Faber, 2008).
Packer, G., 'Betrayed: The Iraqis who trusted America the most', *The New Yorker*, 26 March 2007 <http://www.newyorker.com/magazine/2007/03/26/betrayed–2> [accessed 7 January 2015].
Paget, D., *True Stories? Documentary Drama on Radio, Screen and Stage* (Manchester: Manchester University Press, 1990).
Paget, D., 'Verbatim Theatre: Oral History and Documentary Techniques', *New Theatre Quarterly* 3:12 (1987), pp. 317–36.
Parkert, C., *Witness*, trans. by K. Halliwell (London: Oberon, [1995] 2002).
Pascal, J., *Crossing Jerusalem and Other Plays* (London: Oberon, 2003).
Pinter, H., *Plays 4: Betrayal, Monologue, One For The Road, Mountain Language, Family Voices, A Kind Of Alaska, Victoria Station, Precisely, The New World Order, Party Time, Moonlight, Ashes to Ashes, Celebration* (London: Faber and Faber, 2005).
Poirier, L., *Le chantier stratégique* (Paris: Hachette, 1997).
Pratt, M.L., 'Harm's Way: Language and the Contemporary Arts of War', *PMLA*, 124:5 (2009), Special Issue on 'War', pp. 1515–31.
Presnyakov Brothers, *Terrorism*, trans. by S. Dugdale (London: Nick Hern, 2003).
Rafael, V.L., 'Translation in Wartime', *Public Culture* 19:2 (2007), pp. 239–46.
Raffo, H., *Nine Parts of Desire* (Evanston, IL: Northwestern University Press, 2006).
Rau P., (ed.), *Conflict, Nationhood and Corporeality in Modern Literature* (Basingstoke: Palgrave Macmillan, 2010).
Ravenhill, M., *Product*, in *Plays 2: Mother Clap's Molly House, Product, The Cut, Citizenship, Pool (No Water)* (London: Methuen, 2008).

Ravenhill, M., *Shoot/Get Treasure/Repeat* (London: Methuen, 2008).

Reinelt, J., 'Toward a Poetics of Theatre and Public Events: In the Case of Stephen Lawrence', *TDR: The Drama Review* 50:3 (2006), pp. 69–87.

Retort, *Afflicted Powers: Capital and Spectacle in a New Age of War* (London: Verso, 2005).

Rickman, A., and K. Viner (eds), *My Name is Rachel Corrie* (London, Nick Hern, 2005).

Ricoeur, P., *On Translation*, trans. by E. Brennan (London: Routledge, [2004] 2006).

Roberts, P., *About Churchill: The Playwright and the Work* (London: Faber and Faber, 2008).

Robertson, R., *Globalization: Social Theory and Global Culture* (London: Sage, 1992).

Roger, N., *Image Warfare in the War on Terror* (Basingstoke: Palgrave Macmillan, 2013).

Rogers, J.T., *The Overwhelming* (London: Methuen, 2006).

Rogers, N., 'The Play of Law: Comparing Performances in Law and Theatre', *Queensland University of Technology Law Journal* 8:2 (2008), pp. 429–43.

Rolston, B., 'Assembling the Jigsaw: Truth, Justice and Transition in the North of Ireland', *Race & Class* 44 (2002), pp. 87–105.

Rolston, B., and P. Scraton, 'In the Full Glare of English Politics: Ireland, Inquiries and the British State', *British Journal of Criminology* 45:4 (2005), pp. 547–64.

Salama-Carr, M. (ed.), *Translating and Interpreting Conflict* (Amsterdam: Rodopi, 2007).

Scarry, E., *The Body in Pain: The Making and Unmaking of the World* (Oxford: Oxford University Press, 1985).

Schechner, R., '9/11 as Avant-Garde Art?', *PMLA* 124:5 (2009), Special Issue on 'War', pp. 1820–29.

Schiavenza, M., 'France declares its own "War on Terror"', *The Atlantic*, 10 January 2015 <http://www.theatlantic.com/international/archive/2015/01/france-declares-its-own-war-on-terror/384409> [accessed 13 February 2015].

Sedley, S., 'Public Inquiries: A Cure or a Disease?', *Modern Law Review*, 52:4 (1989), pp. 469–79.

Shakespeare, W., *As You Like It*, in *The Complete Works*, ed. by S. Wells and G. Taylor, Oxford Shakespeare Series (Oxford: Clarendon, 1988).

Shakespeare, W., *Henry V*, in *The Complete Works*, ed. by S. Wells and G. Taylor, Oxford Shakespeare Series (Oxford: Clarendon, 1988).

Shaplin, A., *Pugilist Specialist* (London: Oberon, 2003).

Sierz, A., *Rewriting the Nation: British Theatre Today* (London: Methuen, 2011).

Sierz, A., *The Theatre of Martin Crimp* (London: Methuen, 2006).

Sierz, A., 'To each his Via Dolorosa', *Al-Ahram Weekly*, 5 February 2001 <http://weekly.ahram.org.eg/1998/1948/396_via.htm> [accessed 18 January 2011].

Soans, R., *The Arab-Israeli Cookbook* (London: Aurora Metro, 2005).

Soans, R., *Talking to Terrorists* (London: Oberon, 2005).

Soncini, S., '"A horror so deep only ritual can contain it": The art of dying in the theatre of Sarah Kane', *Altre Modernità* 4 (2010), pp. 116–31 <DOI: 10.13130/2035–7680/695>.

Soncini, S., '"A Job for the Go-Between": Dramatising Translation in Brian Friel and David Edgar', in S. Coelsch-Foisner and H. Klein (eds), *Drama Translation and Theatre Practice* (Frankfurt am Main: Peter Lang, 2004).

Soncini, S., 'New Order, New Borders: Post-Cold War Europe on the British Stage', in R. Littlejohns and S. Soncini (eds), *Myths of Europe* (Amsterdam: Rodopi, 2007).

Soncini, S., 'Shakespeare va alla guerra. Conflitti contemporanei in alcune rivisitazioni sceniche del canone', in R. Ferrari and L. Giovannelli (eds), *The Complete Consort. Saggi di Anglistica in onore di Francesco Gozzi* (Pisa: Plus/Pisa University Press, 2005).

Soncini, S., 'War Images/War of Images: Looking at Contemporary Conflict Through Shakespeare', *Stratagemmi—Prospettive teatrali* 24/25 (2013), pp. 85–113.

Sontag, S., *Regarding the Pain of Others* (New York: Farrar, Straus & Giroux, 2003).

Soto-Morettini, D., 'Trouble in the House: David Hare's *Stuff Happens*', *Contemporary Theatre Review* 15:3 (2005), pp. 309–19.

Spencer, J., 'Performing Translation in Contemporary Anglo-American Drama', *Theatre Journal* 59 (2007), pp. 389–410.

Spencer, J. (ed.), *Political and Protest Theatre after 9/11: Patriotic Dissent* (New York: Routledge, 2012).

Stahlujak, Z., 'Violent Distortions: Bearing Witness to the Task of Wartime Translators', *TTR: traduction, terminologie, rédaction*, 13:1 (2000), pp. 37–51 <http://id.erudit.org/iderudit/037392ar> [accessed 25 April 2015].

Stanley, A., 'A Nation at War: The TV Watch, Lengthy Hours Magnify Strengths and Foibles', *New York Times*, 26 March 2003, Section B, p. 14.

Stauber, J., and R. Sheldon, *Toxic Sludge is Good for You! Lies, Damn Lies and the Public Relations Industry* (Monroe, ME: Common Courage Press, 1995).

Steiner, G., *After Babel: Aspects of Language and Translation* (Oxford: Oxford University Press, 1975).

Stephens, S., *Motortown* (London: Methuen, 2006).

Stephens, S., *Pornography*, in *Plays 2: One Minute, Country Music, Motortown, Pornography, Sea Wall* (London: Methuen, 2009).

Svich, C., 'Physical Poetry: David Greig in Conversation with Caridad Svich', *PAJ: A Journal of Performance and Art* 29:2 (2007), pp. 51–58.

Taylor, D., 'Afterword: War Play', *PMLA* 124:5 (2009), Special Issue on 'War', pp. 1886–95.

Teevan, C., *How Many Miles to Basra?* (London: Oberon, 2006).

Thompson, J., *Palace of the End* (London: Oberon, 2010).

Thorpe, C., *Safety* (London: Nick Hern, 2002).

tucker green, d., *Stoning Mary* (London: Nick Hern, 2005).

tucker green, d., *truth and reconciliation* (London: Nick Hern, 2011).

Venuti, L. (ed.), *Rethinking Translation: Discourse, Subjectivity, Ideology* (London: Routledge, 1992).

Venuti, L., *The Translator's Invisibility. A History of Translation* (London: Routledge, 1995).

Virilio, P., *Strategy of Deception*, trans. by C. Turner (London: Verso, [1999] 2000).

Virilio, P., *War and Cinema: The Logistics of Perception*, trans. by P. Camiller (London: Verso, [1984] 2000).

Wallace, C., *The Theatre of David Greig* (London: Bloomsbury, 2013).

Wallace, N., *In the Heart of America and Other Plays* (New York: Theatre Communications Group, 2001).

Wallace, N., *The Retreating World*, in F. Grace and N. Wallace, *Two Into War* (London: Oberon, 2005).

Wallace, N., *A State of Innocence*, in F. Grace and N. Wallace, *Two Into War* (London: Oberon, 2005).

Walsh, D., *Bloody Sunday and the Rule of Law in Northern Ireland* (Basingstoke: Palgrave Macmillan, 2000).

Walsh, J., (ed.), *The Gulf War Did not Happen: Politics, Culture and Warfare Post-Vietnam* (Aldershot: Arena, 1995).

Waters, S., *World Music* (London: Nick Hern, 2003).

Wertenbaker, T., *Credible Witness* (London: Faber and Faber, 2001).

Whelan, P., *A Russian in the Woods* (London: Methuen, 2001).

White, G.D., '"Quite a Profound Day": The Public Performance of Memory by Military Witnesses at the Bloody Sunday Tribunal', *Theatre Research International* 31:2 (2006), pp. 174–87.

Williams, R., *Days of Significance* (London: Methuen, 2007).

Index